Cultural Heritage and International Law

AF896332

Evelyne Lagrange • Stefan Oeter •
Robert Uerpmann-Wittzack
Editors

Cultural Heritage and International Law

Objects, Means and Ends of International Protection

Springer

Editors
Evelyne Lagrange
IREDIES
Pantheon-Sorbonne University
Paris, France

Stefan Oeter
Faculty of Law
University of Hamburg
Hamburg, Germany

Robert Uerpmann-Wittzack
Faculty of Law
University of Regensburg
Regensburg, Germany

ISBN 978-3-030-07649-8 ISBN 978-3-319-78789-3 (eBook)
https://doi.org/10.1007/978-3-319-78789-3

© Springer International Publishing AG, part of Springer Nature 2018
Softcover re-print of the Hardcover 1st edition 2018
This work is subject to copyright. All rights are reserved by the Publisher, whether the whole or part of the material is concerned, specifically the rights of translation, reprinting, reuse of illustrations, recitation, broadcasting, reproduction on microfilms or in any other physical way, and transmission or information storage and retrieval, electronic adaptation, computer software, or by similar or dissimilar methodology now known or hereafter developed.
The use of general descriptive names, registered names, trademarks, service marks, etc. in this publication does not imply, even in the absence of a specific statement, that such names are exempt from the relevant protective laws and regulations and therefore free for general use.
The publisher, the authors and the editors are safe to assume that the advice and information in this book are believed to be true and accurate at the date of publication. Neither the publisher nor the authors or the editors give a warranty, express or implied, with respect to the material contained herein or for any errors or omissions that may have been made. The publisher remains neutral with regard to jurisdictional claims in published maps and institutional affiliations.

Printed on acid-free paper

This Springer imprint is published by the registered company Springer International Publishing AG part of Springer Nature.
The registered company address is: Gewerbestrasse 11, 6330 Cham, Switzerland

Preface

Cultural heritage is part of the identities of individuals, groups, and communities and not indifferent to states and international organizations. It is also the object of numerous norms and institutions in contemporary public international law.

In armed conflicts, cultural heritage may be damaged inadvertently or even deliberately with a view to destroying cultural identities.

In times of peace, cultural heritage becomes an object of economic exchange in a globalized world. Works of famous painters attain exorbitant prices at international art auctions, and inscribing a site or a local custom on a cultural heritage list is likely to promote tourism. Even in armed conflicts, cultural heritage sites are spoiled in order to sell the objects on the international art and antiques market.

Global exchanges also put intangible cultural heritage under pressure, and local customs or regional and minority languages may disappear.

In the face of such threats, fostering the perceived cultural identity of a community corresponds to a desire for stability and security. However, culture, cultural heritage, and cultural identity are not static concepts. It is in their nature to evolve over time, since encounters between different cultures generate new forms of cultural expressions in addition to endogenous changes. Therefore, the diverse cultural heritage of the world must not be petrified but safeguarded as a unique resource for human progress.

Against this background, the present volume explores current challenges and the responses of international cultural heritage law.

This book has been realized within the long-standing cooperation of the German and the French Societies of International Law. Every 2 years, both Societies organize joint conferences.

Since 2006, the biannual joint conferences have been preceded by young scholars' workshops, which have been generously funded by the German-French University (Deutsch-Französische Hochschule/Université franco-allemande). In November 2016, members of both Societies met in Regensburg for a session on "Religion and International Law." The Regensburg workshop, open to junior researchers, which took place on November 2–3, 2016, was organized by the

University of Regensburg with the support of the Sorbonne Law School (IREDIES). It was dedicated to "Cultural Challenges Facing International Law," with a clear focus on cultural heritage law. Its results are published here, in English and French for the sake of a better diffusion.

The editors owe a debt of gratitude to all those who have assiduously helped to realize this volume: the young authors and members of University staff, especially Lena Springer and Benjamin Manthey in Regensburg, Catherine Botoko and Inès El Hayek at the Sorbonne Law School (University Paris 1 Pantheon-Sorbonne – IREDIES).

Paris, France
Hamburg, Germany
Regensburg, Germany

Evelyne Lagrange
Stefan Oeter
Robert Uerpmann-Wittzack

Contents

Part III Protection in Times of War

Part IV Cultural Identity

List of Contributors

Gabriele D'amico Soggetti Free University of Berlin, Berlin, Germany

Martin Gerner Institut für Auslandsbeziehungen (ifa), Stuttgart, Germany

Jérémy Hall Attaché Temporaire d'Enseignement et de Recherche (ATER), University of Grenoble, Alpes, France

Claudia Maria Hofmann University of Regensburg, Regensburg, Germany

Evelyne Lagrange Sorbonne Law School, Pantheon-Sorbonne University (Paris 1), IREDIES, Paris, France

Amandine Lizot Sorbonne Law School, Pantheon-Sorbonne University (Paris 1), IREDIES, Paris, France

Fabian Michl University of Regensburg, Regensburg, Germany

University of Münster, Münster, Germany

Mariana Monteiro de Matos Institute of International and European Law, Faculty of Law, Georg-August University of Göttingen, Göttingen, Germany

Stefan Oeter University of Hamburg, Hamburg, Germany

Lukas Rass-Masson University Toulouse 1 Capitole, Toulouse, France

Claire Sainte-Beuve Attachée Temporaire d'Enseignement et de Recherche (ATER), University of Picardie Jules Verne, CURAPP-ESS, Amiens, France

Sophie Simon Sorbonne Law School, Pantheon-Sorbonne University (Paris 1), Paris, France

Robert Uerpmann-Wittzack University of Regensburg, Regensburg, Germany

Caroline Westphal University of the Basque Country, Bilbao, Spain

University of Hamburg, Hamburg, Germany

Introduction: Cultural Heritage Law and the Quest for Human Identities

Robert Uerpmann-Wittzack

Abstract This chapter gives an introduction to the rationale of international cultural heritage law. Whereas the frequently used notion of "cultural property" hints on the commercial relevance of cultural goods, "cultural heritage" designates human expressions that constitute the identities of groups and communities. Cultural heritage may be tangible like monuments and paintings or intangible like languages, religious beliefs, or fashion.

UNESCO has adopted a series of conventions for the protection of cultural heritage, ranging from the 1954 Hague Convention for the Protection of Cultural Property in the Event of Armed Conflict to the 2005 Convention on Cultural Diversity. An analysis of these conventions and other international documents shows that, beyond questions of private property law, cultural goods may be attributed to the group where they have been created or to the community where they are located or even to humanity as a whole. Construed in a static way, cultural heritage, which constitutes a given group or community, may be used in order to exclude those who do not belong to the same group or community. Under a dynamic concept, which recognizes the inspiring potential of cultural diversity, by contrast, multiple, multilayered, and contextual identities may be conceived.

1 The Challenges of International Cultural Heritage Law

Culture matters, and so does cultural heritage law. Broadly construed, culture is closely related to the very idea of human civilization. Culture is not preset, but it is made by humankind.[1] Following a definition given by the UN Committee on Economic, Social and Cultural Rights, culture comprises all means "through

[1]Committee on Economic, Social and Cultural rights, General comment No. 21: Right of everyone to take part in cultural life (Art. 15, para. 1 (a), of the International Covenant on Economic, Social and Cultural Rights), 2009, UN Doc. E/C.12/GC/21, para. 12.

R. Uerpmann-Wittzack (✉)
Public and International Law, Faculty of Law, University of Regensburg, Regensburg, Germany
e-mail: robert.uerpmann-wittzack@ur.de

© Springer International Publishing AG, part of Springer Nature 2018

E. Lagrange et al. (eds.), *Cultural Heritage and International Law*,
https://doi.org/10.1007/978-3-319-78789-3_1

which individuals, groups of individuals and communities express their humanity and the meaning they give to their existence, and build their world view representing their encounter with the external forces affecting their lives."[2] According to the Committee, such means comprise "ways of life, language, oral and written literature, music and song, nonverbal communication, religion or belief systems, rites and ceremonies, sport and games, methods of production or technology, natural and man-made environments, food, clothing and shelter and the arts, customs and traditions."[3] Culture thus conceived is not limited to so-called high culture such as art and literature, but it comprises "lifestyles, ways of living together, value systems, traditions and beliefs."[4] So the practice of shaking hands at a meeting and the act of wearing a beard, be it for reasons of fashion or of religious beliefs, are equally elements of a certain culture. Even laws, which reflect a certain way of living together, are expressions of culture. This is particularly true for family law with its underlying role concepts of husbands, wives, and children. Thus, the family statute analyzed by Lukas Rass-Masson in this volume implies options for or against foreign cultures.

Culture is important because it constitutes the identity of individuals, groups, and societies.[5] Hence, the 2005 UNESCO Convention on the Protection and Promotion of the Diversity of Cultural Expressions recognizes "the distinctive nature of cultural activities, goods and services as vehicles of identity, values and meaning."[6] All these expressions of human culture form the cultural heritage of a given group or community. According to the 1970 UNESCO Convention on the Means of Prohibiting and Preventing the Illicit Import, Export and Transfer of Ownership of Cultural Property, cultural heritage is "one of the basic elements of civilization and national culture."[7] Cultural heritage thus represents the identity of a certain group or community. This is recognized by the 2003 UNESCO Convention for the Safeguarding of the Intangible Cultural Heritage, which holds that intangible cultural heritage provides "communities and groups . . . with a sense of identity and continuity."[8]

The same is true for tangible cultural heritage. Confronted with the destruction of world heritage sites in Timbuktu, Mali, by a fundamentalist Islamic group, UNESCO stated that "the loss of heritage . . . can deprive a community of its identity and memory, as well as the physical testimony of its past."[9] The 2015 UNESCO Recommendation concerning the Protection and Promotion of Museums and

---

[2]Ibid., para. 13; see also Hofmann, in this volume, Sect. 2.

[3]Ibid.

[4]UNESCO Universal Declaration on Cultural Diversity, Resolution adopted by the General Assembly at its 20th plenary meeting, 2 November 2001, Preamble para. 5.

[5]See also Hofmann, in this volume, Sect. 3.

[6]UNESCO Convention of 20 October 2005, UNTS 2440, p. 311, Article 1 lit. g.

[7]UNESCO Convention of 14 November 1970, UNTS 823, p. 231, Preamble para. 4.

[8]UNESCO Convention of 17 October 2003, UNTS 2368, p. 3, Article 2 para. 1.

[9]Submission by UNESCO, quoted by International Criminal Court (ICC), *The Prosecutor v. Ahmad Al Faqi Al Mahdi*, Reparations Order, 17 August 2017, ICC-01/12-01/15, para. 14.

Collections, their Diversity and their Role in Society points in a similar direction when it states that museums can "play an important role in . . . building citizenship and reflecting on collective identities."[10]

Although the protection of cultural heritage in armed conflicts marks the very beginning of international cultural heritage law,[11] armed conflict, where cultural heritage is neglected or even deliberately destroyed in order "to disrupt the social fabric of societies,"[12] is only one threat to cultural identity. At the age of globalization and global migration, communities are not only increasingly confronted with different cultures, but cultural identities become ambiguous to a point that people may long for clear-cut identities. In fact, many conflicts are framed today in terms of religious differences. As illustrated by the definition given by the UN Committee on Economic, Social and Cultural rights,[13] religion is part of culture, and debates on Muslim headscarves and veiling in public reflect cultural conflicts. The wish to define one's own identity may lead to concepts of "Leitkultur" (guiding culture)[14] and to the increased reliance on cultural heritage.

However, cultural heritage in a given state is not limited to goods created within that state or by its nationals. Visitors of the Louvre may admire Italian Renaissance paintings, as well as paintings from the Dutch Golden Age, and the National Gallery in Berlin owns important paintings by French impressionists, whereas other impressionist paintings are shown in London or New York. In the colonial age, European museums constituted important collections with objects from all over the world. The bust of Pharaoh Queen Nefertiti in Berlin[15] and the Elgin Marbles originating from the Parthenon temple in Athens and now exposed in London are only two prominent examples of this. According to Article 4 of the 1970 UNESCO Convention on the Means of Prohibiting and Preventing the Illicit Import, Export and Transfer of Ownership of Cultural Property,[16] the cultural heritage of a state encompasses both objects created within the territory of the state and objects properly acquired from abroad.

In a globalized world, cultural property is also the object of international trade, thus involving private, commercial interests. While international trade may be a means of spreading the knowledge of different cultures throughout the world, a

---

[10]Recommendation concerning the Protection and Promotion of Museums and Collections, their Diversity and their Role in Society, adopted by the UNESCO General Conference at its 38th Session, Paris, 17 November 2015, para. 17.

[11]Odendahl (2005), pp. 107 et seq.

[12]UNESCO (n. 9).

[13]See above (n. 3).

[14]See the Bavarian Integration Act (Bayerisches Integrationsgesetz) of 13 December 2016, Bayerisches Gesetz- und Verordnungsblatt 2016, p. 335, which, in its Preamble, refers to a guiding culture forming the fundamental cultural order of society and which aims at implementing this guiding culture throughout the integration process; for a thorough analysis see the contribution of Claudia M. Hofmann, in this volume, Sect. 1 and passim.

[15]See Stoll (2012).

[16]UNESCO 1970 (n. 7).

group, a community, or a state may wish to keep control over the cultural heritage present on its territory, therefore prohibiting its export. Such prohibitions constitute nontariff barriers to trade within the meaning of Article XI GATT, which may be justified under Article XX lit. f GATT. Seen from an individual rights perspective, commercial interests of the private owner collide with state interests. The European Court of Human Right had to deal with such a situation in *Beyeler v. Italy*, where Italy's preemptive right with regard to a painting by van Gogh was at stake.[17]

The apparently growing importance of cultural heritage and the challenges for its protection go hand in hand with an increasing relevance of cultural heritage law. In fact, in Germany alone, three legal scholars have dedicated their habilitation theses to culture and cultural law since 2004.[18] Whereas the following chapters deal with current developments and challenges of international cultural heritage law, this introductory chapter shall address some underlying questions. After terminological clarifications in Sect. 2, the following Sect. 3 seeks to identify the stakeholders of cultural heritage law. While it may be taken for granted that culture constitutes human identities, it is not always certain whose identity should be protected by international law. Finally, the including and excluding effects of cultural heritage and its protection shall be reviewed in Sect. 4.

2 Cultural Property, Heritage, and Goods

French- and German-speaking legal scholars are used to refer to the protection of "biens culturels" or "Kulturgüter." This explains why the term "cultural goods" is used quite frequently in this volume. English-speaking scholars, however, rather prefer two other notions with divergent connotations, i.e. "cultural property" and "cultural heritage." Some hold cultural heritage to be the broadest notion, not being limited to tangible goods.[19] The concept of intellectual property illustrates, however, that there is intangible property, too.

Rather, the term property highlights the material and commercial value of cultural goods,[20] while heritage refers to the immaterial dimension of cultural goods, which may have a nonmaterial value for certain persons, groups, nations, or even humanity as such. Whereas property implies the owner's power to dispose of an object, the concept of heritage implies a sense of duty.[21] In this volume, the material dimension

[17] *Beyeler v. Italy* [GC], no. 33202/96, paras 111–113, ECHR 2000-I; see Michl, in this volume, Sect. 3.1.

[18] Odendahl (2005); Germelmann (2013) with a section on cultural heritage law at pp. 579 et seq.; Lenski (2013) with a section on international cultural heritage law at pp. 269 et seq.; see also the doctoral thesis by von Schorlemer (1992).

[19] Odendahl (2005), p. 390; see also Blake (2015), pp. 6–7.

[20] Prott and O'Keefe (1992), p. 311.

[21] Prott and O'Keefe (1992), pp. 309–311.

of cultural property is at stake when Fabian Michl considers the protection of cultural goods under Article 1 of Protocol No. 1 to the European Convention on Human Rights. Nevertheless, this author explicitly opts for the term "cultural good" in order to avoid the economic implications of cultural property.[22] Other contributions explore the nonmaterial dimensions of cultural heritage protection.

Some international legal documents even use the term "cultural goods" familiar to German and French scholars in their English versions. This is true for the aforementioned General Comment No. 21, where the UN Committee on Economic, Social and Cultural Rights refers exclusively to cultural goods.[23] However, this terminology may be inspired by the juxtaposition of goods and services, which is common in world trade law and which is taken up by the Committee.[24] Similarly, the 2005 UNESCO Convention on the Protection and Promotion of the Diversity of Cultural Expressions refers to "cultural activities, goods and services"[25] and twice to the "heritage of humanity"[26] without any reference to "cultural property" except for one reference to "intellectual property."[27]

Cultural heritage may be tangible or intangible. The contributors to Part I of this volume dealing with linguistic diversity concentrate on a specific aspect of intangible cultural property.[28]

Tangible cultural heritage comprises movable and immovable objects. When Amandine Lizot investigates on the legal framework for international exchanges of museum collections or when Martin Gerner explores safe havens for cultural property, both deal with movable objects. In contrast, the 1972 UNESCO Convention Concerning the Protection of the World Cultural and Natural Heritage[29] analyzed by Claire Sainte-Beuve focuses on immovable objects.

Finally, the contributors to Part IV of this volume transcend the distinctions between tangible and intangible, movable and immovable cultural heritage. In fact, cultural identity, which is the key concept of that part, expresses itself through and relies upon all categories of cultural heritage. Therefore, the cultural-identity-based approach to the protection of indigenous peoples, which has been developed by the UN Human Rights Committee and which is analyzed by Mariana Monteiro de Matos, invariably applies to all aspects of cultural identity, be they tangible or intangible, movable or immovable. It is true, however, that de Matos pays particular attention to land rights and rights to natural resources, which protect the territorial, tangible, and immovable basis of indigenous communities. When Claudia

---

[22]See Michl, in this volume, Sect. 2.1 with references to a series of other languages, which equally follow the concept of cultural goods.

[23]General Comment No. 21 (n. 1), paras 6, 15 lit. b, 16 lit. a, 70.

[24]Ibid., paras 6, 16 lit. a, 22, 43, 49 lit. b, 50 lit. b, 62.

[25]UNESCO 2005 (n. 6), Articles 1 lit. g, 4 no. 4 and passim.

[26]UNESCO 2005 (n. 6), Preamble para. 2, Article 4 no. 1 para. 2.

[27]UNESCO 2005 (n. 6), Preamble para. 17.

[28]See Simon, Westphal, and Oeter, in this volume.

[29]Convention of 16 November 1972, UNTS 1037, p. 151.

M. Hofmann investigates on "Leitkultur," by contrast, the focus shifts to intangible cultural heritage, which is perceived to constitute the identity of a given community. The same is true for the contribution of Lukas Rass-Masson, who analyzes the interplay of legal cultures in family matters.

3 Whose Cultural Heritage? Multiple and Complex Identities

As public international law is made by and governs the relations between sovereign states, one might presume that international cultural heritage law protects the cultural heritage of sovereign states. This is in fact the approach taken by the Hague Regulations Respecting the Laws and Customs of War on Land of 1907,[30] which oblige states to safeguard cultural property in their mutual relations as belligerent parties.[31] In particular, Article 27 of the Regulations exhorts states to spare, inter alia, "buildings dedicated to religion, art, ..." and "historic monuments" during sieges and bombardments.

However, mobile cultural property at least does not necessarily originate from the state where it is located. Leonardo's Mona Lisa in Paris and Nefertiti in Berlin are good examples of this. Nevertheless, foreign objects that have been in a country for a long time may add to this country's identity. Moreover, important collections such as those exposed in the Louvre may be perceived as a cultural achievement of the respective community even if the elements of the collection originate from abroad. Kerstin Odendahl has analyzed these effects in terms of "kulturelle Bindung" worthy of protection.[32] This "cultural link" explains why the 1970 UNESCO Convention attributes objects, which were lawfully acquired and imported into the country, to that country's cultural heritage. According to Article 4 of the 1970 UNESCO Convention, the cultural heritage of a state party comprises

> (c) cultural property acquired by archaeological, ethnological or natural science missions, with the consent of the competent authorities of the country of origin of such property;
> (d) cultural property which has been the subject of a freely agreed exchange;
> (e) cultural property received as a gift or purchased legally with the consent of the competent authorities of the country of origin of such property.

The same attribution follows from the *Beyeler* judgment of the European Court of Human Rights analyzed by Fabian Michl.[33] In *Beyeler*, the European Court

---

[30] Annex to the Hague Convention on Laws and Customs of War on Land, 18 October 1907, US Treaty Series No. 539.

[31] For an overview of Regulations articles applying to cultural property see Germelmann (2013), pp. 625–626. The reciprocal character of obligations under the Hague Regulations is underlined by Article 2 of the Hague Convention (n. 30).

[32] Odendahl (2005), pp. 407 et seq.

[33] Michl, in this volume, Sect. 3.1.

recognized that Italy had a legitimate public interest to make a painting by van Gogh, which had been lawfully on its territory, publicly accessible even though the Dutch artist had painted it in France.[34] In its reasoning, the Court referred to the concept of a universal cultural heritage of all nations in order to explain Italy's legitimate interest. So Italy would act as a proxy of the international community as a whole in protecting the cultural heritage at stake. However, the fact that Italy had invoked the scarcity of van Gogh paintings in Italian museums in order to justify the special protection accorded to the painting[35] hints to another explanation: Italy would have a genuine interest to present world heritage on its proper territory. This could imply that a state's cultural identity derives not only from what was created within the state or by its nationals but also from the cultural treasures presented in its museums and collections of art.

Although cultural heritage conventions lay down rights and obligations of states parties, most of them do not follow a state-centered concept of cultural heritage. The 2003 UNESCO Convention on Intangible Cultural Property attributes cultural heritage to "communities, groups and individuals,"[36] whereas the 2005 UNESCO Convention on cultural diversity refers to "groups and societies."[37] Thus, cultural heritage may be attributable to local or regional groups and communities within a state, and to indigenous communities in particular.[38] This view has been corroborated by the ICC *Al Mahdi* judgment of 2016, which Jérémy Hall analyzes in this volume.[39] When assessing the gravity of the crimes of destroying a series of mausoleums at Timbuktu, the Court referred to the "symbolic and emotional value for the inhabitants of Timbuktu,"[40] and it stated that destroying the monuments "aimed at breaking the soul of the people of Timbuktu."[41] In the same vein, the ICC Reparations Order of 2017 held that "the community of Timbuktu" and its members were the primary victims of the crimes.[42]

Moreover, the attribution of cultural heritage to particular groups and communities has been complemented by the concept of a common heritage of humankind as a whole. As early as in 1954, the Hague Convention for the Protection of Cultural Property in the Event of Armed Conflict stated "that damage to cultural property belonging to any people whatsoever means damage to the cultural heritage of all mankind, since each people makes its contribution to the culture of the world."[43]

---

[34]*Beyeler v. Italy* [GC], no. 33202/96, paras 111–113, ECHR 2000-I.

[35]*Beyeler v. Italy* [GC], no. 33202/96, para. 36, ECHR 2000-I.

[36]UNESCO (2003) (n. 8), Article 1 lit. b.

[37]UNESCO (2005) (n. 6), Article 4 no. 1.

[38]With regard to indigenous communities, see Monteiro de Matos, in this volume.

[39]Hall, in this volume, Sect. 2.1.

[40]International Criminal Court (ICC), *The Prosecutor v. Ahmad Al Faqi Al Mahdi*, Judgment, 27 September 2016, ICC-01/12-01/15, para. 79.

[41]Ibid., para. 80.

[42]ICC 2017 (n. 9), para. 52.

[43]Convention of 14 May 1954, UNTS 249, p. 215, Preamble para. 2.

Since 1972, the UNESCO Convention Concerning the Protection of the World Cultural and Natural Heritage has effectively promoted the common heritage idea. Given that most of the mausoleums of Timbuktu were classified as world heritage sites, the ICC in *Al Mahdi* retained that their destruction did "not only affect the direct victims of the crimes, namely the faithful and inhabitants of Timbuktu, but also people throughout Mali and the international community," and it added that "the entire international community, in the belief that heritage is part of cultural life, ... [was] suffering as a result of the destruction of the protected sites."[44] This identity-creating function of cultural heritage explains why the destruction of cultural heritage sites may even threaten international peace and security, thus giving rise to Security Council action under Chapter VII of the UN Charter.[45]

The 2003 UNESCO Convention on Intangible Cultural Heritage likewise refers to the concept of a "cultural heritage of humanity"[46] and thereby paves the way for the idea that cultural diversity has an inherent value in itself as it is a reservoir for creativity and progress. This idea has been spelled out in the 2005 UNESCO Convention on Cultural Diversity, and consequently, cultural heritage has to be accessible[47] and cultural exchange should be strengthened.[48] This corresponds to Amandine Lizot's proposal that cultural property originating from one country and now located in another country might be shared by both stakeholders—or even more.[49] Thus, the concept of a common cultural heritage transcends state sovereignty.[50]

While the idea of cultural heritage could imply a static concept where objects of the past are conserved for the future, the 2005 UNESCO Convention on Cultural Diversity favors a dynamic concept taking into account that culture and cultural identities are constantly evolving and that heritage is a basis for future creativity. In fact, tangible property may be detached from its original creators and, in the case of movable property, be relocated to another state and, be it movable or not, subsist even after its creators and their societies have vanished. The bust of Nefertiti, for instance, is now far away from its original environment both locally and in time. Even though tangible property such as liturgical objects may need their original context in order to convey their full meaning, intangible property is more contingent on its historical and cultural context. It must be practiced within a given community in order to stay alive. A language, for instance, that lost its last native speaker is

[44]ICC 2016 (n. 40), para. 80.

[45]See Security Council Resolutions 2056 of 5 July 2012, Preamble para. 14, and 2085 of 20 December 2012, Preamble para. 6, with regard to Mali; see generally von Schorlemer (2016), pp. 4–5; see also Oeter, in this volume, Sect. 6, with regard to the security dimension of minority language protection.

[46]UNESCO 2003 (n. 8), Preamble para. 6.

[47]UNESCO 2005 (n. 6), Article 2 Principle 7; see also General Comment No. 21 (n. 1), para. 15 lit. b.

[48]UNESCO 2005 (n. 6), Article 1 lit. c.

[49]Lizot, in this volume, Sect. 3.

[50]See also Eichel (2016), pp. 900 et seq.

called dead, and with the extinction of a language, the entire knowledge system represented by that language disappears.[51] The 2003 Convention on Intangible Cultural Heritage recognizes the importance of keeping intangible cultural property alive through practice within its community of origin. Hence, Article 15 of the Convention calls upon states parties "to ensure the widest possible participation of communities, groups and, where appropriate, individuals that create, maintain and transmit such heritage, and to involve them actively in its management." Although tangible cultural heritage may survive its community of origin, such heritage must also be filled with life in order to keep its full meaning. Therefore, Article 5 lit. a of the 1972 UNESCO World Heritage Convention obliges states parties "to adopt a general policy which aims to give the cultural and natural heritage a function in the life of the community." This is also highlighted by Gabriele D'amico in his contribution to this volume.[52]

4 Inclusion and Exclusion Through a Common Cultural Heritage

As a means of identification, cultural heritage determines the affiliation or nonaffiliation to social groups. In fact, common cultural heritage may constitute a certain social group and distinguish this group from other groups and populations. This is particularly true for indigenous peoples, as is highlighted by Mariana Monteiro de Matos in this volume. The author compares two different approaches to protecting indigenous peoples, i.e. the self-determination approach adopted by the United Nations Declaration on the Rights of Indigenous Peoples and the cultural identity approach followed by the UN Human Rights Committee. Her analysis shows that a cultural identity approach offers higher protection than relying on self-determination. This is highly convincing: if a group is not only constituted by rational choice of free individuals concluding a social contract but is also rooted in tangible and intangible cultural heritage, which constitutes the group's specific identity, then effective protection must take this common cultural heritage into account.

The wish to create adherence also explains the Bavarian attempt to foster a guiding culture (*Leitkultur*)[53] even though a legal act specifically applying to migrants may be the wrong way to make persons adopt a common culture. At the same time, promoting a certain cultural identity risks excluding all those who do not adhere to the same culture.[54] Thus, the Muslim headscarf has become a prominent distinctive sign. A legal ban on wearing Muslim headscarves at work and in public institutions obliges women to make a choice between two different cultures, and if

[51] See Oeter, in this volume, Sect. 2.

[52] D'amico, Sect. 3.

[53] N. 14.

[54] From a philosophical point of view Jullien (2016), pp. 13–14.

they opt for their traditional community, they are excluded from the majority society.[55]

The concept of cultural diversity would open a different way, accepting that one person may identify with more than one culture at one time. According to the UN Committee on Economic, Social and Cultural Rights, the right to participate in cultural life, as laid down in Article 15 para. 1 lit. a of the International Covenant on Economic, Social and Cultural Rights,[56] includes the right "to identify or not with one or several communities."[57] This corroborates the awareness of the 2005 UNESCO Convention on Cultural Diversity "that cultural diversity creates a rich and varied world, which increases the range of choices,"[58] and it is fully in line with the 2012 Ljubljana Guidelines on the Integration of Diverse Societies of the OSCE High Commissioner on Human Rights. These guidelines recognize that diversity "is a feature of all contemporary societies and of the groups that comprise them," and they therefore stipulate that the "legislative and policy framework should allow for the recognition that individual identities may be multiple, multilayered, contextual and dynamic."[59] This explains, for instance, why states should foster minority languages both in the education system and in public life,[60] and it may militate in favor of a family statute open to the values of a foreign legal order.[61]

From this point of view, museum collections may even have a threefold importance, as analyzed by Amandine Lizot.[62] Individual objects belonging to a collection may pertain to the identity of the communities where they come from. At the same time, the collection as such may contribute to the identity of the state where it is placed. Finally, a collection, which represents the cultural richness of the world, forms part of the common heritage of humankind and is, as such, of worldwide interest. This points in favor of international expositions and exchanges not only between the state where the collection is located and the state where its objects originate from but also with third states. Consequently, the 2015 UNESCO Recommendation on Museums and Collections exhorts states to "encourage cooperation and partnerships among museums and cultural and scientific institutions at all levels, including . . . international exhibitions, exchanges and the mobility of collections."[63] Similarly, the idea of coproperty, as proposed by Amandine Lizot,[64] shows that

[55] See also Braun (2017), p. 1358, who neglects, however, that, unlike headscarves, face veils worn by pupils are not only symbols of a different culture but also serious physical barriers to participation in school life.

[56] Covenant of 19 December 1966, UNTS 993, p. 6.

[57] General Comment No. 21 (n. 1), para. 15 lit. a.

[58] UNESCO 2005 (n. 6), Preamble para. 3.

[59] OSCE High Commissioner on National Minorities, Ljubljana Guidelines on the Integration of Diverse Societies & Explanatory Note, 2012, p. 14.

[60] See Simon, in this volume, Sect. 3.2.

[61] See Rass-Masson, in this volume, Sect. 2.2.

[62] In this volume, Sect. 3.1.

[63] UNESCO 2015 (n. 10), para. 31.

[64] In this volume, Sect. 3.1.

cultural heritage does not necessarily belong to one community alone but belongs to a plurality of stakeholders or trustees, which may even comprise the international community as a whole.

References

Blake J (2015) International cultural heritage law. Oxford University Press, Oxford

Braun K (2017) How much veil is too much veil: on the constitutionality and advisability of face veil bans for German public school students. Germ Law J 18:1331–1358

Eichel S (2016) Kulturgüterschutz und common concern-Konzept. Zeitschrift für ausländisches öffentliches Recht und Völkerrecht 76:879–907

Germelmann CF (2013) Kultur und staatliches Handeln. Mohr Siebeck, Tübingen

Jullien F (2016) Il n'y a pas d'identité culturelle: mais nous défendons les ressources d'une culture. Herne, Paris

Lenski C (2013) Öffentliches Kulturrecht. Mohr Siebeck, Tübingen

Odendahl K (2005) Kulturgüterschutz. Mohr Siebeck, Tübingen

Prott LV, O'Keefe PJ (1992) 'Cultural heritage' or 'Cultural property'? Int J Cult Prop 1:307–320. https://doi.org/10.1017/S094073919200033X

Stoll P-T (2012) Where should Nefertiti go? Reflections on international cultural law. In: Hestermeyer HP (ed) Coexistence, cooperation and solidarity. Liber amicorum Wofrum R. Nijhoff, Leiden, pp 303–316

von Schorlemer S (1992) Internationaler Kulturgüterschutz. Duncker und Humblot, Berlin

von Schorlemer S (2016) Der Schutz von Kulturerbestätten als Aufgabe der UN-Sicherheitspolitik. Vereinte Nationen 64:3–8

Part I
Linguistic Diversity

Le Commissaire aux droits de l'homme, un acteur de la protection de la diversité linguistique

Sophie Simon

Abstract Une étude systématique des rapports du Commissaire aux droits de l'homme du Conseil de l'Europe fait apparaître de multiples prises de position sur les questions linguistiques. Si celles-ci ne sont pas véritablement originales par rapport à celles des autres organes de droits de l'homme, la volonté du Commissaire de se saisir des questions relatives à la diversité culturelle et linguistique en particulier ressort nettement de cette étude. Son mandat large le lui permet et la liberté rédactionnelle dont il fait usage l'autorise à ne pas suivre d'argumentaire juridique strict. Ainsi, il ne se réfère pas à une disposition précise d'un traité international ou d'une déclaration spécifique dont il aurait la charge d'assurer le *monitoring*. Davantage mêle-t-il, au gré des besoins et des situations de fait qu'il rencontre, les arguments tirés du principe de non-discrimination à ceux relatifs à la mise en œuvre de droits spécifiques clairement énoncés, tels que le droit à la liberté d'expression. Pareillement, il se fonde sur des éléments constitutifs des sociétés démocratiques qu'il a pour volonté d'aider à construire: pluralisme, intégration et participation de tous aux affaires collectives. Il adopte ainsi un positionnement souple s'adaptant aux besoins concrets des sociétés européennes à la fois diverses et en constante mutation.

1 Introduction

La doctrine s'est longtemps questionnée sur la légitimité d'octroyer aux membres des minorités linguistiques le droit de parler dans une autre langue que la langue officielle[1]. En France notamment, les débats sur ce thème se sont cristallisés autour de la

[1] La conception de l'Etat en tant qu'Etat-nation a fortement marqué les esprits, de sorte que persiste encore l'idée que, dans un même Etat, il est nécessaire que tous partagent la même langue. Pourtant, dans les Etats multiculturels dans lesquels nous vivons, la réalité n'est pas celle d'un monolinguisme absolu. Si des mesures d'uniformisation linguistique ont été appliquées en tant que moyen d'unifier les populations et de faire naître un sentiment national, les langues

S. Simon (✉)
Université Paris 1 Panthéon-Sorbonne, Paris Cedex 5, France

© Springer International Publishing AG, part of Springer Nature 2018

E. Lagrange et al. (eds.), *Cultural Heritage and International Law*,
https://doi.org/10.1007/978-3-319-78789-3_2

ratification de la Charte européenne des langues régionales ou minoritaires[2] et la décision du Conseil constitutionnel déclarant ce traité inconstitutionnel[3]. Une étude systématique des rapports du Commissaire aux droits de l'homme du Conseil de l'Europe fait apparaître de multiples prises de position sur les questions linguistiques. Il en ressort qu'indiscutablement et en raison de son mandat, la protection de la diversité linguistique forme une partie intégrante des droits de l'homme. Sur de nombreux points, cependant, la position du Commissaire n'est pas véritablement originale par rapport à celle des autres organes de droits de l'homme.

Le Commissaire aux droits de l'homme a été créé le 7 mai 1999 par le Comité des ministres du Conseil de l'Europe *via* l'adoption de la Résolution (99) 50 qui institue la fonction de Commissaire et définit son mandat. En application de cette résolution, le Commissaire a pour mission de promouvoir le respect effectif des droits de l'homme et d'aider les Etats membres à mettre en œuvre les normes du Conseil de l'Europe en la matière ; de promouvoir l'éducation et la sensibilisation aux droits de l'homme dans les Etats membres du Conseil de l'Europe ; de déceler d'éventuelles insuffisances dans le droit et la pratique en matière de droits de l'homme ; de faciliter les activités des bureaux nationaux de médiateurs et d'autres structures chargées des droits de l'homme ; et d'apporter conseils et informations concernant la protection des droits de l'homme dans toute la région.

Le Commissaire aux droits de l'homme est rattaché au Secrétaire général du Conseil de l'Europe et est choisi par l'Assemblée parlementaire du Conseil de l'Europe pour un unique mandat de 6 ans. M. Álvaro Gil-Robles, espagnol, a été le premier Commissaire et a occupé ce poste du 15 octobre 1999 au 31 mars 2006. M. Thomas Hammarberg, suédois, lui a succédé le 1er avril 2006. Le Commissaire actuel, Nils Muižnieks, est letton et a pris ses fonctions le 1er avril 2012.

La personnalité du Commissaire en poste donne assurément une couleur à son mandat. Malgré tout, le mode d'action du Commissaire est resté inchangé depuis sa création : le Commissaire n'est pas une institution juridictionnelle et ne peut, dès lors, être saisi de plaintes individuelles. En outre, il ne peut pas adresser directement ses remarques écrites à l'Etat concerné mais il doit les transmettre au Comité des Ministres ou à l'Assemblée parlementaire du Conseil de l'Europe. Enfin, il ne peut pas prononcer de sanction lorsqu'il constate des violations des droits de l'homme. Il doit compter sur les effets moraux de ses prises de position et de la pression publique qui en résulte pour l'Etat mis en cause.

Le Commissaire peut, toutefois, se fonder sur des informations relatives à des violations des droits de l'homme dont sont victimes des particuliers pour en tirer des conclusions et prendre des initiatives visant à améliorer concrètement la sensibilisation aux droits de l'homme et leur protection. De même, et afin de

traditionnellement parlées par certaines minorités, parfois régionales, ont su subsister jusqu'à nos jours. A celles-ci s'ajoutent, de surcroît, les langues parlées par les immigrés.

Sur le modèle politique de l'Etat-nation, dominant au XIXème siècle, voir notamment : Gellner (1983).

[2]Voir notamment : Conseil de l'Europe et Université Robert Schuman (dir.) (2003).

[3]CC, 15 juin 1999, n° 99-412, *Ratification de la Charte européenne des langues régionales.*

collecter des informations et de s'assurer de l'impact de ses actions, il coopère avec les institutions nationales (notamment les défenseurs des droits de l'homme) et internationales (dont les organes chargés du suivi des droits de l'homme des Nations Unies et de ses bureaux spécialisés, l'Union européenne, l'OSCE, etc.) ainsi qu'avec les organisations non gouvernementales.

Pour mener à bien sa mission, les activités du Commissaire sont de trois types : des visites dans les pays et un dialogue avec les autorités nationales et la société civile ; un travail thématique d'information et de conseil sur la mise en œuvre systématique des droits de l'homme ; et des activités de sensibilisation.

Ainsi, les visites dans les Etats membres du Conseil de l'Europe sont au cœur de la pratique du Commissaire. Dans les rapports ou les lettres qui y succèdent, il réalise une évaluation de la situation des droits de l'homme dans les pays visités et adresse des recommandations, indiquant aux autorités concernées comment remédier aux insuffisances constatées, tant dans la législation que dans la pratique. Il a été amené, dans ce cadre, à se prononcer sur des aspects culturels et notamment sur la question de la diversité linguistique, question qu'il a souvent abordée indirectement mais sur laquelle il a, au cours du temps, adopté une position de plus en plus ferme, s'appuyant notamment sur les traités relatifs aux minorités.

Quel est l'apport du Commissaire aux droits de l'homme dans le domaine de la protection de la diversité linguistique, matière encore souvent considérée comme relevant des seules politiques culturelles ?

Les questions linguistiques trouvent toute leur place dans le travail du Commissaire dès lors qu'elles se rapportent à des questionnements relatifs à la mise en œuvre des droits de l'homme (2). En outre, la volonté de protéger les langues les moins parlées oblige à replacer les droits de l'homme dans le cadre plus large des sociétés démocratiques (3).

2 Les enjeux de la diversité linguistique en terme de droits de l'homme

Les organes protégeant les droits de l'homme, juridictions et quasi-juridictions internationales, ont considéré que le libre choix de la langue devait être assuré aux personnes appartenant à des minorités. Cet objectif est réalisé par l'application directe des droits fondamentaux ou du droit à ne pas être discriminé. Le Commissaire aux droits de l'homme suit, dans ses rapports, une logique similaire, demandant que les justiciables ne soient pas victimes de discrimination sur le fondement de la langue (Sect. 2.1) ou appelant à la prise en compte des langues parlées par les individus lors de l'application directe des droits fondamentaux (Sect. 2.2)

2.1 L'égale jouissance des droits et l'égal accès aux services

L'utilisation du principe de non-discrimination en faveur de la diversité linguistique est ancienne car déjà dans son arrêt de 1935, *Ecoles minoritaires en Albanie*[4], la Cour permanente de justice internationale a relevé que dès lors que l'enseignement public a lieu en albanais, l'interdiction totale des écoles privées a pour effet de priver exclusivement les membres des minorités d'un enseignement en leur langue[5]. Suivant cette même ligne, le Comité des droits de l'homme des Nations Unies a été amené à étendre cette jurisprudence au financement des établissements d'enseignement privés[6], ainsi qu'au droit à un procès équitable[7]

[4]CPJI, *Avis consultatif relatif aux écoles minoritaires en Albanie*, 6 avril 1935, Série A/B, n° 64.

[5]La Cour consacre alors le principe d'égalité substantielle et indique que l'égalité en fait, contrairement à l'égalité en droit, peut « rendre nécessaires des traitements différents en vue d'arriver à un résultat qui établisse l'équilibre entre des situations différentes ». Inversement, un traitement identique de la majorité et de la minorité, « dont la condition et les besoins sont différents », peut, dans certains cas, aboutir à une inégalité de fait.

[6]Dans l'affaire *Waldman c. Canada*, le Comité des droits de l'homme a observé que le Pacte n'oblige pas les États parties à financer des écoles religieuses mais que si un État partie décide de financer de telles écoles, il doit le faire pour toutes sans discrimination. Soulignant que les critères présentés par le Gouvernement pour justifier le traitement préférentiel accordé à la minorité catholique romaine (son fondement historique et sa base constitutionnelle) ne pouvaient être considérés comme raisonnables et objectifs, il a conclu à la violation de l'article 26 du Pacte international relatif aux droits civils et politiques (CCPR, *Waldman c. Canada*, Communication n° 694/1996, 3 novembre 1999, UN Doc. CCPR/C/67/D/694/1996).

[7]Dans l'affaire *Dominique Guesdon c. France* dans laquelle était en cause la question de savoir si un Français d'origine bretonne a le droit à un interprète du français au breton durant une procédure pénale à son encontre, se fondant sur les seuls articles 14 et 26 du Pacte, le Comité a considéré que les droits de M. Guesdon n'ont pas été violés étant donné que ni ce dernier ni les témoins ayant été appelés n'étaient incapables de s'adresser au tribunal dans un français « simple mais adéquat ». Selon lui, le droit à un procès équitable n'inclut pas la possibilité pour l'accusé d'utiliser la langue qu'il parle habituellement ou qu'il parle avec le plus de facilité. Le Comité se fonde sur l'impression de la Cour d'appel française qui mentionnait que l'accusé avait des « compétences suffisantes » en français (CCPR, *Dominique Guesdon c. France*, 25 juillet 1990, communication n° 219/1986, UN Doc. A/45/40, Annual Report, 1990, vol. II, pp. 61 et 67-68).

et à l'accès aux administrations publiques[8]. De même, la Cour européenne des droits de l'homme s'est prononcée sur le choix des langues d'enseignement dans les établissements publics[9] et les restrictions linguistiques pouvant entraver

---

[8]Dans l'affaire *Diergaardt et autres c. Namibie*, dans laquelle était en cause une circulaire du Gouvernement demandant aux fonctionnaires publics de ne plus employer la langue afrikaans ni à l'écrit, ni à l'oral (cette circulaire se fondait sur le fait que la Constitution déclare l'anglais comme seule langue officielle), le Comité des droits de l'homme s'est fondé sur l'article 26 du Pacte relatif aux droits civils et politiques pour considérer qu'en l'absence de réponse de l'Etat partie expliquant la raison de la circulaire, la différence de traitement accordée à la communauté Baster n'était pas justifiée. Il a donc conclu à la violation de l'article 26 du Pacte. Le fait que même l'usage oral informel de la langue afrikaans ait été interdit alors que celui-ci était courant et rendu possible notamment par la concentration géographique de la minorité en cause, a certainement motivé le Comité à trancher de la sorte (CCPR, *Diergaardt et autres c. Namibie*, 25 juillet 2000, communication n° 760/1996, § 10.10).

[9]Dans l'affaire relative à *Certains aspects du régime linguistique de l'enseignement en Belgique* du 23 juillet 1968, la Cour européenne des droits de l'homme a mentionné que « le droit à l'instruction serait vide de sens s'il n'impliquait pas, pour ses titulaires, le droit de recevoir un enseignement dans la langue nationale ou dans une des langues nationales, selon le cas ».

Un enseignement dans une autre langue que la langue officielle du pays ou de la région concernée ne peut, en conséquent, être attendu. Ainsi, l'article 2 du protocole 1 ne fonde pas, à lui seul, de droit à bénéficier d'une instruction en langue régionale ou minoritaire. Cependant, examinant la conformité avec l'article 14 de la Convention combiné avec l'article 2 du Protocole, la Cour a admis que la suppression de l'enseignement public en français dans la région de langue néerlandaise entraînait une différence de traitement fondée sur la langue, dès lors qu'elle favorisait le seul enseignement dispensé en néerlandais. Contrairement à la vision du Gouvernement, la Cour n'a pas comparé la situation des membres des deux communautés linguistiques à l'échelle nationale (la minorité néerlandophone étant aussi défavorisée en Wallonie) mais a considéré que l'application de l'article 14 nécessite une comparaison de la situation des individus à l'intérieur de chaque région. Cependant, l'objectif poursuivi par le gouvernement, « la défense de l'homogénéité linguistique de la région », a été considéré légitime par la Cour car il repose sur l'« élément objectif que constitue la région » et s'inspire d'un intérêt public, « celui d'assurer que tous les établissements scolaires dépendant de l'Etat et existant dans une région unilingue, dispensent leur enseignement dans la langue qui est, au premier chef, celle de la région » (p. 43, § 7).

Dans une affaire plus récente, la Cour a assoupli sa jurisprudence. Dans l'arrêt *Chypre c. Turquie* du 10 mai 2001, elle a en effet constaté que si un enseignement au niveau primaire en langue grecque existait bien au Nord de Chypre, celui-ci n'existait plus au secondaire alors même que les autorités turques connaissaient la demande pour un tel enseignement. La Cour a considéré que « la possibilité offerte aux parents chypriotes grecs d'inscrire leurs enfants dans les établissements secondaires du Nord dans les conditions proposées n'[était] pas très réaliste, étant donné que ces enfants y [avaient] déjà effectué leur scolarité primaire dans une école chypriote grecque ». Par conséquent, « le fait que les autorités de la « RTCN », après avoir organisé un enseignement primaire en langue grecque, n'aient pas fait de même pour le secondaire ne [pouvait] que passer pour un déni de la substance du droit en cause » (§ 278). S'agissant de l'existence des établissements enseignant en grec dans le Sud, elle n'[était] pas propre à satisfaire l'obligation imposée par l'article 2 du premier protocole, vu l'impact de cette option sur la vie privée et familiale. Dans ces conditions et en l'absence d'un enseignement secondaire approprié, les Chypriotes grecs du Nord de Chypre subissaient une violation de leur droit au regard de l'article 2 du Protocole n° 1 (§ 280) (Cour EDH [Grande Chambre], *Chypre c. Turquie*, 10 mai 2001, Rec. 2001-IV).

l'accessibilité à un recours[10] ou la participation aux débats dans les assemblées législatives[11].

Sur cette question de l'égale jouissance des droits et de l'égal accès aux services, la position du Commissaire aux droits de l'homme se situe dans la continuité de la jurisprudence internationale, tout comme celle du CERD – Comité pour l'élimination de la discrimination raciale des Nations Unies [12] – ou de l'ECRI – Commission européenne contre le racisme et l'intolérance [13] – d'ailleurs. Faisant suite au constat selon lequel nombreuses personnes méconnaissent, totalement ou partiellement, la langue officielle de leur Etat, le Commissaire s'attache à rappeler l'importance de l'effectivité de la jouissance des droits de l'homme.

Les exemples allant dans ce sens sont multiples. Ainsi, dans un rapport sur la Turquie, le Commissaire aux droits de l'homme a considéré que l'interdiction de parler les langues minoritaires avec les fonctionnaires publics engendre une difficulté de communication et par conséquent un accès particulièrement difficile aux services[14] ; la position désavantageuse dans laquelle se trouvent les membres des minorités dans leurs relations avec les autorités administratives et lors de leurs

[10]La Cour européenne des droits de l'homme s'est prononcée, dans l'affaire *Čonka c. Belgique*, sur la question de la place de la langue lors des arrestations et a considéré que bien que les articles 5§1 et 5§4 ne contiennent pas de référence expresse à la langue, le fait que « l'information sur les recours figurait [, sur le document qui a été remis aux requérants,] en petits caractères et dans une langue qu'[ils] ne comprenaient pas » et qu'« il n'y avait qu'un seul interprète, qui était présent au commissariat mais n'est pas resté avec [eux] au centre fermé », l'accessibilité des requérants à un recours était entravée. Les requérants avaient en effet été privés d'une possibilité réaliste de saisir la juridiction compétente pour statuer sur la légalité de l'ordre de quitter le territoire qui avait été émis à leur encontre et qui justifiait leur détention. En application d'une jurisprudence constante, rappelée ici, « la Convention vise à garantir des droits non pas théoriques ou illusoires, mais concrets et effectifs » (Cour EDH [3ème section], *Čonka c. Belgique*, 5 février 2002, requête n° 51564/99, § 44).

Voir aussi : Cour EDH, *Brozicek c. Italie*, 19 décembre 1989, requête n° 10964/84, Série A vol. 167, § 41 et Cour EDH (4ème section), *Cuscani c. Royaume Uni*, 24 septembre 2002, requête n° 32771/96, § 38 ; Com. EDH, *ISOP c. Autriche*, 8 mars 1962, requête n° 808/60, Ann. 5, p. 108. Une conclusion similaire a été réalisée dans l'affaire : Com. EDH, *X et Y c. Belgique*, 7 octobre 1966, requête n° 2332/64, Ann. 9., p. 419 ; Com. EDH, *Mehmet Mehdi Zana c. Turquie*, 21 octobre 1993, requête n° 18954/91 ; Com. EDH, *Bideault c. France*, 6 octobre 1986, requête n° 11261/84.

[11]La Cour européenne des droits de l'homme, dans l'arrêt *Podkolzina c. Lettonie*, a rappelé qu'en principe l'obligation posée par les Etats d'utiliser une langue spécifique dans les assemblées n'est pas contraire à la Convention et que la subordination du droit de se porter candidat à la condition de démontrer un certain niveau de connaissance linguistique, sous peine d'être radié des listes électorales, ne constitue pas une atteinte aux droits garantis par l'article 3 du premier protocole (Cour EDH, *Podkolzina c. Lettonie*, 9 avril 2002, requête n° 46726/99, § 33).

[12]Le Comité pour l'élimination de la discrimination raciale s'est prononcé à plusieurs reprises sur la relation entre les connaissances linguistiques et la discrimination dans l'accès à certains droits ou services.

Voir notamment : CERD, *Rapport annuel du Comité*, 6 janvier 2012, UN Doc. A/66/18, Géorgie, § 15.

[13]Voir notamment : ECRI, *Troisième rapport sur Chypre*, 14 juin 2005, CRI(2006)17, § 80.

[14]CommDH, *Rapport sur la Turquie*, CommDH(2003)15, § 224.

procédures judiciaires a aussi été rappelée dans un rapport sur la Géorgie[15]. Suivant cette même idée, le Commissaire a invité des autorités lettonnes à vouer une attention particulière à l'usage de la langue russe dans les relations avec les administrations[16] et a recommandé à ces autorités de faciliter l'usage des langues minoritaires en général dans les correspondances écrites entre les membres des minorités et l'administration[17]. Il ne s'agit pas ici d'imposer aux Etats de permettre l'usage de toutes les langues dans tous les domaines de la sphère publique, ce qui engendrerait des frais exorbitants, mais de trouver un juste milieu entrant dans la logique de la justification de la différence de traitement. Fernand de Varennes, dans son étude pour les Nations Unies de 1997 portant sur les droits des personnes appartenant à des minorités linguistiques, a fait état du lien entre les droits des minorités et les obligations des Etats au travers du principe de non-discrimination. Il a souligné, à ce titre, qu'il ne peut être demandé à un Etat de conduire ses activités dans toutes les langues parlées sur son territoire et que toutes les distinctions impliquant une langue ne pouvaient être interdites *via* la non-discrimination. En revanche, les distinctions qui ne sont « pas raisonnables » (« *unreasonable* ») peuvent, et doivent même, être interdites par ce biais. Fernand de Varennes a suivi un raisonnement classique qui se rapporte à la justification et au test de proportionnalité[18]. En application de celui-ci, il a considéré que dans la pratique, lorsqu'il y a un nombre suffisamment important ou concentré d'individus impliqués dans un service de l'Etat ou autre activité telle qu'un enseignement public dans une langue donnée, la non-discrimination pourrait être invoquée avec succès[19]. En effet, les justifications telles que l'homogénéité linguistique d'un territoire ne peuvent plus être admises à l'heure actuelle, en raison de la valeur accordée au pluralisme dans une société démocratique, et la seule justification valable pouvant être soutenue par les Etats est celle d'un coût trop important pour mettre en place des services ne s'adressant qu'à quelques personnes.

De plus, dans une lettre adressée aux autorités slovaques en 2011, le Commissaire a rappelé que l'application des mesures protectrices de la langue officielle doit être mise en balance avec les droits des minorités et notamment les obligations que l'Etat[20] a contractées en ratifiant la Convention-cadre pour la protection des

[15]CommDH, *Rapport sur la Géorgie*, CommDH(2014)9, § 87.

[16]CommDH, *Rapport sur la Lettonie*, CommDH(2007)9, § 44.

[17]*Ibid.*, Recommandation n° 7.

[18]De Varennes F (1997), § 6.

[19]*Ibid.*, § 9.

[20]De même, il avait déjà souligné que la mise en œuvre des mesures protectrices de la langue officielle ne devait pas porter atteinte aux possibilités qu'ont les minorités de préserver leurs propres langues et de l'utiliser en conformité avec la Convention-cadre pour la protection des minorités nationales (CommDH, *Rapport sur l'Estonie*, CommDH(2004)5, § 23). Il a considéré crucial qu'un juste milieu soit trouvé entre la protection de la langue officielle et celles des minorités (CommDH, *Lettre adressée au Gouvernement de la République Slovaque*, CommDH(2011)45, § 3 ; CommDH, *Lettre au Gouvernement Ukrainien*, CommDH(2012)11), et ce bien que, comme il le rappelle, la Commission de Venise ait considéré que la sauvegarde de la langue officielle peut constituer un but

minorités nationales et la Charte européenne des langues régionales ou minoritaires, deux traités adoptés dans le cadre du Conseil de l'Europe et respectivement dédiés à la protection des minorités et de la diversité linguistique. Ainsi, il n'a pas considéré acceptable l'obligation d'utiliser la langue officielle dans les procédures judiciaires, administratives et autres procédures, dans les cas où la personne appartenant à une minorité a une connaissance insuffisante de la langue officielle. Il a, en outre, ajouté que la limitation de l'usage des langues minoritaires dans les communications officielles aux seules aires dans lesquelles les membres des minorités représentent 20 % de la population n'est, pour lui, pas acceptable, pas plus que l'obligation suivant laquelle les personnes privées doivent faire usage de la seule langue officielle dans leurs rapports avec l'administration[21]. En 2004 déjà, dans un rapport sur l'Estonie, il n'avait pas considéré acceptable la limitation de l'usage de la langue minoritaire avec les autorités aux seules zones habitées par 50 % de membres de cette minorité[22]. En effet, le nombre de personnes appartenant à une minorité donnée, de même que sa concentration, sont, dans le cadre de la justification d'une différence de traitement et en application du test de proportionnalité, de nature à justifier la création de services dans cette langue. Ne pas créer de tels services, alors que le nombre de bénéficiaires ou leur concentration sont suffisants, reviendrait donc à discriminer les membres de la minorité en cause. Ces deux éléments, du nombre de personnes appartenant à la minorité et de l'établissement compact de ces personnes sont d'ailleurs des critères que l'on retrouve non seulement dans la Convention-cadre pour la protection des minorités nationales et dans la Charte européenne des langues régionales ou minoritaires, mais aussi dans la pratique du Groupe de travail des Nations Unies sur les minorités[23] ou encore du Haut-commissaire pour les minorités nationales de l'OSCE[24].

Ainsi, le Commissaire aux droits de l'homme prend en compte la situation réelle des minorités pour assurer qu'elles ne sont pas discriminées dans la jouissance de leurs droits fondamentaux. Et fort logiquement, pour pouvoir agir au mieux et protéger les minorités contre d'éventuelles discriminations, il a considéré (tout

---

légitime (CommDH, *Lettre adressée au Gouvernement de la République Slovaque*, CommDH (2011)45, § 3 ; CommDH, *Lettre au Gouvernement Ukrainien*, CommDH(2012)11, § 6). En outre, il a montré sa satisfaction lorsqu'un Etat a ratifié la Charte européenne des langues régionales ou minoritaires et a recommandé à d'autres de faire de même (voir notamment : CommDH, *Rapport sur l'Arménie*, CommDH(2008)4, § 88 ; CommDH, *Rapport sur la Lettonie*, CommDH(2004)3, § 67 ; CommDH, *Rapport sur la Pologne*, CommDH(2003)4, Recommandation n° 5 ; CommDH, *Rapport sur la Turquie*, CommDH(2009)30, §§ 18 et 161 ; CommDH, *Rapport sur la France*, CommDH(2015)1, §§ 40 et 50 ; CommDH, *Rapport sur la Géorgie*, (CommDH2014)9, § 72).

[21]CommDH, *Lettre adressée au Gouvernement de la République Slovaque*, CommDH(2011)45, § 6.

[22]CommDH, *Rapport sur l'Estonie*, CommDH(2004)5, Recommandation n° 3.

[23]Groupe de travail sur les minorités, *Commentaire sur la Déclaration des Nations Unies sur les droits des personnes appartenant à des minorités nationales ou ethniques, religieuses et linguistiques*, 31 mars 2005, UN Doc. E/CN.4/Sub.2/AC.5/2005/2.

[24]HCNM, *Report on the Linguistic Rights of Persons Belonging to National Minorities in the OSCE Area*, March 1999, 31.p., p. 12.

comme l'ECRI[25] et le CERD[26]) qu'il convient de collecter des informations sur la composition ethnique de la population d'un pays donné, faute de quoi les autorités ne peuvent mettre en place les politiques adéquates[27]. Certes, les statistiques ethniques sont visées par des réserves en raison des utilisations néfastes qui pourraient en être faites[28], mais elles constituent l'unique façon de déceler les discriminations systémiques. De plus, la connaissance du nombre de locuteurs d'une langue donnée est nécessaire pour pouvoir analyser les (in)actions des autorités publiques, suivant l'idée développée ci-dessus de la possible justification de la différence de traitement entre les locuteurs de langues parlées par un faible nombre de locuteurs et ceux de langues parlées par un plus grand nombre de locuteurs.

En outre, le Commissaire aux droits de l'homme a demandé aux Etats d'assurer la présence des langues minoritaires dans des domaines tels que l'éducation, les médias écrits et audio-visuels ainsi que la justice. Il fait, pour cela, entrer ces problématiques dans sa mission visant à promouvoir le respect effectif des droits de l'homme.

---

[25]Voir notamment : ECRI, *Quatrième rapport sur la Lituanie*, 13 septembre 2011, CRI(2011)38, § 204.

[26]Voir notamment : CERD, *Rapport annuel du Comité*, 28 novembre 2009, UN Doc. A/64/18, Turquie, § 9 ; CERD, *Rapport annuel du Comité*, 31 octobre 2010, UN Doc. A/65/18, Maroc, § 7 ; CERD, *Rapport annuel du Comité*, 1 novembre 2008, UN Doc. A/63/18, Autriche, § 41.

[27]CommDH, *Rapport sur l'Albanie*, CommDH(2008)8, § 49 ; CommDH, *Rapport sur la Bosnie-Herzégovine*, CommDH(2011)11, § 17 ; CommDH, *Rapport sur la République Tchèque*, CommDH(2013)1, § 7 ; CommDH, *Rapport sur l'Allemagne*, CommDH(2015)20, § 196 ; CommDH, *Rapport sur la Serbie*, CommDH(2009)8, Reommandation n° 22 ; CommDH, *Rapport sur la République Slovaque*, CommDH(2015)21, § 66 ; CommDH, *Rapport sur le Kosovo*, CommDH(2009)23, § 111 ; CommDH, *Rapport sur la Turquie*, CommDH(2010)1, § 55.

Voir aussi : CommDH, *Rapport sur l'Autriche*, CommDH(2012) 28, § 12 ; CommDH, *Rapport sur l'Allemagne*, CommDH(2007)14, § 100.

[28]Le débat sur les statistiques ethniques est complexe tant il comporte d'enjeux. La réflexion sur le sujet a été abordée en France suivant les vœux du Président de la République (discours prononcé à Palaiseau le 17 décembre 2008) qui a souhaité doter la France d'outils statistiques, reposant sur des méthodes objectives et incontestables, dans le but de mesurer sa diversité. Cette réflexion est soutenue par le Conseil représentatif des organisations noires de France et le Conseil représentatif des institutions juives de France, notamment, qui y voient la possibilité d'obtenir des éléments nécessaires à l'élaboration d'outils permettant l'évaluation des discriminations. Les détracteurs des statistiques ethniques attirent cependant l'attention sur les risques de renforcement de la catégorisation ethnique de la société qui serait induite par la prescription de statistiques de cette nature. Ils soulignent que d'autres actions doivent être menées, de façon alternative, et notamment un renforcement substantiel de la lutte contre les discriminateurs. Pour des informations détaillées sur cette question, se référer aux deux rapports publiés le 5 février 2010 par le Comité pour la mesure et l'évaluation des discriminations (COMEDD) et de la diversité et le 24 juin 2009 par la Commission alternative de réflexion sur les « statistiques ethniques » et les discriminations (CARSED).

Voir notamment : Heran F et autres (2010 (consulté le 22 novembre 2017) ; Badinter E et autres (2009).

2.2 L'application directe des droits et libertés fondamentaux

Le Comité des droits de l'homme des Nations Unies et la Cour européenne des droits de l'homme, entre autres, ont considéré que le droit à la liberté d'expression[29] et à la vie privée[30] peuvent être violés par des restrictions à l'usage de la langue de son

[29]Dans l'affaire *Ballantyne, Davidson et McIntyre c. Canada,* le Comité des droits de l'homme des Nations Unies a reconnu que la liberté de choisir la langue dans laquelle on s'exprime, notamment pour les affichages privés, est un aspect du droit à la liberté d'expression et que les droits de la minorité francophone ne justifient pas la restriction suivant laquelle, en application de la législation du Québec, seul le français peut être utilisé dans l'affichage public et la publicité commerciale. En effet, l'interdiction totale de l'affichage rédigé dans une autre langue que le français n'est, pour le Comité, pas proportionnelle à l'objectif poursuivi. (CCPR, *John Ballantyne, Davidson et McIntyre c. Canada*, Communications n° 359/1989 et 385/1989, 31 mars 1993, CCPR/C/47/D/359/1989 et 385/1989/Rev.1).

De la même façon, le Comité des droits de l'homme a souligné que les médias privés sont protégés par la liberté d'expression et de la presse et qu'une interdiction de l'usage d'une langue minoritaire dans la communication audiovisuelle est, par conséquent, constitutive d'une violation de la liberté d'expression (CCPR, *Commentaires sur la République Dominicaine*, 5 mai 1993, CCPR/C/79/Add/18, § 7).

De même, en interprétant les décisions de la Commission européenne *a contrario*, il en ressort que la protection offerte à la liberté d'expression s'étend au droit d'utiliser la langue de son choix dans les activités relevant du domaine privé. Dans l'affaire *Vingt-trois habitants de l'Alsemberg c. Belgique*, elle a conclu à l'irrecevabilité de la requête indiquant que « rien n'empêch[ait] [les requérants] d'exprimer leur pensée librement et dans la langue de leur choix » (Com. EDH, *Vingt-trois habitants d'Alsemberg et de Beersel c. Belgique*, 26 juillet 1963, requête n° 1474/62, Ann. 6, p. 333, p. 343). Dans l'affaire *Clerfayt, Legros et autres*, la Commission a mentionné que la participation aux débats d'une assemblée représentative « sort[ait] [...] du cadre d'une activité de droit privé » (Com. EDH., *Clerfayt, Legros et al. c. Belgique*, 17 mai 1985, requête n° 19650/83, D.R. 42, p. 217). Finalement, dans l'affaire *Fryske Nasjonale Partij c. Pays-Bas*, la Commission a considéré que les requérants « n'[avaient] pas apporté la preuve qu'ils avaient également été empêchés de recourir à la langue frisonne dans d'autres cas » que dans leurs rapports avec l'administration (Com. EDH, *Fryske Nasjonale Partij c. Pays-Bas*, 12 décembre 1985, requête n° 11100/84, D.R. 45, p. 245).

[30]La Cour européenne des droits de l'homme a considéré, dans l'affaire *Chishti c. Portugal*, que l'interdiction faite à un détenu, emprisonné au Portugal, de correspondre en urdu avec sa famille restée au Pakistan (seule langue comprise par ses proches), constituait une ingérence dans son droit au respect de la correspondance. D'après la Cour, l'article 8 de la Convention ne protège pas seulement le contenu de la correspondance, mais aussi la possibilité d'envoyer et de recevoir des lettres. (Cour EDH, *Chishti c. Portugal*, 2 octobre 2003 (recevabilité), requête n° 57248/00). Dans l'affaire *Zakharova c. France*, la Cour a admis que le placement d'un enfant victime de maltraitance, avec interdiction pour sa mère russophone de lui parler sa langue maternelle lors de ses visites, constituait une ingérence dans le respect de la vie privée. La Cour a aussi considéré dans les affaires *Mentzen* alias *Mencena* et *Kuharec* alias *Kuhareca*, que si une transformation de la graphie d'un nom constitue bien une ingérence dans le droit au respect de la vie privée, dans les cas d'espèce qui n'étaient caractérisés que par des adaptations aux règles orthographiques et grammaticales de la langue nationale, ces adaptations étaient justifiées. Soulignant qu'elle ne pourrait mettre en doute l'appréciation de l'Etat que si celle-ci était entachée d'arbitraire, ce qui n'était pas le cas en l'espèce, elle a reconnu une large marge d'appréciation aux Etats dans ce domaine (Cour EDH [4ème section], *Mentzen* alias *Mencena c. Lettonie*, requête n° 71074/01 et *Kuharec* alias *Kuhareca c. Lettonie*, requête n° 71557/01, décisions du 7 décembre 2004).

choix : on peut notamment citer les décisions *Ballantyne, Davidson et McIntyre c. Canada* et *Raihman c. Lettonie* du Comité des droits de l'homme, ou encore les arrêts *Chishti c. Portugal* et *Mentzen* alias *Mencena c. Lettonie* de la Cour européenne des droits de l'homme.

De son côté, si le Commissaire aux droits de l'homme s'est prononcé à de multiples reprises sur l'usage des langues minoritaires dans la vie publique et privée, il ne cite pour autant pas forcément les droits qui seraient violés par les Etats parties qui ne le permettraient pas ou ne le soutiendraient pas suffisamment. Le lien entre l'usage des langues maternelles et la liberté d'expression a malgré tout été mentionné par le Commissaire aux droits de l'homme qui a considéré que l'éducation des membres des groupes minoritaires, tout comme l'enseignement et l'apprentissage des langues maternelles, est une pré-condition à la jouissance de la liberté d'expression par les membres des minorités[31].

En outre, la liberté dont le Commissaire dispose de par son large mandat lui permet de reconnaître un véritable droit à l'usage des langues : ainsi, dans un Rapport sur la Turquie, il a reconnu, en s'appuyant sur la Charte européenne des langues régionales ou minoritaires dont l'Etat en cause n'est pourtant pas partie, le droit inaliénable de tout individu à l'usage de sa langue minoritaire dans la vie tant privée que publique[32]. Nous mentionnons ici, d'ailleurs, que le CERD a aussi reconnu l'existence d'un droit pour chaque individu d'utiliser sa langue maternelle[33]. Il est remarquable, à ce propos, que la dichotomie traditionnellement réalisée entre la sphère privée et la sphère publique[34], par ailleurs largement critiquée

Le Comité des droits de l'homme a aussi eu à se prononcer sur la politique visant à adapter les noms aux règles orthographiques et grammaticales de la langue officielle (en l'espèce, lettone) dans l'affaire *Raihman c. Lettonie*. S'écartant une fois encore de la vision de la Cour européenne, il a considéré que si la protection de la langue officielle (domaine qu'il considère devoir laisser à l'appréciation des Etats parties) est bien un objectif légitime, l'interférence dans les droits du demandeur par l'adjonction forcée d'une terminaison déclinable au nom (et qui en modifie la prononciation), constitue une mesure intrusive non proportionnée à l'objectif poursuivi. Le Comité, se fondant sur sa jurisprudence antérieure qui considérait que l'article 17 comprenait le droit de choisir et de changer de nom, a conclu que la protection de la vie privée protège les individus contre le fait de se voir passivement imposer un changement de nom par les Etats parties (CCPR, *Raihman v. Latvia,* 28 octobre 2010, communication n° 1621/2007, CCPR/C/100/D/1621/2007, § 8.3).

[31] *"minority group members' education and teaching and learning of their mother tongues, [is] a precondition of enjoyment by them of their freedom of expression"* (CommDH, *Rapport sur la Turquie,* CommDH(2009)30, § 2).

[32] *"inalienable right to use their own regional or minority language in private and public life, in accordance with the principles enshrined in the European Charter for Regional or Minority Languages*" (CommDH, *Rapport sur la Turquie*, CommDH(2009)30, § 162).

[33] CERD, *Rapport annuel du Comité*, 28 novembre 2009, UN Doc. A/64/18, Grèce, § 15.

[34] Cette division classique, qui repose sur le principe de la neutralité de la sphère publique, suppose deux préalables : la limitation faite aux individus qui ne peuvent exprimer leurs différences que dans l'espace privé et l'imposition faite aux Etats de traiter tout le monde à l'identique, sans prise en compte des spécificités individuelles. Voir : Martucelli D (1997), p. 62.

par les mouvements communautarien et multiculturaliste[35], ne se retrouve pas dans les prises de position du Commissaire.

De plus, comme le Commissaire l'a rappelé notamment dans un Rapport sur la Lettonie, les Etats ont non seulement un devoir d'abstention mais encore l'obligation de prendre des mesures positives à l'égard des langues minoritaires[36]. Ainsi, il a par exemple encouragé les autorités étatiques azéries à allouer, dans les médias, des espaces et des créneaux aux représentants des minorités leur permettant d'émettre en langues minoritaires[37] et, dans un Rapport sur l'Arménie, il a qualifié de positive l'existence de journaux et programmes radiophoniques en langues minoritaires[38]. Suivant la même logique, le CERD a été amené, à mentionner sa satisfaction lorsque les langues minoritaires sont présentes dans les médias[39] et l'ECRI a régulièrement encouragé les autorités à prendre des initiatives visant à améliorer l'accès des groupes minoritaires aux médias, et notamment à accorder plus de temps d'antenne aux langues minoritaires[40].

Toujours dans le domaine des médias, le Commissaire est allé un pas plus loin dans son dernier rapport sur la Géorgie de 2014 en ne se positionnant plus seulement sur la possibilité pour les locuteurs de langues minoritaires de s'exprimer dans leur langue dans les médias mais en se fondant sur le droit à l'accès à l'information. Il a en effet rapporté le constat du Défenseur des droits géorgien selon lequel, depuis la fermeture d'une chaîne en langue russe, le programme d'informations quotidiennes ne donne pas d'informations détaillées aux membres des minorités. Il mentionne alors qu'en raison du peu d'informations disponibles dans les médias géorgiens dans des langues pouvant être comprises par les membres des minorités, ceux-ci ne reçoivent pas forcément les perspectives locales des affaires. Ils sont également sous-informés sur la situation en Géorgie ; en effet, ils reçoivent principalement les informations d'Arménie, Azerbaijan, Russie et Turquie[41].

Dans le domaine de l'éducation, par ailleurs, nombreuses sont les prises de positions du Commissaire. Dans un rapport sur la Croatie, il a demandé aux autorités de permettre aux enfants roms d'étudier dans leur langue maternelle et a ajouté que les autorités doivent soutenir les cours et le matériel éducatif en romani et bajashi[42].

---

[35]Pour une présentation détaillée et critique de ses deux courants de pensée et leur positionnement à l'égard du libéralisme, voir : Ringelheim J (2006), pp. 32-48.

[36]"*In general I believe the Latvian authorities should endeavour to provide more support to members of language minorities, and allow them to use their mother tongues for official business, as suggested in Article 10 of the framework convention. A gesture of support and magnanimity on the part of the state would certainly be very beneficial in terms of strengthening national cohesion. In addition, it might well motivate members of minorities with inadequate command of the official language to improve their knowledge of Latvian*" (CommDH, *Rapport sur la Lettonie*, CommDH(2004)3, § 75).

[37]CommDH, *Rapport sur l'Azerbaïdjan*, CommDH(2008)2, § 89.

[38]CommDH, *Rapport sur l'Arménie*, CommDH(2008)4, § 147.

[39]CERD, *Rapport annuel du Comité*, 31 octobre 2010, UN Doc. A/65/18, Kazakhstan, § 4.

[40]Voir notamment : ECRI, *Premier rapport sur Arménie*, 8 juillet 2003, CRI (2003)36, § 57.

[41]CommDH, *Rapport sur la Géorgie*, (CommDH2014)9, § 92

[42]CommDH, *Rapport sur la Croatie*, CommDH(2010)20, § 120.

Sur la même thématique, dans un récent rapport sur la Norvège, il a souligné l'importance capitale de l'éducation pour l'émancipation, en l'occurrence, des Roms et leur jouissance des droits de l'homme[43]. De façon similaire, dans un rapport sur l'Arménie, il a accueilli favorablement et qualifié de positive l'existence d'un enseignement des langues minoritaires et celui des littératures correspondantes ainsi que de manuels scolaires en langues minoritaires[44]. De surcroît, et prenant en compte la situation effective en Suède, le Commissaire aux droits de l'homme est allé jusqu'à prendre une position tranchée en faveur de l'enseignement en langue minoritaire et a demandé spécifiquement aux autorités suédoises que tous les enfants sâmes puissent bénéficier d'une éducation dans leurs langues[45]. Pour assurer un tel enseignement, principalement au niveau secondaire, il a, dans plusieurs rapports, demandé aux autorités non seulement de mettre en place des politiques visant à assurer que les futurs instituteurs puissent étudier en langues minoritaires[46] mais encore d'établir, dans les universités, des départements dédiés aux langues minoritaires[47]. Dans un plus récent rapport sur la Géorgie, il a, de même, encouragé les autorités à renforcer leurs efforts afin de délivrer une éducation de qualité aux membres des minorités non seulement en géorgien mais aussi en langues minoritaires à tous les niveaux éducatifs et dans le pays dans son ensemble[48]. Enfin, tout comme le CERD et l'ECRI, il a aussi ajouté que l'enseignement délivré pour les minorités doit être de qualité et a insisté sur la nécessité de prévoir le budget en conséquence[49], de mettre à disposition du matériel scolaire de qualité en langue minoritaire[50] et d'assurer une formation adaptée des enseignants[51].

---

[43]CommDH, *Rapport sur la Norvège*, CommDH(2015)9, §77.

[44]CommDH, *Rapport sur l'Arménie*, CommDH(2008)4, § 147.

[45]CommDH, *Rapport sur la Suède*, CommDH(2007)10, Recommendation n° 12. Le CERD et l'ECRI vont dans le même sens et encouragent les Etats à assurer un enseignement en langue minoritaire ou, au minimum, l'enseignement de ces langues. Voir notamment : CERD, *Rapport annuel du Comité*, 28 novembre 2009, UN Doc. A/64/18, Finlande, § 18 ; CERD, *Rapport annuel du Comité*, 28 novembre 2009, UN Doc. A/64/18, Turquie, § 20 ; ECRI, *Deuxième rapport sur l'Arménie*, 13 février 2007, CRI(2007)1, § 72.

[46]CommDH, *Rapport sur la Lettonie*, CommDH(2007)9, § 61 et recommandation n° 9 ; CommDH, *Rapport sur la Suède*, CommDH(2004)13, § 44.

[47]CommDH, *Rapport sur la Turquie*, CommDH(2009)30, § 164.

[48]CommDH, *Rapport sur la Géorgie*, (CommDH2014)9, page 4.

[49]CommDH, *Rapport sur l'Azerbaïdjan*, CommDH(2008)2, § 87 ; CommDH, *Rapport sur la Lituanie*, CommDH(2007)8, § 58 ; CommDH, *Rapport sur la Norvège*, CommDH(2006)10, § 47.

Voir aussi notamment : ECRI, *Quatrième rapport sur la France*, 15 juin 2010, CRI(2010)16, § 55 ; CERD, *Rapport annuel du Comité*, 6 janvier 2012, UN Doc. A/66/18, Paraguay, § 19.

[50]CommDH, *Rapport sur le Monténégro*, CommDH(2008)25, § 141 ; CommDH, *Rapport sur la Croatie*, CommDH(2010)20, § 150. Voir aussi notamment : ECRI, *Troisième rapport sur l'Arménie*, 8 février 2011, CRI(2011)1, § 77-79 ; CERD, *Rapport annuel du Comité*, 1er octobre 2007, UN Doc. A/62/18, Ex-République yougoslave de Macédoine, § 280.

[51]CommDH, *Rapport sur l'Estonie*, CommDH(2007)12, § 18. Voir aussi notamment : ECRI, *Deuxième rapport sur l'Arménie*, 13 février 2007, CRI(2007)1, § 70 ; ECRI, *First Report on Armenia*, 8 July 2003, CRI (2003) 36, § 45 ; ECRI, *Quatrième rapport sur la Hongrie*, 24 février

De manière générale et en toute logique, le Commissaire aux droits de l'homme a, au surplus, considéré qu'en l'absence de reconnaissance des minorités elles-mêmes, il est difficile de protéger leurs langues[52].

Ainsi donc, le Commissaire aux droits de l'homme, une fois encore comme le CERD et l'ECRI, a adopté une position qui se rapproche non seulement de ce qui est reconnu par le Comité des droits de l'homme en application de l'article 27 du Pacte international relatif aux droits civils et politiques mais aussi des droits reconnus spécifiquement par les traités dédiés aux minorités. Il semble, par là, tenté d'imposer les obligations spécifiques des traités dédiés aux minorités et à la diversité linguistique à tous les Etats membres du Conseil de l'Europe et même aux Etats qui ne seraient pas parties à ces traités. Cette logique paraît d'ailleurs s'inscrire dans la politique globale de l'organisation qui promeut l'unicité des droits de l'homme et des principes fondamentaux ainsi que leur interprétation, dans ce qui est appelé l'« ensemble de normes du Conseil de l'Europe »[53].

Même si la Commission européenne des droits de l'homme a été amenée à reconnaître que la protection d'une minorité linguistique était un but légitime pouvant être poursuivi par les Etats[54] et que des avancées concrètes ont été réalisées par les organes et juridictions internationales de droits de l'homme dans des domaines particuliers pour permettre aux justiciables d'utiliser dans des domaines toujours plus nombreux la langue de leur choix, la protection de la diversité linguistique n'est généralement pas considérée comme une fin en soi mais comme un moyen visant à protéger les droits fondamentaux des locuteurs de ses langues. C'est donc ici que le point de vue du Commissaire aux droits de l'homme est particulier : ses prises de position dépassent le strict cadre des droits de l'homme et font montre de sa volonté d'œuvrer pour une vision élargie des droits de l'homme qui les intègre dans le contexte général des sociétés démocratiques.

2009, CRI(2009)3, § 172 ; CERD, *Rapport annuel du Comité*, 6 janvier 2012, UN Doc. A/66/18, Géorgie, § 15 ; CERD, *Rapport annuel du Comité*, 6 janvier 2012, UN Doc. A/66/18, Arménie, § 15 ; CERD, *Rapport annuel du Comité*, 31 octobre 2010, UN Doc. A/65/18, Kazakhstan, § 9 ; CERD, *Rapport annuel du Comité*, 28 novembre 2009, UN Doc. A/64/18, Finlande, § 18 ; CERD, *Rapport annuel du Comité*, 1er octobre 2006, UN Doc. A/61/18, Guatemala, § 148 ; CERD, *Rapport annuel du Comité*, 1er octobre 2007, UN Doc. A/62/18, ex-République yougoslave de Macédoine, § 280 ; CERD, *Rapport annuel du Comité*, 6 janvier 2012, UN Doc. A/66/18, Norvège, § 18.

[52]CommDH, *Rapport sur la Slovénie*, CommDH(2003)11, § 18.

[53]Voir à ce titre : Secrétaire général du Conseil de l'Europe, *Situation de la démocratie, des droits de l'homme et de l'état de droit en Europe*, 5-6 mai 2014, SG(2014)1-Final, 72p., p. 9.

[54]Com. EDH, *Polacco et Gorofalo c. Italie*, 15 septembre 1997, requête n° 23450/94.

3 La protection des langues, un enjeu pour la démocratie

Il est clair, à la lecture des décisions des organes internationaux de droits de l'homme, qu'il n'y a pas de démocratie sans pluralisme. La protection de la diversité culturelle et linguistique s'inscrit fort logiquement dans ce cadre (3.1). Dans les sociétés culturellement diverses que sont les sociétés européennes, elle rappelle aussi l'existence de besoins croissants : l'intégration et la participation de tous aux affaires collectives (3.2).

3.1 La protection du pluralisme linguistique

Au-delà de la reconnaissance de droits à l'usage de la langue en tant que tels, le Commissaire aux droits de l'homme reconnaît l'intérêt de la protection de la diversité culturelle. Il se place de cette façon dans la continuité des prises de position des juridictions et quasi-juridictions internationales qui ont souligné l'importance du pluralisme pour les sociétés démocratiques et dans ce cadre, notamment, le rôle des langues minoritaires dans les médias. On peut citer dans ce sens deux arrêts de la Cour européenne des droits de l'homme : *Informationsverrein Lentia et autres c. Autriche*[55] et *Association Ekin c. France*[56].

Ainsi, dans un rapport sur la Norvège, le Commissaire a demandé que davantage de financement soit alloué à la restauration et préservation des cultures, langues et héritage culturel des minorités. Il a d'ailleurs souligné, que l'éducation des minorités est particulièrement importante à cet égard[57]. Il a aussi mentionné ce point dans un rapport sur la Bosnie-Herzégovine, soulignant que c'est pour permettre leur préservation que les langues, l'histoire et la culture des minorités devraient être intégrées aux programmes scolaires[58]. Suivant la même logique, il a défini comme nécessaire

[55]La Cour, dans son arrêt *Informationsverrein Lentia et autres c. Autriche*, a souligné l'importance de l'obligation, pour les Etats, de garantir le pluralisme des médias et, en l'espèce notamment, la possibilité laissée aux personnes appartenant à la minorité slovène d'Autriche, d'établir une radio bilingue (Cour EDH, *Informationsverein Lentia et autres c. Autriche*, 24 novembre 1993, Série A vol. 276, §§ 39-43).

[56]Dans l'arrêt *Association Ekin c. France*, la Cour a par ailleurs jugé contraire à l'article 10 de la Convention, la disposition législative française qui permettait au ministre de l'intérieur d'interdire la circulation, la distribution ou la mise en vente de journaux (ou autres écrits) rédigés en langue étrangère ou en provenance de l'étranger, en raison du caractère vague de la législation nationale qui peut mener à l'arbitraire. D'après la Cour, un « tel texte semble heurter de front le libellé même du paragraphe 1 de l'article 10 de la Convention, selon lequel les droits qui y sont reconnus valent 'sans considération de frontière' ». La Cour a rappelé, et ceci est important pour les minorités souvent séparées par les frontières, qu'il est légitime qu'elles bénéficient de la presse ou autres médias en provenance de leur Etat-parent ou de leur minorité sœur se trouvant de l'autre côté d'une frontière (Cour EDH, *Ekin c. France*, 17 juillet 2001, requête n° 39288/98, § 60).

[57]CommDH, *Rapport sur la Norvège*, CommDH(2006)10, § 47.

[58]CommDH, *Rapport sur la Bosnie-Herzégovine*, CommDH(2011)11, § 62. Voir aussi : CommDH, *Rapport sur la Norvège*, CommDH(2006)10, § 47.

à la survie d'une langue minoritaire faiblement parlée et de la culture qui lui est associée le maintien d'une école et du réseau social qu'elle crée (incluant l'école secondaire)[59]. Par ailleurs, il a considéré que le seul enseignement des langues minoritaires dans les zones où les minorités vivent de façon compacte n'est pas suffisant à lutter contre la disparition de ces langues[60].

Pour le Commissaire aux droits de l'homme, il est donc non seulement nécessaire de protéger les langues les moins parlées et les cultures qui y sont associées afin qu'elles ne disparaissent pas mais, pour ce faire, il est aussi indispensable de les enseigner de façon étendue sur un plan géographique ainsi que de les intégrer aux programmes scolaires.

L'intérêt du Commissaire pour le pluralisme et le maintien du multiculturalisme est souligné dans un rapport de 2014 sur l'Ukraine, dans lequel il a affirmé, concernant la Crimée, que le multiculturalisme est une particularité du territoire en question ainsi qu'un atout. Il a ajouté qu'il doit être encouragé et préservé notamment dans les médias, dans les écoles ainsi que dans les institutions publiques. Il a alors questionné le motif pour lequel l'usage de l'ukrainien avait été réduit dans les écoles, soulignant qu'il n'était pas établi de façon certaine que cette réduction ait été réalisée suivant la volonté des parents des enfants scolarisés dans les écoles en cause. En outre, la question de savoir si les parents pouvaient véritablement librement choisir la langue d'enseignement restait ouverte[61]. Le Commissaire a alors encouragé les autorités à faire leur maximum pour favoriser la liberté linguistique dans la région et à fournir les moyens nécessaires pour que tous les individus d'âge scolaire aient accès à une éducation de qualité dans les différentes langues. Enfin, il a encouragé l'usage de méthodologies bilingues et multilingues dans les processus éducatifs[62].

Pourtant, l'enseignement des langues minoritaires n'est pas réduit au seul objectif de préservation de la culture des minorités ; le Commissaire aux droits de l'homme, en plus de rappeler les implications de la liberté d'expression déjà mentionnées[63], a noté que le caractère illégal de l'éducation, du seul fait qu'elle ne soit pas délivrée dans la langue officielle, met clairement les enfants issus des minorités dans une position désavantageuse qui est, pour le Commissaire, difficile à accepter[64]. Il soutient sa position ici par des arguments tirés du principe de non-discrimination et d'autres, relatifs à la mise en œuvre de droits spécifiques clairement énoncés. Ces objectifs sont donc liés et s'enchevêtrent. Ils ne peuvent être séparés que de façon artificielle, raison pour laquelle, dans ses rapports, le Commissaire aux droits de l'homme, qui se veut pratique, les associe plutôt que les sépare.

---

[59]Il s'agissait en l'espèce de la langue sorabe. CommDH, *Rapport sur l'Allemagne*, CommDH (2007)14, § 108.

[60]CommDH, *Rapport sur l'Azerbaïdjan*, CommDH(2008)2, § 87.

[61]CommDH, *Rapport sur l'Ukraine*, CommDH(2014)19, § 26.

[62]CommDH, *Rapport sur l'Ukraine*, CommDH(2014)19, § 27.

[63]CommDH, *Rapport sur la Turquie*, CommDH(2009)30, §§ 2 et 163.

[64]CommDH, *Rapport sur la Turquie*, CommDH(2003)15, § 225.

Pour le Commissaire aux droits de l'homme, un intérêt fondamental de la protection de la diversité linguistique est, comme il l'a rappelé à de multiples reprises, d'ordre sociétal : pour l'intégration des diverses composantes des sociétés nationales et pour le renforcement des démocraties à caractère participatif.

3.2 La place des langues dans l'intégration et la construction de démocraties à caractère participatif

La Commission européenne des droits de l'homme a accepté que la protection d'une minorité soit considérée comme un objectif légitime justifiant une différence de traitement dans le système électoral (*Lindsay et autres c. Royaume-Uni*)[65] et, dans la décision *Polacco and Garofalo c. Italie*, elle a réitéré son raisonnement et a conclu que la protection des minorités linguistiques, poursuivie par la condition de quatre années de résidence continue nécessaire à pouvoir participer à des élections locales, est un objectif légitime[66]. Ainsi, les questions linguistiques entrent dans les questionnements relatifs à la participation des locuteurs des langues minoritaires aux élections et, de façon plus générale, à la vie publique.

Le Commissaire aux droits de l'homme reste dans cette même ligne tout en allant plus loin grâce à des prises de positions précises. Ainsi, sur la question spécifique de l'usage des langues minoritaires dans les procédures électorales, il a considéré que le seul droit d'usage de la langue officielle est trop restrictif et qu'il empêche la participation effective des membres des minorités à la vie politique. En effet, pour le Commissaire, dans les Etats démocratiques, le pluralisme de la société devrait être effectivement reflété dans toutes les manifestations démocratiques et en particulier dans les élections locales et nationales et dans les campagnes électorales qui sont, selon lui, les moyens les plus importants, pour les citoyens, de participer directement aux prises de décisions[67]. Force est de constater que sur ce point la France fait le mouvement inverse. Certes, des tracts électoraux sont fréquemment rédigés non seulement en français mais aussi dans d'autres langues, sans enfreindre le droit français[68], comme c'est le cas en Alsace, en Bretagne, au Pays basque, en Corse, et en région parisienne[69]. Mais, contrairement au régime local antérieur autorisant, en Alsace et en Moselle, le remboursement par l'Etat des affiches et tracts en allemand

[65]La Commission européenne a considéré, dans l'affaire *Lindsay c. Royaume-Uni* du 8 mars 1979, que le système électoral spécifique existant en Irlande du Nord « tenant compte de la situation particulière qui existe [dans cette zone] du point de vue de la majorité et de la minorité doit être considéré comme facilitant la libre expression de l'opinion du peuple » (Com. EDH, *Lindsay et autres c. Royaume-Uni*, 8 mars 1979, requête n° 8364/78, *D.R.* 15, pp. 247-258, 257).

[66]Com. EDH, *Polacco and Garofalo c. Italie*, 15 septembre 1997, requête n° 23450/94.

[67]CommDH, *Rapport sur la Turquie*, Comm(2009)30, § 43.

[68]CC, 20 décembre 2007, n° 2007-3873/3900, Seine-et-Marne 8ème circonscription.

[69]Woehrling J-M (2008), p. 15.

qui accompagnaient les mêmes affiches et tracts en français, l'Etat, depuis 2008, ne prend plus en charge que l'exemplaire en français[70]. Si ce changement de régime accorde maintenant le même traitement sur tout le territoire national, il aurait été plus respectueux des spécificités des minorités d'harmoniser les pratiques non en nivelant vers le bas mais en alignant le sort des documents électoraux de toutes les langues de France, quand le nombre et la concentration des locuteurs le nécessite, sur celui ayant cours, depuis 1919, en Alsace-Moselle.

En outre, afin de favoriser l'intégration des personnes appartenant à des minorités au sein des sociétés nationales, le Commissaire aux droits de l'homme a adopté une position claire s'agissant des médias et du principe de pluralisme : ce principe appliqué aux médias audiovisuels suppose que les différentes vues, informations, opinions, incluant celles des minorités, soient portées à l'attention d'une large audience[71]. Tout comme l'ECRI a l'habitude de le faire[72], il a rappelé le rôle des médias dans le renforcement du dialogue interculturel et la compréhension mutuelle[73]. L'enjeu est ici d'assurer une visibilité aux minorités et à leurs membres, de les valoriser, tout comme leur langue, leur culture et, par conséquent, leur identité propre. Les revendications allant vers une reconnaissance des minorités, de leur culture et de leur langue sont légitimes et doivent être relayées par les médias. Elles ne sont en rien des marqueurs de volontés indépendantistes ou d'insubordination au pouvoir central. A l'inverse, en l'absence d'une écoute attentive et compréhensive ainsi que de réponses cohérentes de la part des autorités, les risques sont ceux de la résurgence de volontés indépendantistes et de non-reconnaissance des autorités en place. L'exemple de la Catalogne semble parlant à ce titre.

Dans le domaine de l'éducation et suivant cette idée de compréhension mutuelle, le Commissaire aux droits de l'homme[74], à l'instar de l'ECRI et du CERD[75], a souligné la nécessité d'intégrer, dans les programmes scolaires, un enseignement interculturel et pluriculturel. De plus, le Commissaire aux droits de

[70]CE, 22 février 2008, n° 312550, 312737, *Mme Uhlrich-Mallet, Association culture et bilinguisme d'Alsace et de Moselle et autres.*

[71]CommDH, *Rapport sur l'Arménie*, CommDH(2011)12, § 107.

[72]Voir notamment : ECRI, *Troisième rapport sur Chypre*, 14 juin 2005, CRI(2006)17, § 90.

[73]CommDH, *Rapport sur la Bosnie-Herzégovine*, CommDH(2008)1, § 83 ; CommDH, *Rapport sur la Pologne*, CommDH(2004)13, § 67 ; CommDH, *Rapport sur la Serbie*, CommDH(2011)09, § 149.

[74]CommDH, *Rapport sur la Bulgarie*, CommDH(2010)1, § 55.

[75]CERD, *Rapport annuel du Comité*, 1 octobre 2007, UN Doc. A/62/18, République tchèque, § 115 ; CERD, *Rapport annuel du Comité*, 6 janvier 2012, UN Doc. A/66/18, Lituanie, § 7 ; CERD, *Rapport annuel du Comité*, 28 novembre 2009, UN Doc. A/64/18, Tunisie, § 18 ; CERD, *Rapport annuel du Comité*, 6 janvier 2012, UN Doc. A/66/18, République Tchèque, § 7 ; CERD, *Rapport annuel du Comité*, 1 octobre 2007, UN Doc. A/62/18, République Tchèque, § 115 ; CERD, *Rapport annuel du Comité*, 31 octobre 2010, UN Doc. A/65/18, Argentine, § 19 ; CERD, *Rapport annuel du Comité*, 31 octobre 2010, UN Doc. A/65/18, Japon, § 7 ; CERD, *Rapport annuel du Comité*, 31 octobre 2010, UN Doc. A/65/18, Kazakhstan, § 7 ; CERD, *Rapport annuel du Comité*, 6 janvier 2012, UN Doc. A/66/18, Géorgie, § 7 ; CERD, *Rapport annuel du Comité*, 6 janvier 2012, UN Doc. A/66/18, Norvège, § 7.

l'homme et le CERD[76] ont tous deux considéré, dans la ligne du positionnement de l'ECRI en faveur du bilinguisme[77], que des ponts entre les locuteurs devaient être maintenus et que si la mise en œuvre des mesures protectrices de la langue officielle ne devait pas empêcher l'enseignement en langues minoritaires[78], l'enseignement en langues minoritaires ne devait pas non plus empêcher les membres des minorités d'apprendre la langue officielle[79]. Il semble logique, pour qu'un Etat puisse fonctionner convenablement, d'attendre des membres des minorités qu'il accueille de savoir parler la langue officielle ou l'une des langues officielles. Mais la capacité à interagir si elle implique la connaissance d'une langue commune, n'implique pas que tout individu parle strictement et uniquement la même langue que tous ses concitoyens. La connaissance d'une langue n'est, en effet, pas exclusive de la connaissance d'une autre. La justification avancée en faveur des politiques d'assimilation à la langue et culture majoritaire est celle de l'unité de la nation ; la justification avancée pour l'imposition de l'usage de langues minoritaires est celle de la sauvegarde de l'identité régionale ou de l'identité de la minorité en cause. Dans aucun de ces deux cas, le test de proportionnalité n'imposera l'obligation de permettre, dans un secteur donné, l'usage unique d'une seule langue, que ce soit la langue officielle ou la langue minoritaire, un usage encadré de l'une et l'autre langue suffisant à assurer tant l'unité de la nation que la protection de la langue en danger.

Les liens étroits entre les droits de l'homme et le respect de la diversité culturelle ont été rappelés à de multiples occasions par le Commissaire qui a notamment souligné, dans un rapport concernant la Turquie, que la protection des droits et des libertés des personnes appartenant à des minorités fait partie intégrante du système européen des droits de l'homme et n'appartient pas au domaine réservé des Etats. Elle est même à l'origine d'une responsabilité collective à la charge de tous les Etats

---

[76]Le CERD a été amené à se prononcer en faveur de l'enseignement bilingue : CERD, *Rapport annuel du Comité*, 6 janvier 2012, UN Doc. A/66/18, Géorgie, § 15 ; CERD, *Rapport annuel du Comité*, 28 novembre 2009, UN Doc. A/64/18, Suriname, § 16 ; CERD, *Rapport annuel du Comité*, 31 octobre 2010, UN Doc. A/65/18, Argentine, § 19.

[77]L'ECRI a souligné les risques liés à la constitution de classes ou d'écoles en fonction de la langue d'enseignement qui aurait, selon lui, « pour effet collatéral une séparation graduelle des enfants dans le système scolaire selon une ligne linguistique et ethnique. Le danger serait que, éduqués dans des langues distinctes, et séparés dès le plus jeune âge, les membres des différentes communautés se côtoient sans se connaître ni communiquer, et perpétuent ainsi méfiance réciproque et intolérance ». La solution proposée par l'ECRI consisterait alors dans le renforcement de l'enseignement plurilingue et « la définition et à la mise en œuvre d'une politique volontariste visant à développer des activités communes scolaires et parascolaires conduisant les enfants de tous profils linguistiques et ethniques à se rencontrer, à se mélanger et à interagir » (ECRI, Quatrième rapport sur l'Ex-République Yougoslave de Macédoine, 15 juin 2010, CRI(2010)19, §§ 33 et 37). La nécessité d'une éducation interculturelle est par ailleurs rappelée fréquemment par l'ECRI, notamment via l'enseignement de l'histoire. Voir notamment : ECRI, 4ème rapport sur Autriche, 2 mars 2010, CRI (2010)2, § 46 ; ECRI, Troisième rapport sur Chypre, 14 juin 2005, CRI(2006)17, § 68.

[78]CommDH, *Rapport sur l'Estonie*, CommDH(2004)5, § 23.

[79]CERD, *Rapport annuel du Comité*, 6 janvier 2012, UN Doc. A/66/18, Géorgie, § 15.

membres du Conseil de l'Europe[80]. Dans la même ligne, il a noté à plusieurs reprises, d'une part, que la protection et la promotion des droits de l'homme des groupes non dominants et des minorités ont toujours été au cœur de son travail et, d'autre part, que l'histoire de l'Europe a montré que la protection des minorités est essentielle à la stabilité, à la sécurité démocratique et à la paix. Il a ainsi souligné que la protection garantie par les Etats aux groupes non dominants est, en fait, le test décisif du respect des principes fondamentaux des droits de l'homme par ces derniers, principes qui doivent s'épanouir dans toute société pluraliste et démocratique[81]. Enfin, il est possible de synthétiser la position du Commissaire aux droits de l'homme sur la question en citant un de ses rapports de 2003 sur la République Tchèque : « Si la démocratie est le pouvoir de la majorité, la qualité de cette dernière se mesure au respect qu'elle accorde à ses minorités »[82].

4 Conclusion

Les prises de position du Commissaire aux droits de l'homme, si elles ne sont pas originales, sont nombreuses et font apparaître sa volonté de se saisir des questions relatives à la diversité culturelle et linguistique en particulier. Son mandat large le lui permet et la liberté rédactionnelle dont il fait usage dans ses rapports l'autorise à ne pas suivre d'argumentaire juridique strict. Ainsi, il ne se rattache pas à une disposition précise d'un traité international ou d'une déclaration spécifique dont il aurait la charge d'assurer le *monitoring*. Davantage mêle-t-il, au gré des besoins et des situations de fait qu'il rencontre, les arguments tirés du principe de non-discrimination à ceux relatifs à la mise en œuvre de droits spécifiques clairement énoncés, tels que le droit à la liberté d'expression. Pareillement, il se fonde sur des éléments constitutifs des sociétés démocratiques qu'il a pour volonté d'aider à construire : pluralisme, intégration et participation de tous aux affaires collectives. Il adopte ainsi un positionnement souple s'adaptant aux besoins concrets des sociétés européennes à la fois diverses et en constante mutation.

---

[80] *The "protection of the rights and freedoms of persons belonging to minorities is an integral part of the European human rights system, which does not belong to the domaine réservé of individual states but constitutes a collective responsibility borne by all member states of the Council of Europe"* (CommDH, *Rapport sur la Turquie,* CommDH(2009)30, § 8).

[81] *The "protection and promotion of the human rights of non-dominant, minority groups in Europe has always been at the heart of the Commissioner's work. European history has indeed shown that the protection of minorities is essential to stability, democratic security and peace. Protection afforded by states to non-dominant groups is in fact a litmus test for the former's effective observance of and respect for the fundamental human rights principles that should flourish in every pluralist, democratic society"* (CommDH, *Rapport sur la Turquie,* CommDH(2009)30, § 7). Voir aussi : CommDH, *Rapport sur la République slovaque,* CommDH(2011)42, § 4 ; CommDH, *Rapport sur l'Italie*, CommDH(2011)26, § 4 ; CommDH, *Rapport sur l'Italie,* CommDH(2012)26, § 62.

[82] CommDH, *Rapport sur la République tchèque*, CommDH(2003)10, § 21.

S'il eût été intéressant de tenter de définir une ligne jurisprudentielle, ou plutôt une ligne claire dans la pratique du Commissaire, cela n'a pas été possible. Le style rédactionnel des rapports a évolué année après année, ce qui ne permet pas véritablement de comparer l'évolution de sa pratique au cours du temps. En outre et une fois encore, le fait est que le Commissaire s'attache plus à aider des Etats à résoudre des situations juridiques ou factuelles compliquées qu'à élaborer, pour lui, une ligne de conduite.

Il nous a semblé malgré tout que les prises de position sur les questions linguistiques ne sont plus aussi nombreuses actuellement qu'elles ne l'étaient il y a encore quelques années et que l'accent est davantage mis sur le discours de haine et les violences inter-ethniques ou encore sur l'intégration des réfugiés. Cette dernière thématique permet malgré tout que soient prises en compte des questions d'ordre culturel ou linguistique, comme cela a été le cas dans le rapport de 2014 sur le Danemark. Le Commissaire aux droits de l'homme y a souligné que même si les conditions de vie matérielles sont adéquates, de nombreux enfants vivant dans des centres pour réfugiés pour des périodes indéfinies développent des désordres psychologiques et d'autres problèmes de développement. Il a poursuivi, ce qui nous intéresse ici particulièrement, en soulignant le rôle de la langue dans l'éducation. Selon lui, de nombreux enfants apparaissent ne pas pouvoir développer les « capacités langagières » de base en raison de l'absence d'éducation dans leur langue maternelle et d'un manque d'accès au système scolaire traditionnel en danois et à des contacts avec la société danoise[83]. Cette prise de position est novatrice car on peut lire entre les lignes, non seulement, que l'accès à l'éducation en langue maternelle n'est pas reconnue aux seules minorités nationales traditionnellement présentes sur le territoire national mais l'est aussi aux nouvelles minorités issues de l'immigration très récente ; qu'en outre, le droit à l'éducation ne serait pas reconnu comme effectif si cette éducation n'était pas réalisée dans la langue maternelle de l'enfant. Ce second point est cependant contrebalancé par la seconde partie de la phrase faisant référence, au titre de second facteur limitant cet apprentissage, à l'absence d'accès à l'éducation traditionnelle en danois.

Le Commissaire aux droits de l'homme est un acteur de la protection de la diversité linguistique à ne pas négliger, tant sa notoriété, sa crédibilité et son autorité sont importantes, à l'intérieur des Etats membres du Conseil de l'Europe et même au-delà. Son apport le plus important semble à cet égard être, comme cela a été mentionné, qu'il s'efforce de replacer les droits de l'homme dans un contexte plus large, un contexte sociétal. Son travail de terrain et sa pratique fondée sur des rapports rendent ses prises de positions certes moins détaillées en terme de théorie juridique mais plus pratiques et souvent facilement applicables.

[83]"*Many children reportedly fail to develop a core language, due to lack of education in their mother tongue and lack of access to mainstream education in Danish and contacts with Danish society*" (CommDH, *Rapport sur le Danemark*, Comm(2014)4, § 22).

Références

Alfredsson G, Grimheden J, Ramcharan B, De Zayas A (eds) (2001) International Human Rights Monitoring Mechanisms. Essays in Honour of Jakob Th. Möller. Martinus Nijhoff, The Hague/Boston/London

Badinter E et autres (2009) Le retour de la race. Contre les « statistiques ethniques ». Rapport de la CARSED (Commission alternative de réflexion sur les « statistiques ethniques » et les discriminations). Editions de l'Aube, Avignon

Benoît-Rohmer F (2001) La Cour de Strasbourg et la protection de l'intérêt minoritaire: une avancée décisive sur le plan des principes ? (En marge de l'arrêt Chapman). In: Rev. trim. dr. h. 48:999-1015

Benoît-Rohmer F (2002) La Cour européenne des droits de l'homme et la défense des droits des minorités nationales. In: Rev. trim. dr. h. 51:563-586

Conseil de l'Europe et Université Robert Schuman (dir.) (2003) La Charte européenne des langues régionales ou minoritaires et la France. Quelle(s) langue(s) pour la République ? Le Dilemme « diversité/unicité », Actes du Colloque organisé par le Conseil de l'Europe et l'Université Robert-Schuman de Strasbourg, Strasbourg, 11-12 avril 2002. Editions du Conseil de l'Europe, Strasbourg

De Varennes F (1996) Language, Minorities and Human Rights. Martinus Nijhoff, The Hague/London/Boston

De Varennes F (1997) To Speak or not to Speak. The Rights of Persons Belonging to Linguistic Minorities. Working paper, 18 avril 1997, UN Doc. E/CN.4/Sub.2/AC.5/1997/WP.6

Gellner E (1983) Nations and Nationalism, Blackwell, Oxford, 1ère édition

Heran F et autres (2010) Inégalités et discriminations. Pour un usage critique et responsable de l'outil statistique. Rapport du Comité pour la mesure de la diversité et l'évaluation des discriminations (COMEDD) présenté à M. Yazid Sabeg, Commissaire à la diversité et à l'égalité des chances. http://www.ladocumentationfrancaise.fr/var/storage/rapports-publics/104000077/0000.pdf (consulté le 22 novembre 2017)

Kymlicka W, Patten A (2003) Language Rights and Political Theory. Oxford University Press, Oxford

Martucelli D (1997) Les contradictions politiques du multiculturalisme. In: Wieviorka M (dir.) Une société fragmentée ? Le multiculturalisme en débat. La Découverte, Paris, pp. 61-82

Nogueira Lopez A, Ruiz Vieytez E, Urrutia Libarona I (2012) Shaping Language Rights: Commentary on the European Charter for Regional or Minority Languages in Light of the Committee of Experts' Evaluation, Editions du Conseil de l'Europe, Strasbourg

Pentassuglia G (2003) Minority Issues as a Challenge in the European Court of Human Rights: A Comparison with the Case Law of the United Nations Human Rights Committee. In: GYIL 4:401-451

Ringelheim J (2006) Diversité culturelle et droits de l'homme. La protection des minorités par la Convention européenne des droits de l'homme. Bruylant, Bruxelles

Woehrling J-M (2008) La question de la propagande électorale bilingue en Alsace-Moselle. Conformation de la suppression du régime local particulier, note sous arrêt, CE, 22 février 2008, n° 312550, 312737, Mme Uhlrich-Mallet, Association culture et bilinguisme d'Alsace et de Moselle et autres. In: Revue du droit local 53:9-15

Minority Languages in Education in Europe: A Contrasting Exercise of the Cases of the Catalan in Catalonia in Spain and the Sorbian in Germany

Caroline Westphal

Abstract The educational system is fundamental concerning the continuity and the development of languages for future generations. Therefore, the education especially in regional and minority languages is crucial for their survival in the future. Concerning regional and minority languages, the European Charter for Regional or Minority Languages, adopted in 1992, entails obligations under Article 8 for education for Germany and Spain. Both countries have found different solutions of implementation of the Charter for Regional or Minority Languages. Whereas in the realm of education the Catalan model is very successful in preserving and maintaining Catalan as a regional and minority language, with Sorbian in Germany this is not the same case. Therefore, I am going to contrast the regulations for these two languages. This article shall examine the challenges that different regional and minority languages face in education, as well as which legal frameworks work well to ensure the future of regional and minority languages.

1 Introduction

Language is a natural consequence of the human nature.[1] It is an instrument and medium of social communication. Language fosters a sense of identity. The coexistence of languages and multilingualism is natural and common. Yet there is always an imbalance between the juridical status of majority and minority languages. As Professor Iñigo Urrutia Libarona wrote in his book on language rights and the Basque educational system, the relations between the law and the language are intense. The right to know and to use a language is connected with the judicial recognition of that language. The educational system is the vehicle of transmission of the knowledge of languages. The educational system is fundamental concerning

[1]Langham Brown (1967), p. 37.

C. Westphal (✉)
Public, International and Comparative Public Law (Professor St. Oeter), University of Hamburg, Hamburg, Germany

© Springer International Publishing AG, part of Springer Nature 2018
E. Lagrange et al. (eds.), *Cultural Heritage and International Law*,
https://doi.org/10.1007/978-3-319-78789-3_3

the continuity and the development of languages for future generations.[2] The educational system is one of the main pillars of society. It functions to shape the future citizens. A society is only as strong as the education of its people. Knowledge is passed on by language, and language is the mean that creates a collective personality and models a collective identity.[3] Especially a regional or minority language needs to be developed and adapted to a changing society. It needs to meet the requirements for modern communication. If a regional or minority language is marginalized in the public realm, then it faces difficulties to survive also in private life. An effective inclusion of regional and minority languages in school education and university curriculum is crucial for survival in the future.[4] All languages are of equal value, and language diversity has to be seen as a cultural richness. Yet the competing use of more than one language leads to complex differentiation difficulties. The knowledge about multilingualism and its recognition and guarantee are focal points of democracy. Education is an important vehicle that involves the right of future generations to learn a regional or minority language. The school system is the crucial medium in order to secure continuity and development of regional and minority languages. Learning the mother tongue is an inalienable precondition for the survival of minorities.

Concerning the protection and promotion of regional and minority languages, there is an international instrument on the European level: the European Charter for Regional or Minority Languages adopted in 1992. It entered into force on March 1, 1998. So far, 33 states have signed the Charter, and in 25 states the Charter entered into force.[5] The European Charter for Regional or Minority Languages creates positive obligations for the states.[6] Therefore, it differs significantly from the Framework Convention for the Protection of National Minorities adopted in 1994. The Framework Convention is an instrument of the European Human Rights Protection. It creates obligations that are not directly applicable but require a transformation by the contracting states. The Framework Convention tries to establish a balance between the guaranteed rights and freedoms of members of national minorities on the one hand and wants to influence national legislation and government policies through general principles and specific obligations on the other hand.[7]

The European Charter for Regional or Minority Languages is strictly speaking not a human rights instrument as it focuses on the languages itself and features an à la carte approach.[8] Against general expectations and initial criticism, this approach proved to be the strength of the Charter. Despite general fears, the states have not chosen the minimum standard but have created a set menu with normative

[2]Urrutia Libarona (2005), pp. 29–30.

[3]Generaltiat de Catalunya (2015), p. 6.

[4]Langenfeld (2011), p. 186.

[5]http://conventions.coe.int/Treaty/Commun/ChercheSig.asp?NT=148&CM=&DF=&CL=GER (accessed on 3 December 2017).

[6]Oeter (2017), p. 551.

[7]Oeter (2017), pp. 551 et seq.; see also idem, in this volume, Sect. 4.

[8]Dunbar (2009), pp. 155 et seq.

ambitions, taking into account the problems of the individual regional or minority language.[9] The Charter does not explicitly grant any form of individual or collective rights for the speakers of vernacular languages.[10] Yet the Charter creates more than one hundred standards and obligations of protection in the central realms of language protection. These standards and obligations are graded by intensity of protection. The states should enter into at least 35 obligations according to the nature of the protected language. In the third section, there are to be found the protection criteria for regional and minority languages in education and schools. The European Charter for Regional or Minority Languages develops several steps for all five relevant realms of education (preschool, primary school, secondary school, technical and vocational school, university and adult education). It starts with school education in the regional or minority language, bilingual school models, classes in the regional or minority language as second or third language and, last but not least, as a minimum guarantee of the duty to offer classes in the regional or minority language for children from the regional minority.

The preservation of a regional or minority language depends significantly on its role in the educational system. Especially, languages that are threatened to disappear and are in a process to become extinct depend on the transmission of knowledge through education. This can also affect languages, such as Danish, that are posed at risk not in their existence but in their importance as language of communication and cultural factor in the regions beyond the original motherland of these languages. In order to preserve regional and minority languages, they have to find their place in the educational system. Otherwise, also the other obligations of the European Charter for Regional or Minority Languages would be ineffective.[11]

States have entered into obligations under the instrument of the Charter according to Article 8, which is specifically dedicated to issues of education. The Charter for Regional or Minority Languages has been implemented with different solutions in Germany and Spain. Whereas in the realm of education the Catalan model is very successful in preserving and maintaining Catalan as a regional and minority language, with Sorbian in Germany this is not the same case. Therefore, I am going to contrast the educational models put forward by the legal regulations for these two languages.

My cognitive interest herewith lies with the structural factors of society and, further, which legal frameworks work well to ensure the future of regional and minority languages. I am going to demonstrate the legislation for models of education in Sorbian in Germany and Catalan in Catalonia. I will not focus on the Catalan in Valencia and the Balearic Islands, which follow a different approach in education. And I will investigate only in compulsory education in Germany and Spain, hence primary and secondary schools.

---

[9]Oeter (2011), p. 7.

[10]Council of Europe (1992), p. 2.

[11]Langenfeld (2011), p. 186.

2 Language Rights in Education Concerning Sorbian in Germany

2.1 The Historical Background

Lower Sorbian, which is also called Wendish, and Upper Sorbian are western Slavonic languages spoken in the region of Lower and Upper Lusatia in the east of Germany. Lower Lusatia is part of the Land of Brandenburg, and Upper Lusatia is part of the Free State of Saxony. The languages are similar to other West Slavonic languages, such as Polish, Czech, and Slovak.[12]

The Sorbian school system is historically unique, especially in Upper Lusatia in the area around Bautzen. These schools in Upper Lusatia are the only case of genuinely mother tongue minority education in state schools in Germany. According to local traditions in the towns, Sorbian is spoken in daily life and children have grown and are growing up with Sorbian as mother tongue. Therefore, local schools are teaching in Sorbian.[13]

The Sorbs came originally from north of the Carpathian Mountains between Oder and Dnjepr until the Elbe and Saale during the migration wave of the Slavs in the sixth century.[14] For the first time, the "surbi" (Sorbs) were officially mentioned in the Fredegar-Chronicle dating back to 659.[15] Until today, the Sorbs were able to preserve their linguistic and cultural independence, yet they never had the opportunity to establish their own state and thus reach political autonomy.

In the history of the Sorbian people, clergymen played a crucial role in the development of an educational system preserving the Sorbian language. The first Sorbian elementary school was a parish school in Bautzen from 1540/1542 till 1821, and religious studies were taught in Sorbian. Furthermore, Sorbian was taught in small schools called *Winkelschulen* and *Winterschulen*, which were founded in towns in Lusatia during the time of the Reformation until the eighteenth century. A compulsory school education did not exist; therefore, there were no regular classes. In the beginning of the eighteenth century, the first textbooks in Sorbian were printed.[16]

In the time of the German Empire (1871–1918), Sorbian was eradicated due to the methods of Germanization. During the Weimar Republic, with the Provisional Law (*Übergangsgesetz*) of 1919, the Sorbs in Saxony gained rights to practice their mother tongue in schools again. In the Prussian part of Lusatia, the Sorbian language was not taken into consideration in schools. Between 1933 and 1945, the Nazi regime tried to definitely solve the "Sorbian national question." All Sorbian

[12]Brězan and Nowak (2016), p. 5.

[13]Oeter (2001), p. 45.

[14]Kunze (2008), p. 9.

[15]Kroll (2014), p. 10.

[16]Budar (2010), p. 173.

associations were prohibited, and Sorbian books and printed matters were destroyed. Sorbian was purposively suppressed in public and survived only in the private realm within the families.[17]

May 1945 marked a new beginning for the Sorbian educational system. The Soviet Military Administration gave the instruction to legally reinitiate Sorbian classes in the schools in Lusatia. The Parliament of Saxony passed a law for the preservation of the rights of the Sorbian population in March 1948, and in September 1950 the Council of Ministers of Brandenburg followed with a regulation for the promotion and development of Sorbian cultural efforts.[18]

The German Democratic Republic entered into the obligation to promote the Sorbs in their free and traditional development according to Article 40 of the Constitution of the GDR. Yet the Sorbs had to develop a Sorbian national consciousness again. Not all members of the Domowina—the Union of Lusatian Sorbs—had a feeling of belonging to the Sorbian people. The foundations for today's Sorbian school system were laid in the early years of the German Democratic Republic. In 1952, the directive to regulate the education in the Sorbian settlement area in Saxony and Brandenburg was passed. This directive introduced two types of schools. Type A implemented schools with Sorbian as the medium of instruction, whereas the Type B schools only offered classes of Sorbian. This system worked well for a long time.

The government of the GDR tried to revaluate the Sorbian language in daily life with the motto "Lusatia is becoming bilingual."[19] The organization of the policy toward the Sorbs was a lengthy process of learning for all sides involved. It was a model of the GDR's nationality policy. In the end, the Sorbian question was considerably promoted in the 40 years of the existence of the GDR and also instrumentalized by the state.[20] The state wanted to integrate the minority in its socialist system. The Domowina was under the mandate of the Central Committee of the Socialist Unity Party of Germany (SED). Hence, the Sorbs could not participate in important government decisions.[21]

The restructuring of society after the German reunification in 1990 influenced politics toward the Sorbs and education in Sorbian immensely.[22] In note 14 to the minutes of Article 35 of the Reunification Treaty of 1990, it is enshrined that the Sorbs have the right to preserve their national identity, language, and culture. Further, the school system was freed from the political baggage of the past. The equality of the Sorbian population and the state promotion and support to preserve their culture and traditions were embedded on regional, federal, and European levels.

---

[17]Budar (2010), pp. 175 et seq.

[18]Budar (2010), p. 176.

[19]*Anweisung zur Regelung der Schulverhältnisse in den sorbischen Siedlungsgebieten des Freistaates Sachsen und des Landes Brandenburg*; Budar (2010), p. 176.

[20]Toivanen (2001), p. 11.

[21]Scholze (2002), p. 54.

[22]Pech (2012), p. 249.

Together with the principle of federalism, the Sorbian school system formed part of the sovereign duty of the federal states (*Bundesländer*) in charge. Ever since, Sorbian and bilingual schools have been established in the school systems of Brandenburg and Saxony.[23]

In the past decades, difficulties have arisen with the provision of education in Sorbian outside the main settlement areas. As a consequence of negative demographic change in Lusatia, schools had to be closed. Thus, a self-contained Sorbian social environment was lost. Sorbian is now an asymmetric minority language. The Sorbs in Upper Lusatia have always wanted autonomy in structural decisions similar to the Danish School Association. Cultural autonomy with their own school authorities would be an option for a couple of schools in Upper Lusatia, yet it is impossible for the federal government to grant such funding due to the limits of the constitutional division of competences. Further, there is no kin state that could provide the indispensable supplementary aid to finance such a costly minority school system.[24]

Ethnic statistics are not allowed in Germany.[25] Hence, the number of Sorbs or Sorbian speakers is unknown. The number of Sorbian speakers is lower than the number of Sorbs (as people perceiving themselves to belong to the Sorbian minority) since a lot of people feel Sorbian but do not have the language capabilities to speak Sorbian. According to officially estimated numbers, there are 60,000 Sorbs in general.[26] Active Sorbian speakers are estimated to be 7000 at most for Lower Sorbian and about 18,000 for the Upper Sorbian language.[27] Since the German reunification, there has been a decrease in birth rates in the east of Germany, as well as in Lusatia. For Lower Sorbian, most speakers are older than 60 years; therefore, the aging population pyramid is a very severe problem. Also in Upper Lusatia, it was more and more challenging to establish Sorbian classes with children with Sorbian as a mother tongue. Because of economic reasons, many younger Sorbs do not live in Lusatia anymore.[28] In general, it can be said that in Lower Lusatia, a special challenge lies in the revitalization of the language, and in Upper Lusatia mainly the preservation of authenticity of the Sorbian and the education of new speakers are the tasks of the political agenda. Hence, lower Sorbian is the minority language within the minority language and therefore even more seriously endangered.[29]

[23]Budar (2010), p. 178.

[24]Oeter (2001), pp. 46–47.

[25]Van Dongera et al. (2017), p. 91.

[26]Kunze (2008), p. 73.

[27]Van Dongera et al. (2017), p. 91.

[28]Brězan and Nowak (2016), pp. 11, 25.

[29]Expert-interview with Ludmila Budar, President of the Sorbian school association, in Bautzen on 10 April 2017.

2.2 *The Current German School System*

In Germany, the legal competence in the domain of education and culture is located on the level of the federal states due to the cultural sovereignty rooted in Article 30 of the German Basic Law.

In general, it can be said that a coherence in the system of promotion for regional or minority languages is absent in Germany. All regional or minority languages in Germany are handled differently, as well as the legal framework differs according to each language, although the socio-linguistic situations are similar. Universal standards do not exist. Furthermore, the financial support of regional and minority organizations and the organization of the educational system differ according to each federal state. School education is a competence of the states and historically shaped by *Länder* traditions. Therefore, considerable inequality results from the current system, and there are privileged and underprivileged language groups that feel discriminated.[30]

In Saxony, the compulsory education is 9 years, according to § 28 para. 2 Saxon Education Act. In Brandenburg, there are 10 years of compulsory education, as stated in § 38 Brandenburg Education Act. In Germany, schools can be run by the state, the district, and the municipality or by private organizations. State schools are most common. Sorbian schools are almost all publicly organized.[31]

2.3 *Laws Governing the Schooling Models in Sorbian in Saxony and Brandenburg*

The federal states, the *Länder*, guarantee in Article 25 of the Brandenburg Constitution and Article 6 of the Constitution of the Free State of Saxony, as well as through the laws, for the Sorbs German citizens the right to express their Sorbian identity and to retain the Sorbian language, culture, and tradition also through schools.[32] In addition, the Education Acts in Brandenburg and Saxony, as well as special regulations (*Verwaltungsvorschriften*), contain the right to learn the Sorbian language in Lusatia. In Brandenburg, the rights of the Sorbs are regulated in § 5 of the Education Act and in the Sorbian-Wendish School Regulation.[33] In Saxony, § 2 of the Education Act is directed at the regulation of Sorbian language and culture at the schools.

[30]Oeter (2001), pp. 36 et seq.

[31]Brězan and Nowak (2016), p. 16.

[32]Brězan and Nowak (2016), p. 25.

[33]Verordnung über die schulischen Bildungsangelegenheiten der Sorben (Wenden) from the 31st of July 2000.

In order to preserve the Sorbian language, Sorbian institutions and associations have created some projects and programs to foster the learning of Sorbian in compulsory school education.

Lower Sorbian is not passed on in the families anymore. Therefore, the educational system plays a vital role for language acquisition. It is the only way of early language acquisition as a second language in kindergarten and school. Thus, drastic measures have to be taken in the future in order to stop the extinction of the language. Analyzed under this perspective, the situation in the Brandenburg school system is very poor. The amount of hours and quality of teaching Sorbian are largely insufficient in order to guarantee an effective second language acquisition.[34]

The great success of kindergartens with the Witaj approach, which features language immersion, shows that there is an interest of parents in the vernacular language, especially since Sorbian, due to the similarities with Polish, can fulfill a bridging function to other western Slavonic languages. Yet there is no guarantee for continuity of classes between kindergarten or preschool and primary school in all towns in the region of Lusatia. Language acquisition with the immersion model at an early age alone does not suffice. There must be options to continue Sorbian classes in primary and secondary schools.[35]

In Saxony, in the 1990s, an integral concept for learning Sorbian inspired by the Breton model in France has been developed.[36] It starts in kindergarten with the Witaj education program. Witaj is the Sorbian word for welcome. Children learn Sorbian in Witaj kindergartens by means of total language immersion. The education program continues at the schools with the educational Concept 2 Plus. According to this model, the Sorbian language is taught as a medium of instruction in the status of mother tongue, second language, and foreign language.[37] In Saxony, the Concept 2 Plus is connected also with bilingual teaching. Generally, the Concept 2 Plus means that Sorbian and German have the status of mother tongues, plus learning of additional languages is promoted. The decline of the main Sorbian-speaking town environment shall be compensated through strengthening the Sorbian as second language.[38] Students shall be literate in Sorbian and German in primary school in this region of Saxony. The pupils study mathematics, general knowledge, music, and sports with German and Sorbian as medium of instruction. It depends on the language qualifications of the teachers and the composition of the classes which language is used more intensely. If there are a lot of students with Sorbian as mother tongue, the teacher speaks mostly Sorbian.[39] Furthermore, the schools have the opportunity to make use of teacher tandems, meaning that there are a Sorbian and a German teacher teaching in the same bilingual class at the same time. While one

[34]Oeter (2001), p. 48.

[35]Oeter (2001), p. 48.

[36]Budar (2009), p. 29.

[37]Kunze (2008), p. 74.

[38]Oeter (2001), p. 47.

[39]Brězan and Nowak (2016), p. 27.

teacher is working with an individual student, the other colleague is responsible for the knowledge transfer. The German teacher teaches the German sequence, whereas the Sorbian colleague is doing the same in Sorbian.[40] This ensures that the students can learn the different subjects according to their linguistic qualifications as native speakers or as learners of the Sorbian or German language.

In addition to that, according to § 4a para. 4 no. 4 Saxon Education Act, it is possible in justified exceptional cases to deviate from the regular minimum number of pupils in a class in order to guarantee the establishment of Sorbian classes for Sorbian pupils. In Saxony, classes in which Sorbian is taught start with the number of five pupils.[41]

In Brandenburg, Sorbian has the status of a second language or foreign language in school education. Hence, the structures differ from the situation in Saxony.[42] Yet it has to be stated that for the Lower Sorbian in Brandenburg, the efforts made in school education are insufficient. The language is drastically on decline, and early childhood language acquisition has been withering away with the last one or two young generations.[43] Furthermore, in Brandenburg, secondary school education for Sorbian is almost nonexistent. The only Lower Sorbian secondary school (*Gymnasium*) in Cottbus is not enough in order to guarantee the necessary continuity of second language acquisition. This school also experiences difficulties with the lack of sufficient teaching personnel in Lower Sorbian. There is no provision of teacher training in Brandenburg either. In order to preserve the language and in order to comply with the obligations resulting from the European Charter for Regional or Minority Languages, new measures have to be taken regarding the training of kindergarten and school teachers in Lower Sorbian.[44]

There are also Witaj kindergartens that practice the full language immersion concept. For the schools, the Sorbian language provisions are to be found in § 4 and § 5 of Brandenburg Education Act. Further, there is the special Sorbian/Wendish School Regulation from the year 2000. These provisions implement the bilingual teaching program also called Witaj.[45] The Witaj-Welcome program in Brandenburg is directed at children in the Sorbian settlement area with the objective to learn Sorbian in early childhood. Witaj also entails bilingual teaching at school. Witaj education in Brandenburg is not based on an integral teaching concept such as in Saxony. The amount of teaching of Sorbian, as well as the number of bilingual classes, differs from school to school. A decisive point for the organization of the

[40]Expert-interview with René Jatzwauk, headmaster of the Sorbian Sixth Form School in Bautzen, on 11 April 2017 in Bautzen.

[41]Expert-interview with Ludmila Budar, President of the Sorbian school association, in Bautzen on 10 April 2017.

[42]Budar (2009), p. 41.

[43]Oeter (2001), p. 47.

[44]Oeter (2001), pp. 49 et seq.

[45]Department for Sorbian/Wendish Education Development (*Arbeitsstelle für sorbische/wendische Bildungsentwicklung Cottbus*): http://www.schulaemter.brandenburg.de/sixcms/detail.php/685404 (accessed on 25 April 2017).

bilingual classes is the language abilities of the teaching personnel. Further, it is a challenge to realize the teaching of Sorbian as in the same class, some students study Sorbian according to the Witaj education program, some students learn it as a foreign language, and some pupils do not take part in Sorbian classes at all.[46]

2.3.1 Primary Education

Compulsory education in the *Länder* Brandenburg and Saxony begins at the age of 6. In Saxony, students take 4 years of primary school, and in Brandenburg there are 6 years of primary education. In Brandenburg, students learn Lower Sorbian, and in Saxony students study Upper Sorbian.

Germany adopted the European Charter for Regional or Minority Languages concerning primary education with the lowest level of protection for the Sorbian. Article 8 b iv of the Charter provides that teaching in or of the regional or minority languages should be available at least as an integral part of the curriculum for those pupils whose families request so and whose number is considered sufficient.

Hence, in Saxony, Sorbian is taught in 23 primary schools, six schools using the Concept 2 Plus. Fourteen primary schools offer the Sorbian language as a foreign language in the Sorbian settlement area in Saxony.[47]

In Brandenburg, there are 22 primary schools teaching the Sorbian language. There are five primary schools that take part in the Witaj bilingual teaching program.[48] Bilingual teaching is possible due to § 7 III (4) administrative directive to the Brandenburg Primary School Act (VV-Grundschulverordnung). In the other primary schools, there is optional language teaching of Sorbian as a second language. The major challenge in that regard herewith is to be found in the problem that children who are native Sorbian speakers are practically nonexistent.[49]

2.3.2 Secondary Education

Secondary education starts in Saxony in the fifth grade and takes 6 years. In Brandenburg, secondary education begins in the seventh grade and takes 4 years. The legislation for secondary and grammar schools can be found in the same documents in which the primary education is regulated.

Also for the secondary school education, Germany adopted the European Charter for Regional or Minority Languages with the lowest level of protection for the Sorbian. Article 8 c iv of the Charter, similarly to Article 8 b iv, provides that teaching in or of the regional or minority languages should be available at least as an

---

[46]Brězan and Nowak (2016), p. 27.

[47]Budar (2010), p. 180.

[48]Budar (2010), p. 180.

[49]Brězan and Nowak (2016), p. 25.

integral part of the curriculum for those pupils whose families request so and whose number is considered sufficient.

Further, there is an administrative directive to the Secondary School Act in Brandenburg (*Sekundarstufe-I-Verordnung*) that states in § 11 that bilingual education is possible. In Brandenburg, the Sorbian/Wendish School Regulation states in § 2 para. 7 and para. 9 that the Sorbian language groups can be taught in two grades together in case there are not enough students for a group in one grade.

Currently, in Upper Lusatia in Saxony, there are 17 secondary schools where Sorbian is taught—three of them with the Concept 2 Plus.[50] The administrative regulation concerning the overview of curriculum requirements (*Verwaltungsvorschrift Stundentafeln*) for Saxony of 28 June 2010 grants the Sorbian grammar school independence for the compulsory education. According to this regulation, the partition of subjects that can be taught in Sorbian and German as medium of instruction is delegated to the responsibility of the school, which mostly decides with a view to the availability of a qualified teaching staff and to pedagogical considerations.

In Brandenburg, there are six secondary schools that teach Sorbian.[51] In addition to that, in Brandenburg, a reform of the Sorbian-Wendish School Regulation is planned at the moment in order to implement a new concept of teaching Sorbian in Lower Lusatia. The draft regulation includes an improvement of bilingual education until the 12th grade.[52]

To summarize, all possibilities to study Sorbian are not compulsory; that is why there are different possibilities: (1) students who only take part in the teaching of Sorbian as a foreign language, (2) students who learn Sorbian as a second language and partly also visit bilingual courses, and (3) students who follow only the bilingual courses.

3 Language Rights in Education in Catalonia in Spain

3.1 Historical Background

Catalan as a Romance language forms part of the Indo-European language family. It is spread over five autonomous communities in Spain: Catalonia, the Balearic Islands, the Valencian country, the eastern part of Aragon, and also a small part of the autonomous community of Murcia. Outside Spain, Catalan is spoken in the department of Eastern Pyrenees in southern France and in the Principality of

---

[50]Budar (2010), p. 180.

[51]Budar (2010), p. 180.

[52]Expert-interview with Dr. Beate Brězan, Director of the WITAJ-Language Center in Bautzen on 13 April 2017.

Andorra. In Italy, there are also some speakers in Alghero in Sardinia.[53] Catalonia today has 7.5 million inhabitants and 6.16 million speakers of Catalan.[54]

The Catalan language came into existence between the eighth and tenth centuries on both sides of the Pyrenees, in the territories of the Carolingian Empire that was part of the counties of the Spanish March.[55] Thereafter, Catalan was the official language on the territory of Catalonia between the eleventh and the eighteenth centuries. Decisive for the development of the Catalan language and the Catalan cultural community has been the period between the ninth century and the thirteenth century parallel to the growing Muslim influence on the Iberian Peninsula.[56] Castile and the Crown of Aragon were united under the joint rule of Ferdinand and Isabella—the Catholic Kings from 1479. Barcelona was the capital of Catalonia having formed part of the Crown of Aragon at that time. King Philip IV wanted to create a powerful absolutist state in 1621. As a consequence, the relations between Castile and Catalonia were heavily strained, and the tension reached its peak with the unsuccessful Revolt of the Reapers (*Revolta dels Segadors*) in 1640.[57]

Again in the early eighteenth century, Catalonia and Castile were at war. Catalonia lost that war against Castile and the 11th of September 1714 marked the end of Catalonia's political power.[58] With the decrees of the *Nueva Planta* 1716 by King Philip V, the process of castilianization was introduced, and the attempt was made to eradicate the national character of Catalonia by the prohibition to use Catalan in public life and the imposition of Castilian as official language.[59] The *Moyano* Law regulated the public school system in 1857 and provided that only Castilian was to be spoken in the classroom.[60]

In the middle of the nineteenth century, a cultural and linguistic renaissance of the regional language started, and Catalans strived to achieve political autonomy in the beginning of the twentieth century.[61] This revivalist movement to promote Catalan culture and the Catalan language was called *Renaixença*.[62] Furthermore, the association *Associació Protectora de l'Ensenyança Catalana* was founded to protect education in Catalan. In the beginning of the twentieth century, harmonization of the Catalan in its administrative, legal, and scientific structures took place.

---

[53] Areny et al. (2013), p. 5.

[54] Fourth periodical report presented to the Secretary General of the Council of Europe in accordance with Article 15 of the Charter for Spain, English Version, Strasbourg 2014, MIN-LANG (2014) PR 5, p. 5.

[55] Generalitat de Catalunya, Catalan, Language of Europe. http://llengua.gencat.cat/permalink/91192f76-5385-11e4-8f3f-000c29cdf219 (accessed on 26 April 2017).

[56] Marì i Mayans (2016), pp. 13, 19.

[57] Guibernau (2000), pp. 55 et seq.

[58] Desfor Edles (1999), p. 317.

[59] Pilar Parea and Mesa (2008), p. 562.

[60] Pons Parera and Vernet I Llobet (2009), p. 147; Marì i Mayans (2016), p. 113.

[61] Berschin et al. (2012), p. 45.

[62] Nogué and Vicente (2004), p. 122.

Decisive for this development were personalities such as Pompeu Fabra or Enric Prat de la Riba.[63] In 1898, Francesc Flos i Calcat founded the first Catalan school *Collegi Sant Jordi*, which was dedicated entirely to education in the Catalan language. An association of local authorities called *Mancomunitat de Catalunya* came into existence in 1914 providing autonomous administration for Catalonia. As first public institution in the modern history of Spain, it determined Catalan as lingua franca.[64] After the coup d'etat of General Primo de Riveira in 1923, Castilian was introduced again as only vehicular language in the schools. The Mancomunitat was definitely dissolved in March 1925.[65]

After the suppression by the dictatorship of General Primo de Rivera had ended, Catalan was reestablished as common language and the laws were abolished that prohibited Catalan schools. The upturn of General Franco and the outbreak of the civil war interrupted these developments. Catalonia's autonomy was revoked by Franco's decree of 5 April 1938.[66] After the Spanish Civil War, the most bitter and longest period of oppression of the Catalan language occurred during the Franco dictatorship (1939–1975). Once again, Catalan was prohibited in schools, and Franco tried to eradicate the Catalan identity.[67]

Yet, some institutions secretly taught Catalan, such as the *Centre d'Influència Catòlica Femenina* founded in 1950. Catalan was maintained by a catholic movement and the political opposition. In the 1960s, a civil movement called *Òmnium Cultural* put forward a campaign for the Catalan language in schools. It raised awareness in society in order to insert Catalan in the school curriculum.[68] The final return of Catalan only succeeded after Franco's death in 1975. A phase of democratization began. With the enacting of the new Spanish Constitution in 1978, the coofficiality of vernacular languages was established.[69] The Constitution further divides Spain into semi-federal regional authorities, the *comunidades autónomas.* These self-governing autonomous communities or *comunidades autónomas* can enact laws and regulate the official language, as well as the language of instruction in schools. Hence, the Constitution delegates to the autonomous communities the competence to determine how they want to develop and promote the regional identity in their territory in which they constitute the majority.[70] The social cohesion in Catalonia made it possible to deal with the socio-cultural changes that emerged

---

[63]Generalitat de Catalunya (2015), p. 21.

[64]Grau Mateu (2014): The *Mancomunitat de Catalunya* was the first democratically legitimate government organ and modernized the cultural and pedagogic institutions in Catalonia.

[65]Arbós i Marín (2008), p. 54; Escribano (2014).

[66]Guibernau (2000), p. 56.

[67]Dowling (2013), p. 3.

[68]Generalitat de Catalunya (2015), pp. 25 et seq, 29 et seq.

[69]Areny et al. (2013), p. 7.

[70]Hofmann (1992), pp. 56 et seq.

with the successive immigration waves and that have heavily changed the physiognomy of the region in a short time.[71]

In the past, there have been two important judgments dealing with the language situation in Catalonia by the Spanish Constitutional Court (*Tribunal Constitucional*). The first judgment, STC 1994/337, states that there is no right deriving from the Constitution to receive education in the regional language. It is rather connected to the competence of the autonomous community to establish such a right. Furthermore, Catalan may constitute the focal point in a bilingual school model as long as Castilian is not excluded as vehicular language in the curriculum. Castilian has to be taught also in the territory of the autonomous community.[72]

The second judgment is the case STC 31/2010 of the Constitutional Court of 28 June 2010. It entails that although Catalan is a language of instruction, it must not be the only medium of instruction in schools as Castilian has to be used due to its character of official language in Spain and thus also in Catalonia. Consequently, "the legitimacy of Catalonia's immersion model" has been challenged by the judgment.[73] This judgment has been heavily criticized as an interpretative judgment and approach of judicial activism as it affects the valid laws in Catalonia.

3.2 *Current Spanish Education System*

In Spain, school attendance is compulsory and free from age six to sixteen, according to Articles 16 and 22 of the Organic Law on Education 2/2006. There are national and regional laws determining the organization of the educational system.

3.3 *Laws Governing the Schooling Model in Catalan in Catalonia*

Catalan is the lingua franca in education in Catalonia. Yet the actual schooling model is the product of different laws and decrees since 1979. The first Statute of Autonomy of Catalonia after the Franco dictatorship, adopted in 1979, attributed in its Article 3 official status to Catalan as Catalonia's own language, whereas Castilian remains official language as well. The government of Catalonia shall ensure the normal and official use of both languages.[74]

---

[71] Siguan (1988), p. 454.

[72] Spanish Constitutional Court, judgment of 23 December 1994, STC 1994/337, para. 10, p. 53.

[73] Arzoz (2012), p. 280.

[74] http://web.gencat.cat/en/generalitat/estatut/estatut1979/titol_preliminar/ (accessed on 27 April 2017).

There are three important laws that determined the design of the educational system in Catalonia. At first, the Law of Linguistic Normalization was passed by the Parliament of Catalonia in 1983 and had as its objective the upgrading of the status of Catalan to a full-fledged modern language used in all domains. Article 14.1 of this law states that Catalan shall be the medium of instruction on all levels of the educational system. Thus, this new law was a means for the normalization of the public use of Catalan and has also been called "a landmark in the history of Catalan language policy."[75] This is due to the fact that it established the Catalan Conjunction Model, which means that a complete immersion of the students in the Catalan language as medium of instruction takes place.[76] Students were not separated along linguistic lines in the classrooms in order to enhance social cohesion. The Catalan Conjunction Model aimed at pupils to be bilingually literate in Catalan and Castilian after compulsory education.[77]

Furthermore, after the 1983 Law was passed, the Catalan government introduced the Linguistic Immersion Programme, which was meant for children with Castilian-speaking parents of the age between 3 and 12 years. The Catalan government supported to guarantee the competence through this pedagogical program. It was implemented in schools with over 75% non-Catalan-speaking pupils in order to create a single Catalan society.[78]

The Catalan Parliament passed the Law on Linguistic Policy in 1998, which reinforced the linguistic policy that was initiated during the 1980s. Articles 20 and 21 of the Law on Linguistic Policy strengthened the role of Catalan as the medium of instruction in education. In 2006, a new Statute of Autonomy of Catalonia was approved. Article 35 of the Statute states that Catalan is still the language of normal use for teaching and learning in the education system. The Catalonian Education Act (*Llei d'educació de Catalunya*) from the year 2009 recalled in Article 11 para. 3 that students were not to be separated in different group classes because of their mother tongue. All schools, private and public, must use Catalan as a normal medium of instruction.

Lastly, the national law for better quality of education called LOMCE 8/2013 based on Article 149.1 para. 30 of the Spanish Constitution was adopted on December 9, 2013. Article 149.1 para. 30 of the Spanish Constitution enables the state to establish basic regulations for the implementation of Article 27 of the Spanish Constitution. The LOMCE law aims to guarantee the observation of the obligations of public authorities in the realm of education. The LOMCE law is based on decision 31 of the Spanish Constitutional Court regarding language rights in education in Catalonia, adopted on June 28, 2010. In the additional provision, 38, the LOMCE law guarantees that education must be in the vernacular language, as well as Castilian. It entails also the right of the parents that their children can receive their school

[75]Areny et al. (2013), p. 11.

[76]Pons Parera (2006), p. 306.

[77]Pons Parera and Vernet I Llobet (2009), p. 165.

[78]Huguet (2004), pp. 412 et seq; Areny et al. (2013), p. 22.

education in Castilian. In case there are no public schools that fulfill the criteria of this right, the Spanish school ministry will compensate for the costs of private school education after an evaluation of the individual case. These costs will be put down to the account of the regional school ministry.[79] This law is supposed to enhance the quality of school education and to harmonize school education. It is the first national law that regulates the medium of instruction in school education. Yet the LOMCE law is disputed by Catalan authorities. Furthermore, the Committee of Experts on the application of the European Charter of Regional or Minority Languages states that "great care should be taken that the offer of this model will not negatively affect the provision of education in regional or minority languages, including their promotion and support structure."[80]

3.3.1 Primary Education

Primary education is the first compulsory stage of education in Spain. Article 16 para. 1 of the Organic Law for Education from 2006 states that it is aimed at pupils from 6 to 12 years old. Concerning the implementation of the European Charter for Regional and Minority Languages, the Spanish state has opted for the highest level of protection of Catalan. According to Article 8 b I of the Charter, primary education is made available in the relevant regional or minority language.

Catalan is the medium of instruction in primary education. The teaching of Spanish begins in primary education, at the first compulsory stage. Although Catalan is the normal language of instruction, Spanish is also taught as a subject (as a minimum requirement), according to Article 11 of the Catalan Law of Education of 10 July 2009. The same is provided for in Article 4 of Decree 119/2015 of 23 June 2015 for primary education.

3.3.2 Secondary Education

Secondary education is compulsory for students from 12 to 16 years, according to Article 22 para. 1 of the Organic Law of Education 2006.

Also for secondary education, Spain chose the highest protection of the Catalan language according to Article 8 c i of the European Charter for Regional or Minority Languages. Hence, education in Catalan is made available in secondary schools.

Catalan is the language commonly used as a vehicular language of teaching and learning. The linguistic plan of each individual school states the decisions regarding the medium of instruction—usually Catalan—and the amount of teaching of

[79]Fourth periodical report presented to the Secretary General of the Council of Europe in accordance with Article 15 of the Charter for Spain, English Version, Strasbourg 2014, MIN-LANG (2014) PR 5, p. 14.

[80]Council of Europe (2016), p. 4.

Castilian and of, at least, one foreign language. According to Article 5 of Decree 187/2015 of 25 August 2015, Spanish is taught as a subject.

According to official results, students are literate both in Catalan and Castilian at the end of compulsory school education. Remarkably, the level of knowledge of Castilian among Catalan students is the same as it is in the rest of Spain. Furthermore, students that are to be integrated into the Catalan educational system later on are able to get special and additional support concerning the Catalan language.[81]

In conclusion, the Catalan immersion model is very successful in primary and secondary education in Catalonia.

4 Evaluation of the Different Education Models

I am now going to evaluate the legislation for education in Sorbian and Catalan, hence the educational models that are pursued by the respective German and Catalan laws.

Most important for the evaluation of laws for regional and minority language education is the demographic context of the speakers of these languages in Spain and Germany. The number of speakers of Sorbian in Germany is quite low (around 25,000) compared to the 6.16 million speakers of Catalan in Catalonia.

This is the reason why the models that are pursued by the respective legislation in both countries differ, and accordingly also the ratification menus under the European Charter for Regional or Minority Languages. Due to the demographic situation in Brandenburg and Saxony with a declining number of students in general, the laws implementing the Witaj-Welcome program and the Concept 2 plus offer a lot of flexibility and autonomy for the individual schools. In addition, this model attempts to achieve as the educational objective a developed state of bilingualism/multilingualism, with the capability of students leaving the school to use the language qualifications in both languages context-specifically.[82]

For Saxony, it can be said that the current system with the Concept 2 Plus seems to work to a large degree. This instrument that promotes a moderate form of teaching in Sorbian and German as mother tongues (or second languages) is the only way to preserve the Sorbian language in the given socio-linguistic context. It is a transparent model that enables the integration in tolerance between pupils who study Sorbian as a second language and those who speak it as a mother tongue. In practical terms, there is no alternative to the Concept 2 Plus.[83]

[81] Areny et al. (2013), pp. 16, 22 et seq.

[82] Fifth periodical report presented to the Secretary General of the Council of Europe in accordance with Article 15 of the European Charter for Regional and Minority Languages for the Federal Republic of Germany, English version, Strasbourg 2013, MIN-LANG (2013) PR 02, p. 36.

[83] Expert-interview with René Jatzwauk, headmaster of the Sorbian Sixth Form School in Bautzen, on 11 April 2017 in Bautzen.

While in some villages in Saxony Sorbian is used in public in daily life and there are many native speakers, which the school models have to take into account, in most regions of the Sorbian settlement area of Saxony (and all the Sorbian areas in Brandenburg) children learn Sorbian only as a second language with German as a mother tongue. As a result, these children must receive their education partly in German.

This flexibility is not the case in Catalonia. There is some pressure on the Catalan model due to the ongoing immigration of Castilian speakers. A challenge further lies in the fact that schools should provide (as a political objective) the incentive to actively use Catalan.[84] Hence, in Catalonia, the school system is dominated by the Catalan immersion model. The function of the early laws of the 1980s and 1990s in Catalonia was to implement this immersion model. Castilian is only taught as a subject in primary and secondary education. The students in Catalonia are not separated in the classrooms on behalf of their mother tongue. The development of the Catalan immersion model is the main reason for the success story of rehabilitation of Catalan in daily life after the brute repression during the Franco dictatorship.

If we want to learn from the Catalans, would there not be the option to introduce the comprehensive immersion model (used in Catalonia) also for the Sorbian language? Probably not! Small minorities face different challenges that have to be taken into account. The demographic situation in Lusatia does not permit the same policy as in Catalonia, namely to implement the Catalan immersion model.

Furthermore, a current challenge to the Sorbian school system in Brandenburg and Saxony is the deficit of adequate teaching personnel. Until 2022, approximately one hundred more teachers will be needed in Sorbian schools. There are different approaches in order to combat this deficit of Sorbian-speaking teachers. Firstly, the Sorbian school association has reached an agreement with the State Ministry for Science and the Arts of Saxony in § 6 of the Higher Education Access Act (*Hoschschulzulassungsgesetz*) about lower entry requirements into university for students who have excellent knowledge in Sorbian if they want to study Sorbian at the Institute for Sorabistics at the University of Leipzig in order to become teachers. These special entry requirements shall apply to other universities and institutions of higher education in Saxony in all subject combinations in the future. In addition, Sorbian-speaking students who are studying to become teachers are getting an employment guarantee in a Sorbian school in Saxony. The Sorbian school association also tries to recruit career changer with Sorbian knowledge in the realm of natural sciences to start teaching at Sorbian schools after a pedagogical training. Last but not least, there is the possibility for teachers from Poland and the Czech Republic to start teaching at Sorbian schools after having completed 1 year of studies at the Institute for Sorabistics at the University of Leipzig.[85] A comparable policy of dedicated support for the training of Sorbian teachers is lacking in Brandenburg.

[84]Galindo et al. (2007), pp. 118 et seq.

[85]Expert-interview with Ludmila Budar, president of the Sorbian school association, Bautzen on 10 April 2017.

In the end, a one-size-fits-all model for education in regional and minority languages does not exist. However, we have to invent typologies for different demographic and socio-linguistic situations.

5 Summary

The objective of the different models presented here is the offering of education in a language that enables children in school to understand the content of the teaching and to preserve the regional and minority languages at the same time. The future—this is the underlying assumption—lies in multilingualism.

Catalan as a regional minority language was oppressed for a long time in the twentieth century. Since 1975, it has become the standard language in the education system in its traditional territory and the first language of instruction for the larger part of the current generation of pupils who have been educated in Catalonia. This is an extremely rare progress in European history.[86]

Catalan is the everyday language of public life in Catalonia. The legislative choice not to separate students along their linguistic abilities in Catalonia is very important. The price to be paid for this is the decision to offer Spanish/Castilian only as a subject and to teach all other courses with Catalan as the medium of instruction. As shown in the evaluation, this is not possible in Lusatia due to the demographic situation. Sorbian is not the everyday language in Brandenburg and Saxony. It is rather spoken, if at all, in the private realm in the families and—as a maximum—as community language in some of the Sorbian villages in the Sorbian core area.

Furthermore, the legal framework for language rights always has to be interpreted in the light of the European Charter for Regional or Minority Languages from 1992. Whereas the Sorbian language enjoys only the basic protection under the Charter, as granted by Germany in its instrument of ratification, the Spanish state has chosen to implement the highest standard of protection to Catalan. In the end, these are adequate decisions for the different tasks that face both language minorities.

The strengthening of multilingualism is the overriding political objective behind these policies. The educational system shall ensure that children, in certain areas historically characterized by the strong presence of a regional or minority language, have access to the heritage language of the community, together with the learning of the national language. The European Charter for Regional or Minority Languages provides for very different options on how to strive for that end. The starting points and socio-linguistic contexts in different parts of Europe (and with different regional and minority languages) vary so much that very different kinds of policies are needed in order to cope with the specific challenges of each situation. The European Charter for Regional or Minority Languages takes up this challenge by offering a very differentiated menu of measures that need to be taken. Yet the

[86]Castellà Surribas and Strubell (2008), p. 136.

challenges lie also outside of the school life, if one wants to ensure the survival of regional and minority languages. It is an interaction between education as the most important vehicle to pass on the knowledge of regional and minority language and other realms such as social, economic, and cultural life; the media; and also the official use of languages within the administration and the judiciary. These realms of language use are also covered by sets of measures provided for in the Language Charter. The options are open for use by the states concerned—they only must be willing to make use of them. The multifaceted cultural heritage of Europe, with its age-old traditions of linguistic diversity, is worth the efforts needed to go the way toward an enhanced protection of regional and minority languages.

References

Arbós i Marín X (2008) Los antecedentes históricos de la autonomía de Cataluña. In: Barceló M, Vintró M (eds) Derecho Público de Cataluña. S. A. Atelier Libros, Barcelona, pp 37–76

Areny M, Mayans P, Forniès D (2013) Regional dossier on the catalan language in education in Spain, 2nd edn. Mercator European Research Centre on Multilingualism and Language Learning, Leeuwarden

Arzoz X (2012) Linguistic minorities in Spain. In: Richter D, Richter I (eds) Language rights revisited – the challenge of global migration and communication. Berliner Wissenschafts-Verlag, Berlin, pp 271–286

Berschin H, Fernández-Sevilla J, Felixberger J (2012) Die spanische Sprache. Verbreitung, Geschichte, Struktur, 4th edn. Georg Olms Verlag, Hildesheim

Brĕzan B, Nowak M (2016) Sorbian. The Sorbian language in education in Germany, 2nd edn. Mercator European Research Centre on Multilingualism and Language Learning, Leeuwarden

Budar L (2009) 10 Jahre Witaj – Modellprojekt des Sorbischen Schulvereins e.V. In: Sorbischer Schulverein (ed) Witaj und 2 Plus – eine Herausforderung für die Zukunft. Lausitzer Druck- und Verlagshaus GmbH, Bautzen, pp 28–43

Budar L (2010) Geschichte des Sorbischen Bildungswesens. In: Budar L (ed) 20 Jahre Sorbischer Schulverein. Sorbischer Schulverein Bautzen, Bautzen, pp 172–184

Castellà Surribas S-J, Strubell M (2008) The Catalan language and monitoring the European Charter for Regional or Minority Languages in Spain. In: Dunbar R, Parry G (eds) The European Charter for Regional or Minority Languages: legal challenges and opportunities. Council of Europe Publishing, Strasbourg, pp 127–146

Council of Europe (1992) Explanatory report – ETS 148 – regional or minority languages, Strasbourg. https://rm.coe.int/16800cb5e5. Accessed 3 Dec 2017

Council of Europe (2016) Recommendation of the Committee of Ministers of the Council of Europe on the application of the Charter by Spain (adopted on 20 January 2016). In: European Charter for Regional or Minority Languages, application of the Charter in Spain, 4th monitoring cycle, Strasbourg. ECRML (2016) 7

Desfor Edles L (1999) A culturalist approach to ethnic nationalist movements: symbolization and Basque and Catalan nationalism in Spain. Soc Sci Hist 23(3):311–355

Dowling A (2013) Catalonia since the Spanish civil war: reconstructing a nation. Sussex Academy Press, Eastbourne

Dunbar R (2009) The Council of Europe's European Charter for Regional and Minority Languages. In: Henrard K, Dunbar R (eds) Synergies in minority protection. Cambridge University Press, Cambridge, pp 155–186

Escribano D (2014) La Mancomunitat de Catalunya i el català: el conflicte de l'oficilaitat lingüística al règim de la Restauració borbònica, Blog publication of 27 March 2014 in the Revista

LLengua i Dret Blog. https://eapc-rld.blog.gencat.cat/2014/03/27/la-mancomunitat-de-catalunya-i-el-catala-el-conflicte-de-loficialitat-linguistica-al-regim-de-la-restauracio-borbonica-daniel-escribano. Accessed 3 Dec 2017
Galindo M, Strubell M, Vila FX (2007) Eine unterdrückte Sprache wird Gravitationszentrum. Die neue Rolle des Katalanischen in der Schule. In: Eßer T, Stegmann T (eds) Kataloniens Rückkehr nach Europa 1976–2006. LIT Verlag Dr. W. Hopf, Berlin, pp 107–120
Generalitat de Catalunya, Catalan, Language of Europe. http://llengua.gencat.cat/permalink/91192f76-5385-11e4-8f3f-000c29cdf219. Accessed 3 Dec 2017
Generalitat de Catalunya, Departament d'Ensenyament (2015) Language in Catalan schools, a model for success. Barcelona
Grau Mateu J (2014), L'ús del català a la Mancomunitat de Catalunya, Blog publication of 5 June 2014 in the Revista LLengua i Dret Blog. http://eapc-rld.blog.gencat.cat/2014/06/05/lus-del-catala-a-la-mancomunitat-de-catalunya-josep-grau. Accessed 3 Jan 2018
Guibernau M (2000) Spain: Catalonia and the Basque country. Parliam Aff 53(1):55–68
Hofmann R (1992) Minderheitenschutz in Europa – Überblick über die völker- und staatsrechtliche Lage. ZaöRV 52(1):1–69
Huguet Á (2004) La educación bilingüe en el Estado español: situación actual y perspectivas. Cultura y Educación 16(4):399–418
Kroll F-L (2014) Geschichte Sachsens. Beck Verlag, München
Kunze P (2008) Kurze Geschichte der Sorben, 4th edn. Domowina Verlag, Bautzen
Langenfeld C (2011) Article 8. In: Boysen S, Hilpold P (eds) Europäische Charta der Regional- oder Minderheitensprachen. Handkommentar. Dike Verlag, Zürich, pp 183–221
Langham Brown R (1967) Wilhelm von Humboldt's conception of linguistic relativity. Walter de Gruyter, Berlin
Marì i Mayans I (2016) Die Katalanischen Länder. Verlag Walter Frey, Berlin
Nogué J, Vicente J (2004) Landscape and national identity in Catalonia. J Polit Geogr 23:113–132
Oeter S (2001) Aus europäischer Sicht: Die Regional- und Minderheitensprachen und ihr Platz in den deutschen Schulsystemen. In: Bundesraat för Nedderdütsch (ed) Mit den Regional- und Minderheitensprachen auf dem Weg nach Europa. Verlag Schuster Leer, Bremen
Oeter S (2011) Vorwort. In: Boysen S, Hilpold P (eds) Europäische Charta der Regional- oder Minderheitensprachen. Handkommentar. Dike Verlag, Zürich, pp 7–10
Oeter S (2017) Conventions on the protection of national minorities. In: Breuer M, Schmahl S (eds) The Council of Europe. Its law and policies. Oxford University Press, Oxford, pp 542–571
Pech E (2012) Ein Staat – eine Sprache? Deutsche Bildungspolitik und autochthone Minderheiten im 20. Jahrhundert. Die Sorben im Vergleich mit Polen, Dänen und Nordfriesen. Domowina Verlag, Bautzen
Pilar Parea M, Mesa R (2008) Las Lenguas de España: Balance de una convivencia milenaria. In: Elvira J, García González J (eds) Lenguas, reinos y dialectos en la Edad Media Ibérica, La construcción de la identidad, Homenaje a Juan Ramón Lodares. Iberoamericana Editorial Vervuert S.L, Frankfurt
Pons Parera E (2006) Estatuto Jurídico de las Lenguas en Cataluña. In: Pérez Fernández JM (ed) Estudios sobre el estatuto jurídico de las lenguas en España, Barcelona, pp 281–324
Pons Parera E, Vernet I Llobet J (2009) La Llengua de l'Ensenyament a les Comunitats Autònomes amb Llengua Pròpia. Revista d'Estudis Autòmics i Federals 8:144–191
Scholze D (2002) Die Situation der Sorben in Vergangenheit und Gegenwart. Eur Reg 10(2):51–56
Siguan M (1988) Bilingual education in Spain. In: Bratt Paulston C (ed) International handbook of bilingualism and bilingual education. Greenwood Publishing Group, New York, pp 449–474
Toivanen R (2001) Minderheitenrechte als Identitätsressource?: Die Sorben in Deutschland und die Saamen in Finnland. LIT Verlag, Münster
Urrutia Libarona I (2005) Derechos lingüísticos y Euskera en el sistema educativo. LETE argitaletxea, Navarre
Van Dongera R, Van der Meer C, Sterk R (2017) Research for CULT Committee – minority languages and education: best practices and pitfalls. European Parliament, Policy Department for Structural and Cohesion Policies, Brussels. http://www.europarl.europa.eu/RegData/etudes/STUD/2017/585915/IPOL_STU(2017)585915_EN.pdf. Accessed 16 May 2017

Intangible Cultural Heritage in Need of Protection: The Case of Regional and Minority Languages

Stefan Oeter

Abstract This chapter explores the relationship between European efforts at protecting regional and minority languages, with a particular focus on the European Charter for Regional or Minority Languages, on the one hand, and UNESCO endeavors at protecting intangible cultural heritage, with a special focus on the 2003 UNESCO Convention, on the other hand. The 2003 UNESCO Convention on the Safeguarding of the Intangible Cultural Heritage is a product of decades of debates in the framework of UNESCO on how to improve the protection of the world's cultural heritage against the onslaught of modernity and globalization. Shifting the perspective to the broad range of intangible cultural heritage produces a certain overlap with traditional undertakings for the protection and promotion of folkloristic practices and rituals and also with the safeguarding of threatened languages. Languages as such are not explicitly covered by the 2003 UNESCO Convention, but the definition of "intangible cultural heritage" is so broad that threatened minority languages can be easily brought under the scope of application.

This opens up a fascinating interface with traditional European efforts at protecting regional and minority languages. The historical evolution of these efforts, and of the treaty regime of the European Charter for Regional or Minority Languages in particular, is described in the chapter. The roots of this treaty, as well as the parallel regime of the Framework Convention for the Protection of National Minorities, may be found in the classic discourses on minority protection. Whereas the Framework Convention is designed as a special human rights treaty, the Language Charter explicitly serves the purpose of contributing "to the maintenance and development of Europe's cultural wealth and traditions," which creates an interesting connection with the 2003 UNESCO Convention. The setup of the regime of protection in the Language Charter is described in detail, and the parallels in treaty design and the convergence of approaches, and also the conceptual differences are analyzed. At the end of the contribution, the question is raised what a comparative

S. Oeter (✉)
German and Comparative Public Law and Public International Law, Faculty of Law, University of Hamburg, Hamburg, Germany
e-mail: stefan.oeter@jura.uni-hamburg.de

© Springer International Publishing AG, part of Springer Nature 2018

E. Lagrange et al. (eds.), *Cultural Heritage and International Law*,
https://doi.org/10.1007/978-3-319-78789-3_4

perspective might add to the two parallel endeavors, which up to now take few cognizance of each other.

1 The Protection of Immaterial Cultural Heritage

The cultural heritage of humankind is severely threatened. Processes of modernization and globalization lead to a strong bias in favor of the new and innovative, the modern and cosmopolitan. Emanations of traditional forms of life, and cultural heritage in general, all too often seem to stand in the way of modernity and are thus becoming marginalized, if not destroyed altogether. During the twentieth century, the world became aware of the resulting problems, with a constant loss of traditional ways of life and its cultural expressions. As UNESCO was formulating already in 1993 in its guidelines for the "Living Human Treasures" program, "Unfortunately a number of its manifestations ... have already disappeared or are in danger of doing so. The main reason is that local intangible cultural heritage is rapidly being replaced by a standardized international culture, fostered not only by socio-economic 'modernization' but also by the tremendous progress of information and transport techniques."[1]

A growing consciousness of the threats that overshadow our cultural heritage was developing from 1970 onward, leading to calls for an institutionalization of some kind of protective regime.[2] At national level, schemes of monument protection, and safeguarding cultural heritage, had been developing since the nineteenth century[3]—but at international level, some sort of coordinating scheme for these efforts was lacking. UNESCO served as a catalyst to develop the needed international legal instruments.[4] The 1972 World Heritage Convention was the first result of such efforts at international regime building.[5] Focused on buildings and cultural monuments, this Convention could build on the long-standing developments at national level as far as the protection of material cultural heritage is concerned.[6] Schemes for the protection of outstanding natural sites were also included in the realm of the 1972 World Heritage Convention.[7]

Intangible cultural heritage came to the forefront of UNESCO's activities only at a later stage. There had been some normative and operational activities in the organization during the 1970s, 1980s, and 1990s dedicated to intangible cultural

[1]Citation from Blake (2015), p. 151 fn. 4.

[2]See Blake (2015), pp. 4–6; von Schorlemer (1992), pp. 36–38.

[3]See Jensen et al. (2010).

[4]See Forrest (2010), pp. 31–41; Cameron and Rössler (2013), pp. 1–26.

[5]See Forrest (2010), pp. 227–285, and in detail Francioni (2009).

[6]See as a critical analysis Gillman (2010), in particular pp. 9–63, 65–98.

[7]See Forrest (2010), pp. 240–241.

heritage,[8] but these activities condensed in efforts at drafting a dedicated convention on the protection of intangible cultural heritage only later, around the year 2000.[9] It took some years until the 2003 Convention for the Safeguarding of the Intangible Cultural Heritage materialized as standard under international law. This movement required employing a broader and more "anthropological" notion of cultural heritage, covering intangibles such as language-bound practices and expressions, oral traditions, and local know-how, largely independent of material culture.[10]

The 2003 Convention for the Safeguarding of the Intangible Cultural Heritage[11] now has become the main instrument for dealing with issues of threatened cultural heritage beyond the traditional scheme of the protection of cultural objects and natural sites.[12] The notion of "intangible cultural heritage," however, is very broad and sweeping and tends to cover an extremely wide spectrum of social and cultural practices and emanations of traditional forms of culture.[13] The definition in Article 2 of the 2003 Convention is of limited help in this regard.[14] In a general clause in Article 2 (1), the Convention provides: "The 'intangible cultural heritage' means the practices, representations, expressions, knowledge, skills – as well as the instruments, objects, artefacts and cultural spaces associated therewith – that communities, groups and, in some cases, individuals recognize as part of their cultural heritage." Being aware that this is extremely broad, the Convention attempts to give some more concrete shape to this notion of "intangible cultural heritage" by providing in Article 2 (2) as follows:

> The "intangible cultural heritage", as defined in paragraph 1 above, is manifested inter alia in the following domains:
>
> (a) oral traditions and expressions, including language as a vehicle of the intangible cultural heritage;
> (b) performing arts;
> (c) social practices, rituals and festive events;
> (d) knowledge and practices concerning nature and the universe;
> (e) traditional craftsmanship.

The broad and sweeping definition makes it difficult to identify the most serious threats and the kinds of cultural expressions urgently in need of schemes of protection. What we know, however, from the list of specific emanations of "intangible cultural heritage" in Article 2 (2) of the 2003 Convention is the fact that the concept of protected heritage under the Convention may include language. The formula used

[8]See Blake (2015), pp. 159–162; Forrest (2010), pp. 363–366; Aikawa-Faure (2009), pp. 13–44; see also—as a critical perspective—Testa (2016), pp. 221–243.

[9]See Blake (2015), pp. 163–168; Forrest (2010), pp. 365–366.

[10]See Blake (2015), p. 151.

[11]Convention for the Safeguarding of the Intangible Cultural Heritage of 17 October 2003, entered into force 20 April 2006, UNTS 42671.

[12]See on the 2003 Convention Blake (2015), pp. 168–181; Lixinski (2013), pp. 29–55.

[13]Andris (2014), pp. 133–147; Munjeri (2009), pp. 131–149.

[14]Forrest (2010), pp. 371–373.

in Article 2 (2) is ambiguous—it inevitably had to be since there was no agreement whether languages should be covered as such.[15] Some states strongly supported the inclusion of languages as a domain of intangible cultural heritage, while others strongly rejected the idea. For many states, treating language as a form of intangible cultural heritage is an extremely sensitive issue, and they object against this because they fear that giving too much significance to minority languages may lead (eventually) to secessionist tendencies.[16] The resulting compromise formula reflects this disagreement—it covers to a certain degree "language as a vehicle of the intangible cultural heritage" and thus opens the possibility for member states to include the safeguarding of languages into the ambit of protection of the 2003 Convention while at the same time allowing other states to deny that languages "as such" are covered by the Convention.

That languages may be brought in principle under the coverage of the 2003 Convention is not astonishing since language is one of the most important bearers of societal knowledge systems, intimately linked to cultural memory and basis of social communication.[17] With the extinction of a language, the knowledge system linked to such a language tends to be dead as well, thus destroying the (intangible) cultural heritage closely intertwined with the language and the knowledge system bound to such language. In such a perspective, threatened languages are some of the "practices, representations, expressions" most urgently in need to be safeguarded under the protective scheme of the Convention.

With the term "safeguarding," the Convention also has opted for a very comprehensive notion that not only covers classic "protection" actions but comprises also a wide array of measures of "promotion," in the sense of providing the conditions within which the intangible cultural heritage can continue to be created, maintained, and transmitted.[18] Basic level of "safeguarding" is the national level of arrangements of protection and promotion, with measures aimed at ensuring the continuing viability of intangible cultural heritage.[19] These national measures are supplemented by an international arrangement, with a system of two lists framed according to the established model of the 1972 World Heritage Convention, with some adaptations to the specific needs of intangible cultural heritage.[20]

[15] Blake (2015), p. 171.

[16] Blake (2015), p. 189.

[17] There are a number of activities under the 2003 UNESCO Convention that cover in essence issues of language protection—see Blake (2015), p. 171.

[18] See Blake (2015), p. 172.

[19] See Forrest (2010), pp. 374–376; Blake (2015), p. 176.

[20] As far as the system of lists is concerned, see Forrest (2010), pp. 377–380; Blake (2015), pp. 173–175.

2 Language as Intangible Cultural Heritage in Need of Protection

Are languages really threatened and thus in need of protection? If looked upon from the perspective of established national languages, this question may sound absurd for most Europeans. Their national languages are in official use in state institutions, dominate societal communication in large communities of several millions of people, and represent a rich heritage of poetry, novels, scientific literature, theater, music, etc. There are some signs that even these consolidated national languages might be threatened in some domains, such as science and higher education—but in general, they still seem safe in their position as dominant means of social communication and artistic expression. This is different, however, with regional or minority languages.[21] Their number is much higher than the number of established national (official) languages, and most of these languages suffer from severe phenomena of marginalization. There are admittedly some regional languages that represent vibrant linguistic communities with dynamic cultures—such as Catalan, Welsh, or Western Frisian.[22] Most of these regional and minority languages, however, are used by rather limited numbers of speakers nowadays, ranging from some hundred to some tens of thousands. Even regional languages such as Low German that used to be the main means of expression of the population of entire Northern Germany, with millions of speakers some one or two generations ago, are in dramatic decline, with fewer and fewer speakers in the young generations.[23]

These languages usually are not in official use in state authorities, in the administrative sphere, as well as in the court system. Even if enjoying some kind of a subsidiary status of "co-officiality," they tend to be of marginal practical importance, with speakers preferring to use the main "national" language in order to avoid being perceived as "trouble-makers" molesting the administration.[24] The offer of radio and television programs in these languages tends to be very restricted, often there is practically no written press, and book production in these languages usually is minimal. The result is more or less the same as was described in the UNESCO guideline cited above for other kinds of intangible cultural heritage—a number of these languages "have already disappeared or are in danger of doing so." The main reason for this process of rapid loss of cultural heritage "is that local intangible cultural heritage is rapidly being replaced by a standardized international culture, fostered not only by socio-economic 'modernization' but also by the tremendous progress of information and transport techniques," not to mention strong trends toward "acculturation" to the dominant "national" cultures imposed by state institutions, media, and the needs of a rapidly modernizing economy.

---

[21] See in detail Oeter (2010), pp. 139–158.

[22] See as an example for this Strubell and Boix-Fuster (2011).

[23] Oeter (2007), pp. 128–131.

[24] Oeter (2014), pp. 88–90.

A large number of regional and minority languages in Europe are severely threatened by extinction.[25] In terms of safeguarding the cultural heritage, this would be a tragedy. With the extinction of a language, the entire knowledge system represented (and supported) by such language gets lost. Even its literary artifacts, its poems, novels, theater plays, music pieces become largely unintelligible and perish from collective memory, are at best stored in archives where some specialized academics might still be able to work with them. The reasons for such loss are manifold, but their main cause lies in the language hierarchies established by modern states.[26] With the establishment of one "national" language of official status, all the other languages traditionally used on the territory of such state over time tend to lose most of its functionality to its speakers. For some generations, the emotional value of using such language as bearer of family heritage and as an expression of cultural identity might still compensate for the loss of functionality. At a certain stage, when the use of such a language becomes limited to the inner circle of families (and perhaps a close-knit village community at most), its functional value as means of social communication has suffered so much that coming generations tend to shift to the majority language, in particular in educating their children, in order to grant children equal chances in a complex society where social stratification is largely built upon formal education. The result of such "language shift"[27] is the loss of language transfer in families—a development that inevitably will lead to the extinction of the language if state and society are not taking decided measures against that trend.

If this trend toward loss of functionality and then "language shift" shall be reversed, or at least brought to a halt, strong institutional safeguards must be built into the political, administrative, and social arrangements upon which a society is built.[28] The loss of language transfer in families must be compensated by early childhood language acquisition in educational establishments, in particular kindergarten, preschool institutions, and primary school. In order to raise the functionality of the language, media use must be significantly expanded, book production and cultural activities in the language must be incentivized, and some degree of use must also be allowed in official communication with the administration, courts, and public services.[29]

---

[25] See Haarmann (2006), pp. 344–350.

[26] See Grillo (1989).

[27] See Fishman (1991), pp. 39–80.

[28] Fishman (1991), pp. 10–38.

[29] Fishman (2001), pp. 1–21.

3 European Efforts at Protecting Minority Languages

Whereas UNESCO deals with the complex of threatened languages and protection of linguistic heritage as a subfield of the protection of "intangible cultural heritage," the European legal tradition has confronted the problem under the heading of "minority protection." The political origins of the European endeavors in that regard are much different from the UNESCO discourse. Whereas UNESCO debates on the protection of "intangible cultural heritage" are a relatively recent phenomenon, dating back to the last quarter of the twentieth century, the European strand of minority protection is much older, dating back to the years after the end of the First World War.[30] Background of these debates was a problem of high politics. With the establishment of new "nation states" in a cultural space traditionally characterized by an extremely high degree of cultural diversity, one could easily foresee that attempts at forcible "nation-building," oriented toward the idea of a homogeneous "nation" with one language, one culture, and a unified historical memory, would lead to serious political conflicts. The great powers that dominated the post-World War I order thus tried to infuse some dose of moderation in the new political setup. Tools of such moderation were minority protection clauses in the peace treaties establishing the new order, together with a series of (unilateral) declarations of minority protection exerted from a number of the newly established states.[31] The system was well intended but never functioned properly, mostly due to the great powers soon losing interest in putting pressure on the states concerned to take these clauses seriously.[32]

After 1945, the concept of minority protection looked outdated and found no immediate successor. However, it experienced a revival in the 1980s and found its way into positive international law at the regional level in Europe after 1990.[33] Background of this revival was the resurgence of significant minority problems after the fall of the iron curtain—minority problems that posed severe security threats. The first institution that was mandated to take up these problems and work with them was the Conference (and then Organization) for Security and Cooperation in Europe (OSCE). It soon developed some standards of a soft-law nature and entrusted a new institution, the High Commissioner for National Minorities (HCNM), with the task of mediating in sensitive minority conflicts.[34]

The standard setting and monitoring of undertakings of minority protection later became an important activity for the profile of the Council of Europe (CoE).[35] Contrary to a number of fields of operation traditionally dealt with by the Council of Europe where the European Union has developed a strong competential portfolio

[30]See Jackson Preece (1998), pp. 67–94.

[31]Hilpold (2006), pp. 156–189.

[32]Ibid., pp. 183–187.

[33]Thornberry and Martín Estébanez (2004), pp. 7–10.

[34]See in detail Höhn (2005), pp. 7–170, 291–370.

[35]Oeter (2017), pp. 541–547, 570–571.

and has taken over the initiative in standard setting, minority protection is still a unique endeavor of the Council of Europe. A certain parallelism with the work done by the High Commissioner for National Minorities (HCNM) in the framework of the OSCE has subsided,[36] but in essence both lines of operation are complementary and there exists a relatively clear division of labor between CoE and OSCE. Whereas the OSCE and its HCNM concentrate their efforts mostly on conflict prevention and conflict management, the Council of Europe has developed a strong competence in standard setting and in monitoring the implementation of such standards in routine cases. The European Union has largely avoided activities in the field of minority protection since this issue is too politically sensitive to reach a consensus among its member states.[37] Minority protection is an important issue in preaccession processes and thus taken into consideration in the set of criteria known as "Copenhagen criteria." The EU, however, does not have its own standards for minority protection and in these cases mostly relies on the CoE standards.[38]

The two specialized CoE instruments dedicated to the issue of minority protection are the Framework Convention for the Protection of National Minorities (FCNM)[39] and the European Charter for Regional or Minority Languages (ECRML).[40] Both are clearly products of the same phase of an intensified political attention to minority problems in Europe after 1990. The texts of both treaties have been negotiated in the early 1990s on more or less parallel tracks, although the origins of both instruments are rather diverse. Whereas the FCNM is clearly a product of the immediate aftermath of 1990, the ideological origins of the Language Charter go back to the Galway Declaration of 1975 and are linked to the regionalism movement of the 1970s.[41] With Recommendation 928 of the Parliamentary Assembly, the Council of Europe adopted in 1981 the initiative to draft a legal instrument on the protection of minority languages. In a follow-up move, the Conference of Local and Regional Authorities of Europe decided in 1984 to set up a group of experts entrusted with the task of drafting such an instrument. The expert group elaborated a first draft, which was adopted by the Conference in 1987 and by the Parliamentary Assembly of the CoE in 1988.[42] The Committee of Ministers was reluctant to embrace the proposal and first set up an Ad Hoc Committee of Experts, which was given the mandate to revise the draft. The new draft was presented in a fortunate moment in 1992 because

[36]See Drzewicki (2014), pp. 25–51.

[37]See Toggenburg (2004), pp. 1–36.

[38]Sasse (2004), pp. 59–84.

[39]Framework Convention for the Protection of National Minorities, adopted on 1 Feb. 1995, entered into force in 1 Feb. 1998, ETS No. 157.

[40]European Charter for Regional or Minority Languages, adopted on 5 November 1995, entered into force on 1 March 1998, ETS No. 158.

[41]Woehrling (2005), p. 23.

[42]See Scherer-Leydecker (1997), pp. 146/47; see also the Explanatory Report to the European Charter for Regional or Minority Languages, paras. 3–8.

member states of the Council of Europe at that time felt a strong pressure to develop legal instruments dealing with the protection of minorities.

At that stage, the European states had decided, in a move parallel to the drafting of the Language Charter, that a solid minority rights instrument was needed in order to be able to cope with the problems of ethnic conflict.[43] Explicit legal guarantees enshrined in a multilateral legal instrument should—thus was the intention—safeguard a series of rights granting minority members protected domains in education, culture, the media, and public administration. Several draft conventions were prepared by various organs of the Council of Europe, like the Venice Commission draft and a proposal for a minority-related Additional Protocol to the European Convention on Human Rights.[44] However, one after the other, the ambitious projects of "progressive" minority rights instruments failed. The project of a "European Charter for Regional or Minority Languages" constitutes, together with the Framework Convention on the Protection of National Minorities, the two survivors of that cumbersome attempt at standard setting.[45]

Compared to the instruments that most international lawyers had strived for, the Language Charter constitutes a very peculiar regime, due to its so-called à la carte approach.[46] Such an "à la carte" construction is not a complete novelty—at least the European Social Charter, the Council of Europe instrument that codifies economic and social rights, follows a comparable model. The draft Charter was adopted by the Committee of Ministers and opened for ratification in 1992, but it came into force only in 1998, after it had been ratified by the minimum number of five states. Even after that date, it took quite a time until a significant number of Council of Europe member states went to ratification. Today, however, more than half of the member states have become contracting parties.

The original drafts were very much influenced by the ideologies of regionalism and then of traditional minority protection. Over the nearly 10 years of drafting, undertaken by various committees and drafting groups, the shape of the project changed considerably, however. This becomes evident if one looks to the preamble of the Charter, which includes an explicit commitment to the values of "interculturalism and multilingualism."[47] Linked to such commitment, the preamble also emphasizes the following:

> Considering that the protection of the historical regional or minority languages of Europe, some of which are in danger of eventual extinction, contributes to the maintenance and development of Europe's cultural wealth and traditions ...

---

[43]See Boysen (2011), para. 10.

[44]Relating to these draft instruments, see Scherer-Leydecker (1997), pp. 151–159; see also Woehrling (2012), pp. 12–13.

[45]Oeter (2017), pp. 545–546.

[46]See Pentassuglia (2002), pp. 130–131, and Boysen (2011), para. 15.

[47]Concerning the values underlying the Charter (and expressed in its Preamble) see Boysen (2011), para. 2, and Präambel paras. 22 et seq.

This passage from the preamble is peculiar since it departs considerably from the wording of traditional endeavors at minority protection and takes up the UNESCO discourse on intangible cultural heritage. The drafting history of the Charter had started with a much narrower mission—the original intent of the various drafting exercises in the 1980s and early 1990s had been linked to traditional concepts of protecting autochthonous minorities, with its inherent focus on collective rights.[48] But the complex and cumbersome drafting process led to a significant shift in emphasis—a shift that has infused a great dose of modernity into the endeavor. The Charter in the end became more an instrument of standard setting in the complex field of managing diversity and protection of cultural heritage than a traditional minority rights treaty.[49] The Charter accordingly avoids any formulation in categories of individual or collective rights.[50] Instead, it uses the terminology of "objective standards,"[51] directed at binding the member states in its formulation and operation of language policies. Nevertheless, the drafters of the Charter could not avoid creating substantive obligations that might give rise to subjective rights as a consequence.[52]

In contrast to the Language Charter, the Framework Convention was from the outset designed as a human rights instrument. Starting point was Recommendation 1134 (1990) of the Parliamentary Assembly calling for an instrument protecting certain minimum rights of members of minorities.[53] The initiative shifted to the Steering Committee for Human Rights (CDDH), which based its workings on a draft Convention prepared by the Venice Commission. In Recommendation 1177 (1992), however, the Parliamentary Assembly criticized the weaknesses of this draft and opted for the project of an Additional Protocol to the ECHR.[54] As a reaction, the Committee of Ministers called upon CDDH to prepare binding standards on minority protection. The newly created Committee of Experts for the Protection of National Minorities (DH-MIN) was subsequently mandated with the task of elaborating an instrument that got stuck in its work—and only the 1993 Vienna Summit of the Council of Europe infused some new momentum into the exercise, by calling upon the Committee of Ministers "to draft with minimum delay a framework convention specifying the principles which contracting States commit themselves to respect, in order to assure the protection of national minorities."[55] As a reaction to

[48]See the Explanatory Report to the Charter, paras. 3 et seq.—published (together with the text of the treaty) as a booklet by the Council of Europe Publishing; available also at the CoE website—https://www.coe.int/en/web/european-charter-regional-or-minority-languages/text-of-the-charter. Accessed 15 Dec. 2017.

[49]See also Boysen (2011), para. 11, and Woehrling (2005), p. 20.

[50]See, for example, Pentassuglia (2002), p. 130.

[51]Boysen (2011), para. 11; Woehrling (2012), p. 17.

[52]See also Boysen (2011), para. 13.

[53]Hafner (2015), para. 34.

[54]Ibid., para. 36.

[55]Ibid., paras. 44/45; see also Thornberry and Martín Estébanez (2004), pp. 89–90.

this call, the Committee of Ministers instituted an Ad Hoc Committee for the Protection of National Minorities (CAHMIN), which in a time frame of less than a year drafted the Framework Convention on the Protection of National Minorities (FCNM).[56] The bases of the substantial part of the FCNM are the human rights enshrined in the European Convention on Human Rights, adapted to the specific circumstances of minorities. Heavy debates ensued over the control mechanism that should take care of the implementation of these standards.[57] At the end, CAHMIN opted, like in the Language Charter, for the classical modalities of a state reporting procedure with an Advisory Committee as a treaty body monitoring the implementation of the Convention. Individual applications based on the Framework Convention to an international body are thus excluded. The draft was adopted by the Committee of Ministers on February 1, 1995, and laid open to signature and ratification. The Framework Convention entered into force in early 1998. Only 4 years later, in 2002, it had already reached a number of 34 member states, a number that has gone up to 39 to date.[58] This broad acceptance distinguishes the Framework Convention from the Language Charter, which has been ratified only by 25 CoE member states.

Both conventions cover more or less the same policy challenge and seem to double the efforts toward minority protection. A look into the practice at a first glance might confirm such an impression since some of the Thematic Commentaries of the Advisory Committee, such as Commentary No. 1 on Education from 2006 and Commentary No. 3 on Language Rights, laid open a strong degree of overlap between the conventions.[59] At the same time, however, both conventions show a clear relation of complementarity.[60] It is true, both stem more or less from the same historical sources—the concept of minority protection. However, when looking into the details of the drafting history, both treaties prove to be results of completely different political movements—and of different actors supporting these movements. In essence, the Language Charter is a child of the regionalism movement of the 1970s and 1980s, with the Conference of Local and Regional Authorities of Europe as its main supporter in the first phase and the support of the Parliamentary Assembly as an additional driving force. The background of the movement leading to the FCNM is much more rooted in high politics and has a lot to do with the ethno-political cleavages and conflicts coming to the surface of European politics in the years after 1990.[61] The first arena where such problems were ventured and solutions were sought had been the OSCE, with the creation of the OSCE High Commissioner

---

[56]See on the negotiations in CAHMIN Hafner (2015), paras. 46–49.

[57]Ibid., para. 48.

[58]See e.g. Hofmann (2015), para. 23.

[59]The Advisory Committee's thematic commentaries are available at the CoE website—http://www.coe.int/en/web/minorities/thematic-commentaries. Accessed 15 Dec. 2017; see also Lantschner (2010), pp. 275–284.

[60]Boysen (2011), para. 10.

[61]See Boysen (2011), para. 10.

as the major result of such search for a new ground. But the feeling that some binding legal standards were needed in addition to the "soft law" standards of the OSCE brought the Council of Europe into the forefront. It was only in the context of the Council of Europe that states could manage to negotiate such legally binding instruments and were able to underpin them by institutional mechanisms of monitoring.

It is evident that the orientation of both treaty regimes shows strong differences. The ideational background of the "high politics" projects of a comprehensive treaty on the protection of minorities clearly was the language of human rights. It is no accident that the most far-reaching project of such a type of treaty was a (proposed) Additional Protocol to the ECHR on minority rights.[62] Even the Framework Convention on the Protection of National Minorities, although in substance much weaker than the original projects, still is phrased explicitly in terms of human rights. The drafters made clear that the document intends to safeguard the human rights of the members of national minorities, and they attempted to find formulations that cover all the human rights aspects of measures of protection and promotion in favor of minorities (respectively their members).[63] In order not to overburden member states with a too far-reaching rights language, the concrete formulations had to be watered down by a large number of softening formulations, limitation clauses, and in-built reservations.[64]

The ambition of the drafters of the Language Charter went into a completely different direction. The various drafting groups knew from the beginning that one cannot do justice to the needs and purposes of language protection by using a mere human rights language. If there is a human rights language adequate to these problems, it is the language of social, economic, and cultural rights. Protection and promotion of languages require in its essence a series of positive actions of states.[65] Educational offers are needed, radio and television programs in these languages must be provided, cultural and social activities must be supported by the state, options of usage in communication with state authorities should be created, and the use of these languages in social life needs to be encouraged. It is difficult, if not impossible, to formulate these needs of "positive action" in the language of absolute rights. The resource basis of states—even inside a regional community as the Council of Europe—is extremely divergent. The sociolinguistic situations differ enormously—and accordingly the needs of positive action, as well as the options that are politically feasible. The resulting path into an "à-la-carte" approach according to the (preexisting) model of the European Social Charter seemed much more promising in this regard than a traditional human rights approach.[66] Accordingly, the Language Charter takes a clearly complementary approach to the human

[62] Klebes (1993), pp. 148–152.

[63] See only Thornberry and Martín Estébanez (2004), p. 92.

[64] Ibid., p. 92; see also Hofmann (2015), p. 73 at para. 19.

[65] See Woehrling (2005), p. 27, and Boysen (2011), para. 22.

[66] See Boysen (2011), para. 11.

rights perspective of the FCNM. FCNM and Language Charter are devoted to the same problem area, but they take alternative routes and cover different aspects of the protection of political, social, and cultural rights of minorities. Both instruments try to fill some major lacunae in the overall setup of the European legal order—a setup that is not yet really completed as far as the protection of cultural diversity in Europe is concerned.[67]

4 The European Charter for Regional or Minority Languages

Despite its roots in the traditional concepts of minority protection "à la européenne," the European Charter for Regional or Minority Languages has infused a strong degree of modern protection of intangible cultural heritage in its construction. The preamble of the Charter makes that evident, with its formula "that the protection of the historical regional or minority languages of Europe ... contributes to the maintenance and development of Europe's cultural wealth and traditions." This formula takes up the language of the debates on the protection of intangible cultural heritage and puts the objective of protection and promotion of regional and minority languages in the framework of the efforts of safeguarding cultural heritage. The object of protection covered by the Charter, the phenomenon of marginalized, and sometimes even severely threatened, regional and minority languages, clearly embodies an emanation of intangible cultural heritage. The broad and comprehensive notion of "safeguarding" used by the 2003 Convention also converges with the Charter's focus on "protection and promotion" of regional and minority languages since the protective regime of the Language Charter does not only envisage classic methods of "protection" of cultural heritage but also envisages a broad range of measures that are needed to create the social and institutional conditions necessary for the survival and further development of a language as a living means of communication.[68]

The reference to the "maintenance and development of Europe's cultural wealth and traditions" is not a purely rhetorical gesture but has also been formative for the construction of the operative parts of the Charter. In order to avoid, as far as possible, any language of human rights, the drafters did its utmost to keep the treaty in the design of an objective regime on the protection of cultural heritage (and of diversity management). With the model of the European Social Charter as a structural source of inspiration, and the resulting path decision for an "à la carte" approach, this meant that states kept a lot of leeway in determining the scope of ratification. In the process of drafting the ratification instrument, states had—not surprisingly—a tendency to

---

[67]Concerning the deficiencies of EU law in that regard see Toggenburg (2015), pp. 52–67; de Witte (2004), pp. 205–241.

[68]Oeter (2017), pp. 558–566.

take the existing state of internal legislation as a given basis of their instrument of ratification. Contrary to initial fears by most of the proponents of an improved standard of minority protection, however, the preexisting legislative state of the art served only as a starting point, mostly because the ratifying states often tried to take the minority communities politically on board, which implied that states had to make more ambitious political pledges than originally intended, incorporating a considerable portion of normative ambition into the instrument of ratification.[69] As a result, the instrument of ratification often promised far-reaching reforms of national language policy, at least if taken at face value. This did not preclude that the practical implementation in a number of cases tended to step back and to delay the realization of the promises made with the ratification of the Charter.

It must be stressed again: the Charter does not protect minorities as social groups. It also does not envisage directly the protection of individual rights of members of minorities.[70] The Charter is a treaty designed to set standards for the formulation and implementation of language policies.[71] The primary object of protection thus is not minorities as groups or individual members of such minority groups but "languages" as a cultural phenomenon.[72] No doubt, the protection of languages in practical detail means also—as a more or less inevitable consequence—protecting the speakers of a minority language in its linguistic rights. Indirectly, the Charter thus protects also individual rights and constitutes (at least indirectly) a human rights instrument.[73] But the political understanding upon which the project of the Charter was based stressed the question of language maintenance as primary objective of the Charter, thus the "objective" character of the instrument. The Charter accordingly speaks of "languages" and of "speakers" of such languages as its objects of protection, not of "minorities" or "linguistic communities." The Charter deliberately avoids any use of collective rights concepts in its wording; nevertheless, it cannot avoid protecting in substance members of linguistic minorities—and indirectly also minorities as collective units.[74] It is also beyond dispute that the Charter, although not an explicit human rights instrument, provides in a number of cases for individual rights bearing human rights character.[75] One must only read obligations like Article 8 para. 1 (b), which provides for various schemes of guaranteed primary school education in minority languages—education in the relevant minority language, a substantial part of education in the language, or the teaching of the language as an integral

[69]See, as an example, the description of the German process for preparing ratification in Oeter and Walker (2006), pp. 259–265.

[70]See Woehrling (2005), p. 27.

[71]See Pentassuglia (2002), p. 130; see also the explanatory report to the European Charter for Regional or Minority Languages, para. 11, as well as Boysen (2011), para. 11.

[72]See Boysen (2011), para. 11, and Woehrling (2012), pp. 16–18.

[73]See in that direction the explanatory report to the European Charter for Regional or Minority Languages, paras. 11 and 13; see also Woehrling (2005), p. 31.

[74]See also the explanatory report to the European Charter for Regional or Minority Languages, para. 11.

[75]See more in detail Boysen (2011), para. 12, and Woehrling (2005), p. 31.

part of the curriculum—with a final option "to apply one of the measures provided for under i to iii above at least to those pupils whose families so request and whose number is considered sufficient." It is difficult to interpret such a clause without ending up in some kind of a "human rights dimension," granting a right for the parents and children concerned.[76]

There are two operative parts that make up the Language Charter, Part II and Part III.[77] Part II provides for a "minimum code" of elementary standards meant to create obligations for states vis-à-vis all minority and regional languages that exist upon the territory of a member state. There is no "menu" concerning Part II—the (programmatic) standards laid down in this part are binding in all its aspects and apply to each minority language covered.[78] The standards as such, however, are rather vague and are more formulated as policy objectives than as concrete legal standards that could be applied directly by administrative authorities and courts.[79] The "chapeau" of Article 7 accordingly requires that "In respect of regional or minority languages, within the territories in which such languages are used and according to the situation of each language, the parties shall base their policies, legislation and practice on the following objectives and principles: . . ." A list of elementary objectives and principles of protection of minority languages follows after this chapeau, phrased in rather abstract terms, such as "the recognition of the regional or minority languages as an expression of cultural wealth," "the need for resolute action to promote regional or minority languages in order to safeguard them," "the facilitation and/or encouragement of the use of regional or minority languages, in speech and writing, in public and private life," and "the provision of appropriate forms and means for the teaching and study of regional or minority languages at all appropriate stages."[80]

Part III is the technical core of the Language Charter. It contains the specific "menu" of protection for recognized minority languages with options of a much more concrete nature than the abstract principles and objectives of Part II.[81] The Charter contains a list of nearly 100 options of specific measures in favor of minority languages, under which a state must select at least 35 options per protected language.[82] States "are free, within certain limits, to determine which of these provisions will apply to each of the languages spoken within their frontiers."[83] It has often been asked why the drafters have chosen such a complex structure based upon

[76] See more in detail Langenfeld (2011), at p. 191 para. 6.

[77] As to the differences between Part II and Part III see the explanatory report to the European Charter for Regional or Minority Languages, paras. 38–41; see also Boysen (2011), para. 14, and Woehrling (2005), p. 29.

[78] Explanatory report, para. 39; see also Boysen (2011), Art. 2 para. 2.

[79] See also Boysen (2011), Art. 2 para. 4, and Dunbar (2012), pp. 187–190.

[80] See the explanatory report to the European Charter for Regional or Minority Languages, paras. 58–75; see also Woehrling (2005), pp. 106–117.

[81] See Boysen (2011), Art. 2 paras. 6 et seq.

[82] Art. 2 para. 2 EChRML; see also the explanatory report, paras. 43–47.

[83] Explanatory report, para. 22.

an optional menu. One should be aware, however, that the task to protect and promote minority languages in operational details of language policy requires more than a broad set of civil and political rights of a general nature. The protection of minority languages in its essence is about positive obligations of states in the fields of education, media, culture, official use in administration and courts.[84] Minority languages cannot be protected by simply obliging states to abstain from harmful acts. As the Advisory Committee on the Framework Convention for the Protection of National Minorities notes in its Third Thematic Commentary on the Language Rights of Persons Belonging to National Minorities, "preventing assimilation requires not only abstention from policies clearly aimed at assimilating persons belonging to national minorities into the mainstream society."[85] It also implies positive action in order to "promote the conditions necessary for persons belonging to national minorities to maintain and develop their culture, and to preserve the essential elements of their identity, namely their religion, language, traditions and cultural heritage," as is stated in Article 5 of the Framework Convention. This will, the Advisory Committee argues, "often require the active promotion and encouragement of the use of minority languages in order to prevent their disappearance from public life, and the creation of an environment more conducive to the use of these languages."[86]

If a sensible degree of protection and promotion of minority languages shall be achieved, states must take a broad range of positive measures, which includes in particular providing certain types of education in minority languages at state schools, offering programs in minority languages in public service radio and television, and enabling speakers to use (at least in certain contexts) their language before administrative authorities and courts.[87] Article 8 thus provides for a wide range of educational options, with models of education in the minority language (as a medium of instruction), bilingual types of education, and models of education in the official state language with a certain level of teaching of the minority language (as an additional language taught in school).[88] Article 9 envisages a differing degree of possibilities of using minority languages in the judicial system, ranging from ambitious models with courts operating in a minority language to various degrees of language use by speakers as accused or civil party (with interpretation at the cost of the state) to rather minimal options of having a possibility to hand in at least written documents in minority languages.[89] Rather similar options exist with regard to language use in the administration provided for in Article 10, where usually only regional and local administrations open up to various degrees of minority language

[84] See Woehrling (2005), p. 27, and Boysen (2011), para. 22.

[85] Advisory Committee FCNM, Thematic Commentary No. 3, para. 29.

[86] Ibid.

[87] Oeter (2017), para. 35.

[88] See also the contribution of Westphal in this volume.

[89] Pla Boix (2012), pp. 301–336.

use.[90] There are obvious reasons behind the limited amount by which states make use of these options. Official use before courts and administrations requires a specific organization of the court system and the administration and implies the recruitment of personnel with specific linguistic capabilities.[91] More or less, the same is true as far as media are concerned, the field regulated in Article 11. Options range here from entire TV and radio stations operating in minority languages to programs broadcast in these languages, support for the production of audiovisual works in minority languages, the training of journalists and media staff in these languages, and support given to minority language newspapers.[92] Article 12 envisages various measures of support for cultural activities in minority languages,[93] whereas Article 13 offers a range of measures encouraging the use of minority languages in economic and social life, with a practical priority in the operation of health systems (in particular hospitals) and homes for the elderly with service offers in minority languages.[94] Article 14 finally covers transfrontier exchanges, either in the framework of bilateral agreements with other states where the same languages are used or via cooperation across borders of regional and local authorities.

The typical forms of abstract, all-embracing formulations characteristic of human rights instruments would make it difficult to oblige states to take all these specific kinds of positive measures. If one wants to spell out these positive obligations in a manner as concretely as possible, it makes sense to work with a catalog of options as it is used in the Language Charter. With the various options set out in the text of Part III, the envisaged positive measures gain a degree of concreteness that would never be achieved in a catch-all formula typically used in standard human rights treaties. The recourse to a "menu structure" like in the Social Charter thus was a logical step to be taken for the drafters of the Charter. The Charter as a result manages to become very technical in its construction of the undertakings, binding the states to rather precise and concrete obligations. States have a choice which obligations they want to take, but if they have taken a set of obligations, they have much less leeway in arguing that a certain policy conforms to its undertakings than they have under a broad and sweeping instrument like the Framework Convention.[95]

[90]See more in detail Engbers (2012), pp. 337–371.

[91]Boysen (2011), Art. 2 para. 6; see also Dunbar (2010), pp. 178–180.

[92]See Dunbar and Moring (2012), pp. 373–424.

[93]See Craig (2012), pp. 425–444.

[94]See Urrutia Libarona (2012), pp. 445–484.

[95]See already Oeter (2004), p. 135.

5 Monitoring Practice Under the Language Charter

As far as compliance control is concerned, the European Charter for Regional or Minority Languages follows the common approach of Council of Europe conventions in the human rights field and sets out a standard reporting procedure.[96] Member states have to submit reports on their policies pursued in accordance with Part II of the Charter and on the measures taken in application of those provisions of Part III chosen by them, in a format that is prescribed by a standard form adopted by the Committee of Ministers.[97] The reports are presented to the Secretary General of the Council of Europe. At the same time, the reports must be made public in the country concerned.[98] The Secretary General forwards the reports to the Committee of Experts established under the Charter, which has the responsibility of examining the reports in detail. The Committee of Experts is composed of one member per each contracting party, appointed by the Committee of Ministers for a term of 6 years.[99] The composition of the Committee of Experts is rather heterogeneous in terms of personal and professional background. Nearly half of the members are law professors or scholars with a particular expertise in social rights and minority rights; the other most important group comprises linguists and social scientists specialized in sociolinguistic issues.[100] Roughly a third of the Committee's members belong to linguistic minorities themselves.

In the process of monitoring the implementation of the Charter, the involvement of civil society is of extreme importance. The Charter itself invites "bodies or associations legally established in a Party," which means primarily recognized minority bodies or associations, to "draw the attention of the committee of experts to matters relating to the undertakings entered into by that Party under Part III of this Charter."[101] Associations or bodies representing minorities or struggling for the rights of minorities thus may not only brief the Committee's members behind the scene, like this is done at the UN level, but are explicitly allowed to act openly, to submit formally statements, pieces of information, and critical comments to the reports of states. The Committee may "take account of this information" in the preparation of its report, may include it in its statements of facts, may openly refer to it.[102] Legal arrangements alone cannot guarantee a loyal implementation of the set of undertakings ratified under the Charter; societal pressure is needed in that regard, as well as political debate and public attention—and without engaged and professional

[96] See more in detail Pentassuglia (2002), pp. 201–202, and Oeter (2004), pp. 136–140.

[97] Explanatory report to the Charter, para. 127; see also, more in detail, Woehrling (2005), pp. 246–250; Rein (2011), p. 365 paras. 12–17; Lasagabaster (2012), pp. 519–522.

[98] Art. 15 para. 2 ECRML; see also Boysen (2011), Art. 6 paras. 1–6.

[99] See the explanatory report, para. 131, and more in detail Rein (2011), Art. 17 paras. 3–10; see also Lasagabaster (2012), p. 528.

[100] Oeter (2004), p. 137; Rein (2011), Art. 17 para. 7.

[101] See also the explanatory report, paras. 128–29.

[102] See also Rein (2011), Art. 16 paras. 10–12.

NGOs mobilizing the public and orchestrating political pressure, implementation of the conventional standards often becomes deficient.[103] Thus, a (triangular) dialog with the respective authorities and civil society is needed in order to improve the state of implementation. This dialog usually "is carried on in the first place in the form of written questions and answers"[104] but is complemented in a later stage by an "on-the-spot visit" of the working group dealing with the state report (usually consisting of three ComEx members).[105] The resulting evaluation report is finally presented to the Committee of Ministers, the political steering organ of the Council of Europe, which adopts recommendations addressed to the member states based on the findings of the Committee of Experts.[106]

If one tries to give an assessment of the impact of these elaborate monitoring procedures, the findings are mixed. At its essence, the instrument is much more effective as thought at the outset. After the adoption of the draft of the Charter and the Framework Convention, most observers thought that these two conventions were relatively weak in wording and would remain a more or less symbolic exercise.[107] This judgment has been proven to be wrong. Both conventions (and its institutional mechanisms) have heavily influenced the minority policies of member states and thus have made an impact on national legislation and administrative practices in the member states of the conventions. The degree to which such impact can be observed varies inevitably.[108] Some states, like Norway, are rather sensitive toward international criticism and develop strong ambitions to improve the state of affairs when outside critics have a point to be made. Other states, like Russia, do not care much about critical reports from Council of Europe bodies. Most states are somewhere in between these two poles. Outside critique might exert a significant influence, depending on the political sensibilities and the power arrangements at an internal level. Sometimes states react with great responsiveness and develop serious reform projects; in other cases, states (and this may even be the same states) remain stubborn and ignore outside critics. The result of expert monitoring and critical evaluation of the implementation record (with all its strengths and weaknesses) depends very much on internal publics and the strength of civil society organizations. Where the general public is sensitive toward claims of injustice and discrimination and has a sense for the virtues of cultural diversity, critical monitoring might make quite an impact. When strong NGOs in the fields of minority issues and human rights take up the cause and give an enhanced visibility to the findings of international monitoring,

[103]Gramstad (2010), p. 33.

[104]Biennial report by the Secretary General to the Parliamentary Assembly on the Application of the European Charter for Regional or Minority Languages, Doc. 8879 of 18 October 2000, p. 2. https://www.coe.int/en/web/european-charter-regional-or-minority-languages/secretary-general-reports. Accessed 28 Dec. 2017.

[105]See on the importance of the 'on-the-spot visits' for the work of the ComEx Rein (2011), Art. 16 para. 15, and Oeter (2004), p. 139.

[106]See more in detail Oeter (2017), para. 44.

[107]Oeter (2017), para. 49.

[108]Ibid.

this might change a lot. General publics in nation states, however, even in Western Europe, tend to be often rather ignorant toward issues of cultural diversity management (and minorities). And particularly in the problem countries, NGOs are often feeble and lack professionalism and organizational strength. As a result, the findings of monitoring bodies may remain without strong resonance in the most problematic cases.[109]

6 Conclusions: Are There Lessons to Be Learned?

The connecting lines that characterize the relation between the Council of Europe's European Charter for Regional or Minority Languages of 1992 and the UNESCO Convention for Safeguarding Intangible Cultural Heritage of 2003 are striking.[110] Not only the objectives of both treaties show a strong convergence, but even in its technical construction of the operative provisions there exist considerable parallels. Both conventions pursue the objective to safeguard important parts of our cultural heritage, in the form of intangible cultural heritage.[111] Although languages are not as such explicitly objects of protection under the 2003 UNESCO Convention, there are good reasons to categorize regional and minority languages as inseparable parts of oral traditions and expressions that undoubtedly belong to the core of intangible cultural heritage. The Language Charter itself singles out (in its preamble) the "maintenance and development of Europe's cultural wealth and traditions" as one of its primary objectives—a cultural wealth to which the manifold regional and minority languages (and the cultures represented by them) definitely belong. The purpose of both instruments is the safeguarding of the cultural heritage, with an understanding of "safeguarding" that is going much beyond classic tools of "protection," encompassing (as the language of the Charter calls it) also the "promotion" of the cultural practices, expressions, and skills that form the basis of language-centered social interaction. This task of protection and promotion must inevitably comprise the creation of favorable institutional and social arrangements in which the intangible cultural heritage is embedded and can dynamically develop.

Admittedly, the 2003 UNESCO Convention is the more recent instrument, with a much broader coverage than only the protection and promotion of languages. The philosophy behind the two conventions, however, is more or less the same. There are traditional embodiments of inherited culture upon which these cultures rest—and these embodiments are threatened by modernity, in all its aspects. If the specific cultural heritage in need of protection would perish, our cultural memory would impoverish considerably because entire cultures would fall out of the collective memory (except some traces in archives). The maintenance and development of our

[109] Ibid.

[110] See also Blake (2008), pp. 19–22.

[111] See Haider Quercia (2010), pp. 749–759.

cultural wealth and traditions thus call for decided action in order to enable the survival of the crucial elements of cultural heritage, a survival that inherently needs the creation of favorable social and institutional conditions.

This might sound as if the European Charter for Regional or Minority Languages constitutes only a specialized instrument supplementing the general endeavor of "safeguarding" intangible cultural heritage pursued by the 2003 UNESCO Convention. However, construing the relationship between both conventions in such a limited perspective of "lex specialis" would not do justice to the contributions that the Language Charter might deliver to the global endeavor of safeguarding the world's cultural heritage. The Council of Europe's Language Charter is much more than an attempt at concretizing the concept of safeguarding intangible cultural heritage, with a special focus on marginalized languages. It constitutes an innovative, one could say even experimental, treaty regime that has been testing out the instrumentalities needed for safeguarding a specific kind of intangible cultural heritage deeply embedded in political power structures, social formations, cultural practices, and communicative interactions. Safeguarding such intangible cultural heritage cannot be done with a "museological" approach and recording, archiving certain practices and expressions. The survival and dynamic development of such cultural heritage need a sociological and institutional dimension and finally end up in highly political issues.

This is a lesson that the European Charter for Regional or Minority Languages tells us in utmost clarity. Its roots are to be found in the high politics enterprise of minority protection, as it has developed in Europe throughout more than a century. Its background is not only preservation of cultural heritage but also conflict prevention and conflict management, thus primordial challenges of high politics. Europe had to learn throughout the twentieth century that neglecting the cultural needs of minorities can lead directly into armed conflict—a lesson still today not fully incorporated into the setup of European statehood. By linking international cultural heritage law to these roots of (highly politicized) minority protection, we could keep alive in memory that safeguarding intangible cultural heritage is not a pure issue of culture but has a dimension of high politics in the background.

The toolbox of traditional minority protection has some added value for the endeavor of safeguarding intangible cultural heritage. Cultural heritage becomes threatened because it is growingly marginalized in the wake of "modernization." The protection and promotion of the cultural practices, expressions, and skills defined as "intangible cultural heritage" require a reshaping of the social and institutional environment in which they are embedded. The measures designed to "safeguard" such cultural heritage can thus not be limited to the cultural practices and expressions as such but must address also the social, political, and economic conditions under which the bearers of such heritage live and that enable (or disable) them to maintain the practices constitutive of the cultural heritage. The experience with the Language Charter makes that crystal clear for the issue area of threatened languages. The tool box needed here is quite challenging and has very sensitive political dimensions and at the end calls for decided action in the field of language policy. Informal education and, even more, formal education are of crucial importance, as well as the structure of media offers and usage patterns; state support for cultural institutions, organizations, and activities; and also the expansion of functionalities of a language by opening up administrative and judicial communication for certain types of use of minority languages. This is far from trivial, annoys adherents of classic "nation state" projects, and must inevitably face strong political opposition from time to time. The tool box is there and has been tested for quite some time; that is the lesson to be distilled from 20 years of experience with the Language Charter. We know more or less what works under specific conditions—and a close look into the specific social, institutional, and political conditions is definitely needed. "One size fits all" does not work; we need very differentiated menus of measures protecting and promoting our cultural heritage. There is a strong repertory of best practices embodied in the menus of ratification and the corresponding practice of states, and the monitoring work of the treaty body under the Charter has helped to lay that repertory open (together with a mirroring repertory of bad practices). Safeguarding intangible cultural heritage, and in particular languages as an embodiment of such heritage, needs a comprehensive approach that looks upon the whole range of social conditions and legal and institutional arrangements that frame the cultural practices and expressions in need of protection.

At the same time, it is interesting to note that both conventions work with rather flexible sets of obligations. The range of national safeguarding measures, as well as the system of the two lists with its linked action plans, allows a huge degree of flexibility under the 2003 UNESCO Convention; the same is true for the "à la carte" approach of Part III of the Language Charter enabling states to tailor very specific menus of protection and promotion. This points to an in-built need of flexible and differentiated arrangements if the task of "safeguarding" shall really be achieved.

The institutional setup intended to monitor the implementation of the undertakings seems more advanced in the case of the Language Charter. This has a lot to do with the linkage to traditional patterns of human rights protection inside the Council of Europe. A formalized state reporting procedure with a strong (and truly independent) treaty body consisting of independent experts has been established as the standard pattern for compliance control mechanisms in the Council of Europe and was thus taken over when drafting the Charter, although the Charter was definitely not intended to constitute a human rights instrument. The dense but at the same time informal interaction of the Committee of Experts for the Language Charter with NGOs and the language communities concerned enables the expert body to orchestrate some pressure from civil society that is often needed to improve the implementation record. In this regard, an intergovernmental committee, as is standard in UNESCO regimes, is much more handicapped. It might exert strong peer-group pressure from states but tends all too often to fall into routines of complacency typical of intergovernmental environments where the search for consensus is deeply encoded.

The experience with the Language Charter of the Council of Europe thus presents us with an interesting, to a certain degree contrasting, lesson on the intricacies but also chances of safeguarding intangible cultural heritage. UNESCO and its epistemic community of culture diplomats and cultural experts could learn a lot from this experience. At the same time, the Council of Europe and its specific community of diplomats, bureaucrats, experts, and civil society representatives could profit a lot from taking into consideration the ongoing work—and the results—of UNESCO's endeavor to safeguarding our intangible cultural heritage. As mentioned above, the objectives are more or less the same, the technical and institutional approaches converge strongly, but the background experiences and knowledge formations that dominated the formation (and dominate the subsequent practice) of these regimes differ a lot. Just because the epistemics of the related endeavors are starkly contrasting, the potential for mutual learning is considerable.

References

Aikawa-Faure N (2009) From the proclamation of masterpieces to the convention for the safeguarding of intangible cultural heritage. In: Smith L, Akagawa N (eds) Intangible heritage. Routledge, London, pp 13–44

Andris S (2014) 'Call for Intangible Cultural Heritage': Das Suchen und Finden des UNESCO-Kulturerbe nimmt kein Ende. Schweizerisches Archiv für Volkskunde 110(2):133–147

Blake J (2008) The international legal framework for the safeguarding and promotion of languages. Mus Int 60(3):14–25

Blake J (2015) International cultural heritage law. Oxford University Press, Oxford

Boysen S (2011) Einführung. In: Boysen S et al (eds) Europäische Charta der Regional- oder Minderheitensprachen: Handkommentar. Dike, Zürich, pp 23–39

Cameron C, Rössler M (2013) Many voices, one vision: the early years of the world heritage convention. Ashgate, Farnham

Craig E (2012) Article 12. Cultural activities and facilities. In: Nogueira López A et al (eds) Shaping language rights. Council of Europe, Strasbourg, pp 425–444

de Witte B (2004) Language law of the European Union: protecting or eroding linguistic diversity? In: Craufurd Smith R (ed) Culture and european law. Oxford University Press, Oxford, pp 205–241

Drzewicki K (2014) Minority policies of the OSCE. In: Thürer D (ed) International protection of minorities – challenges in practice and doctrine. Schulthess, Zürich, pp 25–51

Dunbar R (2010) The charter as a living instrument: legal challenges and perspectives. In: Council of Europe (ed) Minority language protection in Europe: into a new decade. Council of Europe Publishing, Strasbourg, pp 171–186

Dunbar R (2012) Article 7 - objectives and principles. In: Nogueira López A et al (eds) Shaping language rights. Council of Europe, Strasbourg, pp 185–244

Dunbar R, Moring T (2012) Article 11 – media. In: Nogueira López A et al (eds) Shaping language rights. Council of Europe Publishing, Strasbourg, pp 373–424

Engbers J (2012) Article 10 – administrative authorities and public services. In: Nogueira López A et al (eds) Shaping language rights. Council of Europe Publishing, Strasbourg, pp 337–372

Fishman JA (1991) Why is it so hard to save a threatened language? In: Fishman JA (ed) Can threatened languages be saved? Reversing language shift, revisited, 9th edn. Multilingual Matters, Clevedon, pp 1–21

Fishman JA (2001) Reversing language shift: theoretical and empirical foundations of assistance to threatened languages. Multilingual Matters, Clevedon

Forrest C (2010) International law and the protection of cultural heritage. Routledge, London

Francioni F (ed) (2009) The 1972 world heritage convention: a commentary. Oxford University Press, Oxford

Gillman D (2010) The idea of cultural heritage. Cambridge University Press, Cambridge

Gramstad S (2010) The charter's monitoring mechanism: a practical perspective. In: Council of Europe (ed) Minority language protection in Europe: into a new decade. Council of Europe Publishing, Strasbourg, pp 29–34
Grillo RD (1989) Dominant languages: language and hierarchy in Britain and France. Cambridge University Press, Cambridge
Haarmann H (2006) Weltgeschichte der Sprachen. CHBeck, München
Hafner G (2015) Die Entwicklung des Rechts des Minderheitenschutzes. In: Hofmann R et al (eds) Rahmenübereinkommen zum Schutz nationaler Minderheiten: Handkommentar. Nomos, Baden-Baden, pp 27–45
Haider Quercia U (2010) The distinction of minority language protection and language as a cultural heritage in Italy. The case of the piedmontese dialect. Eur Yearb Minor Issues 9:749–759
Hilpold P (2006) Minderheitenschutz im Völkerbundsystem. In: Pan C, Pfeil BS (eds) Zur Entstehung des modernen Minderheitenschutzes in Europa. Handbuch der europäischen Volksgruppen, vol 3. Springer, Wien, pp 156–189
Hofmann R (2015) Das Rahmenübereinkommen zum Schutz nationaler Minderheiten: Einführung, Überblick, Würdigung. In: Hofmann R et al (eds) Rahmenübereinkommen zum Schutz nationaler Minderheiten: Handkommentar. Nomos, Baden-Baden, pp 68–86
Höhn C (2005) Zwischen Menschenrechten und Konfliktprävention: Der Minderhei-tenschutz im Rahmen der Organisation für Sicherheit und Zusammenarbeit in Europa (OSZE). Springer, Berlin
Jackson Preece J (1998) National minorities and the European nation-states system. Clarendon, Oxford
Jensen L, Leerssen J, Mathijsen M (eds) (2010) Free access to the past: romanticism, cultural heritage, and the nation. Brill, Leiden
Klebes H (1993) Der Entwurf eines Minderheitenprotokolls zur EMRK. Europäische GrundrechteZeitschrift (EuGRZ) 20:148–152
Langenfeld C (2011) Artikel 8 – Bildung. In: Boysen S et al (eds) Europäische Charta der Regional- oder Minderheitensprachen: Handkommentar. Dike, Zürich, pp 183–221
Lantschner E (2010) Evolution and value of the thematic commentaries of the advisory committee of the framework convention for the protection of national minorities. Eur Yearb Hum Rights Issues 2:275–284
Lasagabaster I (2012) Articles 15 to 17 – application of the charter. In: Nogueira López A et al (eds) Shaping language rights. Council of Europe Publishing, Strasbourg, pp 517–534
Lixinski L (2013) Intangible cultural heritage in international law. Oxford University Press, Oxford
Munjeri D (2009) Following the length and the breadth of the roots: some dimensions of intangible heritage. In: Smith L, Akagawa N (eds) Intangible heritage. Routledge, London, pp 131–149
Oeter S (2004) The European Charter for Regional or Minority Languages. In: Pentassuglia G (ed) Mechanisms for the implementation of minority rights. Council of Europe Publishing, Strasbourg, pp 131–158
Oeter S (2007) Status der Regional- und Minderheitensprachen aus verfassungs- und völkerrechtlicher Sicht. Niederdeutsches Jahrbuch 130:127–150
Oeter S (2010) Mehrsprachigkeit als Last oder als Bereicherung? In: Vogt MT (ed) Minderheiten als Mehrwert. Peter Lang, Frankfurt am Main, pp 139–158
Oeter S (2014) Council of Europe – the European Charter for Regional or Minority Languages. In: Thürer D (ed) International protection of minorities – challenges in practice and doctrine. Schulthess, Zürich, pp 59–94
Oeter S (2017) Conventions on the protection of national minorities. In: Schmahl S, Breuer M (eds) The Council of Europe: its law and policies. Oxford University Press, Oxford, pp 542–571
Oeter S, Walker A (2006) The case of the Federal Republic of Germany. In: Spiliopoulou Åkermark S et al (eds) International obligations and national debates: minorities around the Baltic Sea. The Åland Islands Peace Institute, Mariehamn, pp 227–299
Pentassuglia G (2002) Minorities in international law: an introductory study. Council of Europe Publishing, Strasbourg

Pla Boix AM (2012) Article 9. Judicial authorities. In: Nogueira López A et al (eds) Shaping language rights. Council of Europe Publishing, Strasbourg, pp 301–336
Rein D (2011) Artikel 15. In: Boysen S et al (eds) Europäische Charta der Regional- oder Minderheitensprachen: Handkommentar. Dike, Zürich, pp 361–368
Sasse G (2004) Minority rights and EU enlargement: normative overstretch or effective conditionality? In: Toggenburg GN (ed) Minority protection and the enlarged European Union: the way forward. Open Society Institute, Budapest, pp 59–64
Scherer-Leydecker C (1997) Minderheiten und sonstige ethnische Gruppen. Eine Studie zur kulturellen Identität im Völkerrecht. Berlin-Verlag Spitz, Berlin
Strubell M, Boix-Fuster E (eds) (2011) Democratic policies for language revitalisation: the case of Catalan. Palgrave Macmillan, Basingstoke
Testa A (2016) From folklore to intangible cultural heritage: observations about a problematic filiation. Österreichische Zeitschrift für Volkskunde 119:221–243
Thornberry P, Martín Estébanez MA (2004) Minority rights in Europe. A review of the work and standards of the Council of Europe. Council of Europe Publishing, Strasbourg
Toggenburg GN (2004) Minority protection in a supranational context: limits and opportunities. In: Toggenburg GN (ed) Minority protection and the enlarged European Union: the way forward. Open Society Institute, Budapest, pp 1–36
Toggenburg GN (2015) Das Recht der Europäischen Union und das Rahmenübereinkommen zum Schutz nationaler Minderheiten. In: Hofmann R et al (eds) Rahmenübereinkommen zum Schutz nationaler Minderheiten: Handkommentar. Nomos, Baden-Baden, pp 52–67
Urrutia Libarona I (2012) Article 13 – economic and social life. In: Nogueira López A et al (eds) Shaping language rights. Council of Europe Publishing, Strasbourg, pp 445–484
von Schorlemer S (1992) Internationaler Kulturgüterschutz. Duncker und Humblot, Berlin
Woehrling J-M (2005) The European Charter for Regional or Minority Languages: a critical commentary. Council of Europe Publishing, Strasbourg
Woehrling J-M (2012) Introduction. In: Nogueira López A et al (eds) Shaping language rights. Council of Europe Publishing, Strasbourg, pp 11–31

Part II
Other Cultural Goods and Heritage

Réflexions sur la circulation internationale des collections muséales: De l'immunité à la copropriété ?

Amandine Lizot

Abstract Le musée du XXIème siècle renforce son ancrage international par l'exercice exponentiel de ses activités dans la sphère internationale. Symptomatiques de ce mouvement d'internationalisation, les prêts transnationaux de collections muséales, en vue d'expositions internationales, s'affirment désormais comme une des activités essentielles du musée. Bien que leur mise en œuvre soit en adéquation avec les missions muséales et la destination des collections, elle est entravée par les risques d'actions en revendication devant les juridictions de l'Etat emprunteur. En l'absence d'un instrument de droit international réglementant la circulation paisible des collections muséales, le droit international peine en effet à leur octroyer un régime juridique adapté. Le recours aux immunités d'Etat est encore fréquent. Or, force est de constater que, malgré le développement de ces régimes d'insaisissabilité des œuvres prêtées, l'insécurité juridique des prêts persiste. L'inadaptation du régime international des immunités aux collections muséales pourrait découler de l'absence de prise en considération effective des intérêts et droits matérialisés par ces objets. En s'inspirant d'un statut juridique fondé sur ces intérêts partagés, la copropriété, des pistes de réflexions peuvent être envisagées pour réconcilier droit international et prêts de collections muséales.

1 Introduction

Les musées du XXIème siècle confrontent le droit international à la difficulté d'appréhender une institution se multipliant (en passant de 22 000 en 1975[1] à plus de 54 600 en 2016[2]) et s'internationalisant progressivement. Si le musée demeure, par ses

[1]Hudson, Nicholls (1975).

[2]Lochar, Meinhold (2016).

A. Lizot (✉)
Institut de recherche en droit international et européen de la Sorbonne (IREDIES), Université Paris 1 Panthéon-Sorbonne, Paris Cedex 5, France
e-mail: Amandine.Lizot@malix.univ-paris1.fr

© Springer International Publishing AG, part of Springer Nature 2018

E. Lagrange et al. (eds.), *Cultural Heritage and International Law*,
https://doi.org/10.1007/978-3-319-78789-3_5

statuts, une entité de droit national, il exerce également ses missions « traditionnelles/conventionnelles » hors de la sphère nationale, tout en développant des fonctions « nouvelles/contemporaines » liées à une société ouverte sur l'extérieur[3]. L'activité muséale s'intègre dorénavant dans un réseau complexe de flux internationaux d'informations, de financements, d'indivus et de collections muséales[4]. La réglementation existante se révèle dès lors insuffisante pour encadrer cette évolution. Le premier instrument international ayant exclusivement pour objet les musées, la Recommandation concernant les moyens les plus efficaces de rendre les musées accessibles à tous de 1960 (Recommandation de 1960), porte en effet seulement sur l'accessibilité. Prenant acte de l'« ampleur des changements socioéconomiques et politiques qui ont affecté le rôle et la diversité des musées » (préambule), l'Organisation des Nations Unies pour l'Education, la Science et la Culture (UNESCO) adopte une Recommandation sur la protection et la promotion des musées et de leurs collections en 2015 (Recommandation de 2015). Plus de cinquante ans après la pose des premiers jalons, le musée est l'objet exclusif d'un instrument international visant à en appréhender la complexité.

Si la Recommandation de 2015 définit traditionnellement les musées comme des institutions permanentes, à but non lucratif, dont les missions consistent à acquérir, conserver, rechercher, communiquer et exposer le patrimoine culturel de l'humanité et l'environnement[5], ils sont désormais encouragés à internationaliser leurs activités. Dans le cadre de la communication (§ 10), fonction primordiale des musées, l'Etat est ainsi débiteur d'une obligation molle consistant à encourager le développement des expositions, des échanges internationaux et de la mobilité des collections (§ 31). La circulation des collections entraîne l'élargissement du public sensibilisé, permettant également au musée d'accomplir sa mission d'éducation (§ 12). Elle favorise aussi le développement de liens entre les cultures et la constitution d'une identité collective et participe, ce faisant, à la réalisation du rôle social de l'institution (§§ 16-17)[6].

En adéquation avec les missions du musée, l'organisation d'expositions internationales se justifie également par la nature spécifique des collections muséales. Dans la Recommandation de 2015, les collections muséales sont décrites comme constituées du « patrimoine matériel et immatériel de l'humanité » (§ 4) dont les musées seraient « dépositaires » (préambule). En tant que patrimoine de l'humanité, les collections muséales présentent un intérêt commun pour la communauté internationale[7]. Cette qualité ne conduit néanmoins pas à les sortir

---

[3]UNESCO, Comité spécial d'experts techniques et juridiques (2015) Un nouvel instrument normatif international: Projet de recommandation de l'UNESCO concernant la protection et la promotion des musées, de leur diversité et de leur rôle dans la société, 3, p. 2.

[4]Mairesse (2012), pp. 14-15 et pp. 44-48.

[5]Recommandation de 1960 (§ 1), Recommandation de 2015 (§ 4). L'inclusion du patrimoine immatériel dans les collections muséales en 2015 doit cependant être relevée.

[6]L'organisation d'expositions est également un atout pour attirer de nouveaux publics, développer des réseaux avec des professionnels étrangers, récolter des donations et des sponsors, tout en augmentant le prestige de l'institution.

[7]Convention pour la protection des biens culturels en cas de conflit armé (1954), Convention concernant les mesures à prendre pour interdire et empêcher l'importation, l'exportation et le

du patrimoine dont elles relèvent, que ce patrimoine soit privé ou public. Les collections publiques sont par ailleurs complexes à définir en droit international car les sources normatives internationales en ont une appréciation distincte. Le caractère public des collections découle tantôt de leur rattachement à une personne publique par un titre de propriété ou un financement significatif[8], tantôt de l'intérêt public de l'institution à laquelle elles sont affectées[9]. Un objet de propriété privée peut donc être inclus dans les collections publiques si l'institution le conservant remplit les critères du financement ou de l'intérêt public[10]. En partant de ce constat, les collections muséales publiques désignent l'ensemble des collections gérées par des institutions muséales publiques[11]. Ces collections matérialisent un intérêt partagé par, d'une part l'Etat d'origine du musée, débiteur d'obligations molles relatives à leur gestion[12] et d'une obligation de comportement relative à leur protection[13] et, d'autre part la communauté internationale[14]. Facilitant l'accessibilité au patrimoine culturel de l'humanité et correspondant aux missions des musées, les expositions internationales sont donc des manifestations essentielles à l'accomplissement des finalités de l'institution.

Or, la réalisation opérationnelle de ces finalités est entravée par l'absence d'un régime juridique international adapté. Le prêt d'un objet expose en effet l'institution à des revendications devant les juridictions de l'Etat emprunteur. Deux types de revendications peuvent notamment entraîner la saisie des collections prêtées[15]. En premier lieu, des créanciers peuvent exercer des mesures de contrainte sur l'objet en vue de faire exécuter un jugement qui leur est favorable. L'issue du litige est alors incertaine, comme le démontre notamment l'analyse de la jurisprudence américaine. Si, en application du *Foreign Sovereign Immunities Act* (FSIA) de 1976[16], les Etats sont en principe protégés des mesures d'exécution forcée, cette règle n'est pas

---

transfert de propriété illicites de biens culturels (1970), Convention du patrimoine mondial (1972), Convention UNIDROIT (1995), Convention pour la sauvegarde du patrimoine culturel immatériel (2003), Convention sur la protection et la promotion de la diversité des expressions culturelles (2005).

[8]Directive 2014/60/UE (refonte) du 15 mai 2014, article 2.

[9]Convention UNIDROIT, article 7 d).

[10]Cornu et al. (2012), pp. 309-331.

[11]Dans cette contribution, les collections muséales publiques sont appréhendées comme l'ensemble des objets de musée rattachés à l'Etat par un lien de propriété, de possession ou de contrôle.

[12]Voir notamment: Préambule alinéa 8, § 3, § 10, § 16, § 20, § 21.

[13]Le paragraphe 22 stipule que les Etats membres devraient adopter les mesures appropriées pour assurer la protection et la promotion des musées sous leur juridiction ou sous leur contrôle. Les collections muséales relèvent également de la catégorie juridique des biens culturels à l'égard desquels l'Etat est débiteur d'une obligation de protection (Voir notamment: article 5 de la Convention de 1970).

[14]Consulter notamment les dispositions sur: dialogue interculturel, cohésion sociale, développement durable, droits de l'homme, (préambule), patrimoine de l'humanité (§ 4), transmission aux générations futures (§ 6, § 24).

[15]Van Noudenberg (2010), pp. 184-196, et Chechi (2014), pp. 76-77.

[16]Pub.L.N°.94-583, 90 Stat. 2891.

uniformément appliquée en matière d'activités terroristes. Ainsi, dans la jurisprudence *Rubin v. Islamic Republic of Iran*, les victimes d'une attaque terroriste, ayant impliqué l'Iran, requièrent l'exécution d'un jugement par la saisie de biens culturels iraniens prêtés à des institutions américaines[17]. La Cour considère que l'exception au FSIA, permettant de soustraire les Etats soutenant le terrorisme au bénéfice de l'immunité[18], ne saurait servir de fondement juridique, indépendamment du FSIA, à l'exercice de mesures de contrainte à l'égard des biens iraniens[19]. C'est pourtant la solution inverse qui est suivie dans la jurisprudence *Bennett v. Islamic Republic of Iran*[20]. Du fait de cette insécurité juridique, les prêts sont compromis, comme en témoigne le refus du Musée d'art contemporain de Téhéran de prêter une œuvre de Gauguin à la *National Gallery of Art* de Washington en 2009[21]. En second lieu, une action en revendication de la propriété de l'objet de musée peut être intentée. Le différend porte alors sur la détermination du titulaire du droit réel et de la validité du transfert de propriété. Les risques de revendication et l'insécurité juridique entourant l'encadrement du prêt international d'objets de musée risquent donc d'entraver la circulation des collections muséales.

Quels outils et quelles solutions le droit international peut-il fournir pour favoriser les prêts internationaux de collections muséales publiques ? L'enjeu de cette contribution est de démontrer que si le droit international est actuellement lacunaire en raison d'une spécificité insuffisante du régime juridique des immunités aux collections muséales (2), des pistes de réconciliation semblent envisageables en s'inspirant des possibilités offertes par le régime de copropriété (3).

2 Les lacunes des régimes d'immunités en matière de prêts internationaux de biens culturels

L'Etat dispose sur son territoire de compétences pleines et exclusives. Elles découlent de sa souveraineté[22]. En application de cette souveraineté, un bien prêté à un Etat étranger est régi par la loi de situation de cet Etat (*lex rei sitae*). Pour protéger les biens prêtés d'un contrôle exercé par l'Etat sur le territoire duquel ils se situent temporairement, le droit international reconnaît des immunités d'exécution. L'immunité d'exécution est une « exemption qui permet à certaines entités et personnes (Etats [...]) d'échapper sur leurs personnes ou sur leurs biens à toute

[17]*Rubin v.Islamic Republic of Iran* 830 F.3d 470 (7th Cir. 2016).

[18]28 U.S.C. § 1605A et § 1610(g).

[19]*Rubin v.Islamic Republic of Iran* 830 F.3d 470 (7th Cir. 2016). D. 28 U.S.C.§1610(g).

[20]*Bennett v.Islamic Republic of Iran*, 825 F.3d 949, 965 (9th Cir. 2016).

[21]Mehr News Agency, *Iran rejects U.S. National Gallery of Art's request for Gauguin painting*, http://en.mehrnews.com/news/33337/Iran-rejects-U-S-National-Gallery-of-Art-s-request-for-Gauguin, Consulté le 1er mars 2016.

[22]*Palmas (Miangas), île*, Etats-Unis/ Pays-Bas (1928), RSA, vol. II, p. 281.

mesure de contrainte ou d'exécution forcée de la part des autorités de l'Etat de séjour ou d'un Etat tiers »[23]. Appliquée aux biens d'Etat, l'immunité d'exécution empêche donc toute mesure de contrainte à l'égard de biens affectés à des fonctions d'autorité. Les collections muséales en prêt jouissent ainsi en principe d'un régime d'immunité des biens affectés à l'exercice de services publics à l'étranger (2.1), auquel peuvent s'adjoindre, ou se substituer, des normes internes garantissant l'insaisissabilité (2.2). En faisant prévaloir la propriété de l'Etat, ces dispositions internationales et internes peuvent cependant être incompatibles avec certaines obligations internationales dont les Etats sont débiteurs et/ou avec les droits et intérêts d'autres sujets de droit résultant de la spécificité des collections muséales (2.3).

2.1 *Insuffisance du régime international des immunités*

Assimilées aux biens d'Etat, les collections muséales sont régies par les normes internationales relatives aux immunités des biens de propriété publique. Ces normes sont codifiées dans la Convention des Nations Unies sur les immunités juridictionnelles des Etats et de leurs biens de 2004 (Convention de 2004)[24]. Bien que la convention ne soit pas encore entrée en vigueur, à défaut des trente ratifications requises (article 30), la Cour internationale de Justice (CIJ) considère certaines de ses dispositions comme le reflet d'une coutume internationale en la matière. La CIJ reconnaît ainsi, dans son arrêt *Immunités juridictionnelles de l'Etat*, le caractère coutumier de l'article 19 de la Convention de 2004[25]. Elle constate l'existence d'une « pratique bien établie » exigeant « qu'il existe au minimum une condition qui doit être remplie pour qu'une mesure de contrainte puisse être prise à l'égard d'un bien appartenant à un Etat étranger: que le bien en cause soit utilisé pour les besoins d'une activité ne poursuivant pas des fins de service public non commerciales [...] »[26]. Selon l'article 19 de la Convention de 2004, aucune forme de contrainte ne peut en effet être exercée sur les biens d'Etat sauf s'ils sont « spécifiquement utilisés ou destinés à être utilisés par l'Etat autrement qu'à des fins de service public non commerciales » (c). Alors que la finalité non commerciale des expositions pourrait justifier leur inclusion dans cette définition générale, une autre solution est pourtant privilégiée par la Convention.

C'est à l'article 21 de la convention que les biens d'Etat utilisés à des fins d'expositions bénéficient de dispositions leur étant consacrées. Ils entrent d'abord dans le champ d'application de son alinéa 1d) évoquant les « biens faisant partie du patrimoine culturel de l'Etat [...] qui ne sont pas destinés à être mis en vente ». Ils

---

[23]Salmon (2001), p. 559.

[24]A ce jour, 28 Etats sont signataires et 21 sont parties à la Convention.

[25]*Immunités juridictionnelles de l'Etat (Allemagne c. Italie; Grèce (intervenant))*, arrêt, C.I.J. Recueil 2012, p. 99, § 118.

[26]*Idem.*

sont ensuite visés par son alinéa 1e) dont le libellé mentionne spécifiquement les « biens faisant partie d'une exposition d'objets d'intérêt scientifique, culturel ou historique qui ne sont pas mis ou destinés à être mis en vente ». L'article 21 dresse une liste de catégories de biens considérés comme étant utilisés à des fins de service public non commerciales. L'évocation spécifique des biens à destination d'expositions internationales est particulièrement significative dans cette liste pourtant non exhaustive. Le terme « notamment » semble en effet indiquer une catégorie ouverte. L'inclusion expresse des biens prêtés dans la catégorie des biens considérés comme utilisés à des fins non commerciales témoigne du risque d'une qualification du prêt comme acte commercial.

Dans les travaux préparatoires à la convention menés par la Commission du droit international, c'est pourtant seulement à partir de 1986 que les biens à destination des expositions internationales ont été intégrés dans les catégories de biens considérés comme utilisés à des fins de service public non commerciales[27]. Seul le patrimoine culturel, dont relèvent par ailleurs les biens culturels prêtés lors d'expositions, est mentionné dans l'ancien article (24.1.*e*). Le rapporteur spécial justifie l'octroi d'un statut dérogatoire aux biens culturels, par le fait qu'« ils sont en soi inviolables ou qu'ils représentent pour la nation une valeur inhérente les rendant insaisissables »[28]. En 1986, le comité de rédaction fait état d'un article « considérablement modifié et remanié à la lumière du débat de la commission »[29]. Le patrimoine culturel constitue toujours une catégorie, mais s'y ajoute désormais une nouvelle disposition consacrant une catégorie spécifique aux biens destinés à des expositions internationales. Cette adjonction semble être la conséquence du fait que ces biens permettent l'exercice d'une mission de service public à l'étranger. Les commentaires de l'article confirment cette interprétation en excluant de la catégorie les « biens d'Etat exposés à des fins industrielles ou commerciales »[30].

L'article 21 est actuellement considéré comme l'expression d'une coutume émergente en matière d'immunités d'exécution octroyées aux biens culturels publics faisant l'objet d'un prêt temporaire[31]. Aucune réserve au traité de 2004 ne vise directement l'article 21. Selon cet article, les biens faisant partie d'expositions internationales jouissent donc du régime favorable des immunités d'exécution antérieurement (article 18) et postérieurement (article 19) au jugement. Ces immunités protègent les Etats de toute mesure d'exécution ayant pour objet les biens sur lesquels ils détiennent un titre de propriété. Contrairement aux autres biens de droit commun (article 19), aucune exception à la reconnaissance de l'immunité de l'Etat ne peut être soulevée en raison de la nature, de la finalité des actes et de l'affectation des biens faisant partie d'une exposition (article 21). Avec

[27]Commission du droit international (1986), p. 182.

[28]Commission du droit international (1985), p. 43, § 106.

[29]Commission du droit international (1986), pp. 182-183, § 106.

[30]Commission du droit international (1991), pp. 61-62, Commentaire, Paragraphe 1, 7).

[31]Van Woudenberg (2012), p. 434, et Frigo (2016), p. 469, note 572.

ces mesures, la convention semble poser la pierre angulaire d'un régime juridique international favorisant la circulation des collections muséales.

Malgré les efforts de la convention, certains doutes subsistent sur l'efficacité de la protection instaurée.

L'interprétation de la finalité non commerciale des expositions de biens culturels libellée dans les commentaires de l'article 21 soulève d'abord quelques questionnements[32]. Dans la lignée de l'alinéa 1.*e*), l'interprétation la plus pertinente de la finalité non commerciale serait d'exclure de la catégorie les expositions destinées à des manifestations lucratives (ex: salons, foires)[33]. Or, la doctrine craint qu'une interprétation stricte de la notion de finalité économique exclut toutes les expositions dont l'accès serait conditionné au paiement d'une redevance par le visiteur[34]. L'incertitude concernant la qualification commerciale est renforcée par la multiplication considérable des recettes de billetterie générées par le prêt de biens culturels de renommée internationale. Entre le 24 octobre 2012 et le 29 avril 2013, le prêt du tableau *Le cri* d'Edvard Munch, par la *National Gallery* d'Oslo au Musée d'art Moderne de New-York, a ainsi attiré 1,02 million de visiteurs[35]. La finalité non commerciale étant un élément essentiel des immunités, les retombées économiques de telles manifestations risquent de remettre en cause l'immunité octroyée aux objets destinés à des expositions internationales.

Une autre incertitude concerne l'interprétation de la disposition spécifiant que seul le patrimoine culturel sur lequel l'Etat dispose d'un titre de propriété relèverait de la catégorie de l'article 21.1.*d*[36]. Les objets de musée sur lesquels l'Etat ne dispose pas d'un titre de propriété risquent donc d'être exclus du champ d'application de l'article 21[37].

Malgré l'émergence de l'article 21 au rang de coutume internationale, la protection octroyée est donc insatisfaisante tant en raison de l'interprétation incertaine de la finalité non commerciale que de son champ d'application restreint aux propriétés de l'Etat.

2.2 *Insuffisance des dispositions normatives internes subsidiaires aux immunités internationales*

Afin de favoriser la continuité des échanges internationaux, les Etats se dotent de normes d'insaisissabilité. Ces dispositions garantissent légalement les biens culturels

[32]Commission du droit international (1991), pp. 61-62, Commentaire, Paragraphe 1, 7).

[33]Article 31, Convention de Vienne sur le droit des traités (1969).

[34]O'Keefe, Tams (2013), p. 345.

[35]Lending Art Exhibitions Worldwide by Number of Total Visitors in 2013. http://www.statista.com. Consulté le 1er mars 2017.

[36]Commission du droit international (1991), pp. 61-62, Commentaire, Paragraphe 1, 6).

[37]O'Keefe, Tams (2013), p. 345.

de toute saisie par les Etats étrangers durant la période du prêt[38]. Leur application assure ainsi aux Etats prêteurs leur droit de libre disposition sur les biens exposés[39].

Ces législations internes ont vocation à compléter le régime international des immunités des biens d'Etat, ou à s'y substituer. Certains Etats, tels la France (1994), la Suisse (2005), et l'Autriche (2003), ont adopté des normes d'insaisissabilité avant la signature et la ratification de la Convention de 2004. D'autres Etats, comme le Royaume-Uni (2007)[40], se sont dotés de législations d'insaisissabilité après la signature, non suivie de ratification, de ladite convention. Bien qu'ils ne soient pas signataires de la Convention de 2004, certains Etats, comme les Etats-Unis (1965) et l'Allemagne, ont également adopté de telles législations. Dans les quelques Etats qui ne sont actuellement pas dotés de régime d'immunité pour les œuvres prêtées, à l'instar de l'Italie, des projets de législation sont en cours de discussion[41]. Un nombre croissant d'Etats se dotent ainsi de normes juridiques internes. Ces normes s'ajoutent parfois, ou se substituent souvent, au régime de droit international.

Si, dans la continuité de la convention de 2004, certains Etats octroient l'immunité aux biens dès réunion des critères posés par l'instrument normatif (Belgique), une majorité d'Etats la conditionne à l'accomplissement de formalités internes préalables. Ainsi, la norme interne peut exiger l'acceptation de la demande par l'administration étatique (Québec), sa publication pendant un laps de temps déterminé (Royaume-Uni) et ce, sans objection (France et Suisse), ou encore une acceptation par décision judiciaire (Etats-Unis)[42]. A l'unité matérielle des réglementations d'insaisissabilité s'opposent donc la diversité et la complexité de leur mise en œuvre. Avant tout prêt de collections muséales à l'étranger, les institutions doivent s'informer et accomplir les formalités spécifiquement en vigueur dans l'Etat du prêt, pour pouvoir bénéficier de leur immunité. Ainsi, en 2012 le tableau *Cristo Portacroce* de la Pinacothèque de la Brera (Italie), bien culturel propriété de l'Etat italien et prêté au *Mary Brogan Museum* de Tallahasee (Etats-Unis), a été saisi car les formalités administratives requises pour obtenir l'immunité n'avaient pas été accomplies[43]. Les mesures internes subsidiaires semblent moins favorables aux prêts d'objets de musée du fait de la complexité de leurs formalités administratives préalables. Elles s'opposent d'ailleurs à l'octroi automatique de l'immunité aux biens prêtés pour des expositions, octroi automatique que permettra la convention de 2004 après son entrée en vigueur.

Ces dispositions normatives spéciales peuvent cependant se révéler plus opportunes pour la circulation des collections muséales au regard de leur champ d'application. En premier lieu, les normes internes d'insaisissabilité ne sont pas

[38]Van Woudenberg (2010), pp. 184-96.

[39]Chechi (2015), p. 286.

[40]Tribunals, Courts and Enforcement Act 2007 (Commencement No.2) Order 2007, SI2007/3 613. Voir à ce sujet: O'Connell (2006).

[41]Frigo (2016), p. 467, § 255.

[42]Pour une analyse détaillée: Knerly, Stephen (2009).

[43]Frigo (2016), p. 471.

toutes restreintes aux biens sur lesquels l'Etat a un titre de propriété. Si, dans la continuité de l'instrument international de 2004, le critère de la propriété publique est une condition d'inclusion dans la catégorie pour certains Etats (France), d'autres Etats s'en affranchissent pour y intégrer également les biens privés (Allemagne, Royaume-Uni, Suisse)[44]. Ce faisant, les législations internes subsidiaires permettent une protection plus adaptée aux collections muséales sur lesquelles l'Etat ne dispose pas toujours d'un titre de propriété. En second lieu, en application des normes internes d'insaisissabilité, les biens culturels peuvent dans certains cas bénéficier à la fois d'immunités d'exécution et d'immunités de juridiction. Sur le fondement de l'*Immunity from Seizure Act* (1965), un bien culturel en prêt aux Etats-Unis pour une exposition temporaire ne peut par exemple être l'objet de mesures de contrainte ou de revendications de sa propriété.

L'immunité dont jouissent les biens culturels n'est cependant pas absolue dans les législations internes. Dans la Convention de 2004, le libellé de l'article 21 impose de qualifier d'activités de service public non commerciales les expositions internationales de biens culturels. L'absence d'une telle clause dans les normes internes d'insaisissabilité risque d'entraîner la qualification juridique des prêts de collections muséales comme actes de *jure gestionis*.

Ainsi, en 2004, un groupe d'héritiers du peintre russe Kasimir Malevitch dépose une requête en restitution portant sur quatorze tableaux appartenant à la Ville d'Amsterdam (Pays-Bas) et exposés temporairement au Musée Guggenheim de New-York et à la *Menil Collection* de Houston (Etats-Unis). Deux normes nationales d'insaisissabilité sont alors en vigueur dans l'Etat emprunteur. Ayant accompli les formalités administratives requises, la ville d'Amsterdam est en principe protégée par l'*Immunity from Seizure Act* (IFSA) lui garantissant l'immunité de saisie. Or, les héritiers du peintre s'appuient sur une législation nationale ultérieure: le *Foreign Sovereign Immunity Act* (FSIA). Cette législation consacre le passage d'un régime d'immunité absolue à un régime d'immunité restreinte aux seules activités *jure imperii*. La Cour fait droit à la demande des héritiers. Elle fonde son appréciation non pas sur l'objectif poursuivi par le prêt mais sur la nature de la transaction. Le prêt est ainsi qualifié d'activité commerciale et donc, d'acte *jure gestionis* ne bénéficiant pas des immunités d'Etat. Un règlement à l'amiable permet finalement aux parties de s'accorder sur un partage du titre de propriété sur les collections litigieuses. Les héritiers du peintre obtiennent la propriété sur cinq peintures alors que la ville d'Amsterdam conserve son titre de propriété sur les autres œuvres. Ce litige illustre le fait qu'à la suite d'une exposition internationale, alors même qu'une norme nationale d'insaisissabilité est en vigueur dans l'Etat emprunteur, la collection publique peut être démembrée.

Les normes d'insaisissabilité sont parfois même oubliées lors de revendications de la propriété d'une œuvre[45]. Dans le cas du prêt d'une œuvre d'Egon Schiele par le Musée Léopold (Autriche) au *Museum of Modern Art* (Etats-Unis), l'œuvre est ainsi

[44] Frigo (2016), p. 471, note 576.

[45] Frigo (2016), pp. 465-67, § 255.

retournée à son Etat d'origine treize ans après l'exposition. Les normes nationales d'insaisissabilité n'ont été d'aucun secours en l'espèce et c'est un accord entre le gouvernement américain, la Fondation du Musée Léopold et les héritiers qui permet le retour de l'œuvre[46]. Certes l'œuvre réintègre les collections publiques autrichiennes mais ce, en contrepartie d'une importante compensation financière[47].

Législations subsidiaires ou complémentaires au régime international, les dispositions normatives d'insaisissabilité sont donc insuffisantes pour garantir l'immunité des objets de musée prêtés. L'absence d'immunité absolue en matière de collections muséales permet néanmoins d'éviter que les immunités se heurtent à d'autres normes.

2.3 Incompatibilité des immunités et du régime spécifique des collections muséales

Les dispositions internationales et internes en matière d'immunités peuvent se révéler incompatibles avec certaines obligations internationales dont les Etats sont débiteurs et/ou avec les droits et intérêts d'autres sujets de droit résultant de la spécificité des collections muséales.

Si les immunités d'exécution prennent parfois en compte la nature spécifique des biens d'Etat affectés à des fins de service public non commerciales[48], elles semblent toutefois indifférentes à cette considération concernant les collections muséales. Or, les collections muséales ont une nature spécifique. En sus d'être rattachables à la catégorie juridique des biens d'Etat, elles relèvent de la catégorie juridique des biens culturels. Les biens culturels sont notamment constitués des « biens, meubles ou immeubles, qui présentent une grande importance pour le patrimoine culturel des peuples, tels que [. . .] les œuvres d'art, les manuscrits, livres et autres objets d'intérêt artistique, historique ou archéologique, ainsi que les collections scientifiques »[49]. En raison de cette absence de prise en compte de la spécificité des collections muséales, le régime des immunités risque d'être en contradiction avec les normes relatives au patrimoine culturel. Les immunités des collections muséales prêtées peuvent en effet être incompatibles avec certaines obligations relatives au patrimoine culturel dont les Etats sont débiteurs. Les Etats parties au Premier protocole à la Convention pour la protection des biens culturels en cas de conflit armé de 1954 (§ 3), à la Convention concernant les mesures à prendre pour interdire et empêcher l'importation, l'exportation et le transfert de propriété illicites de biens culturels de 1970 (§ 7), à la Convention d'Unidroit sur les biens culturels volés ou illicitement exportés de

[46] *Idem.*

[47] *Idem.*

[48] Consulter notamment Salmon (2014) sur les immunités d'exécution des comptes bancaires des missions diplomatiques et consulaires.

[49] Convention pour la protection des biens culturels en cas de conflit armé (1954), Article 1, alinéa a.

1995 (article 3) et les Etats membres de l'Union européenne[50] sont ainsi débiteurs d'une obligation de restitution[51]. La restitution désigne le retour d'un bien culturel pillé, spolié lors d'un conflit armé, volé ou provenant de fouilles illicites, à son Etat de provenance[52]. Enjeu croissant des relations internationales, la restitution d'objets de musée est une question traitée dans un grand nombre de normes d'autorégulation édictées par la communauté muséale mondiale[53]. *Prima facie*, malgré cette reconnaissance croissante dans l'ordre international, les ordres juridiques internes ne feraient pas nécessairement prévaloir le respect de ces obligations internationales. Interrogés à ce sujet[54], les Etats-Unis déclarent que le conflit entre l'obligation internationale de restitution découlant de la Convention de 1970 et la norme nationale d'insaisissabilité de 1965 se résoudrait par la prévalence de la législation nationale. Dans la mesure où, en cas de conflit, une loi *postérieure* est censée prévaloir, cette déclaration surprend. N'étant pas d'application directe, la Convention serait transposée par une norme interne qui lui conférerait, dès lors, une valeur normative équivalente à celle de la législation de 1965. Ce positionnement ne reflète néanmoins pas la tendance générale qui voit les obligations internationales prévaloir sur les normes internes d'insaisissabilité[55]. Au Royaume-Uni par exemple, l'application de la norme d'insaisissabilité est conditionnée à sa conformité aux obligations communautaires ou internationales[56]. Au niveau international, plusieurs obligations *de lege ferenda* sont d'ailleurs proposées dans ce sens. L'*International Law Association* (ILA) confirme par exemple ce positionnement dans son *Draft Convention on Immunity from Suit and Seizure for Cultural Objects temporarily Abroad for Cultural, Educational or Scientific Purposes* (2014). Evoquant spécifiquement les expositions internationales (7ème considérant), l'ILA affirme que les immunités de saisie ne s'appliquent pas en cas d'incompatibilité avec une norme internationale ou régionale dont l'Etat serait débiteur (article 5). L'article évoque d'ailleurs les obligations découlant des conventions de 1970 et de 1995, ainsi que celles fondées sur la directive 93/7/CEE. Dans son *Final Report and Recommendations to the Cultural Affairs Committee on Improving the Means of Increasing the Mobility of Collection*, un groupe européen d'experts sur la mobilité incite les

[50]Directive 93/7/CEE et directive 2014/60/UE.

[51]Perrot (2005).

[52]Cornu et al. (2012), p. 859.

[53]Voir notamment: *Guidelines Concerning the Unlawful Appropriation of Objects during the Nazi Era* par l'*American Association of Museums* (1999), Recommandation concernant la restitution des œuvres d'art appartenant à des juifs par l'ICOM (1999).

[54]Van Woudenberg (2012), p. 160, note 238.

[55]Frigo (2016), pp. 472-74, §§ 259-260.

[56]Article 135 (A) (b), Tribunals, Courts and Enforcement Act 2007 (Commencement No.2) Order 2007, SI2007/3 613.

Etats à la vigilance quant à la compatibilité des garanties d'insaisissabilité avec leurs obligations internationales (recommandations 15-16)[57].

Les immunités accordées aux collections muséales risquent particulièrement de se heurter à des normes fondamentales comme les droits de l'homme. Evoquant l'atteinte portée au droit de propriété par le régime des immunités, Alessandro Chechi décrit une « relation ambivalente entre les immunités et le droit de propriété »[58]. Les immunités privent les particuliers du droit d'agir en justice afin d'établir leur propriété sur une œuvre. L'analyse de la pratique témoigne d'ailleurs d'une prise en compte croissante des droits des individus dans les normes d'insaisissabilité. Dans la Loi fédérale suisse sur le transfert international des biens culturels de 2003, le retour est ainsi conditionné à l'absence d'objection au titre de propriété après une publicité de trente jours (article 11.3). Cette tendance est également notable au niveau international. Si la gravité de la violation ou du caractère impératif de la règle violée ne limitent pas l'immunité de l'Etat dans la Convention de 2004, il est cependant remarquable que plusieurs Etats y apportent des réserves conditionnant les effets juridiques des dispositions au respect des principes concernant la protection des droits de l'homme[59]. De même, dans la proposition doctrinale défendant la thèse d'une règle coutumière émergente qui accorderait l'immunité à un bien culturel de propriété publique prêté, le domaine d'application de ladite règle serait limité aux seuls biens culturels n'ayant pas fait l'objet d'une violation grave du droit international ou n'étant pas soumis à une obligation internationale de restitution[60].

Les règles sur le droit d'un Etat à bénéficier d'immunités sont étendues aux collections muséales. Or, les collections muséales n'en conservent pas moins un particularisme tenant à leur nature de patrimoine culturel. Il en résulte que la réglementation relative aux biens culturels et les régimes juridiques des immunités peuvent se révéler incompatibles. Les raisons de cette incompatibilité se situent dans les intérêts partagés matérialisés par les collections muséales. Ces intérêts sont en effet cristallisés lors des revendications de la propriété d'un objet de musée. Or, la reconnaissance progressive des droits et intérêts des individus et/ou des communautés entraîne une évolution du droit international et un développement corrélatif de limites aux immunités d'Etats. Si les immunités visent à faire respecter les biens « en rapport direct avec la souveraineté territoriale d'un autre Etat »[61], leur bien-fondé et leur efficacité peuvent soulever des questions quand elles sont appliquées à des biens culturels dont la propriété est litigieuse.

[57]OMC Expert Working Group on the Mobility of Collections (2010).

[58]Chechi (2015), p. 288.

[59]Italie, Norvège, Suède et Suisse.

[60]Van Woudenberg (2012), p. 444.

[61]Daillier et al. (2009), p. 497.

3 La copropriété, une piste de réconciliation entre le droit international et le prêt de biens culturels?

Le constat préliminaire est donc celui d'une inadaptation. Malgré un renforcement notable des régimes consacrant l'immunité des biens prêtés, tant dans l'ordre international que dans les ordres juridiques internes, la circulation des collections reste entravée par l'insécurité juridique. Dès lors, il est proposé de repenser la réglementation internationale actuelle en l'éloignant de la prérogative étatique de l'immunité pour la recentrer sur la spécificité des collections muséales (3.1). La spécificité des collections résulte du fait qu'elles matérialisent un intérêt partagé. C'est en raison de cet intérêt partagé qu'elles sont l'objet de revendications fondées sur le titre de propriété. Si son efficacité doit nécessairement être relativisée (3.3), un régime juridique conciliant les différents intérêts en présence pourrait inspirer des pistes de réconciliation entre le prêt des collections et le droit international (3.2).

3.1 Des collections muséales matérialisant un intérêt partagé

L'analyse de la réglementation actuelle du prêt de biens culturels témoigne d'une dichotomie entre les sources nationales et internationales. L'élaboration d'un régime juridique adapté nécessite donc la détermination préalable du type de normes à favoriser.

La spécificité des collections muséales découle de leur matérialisation des différents intérêts en présence. L'intérêt est un « avantage matériel ou moral non juridiquement protégé que présente pour une personne une situation donnée » [62]. En matière de collections muséales, plusieurs intérêts peuvent être observés. L'intérêt est d'abord individuel quand il désigne le droit de propriété d'un propriétaire privé sur les collections muséales. Ce droit peut être acquis (prêt d'une œuvre à une institution muséale), ou faire l'objet de prétentions (dans le cas de revendications de la propriété). L'intérêt collectif peut ensuite désigner l'intérêt d'une communauté culturelle sur un objet de musée. Cet intérêt fait l'objet d'une reconnaissance croissante. Les interactions entre les droits de propriété et les droits de l'homme permettent désormais par exemple de protéger les biens culturels car ces derniers expriment une identité culturelle spécifique[63]. Les biens culturels reflètent en effet des particularismes spirituels et culturels communautaires dont la préservation fait partie intégrante de la protection de l'identité culturelle communautaire[64]. Ces collections « ont un caractère dépassant la propriété normale, pouvant aller jusqu'à de fortes affinités avec l'identité nationale, régionale, locale, ethnique,

[62]Salmon (2001), p. 596.

[63]Francioni (2012), p. 722.

[64]Blake (2000), p. 82.

religieuse ou politique »[65]. Cet intérêt se manifeste notamment lors de revendications en retour présentées par des Etats autrefois colonisés, des peuples autochtones ou des minorités. Le retour du bien provenant de la collection muséale est perçu comme une étape déterminante pour la construction d'une autonomie politique et/ou culturelle[66]. La question se pose de savoir si les collections muséales matérialisent également un intérêt pour la communauté internationale. Si dans la Recommandation de 1960 la perception des collections relève essentiellement du nationalisme, une évolution de perception est remarquable dans la Recommandation de 2015. Cette dernière reconnaît aux collections muséales une valeur universelle. D'après le libellé de la Recommandation de 2015, les collections muséales sont constituées du « patrimoine matériel et immatériel de l'humanité et de son environnement »[67]. Les Etats membres doivent favoriser la coopération internationale en encourageant « les expositions et échanges internationaux et la mobilité des collections » (article 31). L'intérêt de la communauté internationale pour les collections muséales est ainsi reconnu par un instrument international.

L'une des spécificités des collections muséales tient ainsi au fait qu'elles matérialisent les multiples intérêts entourant les objets de musée. Ces intérêts ne sauraient néanmoins être résumés à l'opposition dualiste, entérinée de longue date par les théoriciens, entre le « nationalisme culturel » et l'« internationalisme culturel »[68]. Comme leurs terminologies l'indiquent, ces catégories doctrinales opposent deux approches du patrimoine culturel. Une présentation simplifiée permet d'en saisir la teneur. Concevant le patrimoine culturel comme une valeur nationale, le nationalisme culturel se caractérise par la volonté d'adopter des mesures restrictives permettant la conservation des biens dans les frontières nationales. A l'inverse, concevant le patrimoine culturel comme une valeur universelle, l'internationalisme culturel favorise plutôt les mesures libérales permettant la circulation des biens. Cette division est inapplicable aux collections muséales dans la mesure où les intérêts qu'elles matérialisent ne sont pas mutuellement exclusifs. C'est parce qu'ils sont témoins d'une identité culturelle spécifique que les biens culturels intègrent les collections muséales. Or, c'est précisément en raison de ce rôle dans l'identité culturelle d'un peuple, que les biens culturels présentent également un intérêt collectif pour leur communauté d'origine. Les intérêts partagés sont inhérents aux collections car ils sont à l'origine de leur constitution.

La prise en compte effective de ces différents intérêts en présence permet d'ailleurs d'enrichir le potentiel informatif d'un objet de musée. Cette prise en compte peut notamment être illustrée par les Musées Nationaux de Récupération (MNR) en France. Cette appellation désigne des musées nationaux dépositaires d'œuvres spoliées par les nazis et conservées dans l'attente de retrouver leurs

---

[65]ICOM (2006), article 6.

[66]Vrdoljak (2008), p. 9.

[67]Recommandation de 2015, § 4.

[68]Francioni (2013), p. 11.

propriétaires ou leurs ayants droit[69]. Identifiables par le préfixe MNR précédant leur numéro d'inventaire, ces objets de musée ont un intérêt individuel pour les propriétaires légitimes ou leurs ayants droit. Cet intérêt individuel est reconnu par l'octroi d'un statut juridique spécifique. Néanmoins, cet intérêt n'est pas considéré comme exclusif d'un intérêt universel. Ainsi, le statut juridique permet la mise à disposition temporaire de ces œuvres au public, dans l'attente de leur revendication par leurs propriétaires ou leurs ayants-droit. La prise en compte de cet intérêt individuel, et sa publicité auprès du public, permet d'enrichir le potentiel informatif de l'œuvre en en faisant un témoin de la barbarie des campagnes de spoliations nazies. Les intérêts concurrents sur les collections muséales ne doivent donc pas nécessairement être conçus comme mutuellement exclusifs. Il est ici plus opportun de raisonner en termes d'intérêts partagés.

En raison de cet intérêt partagé, la circulation des collections doit être favorisée et ce, même si elle conduit, et c'est là également un corollaire de cet intérêt partagé, à la multiplication des revendications. L'immobilisme des collections dans les frontières nationales est contraire à la réalisation de l'ensemble des intérêts en jeu. La circulation transfrontalière nécessite donc un mécanisme de droit international dépassant la vision désormais obsolète d'un droit de propriété unique sur l'œuvre.

3.2 Propositions pour un régime juridique de copropriété pour les collections muséales

L'élaboration d'un régime international plus adapté aux différents intérêts en présence pourrait s'inspirer des revendications en retour et en restitution. Ces dernières sont, pour une part, la conséquence de l'inadaptation du régime actuel à la spécificité des collections muséales. Pour une autre part, leurs méthodes de résolution tentent de mettre en balance des intérêts concurrents sur un bien culturel. Depuis 2005, Marc-André Renold identifie une évolution en faveur de solutions alternatives en matière de restitution, selon le principe de la *Caring and Sharing alternative*[70]. En 2006, le Comité sur le droit du patrimoine culturel de l'ILA adopte en effet une résolution incitant notamment les musées – spécifiquement mentionnés – à suivre les directives du Conseil international des musées (ICOM). Les directives encouragent les musées à répondre aux revendications par des moyens alternatifs comme le prêt, les copies ou le management et le contrôle partagés[71]. Marc-André Renold estime que le management et le contrôle partagés vont dans le sens de régimes de copropriété ou de copossession. Ces solutions fondées sur l'instauration de mécanismes de copropriété, proposent de dépasser la conception du droit de propriété unique de l'œuvre en consacrant l'intérêt partagé.

---

[69]Site Rose-Valland. Musées Nationaux de Récupération. http://www.culture.gouv.fr/documentation/mnr/MnR-pres.htm. Consulté le 1er mars 2017.

[70]Renold (2015), pp. 169-170.

[71]International law association, Résolution n° 4/2006, Cultural Heritage Law, Article 3, i).

Comme le démontre Marc-André Renold, la méthode traditionnelle de résolution des litiges en matière de propriété consiste à reconnaître un titre exclusif à l'une ou l'autre des parties. Pour permettre la reconnaissance d'un titre de propriété partagé, il propose de repenser cette méthode de résolution par le biais d'un mécanisme de copropriété. Ce régime permet de partager la propriété d'une œuvre entre plusieurs personnes ayant chacune un titre de propriété sur une quote-part spécifique de l'œuvre.

Ce régime de copropriété est illustré par l'affaire portant sur la propriété des mosaïques murales provenant du site aztèque de Teotihuacan et conservées au Musée des Beaux-Arts de San Francisco (Etats-Unis). Ces collections muséales sont en effet divisées, à parts égales, entre l'institution étasunienne et le *Mexican National Museum* (Mexique)[72]. La copropriété résulte de négociations menées à partir de 1978. Après l'échec de l'action en restitution alors intentée par le Mexique, le musée entame un processus de négociation. L'institution muséale déclare chercher à garantir la préservation optimale des œuvres, à favoriser le partage des connaissances et à reconnaître leur importance pour l'Etat d'origine[73]. En justifiant de la sorte son initiative, le musée témoigne d'une prise en compte effective de l'intérêt des collections pour les différentes parties en présence. La prise en compte de ces intérêts inspire le choix d'un nouveau statut juridique fondé sur la copropriété. Un accord partage en effet entre les parties la propriété des œuvres et leurs coûts de conservation. Si la solution juridique présente un intérêt certain, la cohérence d'une division matérielle de l'œuvre est questionnable au point de vue patrimonial. Comme le dirait Quatremère de Quincy, érudit français, « diviser c'est détruire »[74]. Une telle division est d'ailleurs souvent inenvisageable. Ainsi, l'œuvre *Paysage avec Cheminées* peinte par Edgar Degas est en prêt à l'*Art Institute of Chicago* (Etats-Unis) lorsqu'elle fait l'objet d'une revendication présentée par les héritiers d'une victime de l'holocauste[75]. Après une phase contentieuse analysant essentiellement des questions de propriété, le litige est résolu à l'amiable. Le titre de propriété est partagé entre le particulier, jusqu'alors propriétaire exclusif de l'œuvre, et les héritiers. Une fois le titre de propriété établi, se pose le problème de la possession effective de l'œuvre. Le Musée de Chicago bénéficie du transfert des droits du particulier, et achète les parts des héritiers. En conséquence, le tableau entre dans les collections permanentes du musée. Cette affaire témoigne des lacunes d'un régime de copropriété qui se contente de déplacer la question litigieuse de la propriété vers la possession effective.

---

[72]Renold C, Chechi A, Renold M.-A, Murals of Teotihuacàn – Fine Arts Museums of San Francisco and National Institute of Anthropology and History. In: ArThemis. Accessible par: https://plone.unige.ch/art-adr/cases-affaires. Consulté le 30 Novembre 2017.

[73]*Idem.*

[74]De Quincy Q (1815) Lettres sur le préjudice qu'occasionneroient aux Arts et à la Science, le déplacement des monumens de l'art de l'Italie, le démembrement de ses Ecoles, et la spoliation de ses Collections, Galeries, Musées, etc, p. 25.

[75]Bandle A.L, Chechi A, Renold M-A, Case Landscape with Smokestacks – Gutmann Heirs and Daniel Searle. In: ArThemis. Accessible par: https://plone.unige.ch/art-adr/cases-affaires. Consulté le 30 Novembre 2017.

Il convient de déterminer si l'exercice des fonctions muséales est conditionné à la détention de l'objet et à la reconnaissance d'un titre de propriété du musée sur l'objet. En premier lieu, la possession de l'œuvre semble être un prérequis essentiel à l'accomplissement des fonctions muséales. Les missions de préservation, de recherche, de communication et d'éducation[76] impliquent en effet l'accès du personnel de musée aux collections. Le musée doit également mettre ses œuvres à disposition du public[77]. En second lieu, le titre de propriété ne semble pas être indispensable. La détention de l'œuvre semble en effet suffisante à l'accomplissement des finalités muséales. De plus, les incertitudes concernant la légalité du titre de propriété des musées sur leurs collections peuvent aussi empêcher la mise en œuvre des fonctions muséales. Les institutions peuvent en effet être tentées de conserver des œuvres acquises dans des circonstances inconnues, et/ou suspectes, à l'abri dans leurs réserves[78]. Dans ces conditions, les missions muséales impliquant l'accessibilité aux œuvres ne peuvent pas être exercées. En définitive, seule la possession effective de l'œuvre semble nécessaire à l'accomplissement effectif des finalités muséales.

Dès lors le prêt, également proposé comme méthode alternative de résolution des demandes en restitution par le Comité sur le droit du patrimoine culturel de l'ILA, peut trouver à s'appliquer[79]. Il est ainsi notable que le conflit opposant le Nigéria au Musée du Quai Branly (France), au sujet de la propriété d'objets Nok et Sokoto, se soit résolu par un prêt. La propriété du Nigéria est reconnue sur ces œuvres illégalement exportées de son territoire par le passé. L'institution obtient un titre légal de détention lui permettant de poursuivre l'accomplissement de ses fonctions muséales. Le prêt permet ainsi au musée de continuer à exposer l'œuvre tout en posant les fondements d'une collaboration durable avec l'Etat d'origine. Si la qualification de restitution est contestable dans ce litige où le bien reste physiquement en possession de l'institution[80], le conflit est néanmoins résolu par une dissociation entre la propriété et la possession de l'œuvre. Comme le souligne Raphaël Contel, ce prêt conduit à une inversion des rapports traditionnels entre la propriété et la possession. C'est en effet habituellement l'Etat de provenance du bien qui bénéficie du prêt d'un bien culturel afin de permettre son utilisation par la population, par exemple à des fins de rites cultuels[81]. Encore faut-il préciser que malgré les avantages du prêt, il présente l'inconvénient de laisser une faible marge de manœuvre au musée pour la gestion des biens. L'accomplissement effectif des finalités muséales, en termes de circulation des œuvres, de conservation, d'exposition et de recherche, nécessite en effet un pouvoir de fait sur la chose (*corpus*) et l'exercice des prérogatives inhérentes à la propriété (*animus*).

---

[76]Recommandation de 2015, III.

[77]ICOM (2006), 3.2.

[78]Chechi (2014), p. 44.

[79]International law association, Résolution n° 4/2006, Cultural Heritage Law, Article 3, i).

[80]Cornu, Renold (2009)

[81]Contel (2012), p. 188.

En s'inspirant de la dissociation permise par le mécanisme du prêt, entre le titre de propriété et la possession effective d'une œuvre, il est envisageable de proposer un régime de copropriété adapté aux collections muséales. Le régime de la copropriété permet au musée de détenir le bien sans porter atteinte au droit de propriété d'un Etat étranger et/ou de sujets internes. Il faut noter néanmoins que contrairement au régime du prêt, la copropriété impose une véritable gestion partagée du bien en imposant aux parties de coopérer dans l'exercice des prérogatives de la propriété[82]. La libre disposition de l'institution sur ces biens est donc relative car, encadrée par ce principe de gestion partagée.

3.3 *Une efficacité de la copropriété à relativiser*

Si la copropriété suggère des pistes de réflexion pour adapter le régime juridique des collections aux intérêts partagés qu'elles matérialisent, son efficacité est néanmoins relative.

La première limite du régime de copropriété concerne les normes juridiques susceptibles de fonder un nouveau statut pour les collections muséales. En l'état actuel du droit positif, les dispositions concernant leur statut juridique sont rares. Dans la Recommandation sur la protection et la promotion des musées et des collections (2015), la question de la propriété des collections est laissée en suspens en « l'absence de consensus à leur sujet dans la communauté internationale des musées »[83]. Cette lacune pourrait être attribuée à l'état embryonnaire de la réglementation internationale en matière de collections muséales. La recommandation de 2015 est en effet le premier instrument normatif à visée exhaustive qui leur soit spécifiquement consacré[84]. La reconnaissance progressive de la diversité culturelle en droit international et la protection de l'identité culturelle en découlant[85] peuvent conduire à l'évolution de l'activité normative vers une meilleure prise en compte des cultures de provenance des collections muséales. La Recommandation de 2015 impose déjà une obligation molle aux Etats de « prendre les mesures appropriées pour encourager et faciliter le dialogue et le développement de relations constructives entre ces musées et les populations autochtones concernant la gestion de ces collections et, le cas échéant, leur retour et leur restitution conformément aux lois et politiques applicables » (§ 18). La consécration de plusieurs articles du *Code de l'ICOM pour les musées*[86] à la gestion des

[82]Renold (2015), pp. 169-170.

[83]UNESCO, Comité spécial d'experts techniques et juridiques (2015) Un nouvel instrument normatif international: Projet de recommandation de l'UNESCO concernant la protection et la promotion des musées, de leur diversité et de leur rôle dans la société, 6), p. 4.

[84]UNESCO (2011), p. 64.

[85]Frigo (2016), pp. 48-55.

[86]Norme de droit mou, ce code de déontologie est un outil d'autorégulation adopté par une ONG représentative de la communauté muséale internationale, et placé en tête des instruments promus par l'UNESCO les plus utilisés.

restes humains et des objets sacrés témoigne d'une sensibilisation accrue de la communauté internationale des musées au lien unissant un bien à sa culture d'origine. Cette sensibilisation des acteurs concernés et l'évolution normative en faveur de la diversité culturelle pourraient favoriser le développement de la réglementation internationale vers un régime juridique favorisant les intérêts partagés. Dès à présent, des régimes de copropriété pourraient ainsi être instaurés par le biais de conventions bilatérales. Ces conventions seraient conclues entre les Etats d'origine des musées et les Etats de provenance des collections. Des accords similaires ont ainsi été conclus en matière de prêt de biens culturels. A la suite de la conclusion d'un *Memorandum of Undersanding* entre l'Italie et les Etats-Unis (2001), l'Italie a par exemple conclu plusieurs accords avec le *Cleveland Museum* (2008)[87].

La deuxième limite à la copropriété est son conditionnement à la bonne entente des parties. Une œuvre pourrait en effet sortir des collections muséales du fait d'un désaccord entre les parties ou d'une volonté de mettre fin au régime de copropriété. Ainsi, en 1996, la réunion du fragment représentant l'*Archange Raphaël,* propriété du Conseil Municipal de La Haye, et du fragment figurant *La prière de Tobias et Sarah,* propriété de l'Etat des Pays-Bas, permet la reconstitution du tableau initial[88]. Dans un premier temps, l'œuvre unifiée est ainsi soumise à un régime de copropriété dont le ratio est établi en fonction de la valeur individuelle des deux panneaux: 76 % pour l'Etat et 24 % pour le Conseil Municipal. Dans un deuxième temps, en 2006, un particulier obtient la restitution du panneau illustrant *La prière de Tobias et Sarah.* La propriété des 76 % de l'œuvre unifiée est ainsi transférée de l'Etat au particulier. Dans un troisième temps, le particulier et le Conseil Municipal décident de mettre fin au régime de copropriété sans compromettre l'intégrité de l'œuvre (1.3-4). Le comité de restitution[89], en charge de l'affaire, constate qu'aucun copropriétaire ne peut se voir imposer le maintien dans un régime de copropriété contre son gré (2.4). Il reconnaît également l'importance de préserver l'unité de l'œuvre (3.v). La première solution proposée par ce comité de restitution est intéressante car il suggère au Conseil Municipal de racheter au particulier ses 76 % de l'œuvre, soit le panneau de *La prière de Tobias et Sarah.* L'œuvre pourrait ainsi rester dans les collections du Musée de Brédius (4.3). Dans l'esprit de coopération à l'origine du régime de copropriété de l'œuvre, les deux parties s'accordent initialement pour favoriser les finalités muséales en garantissant le maintien de cette œuvre dans les collections publiques. Cependant, en raison de l'impossibilité pour le Conseil Municipal de réunir des fonds nécessaires (4.5), le bien sort finalement des collections muséales et devient propriété exclusive du particulier (4.7). Si le régime de la copropriété permet

[87]Chechi A, Brandle A.L, Renold M-A (2013), Case 14 Antiquities – Italy and Cleveland Museum of Art. In: ArThemis. Accessible par: https://plone.unige.ch/art-adr/cases-affaires. Consulté le 30 Novembre 2017.

[88]Site du comité: http://www.restitutiecommissie.nl/en/recommendations/recommendation_393.html. Consulté le 1er mars 2017.

[89]*Advisory Committee on the Assessment of Restitution Applications for Items of Cultural Value and the Second World War in The Hague.*

d'appréhender l'intérêt partagé à travers le filtre du droit, la pérennité de sa mise en œuvre est donc questionnable.

La troisième limite à la copropriété est également liée à l'exigence de concordance des volontés. La nature spécifique de certaines collections, comme celles des objets sacrés, pourrait en effet être incompatible avec un régime limitant la détention effective du bien à un seul copropriétaire. Certaines dispositions du *Code de l'ICOM pour les musées* renforcent d'ailleurs l'importance de la prise en compte du lien unissant le bien à sa culture d'origine. Les institutions doivent les traiter (2.5), les étudier (3.7) et les exposer (4.3) en accord avec, « lorsqu'ils sont connus, les intérêts et croyances de la communauté ou des groupes ethniques ou religieux d'origine ». Sur le fondement de la Recommandation de 2015, l'Etat doit également « prendre les mesures appropriées pour encourager et faciliter le dialogue et le développement de relations constructives entre ces musées et les populations autochtones concernant la gestion de ces collections » (§ 18). Les musées sont donc tenus de respecter et de coopérer avec les cultures de provenance de leurs collections. Or, la possession d'un bien par le musée peut être incompatible avec l'exercice de pratiques culturelles nécessitant l'accessibilité du bien. L'exercice de ces pratiques peut en effet être conditionné à l'accessibilité du bien. Selon Patrick J.O'Keefe, les entités qui « détiennent des objets sacrés dans des collections d'objets d'art ou d'histoire exercent une tutelle temporaire et doivent reconnaître la supériorité du droit moral de ceux qui en ont besoin pour leur pratique religieuse »[90]. Les demandes en retour pourraient se fonder sur la Déclaration des Nations Unies sur les droits des peuples autochtones (11.2, 12.1), le code de déontologie de l'ICOM (4.4) ou les instruments internationaux relatifs aux droits de l'homme. Dès lors, un régime de copropriété permettant à l'institution muséale d'être détentrice de l'objet, ne saurait être satisfaisant dans la mesure où « [l]es peuples autochtones ont [...] le droit d'utiliser leurs objets rituels et d'en disposer »[91]. Dans le cas spécifique des objets sacrés, et en cas d'impossibilité de retour des biens culturels, les échanges ou les prêts sur le long terme pourraient donc être préférés au régime de la copropriété[92].

Si la copropriété n'est pas une solution généralisable, elle inspire néanmoins des pistes de réflexion non négligeables.

4 Conclusion

Ces réflexions inspirées par le statut juridique de la copropriété visent à repenser l'encadrement international des collections muséales afin d'en faciliter la circulation transfrontalière.

[90]O'Keefe (2011), p. 251.

[91]Déclaration des Nations-Unies sur les droits des peuples autochtones (2006), Article 12, § 1.

[92]Contel (2012).

En l'état actuel du droit, les réglementations, tant nationales qu'internationales, assurent l'insaisissabilité, par le biais des immunités, des collections muséales prêtées. Ces immunités sacralisent la propriété de l'Etat sans prendre en compte la spécificité des objets de musée par rapport aux autres biens de propriété publique. Or, la spécificité des collections muséales résulte justement des intérêts partagés qu'elles matérialisent. En faisant abstraction des questions de fond portant sur la légalité du titre de propriété, les régimes d'insaisissabilité des collections muséales doivent en définitive gérer les conséquences d'un régime inadapté. Les revendications relatives à la propriété de l'objet de musée ne sont que la cristallisation d'un intérêt partagé actuellement négligé par les régimes d'immunité. L'appréhension de cet intérêt partagé semblerait ainsi nécessiter l'évolution du régime juridique actuel des collections vers une gestion partagée. Si la copropriété n'est pas une solution absolue et généralisable, elle inspire néanmoins des pistes de réflexion afin d'élaborer un régime juridique prenant en compte cet intérêt partagé tout en permettant un exercice effectif des finalités muséales. La caractéristique même des collections muséales relève de leur lien intrinsèque à l'identité d'individus et/ou de communautés, et seule une prise en considération de ce lien spécifique peut permettre l'élaboration d'un régime juridique international adapté.

L'encadrement juridique de la circulation internationale des collections est symptomatique d'une difficulté rencontrée par le droit international dans l'appréhension d'un objet juridique transcendant les catégories juridiques classiques. Peinant à suivre l'internationalisation progressive des musées, la réglementation internationale actuelle est désormais obsolète pour appréhender les changements affectant leurs activités. Le renouveau des fonctions muséales dans l'ordre international pourrait cependant faire l'objet d'une reconnaissance croissante par le droit international avec les débats actuels autour des réseaux internationaux de refuges du patrimoine culturel en péril.

Références

Blake J (2000) On Defining the Cultural Heritage. In: ICLQ 49(1):61-85

Chechi A (2014) The settlement of International Cultural Heritage Disputes. OUP, Oxford

Chechi A (2015) State Immunity, Property Rights, and Cultural Objects on Loan. In: IJCP 22 (2-3):279-299

Commission du droit international (1985) Annuaire, vol 2. Nations-Unies, New-York

Commission du droit international (1986) Annuaire, vol 1. Nations-Unies, New-York

Commission du droit international (1991) Annuaire, vol 2. Nations-Unies, New-York

Contel R (2012) Echange, prêt et coopération culturelle: Solutions en matière de restitution de biens culturels. In: Chechi A, Renold M.-A, Bandle A.-L (eds) Resolving disputes in cultural property. Schulthess, Zurich, pp. 175-210

Cornu M, Renold M.-A (2009) Le renouveau des restitutions de biens culturels: les moyens alternatifs de règlement des litiges. In: JDI 2:493-533

Cornu M, Wallaert C, Fromageau J (2012) Dictionnaire comparé du droit du patrimoine culturel. CNRS, Paris

Daillier P, Forteau M, Pellet A (2009) Droit international public, 8ème éd. LGDJ, Paris

Desvallées A, Mairesse F (éds) (2010) Concepts clés de muséologie. Armand Colin, Paris
Francioni F (2012) Public and Private in International Protection of Cultural Goods. In: EJIL 23:719-730
Francioni F (2013) Plurality and Interaction of Legal orders. In: Francioni F, Gordley J (eds) Enforcing International Cultural Heritage Law. OUP, Oxford, pp. 9–21
Frigo M (2016) Circulation des biens culturels, détermination de la loi applicable et méthodes de règlement des litiges. Triangle bleu, Maubeuge
Hudson K, Nicholls A (1975) The Directory of World Museums. Columbia University Press, New York
ICOM (2006) Code de déontologie pour les musées. http://icom.museum/fileadmin/user_upload/pdf/Codes/code_ethics2013_fr.pdf. Consulté le 01 mars 2017
Knerly Jr Stephen J (2009) International Loans, State Immunity and Anti-Seizure Laws. In: Ali-Aba Course of Study-Legal Issues in Museum Administration. http://www.lending-for-europe.eu/fileadmin/CM/public/training/Antwerp/ALI-ABA_2009__Summary_of_Seizure_Laws.pdf. Consulté le 1er mars 2017
Lochar R, Meinhold A (2016) Museums of the World, 23[d] éd. De Gruyter Saur, Munich
Mairesse F (2012) Etude sur l'opportunité, l'étendue, les raisons et la valeur ajoutée d'un instrument normatif sur la protection et la promotion des musées et des collections (aspects muséaux). http://www.unesco.org/fileadmin/MULTIMEDIA/HQ/CLT/pdf/Mairesse_Etude_preliminaire_-_aspects_museaux_04.pdf. Consulté le 1er mars 2017
O'Connell A (2006) Immunity from Seizure: An Overview. In: AAL 11(1):1-22
O'Keefe PJ (2011) Le rapatriement d'objets sacrés. In: Prott Lyndel V (éds) Témoins de l'Histoire. Unesco, Paris, pp. 241-255
O'Keefe R, Tams CJ (2013) The United Nations Convention on Jurisdictional Immunities of States and their Property: A Commentary. OUP, Oxford
OMC Expert Working Group on the Mobility of Collections (2010) Final Report and Recommendations on the cultural affairs commmittee on improving the means of increasing the mobility of collections. http://www.lending-for-europe.eu/fileadmin/CM/internal/OMC/OMC_Mobility_of_Collections_Report_Rome_7_July10.pdf. Consulté le 1er mars 2017
Perrot X (2005) De la restitution internationale des biens culturels au XIXème et XXème siècles: vers une autonomie juridique. Thèse, Université de Limoges
Renold M-A (2015) Cultural Co-ownership: Preventing and Solving Cultural Property Claims. In: IJCP 22(2-3):163-176
Salmon J (2001) Dictionnaire de droit international public. Bruylant, Bruxelles
Salmon J (2014) L'immunité d'exécution des comptes bancaires des missions diplomatiques et consulaires. In: Alland D, Chetail V, De Frouville O, Viñuales JE (éds) Unité et diversité du droit international. Martinus Nijhoff, Leiden Boston, pp. 447-475
UNESCO (2011), Actes de la Conférence générale: 36ème session, vol 1. http://unesdoc.unesco.org/images/0021/002150/215084f.pdf. Consulté le 01 mars 2017
Van Woudenberg N (2010) Immunity from Seizure: A Legal Exploration. In: Petersson S et al (eds) Encouraging Collections Mobility: A Way Forward for Museums in Europe. http://www.lending-for-europe.eu/fileadmin/CM/public/handbook/Encouraging_Collections_Mobility_A4.pdf. Consulté le 01 mars 2017
Van Woudenberg N (2012) State Immunity and Cultural Objects on Loan. Martinus Nijhoff, Leyde
Vrdoljak AF (2008) International Law, Museums and the Return of Cultural Objects. CUP, Cambridge

The Protection of Cultural Goods and the Right to Property Under the ECHR

Fabian Michl

Abstract This chapter analyses the case law of the European Court of Human Rights on matters of cultural goods' protection. State measures protecting cultural goods usually amount to interferences with private property rights and therefore must comply with Article 1 of Protocol No. 1 to the ECHR. In a number of judgments, the Court has set out the requirements of the right to property in detail. It has shown itself understanding towards the need for preserving cultural heritage while remaining sensitive to abuses of public power or, more broadly, to 'bad governance' in this field. Despite this balanced approach, particular judgments engender criticism as they display implicit biases in the Court's reasoning, either towards the right holder (applicant bias) or the State (State bias) in question.

1 Introduction

The European Convention for the Protection of Human Rights and Fundamental Freedoms (hereafter 'ECHR' or 'Convention') was not drafted as an instrument for the protection of cultural goods. As its official title proves beyond doubt, it is a legal document designed to protect human rights and fundamental freedoms. Above all, Convention law takes an interest in the individual, not in collective settings, such as society, State and culture. To be sure, individuals pursue their life plans within these settings; individual liberties are of little value without a society that makes human life possible in the first place. It is, however, the purpose of the ECHR to protect individual spheres from excessive intrusions of those who exert public powers to maintain State and society.[1]

[1]For a general account of the institutionalisation of fundamental rights see MacCormick (2007), pp. 195–201.

F. Michl (✉)
Public Law and Constitutional Theory, University of Münster, Münster, Germany
e-mail: fabian.michl@uni-muenster.de

© Springer International Publishing AG, part of Springer Nature 2018

E. Lagrange et al. (eds.), *Cultural Heritage and International Law*,
https://doi.org/10.1007/978-3-319-78789-3_6

The preservation of cultural achievements embodied in 'cultural goods' does therefore not rank among the express goals of Convention law. It can rather be seen as an interference with individual rights and freedoms, which must be justified by public interest in order to be compatible with ECHR safeguards. There is, it is noted, a number of cases in which the European Court of Human Rights (hereafter 'the Court') has recognised what one may call 'cultural rights'. From this case law follows that culture may have implications worthy of human rights protection. Some of these aspects are discussed in other chapters of the present volume. The bulk of cases relating to cultural matters is, however, of different nature. These cases deal with the conflict between State measures aiming at the protection of cultural goods on the one hand and the owner's proprietary interest on the other hand. From the viewpoint of Convention law, public preservation measures constitute interferences with the right to property that the owner of the protected good enjoys by virtue of Article 1 of Protocol No. 1 to the Convention (hereafter 'P1') as they come along with restrictions of the use of property or may even result in expropriations.

I shall demonstrate how Convention law attempts to solve this conflict between public interest and individual rights by summarising the relevant case law of the Court. Before embarking on this legal *tour d'horizon*—for anything more than a brief survey would go beyond the constraints of this contribution—I shall outline the legal framework within which the Court adjudicates on matters of cultural goods' protection. With this case law in mind, I would like to make some critical remarks concerning the diverging standards of adjudication governing the Court's practice. This jurisprudential deficiency warrants the conclusion that despite there being some discernible aspects of a reliable doctrine, the Court's case law is still characterised by an objectionable degree of inconsistency, which is capable of jeopardising the acceptance of the Court's authority within this field.

2 Legal Framework

The relevant legal framework comprises, on the one hand, international legal documents aimed at protecting cultural goods and, on the other, the guarantee of the right to property (Article 1 P1).

2.1 Protection of Cultural Goods

Over the last 70 years or so, international law has seen a steady increment of legal rules geared towards the protection of cultural goods. The starting point came with the signing of the Convention for the Protection of Cultural Property in the Event of Armed Conflict, the so-called Hague Convention 1954. In 1970, UNESCO adopted the Convention on the Means of Prohibiting and Preventing the Illicit Import, Export and Transfer of Ownership of Cultural Property (UNESCO Anti-Trafficking

Convention 1970), which, only 2 years later, was joined by the seminal Convention Concerning the Protection of the World Cultural and Natural Heritage (UNESCO World Heritage Convention 1972). The temporary end to this development was reached by the UNESCO Convention for the Safeguarding of the Intangible Cultural Heritage, adopted in 2003. The titles of the mentioned treaties already adumbrate some conceptual intricacies. While the 1954 Hague Convention and the 1970 UNESCO Convention speak of 'cultural property', the UNESCO Conventions of 1972 and 2003 relate to 'cultural heritage'.[2] Terminological confusion intensifies when considering the other authentic linguistic versions. The French texts, for example, employ the term *biens culturels* and *patrimoine culturel* respectively.[3] Notwithstanding the widespread use of the notion of 'cultural property', the term 'cultural good' appears to be more suitable for the present purpose. It avoids the equivocation of the term 'property', which may denote either someone's legal position in the sense of ownership or the object to which this position refers.[4] In addition, 'cultural goods' squares semantically with the correspondent expressions in other international languages, notably the French *biens culturels*, Spanish *bienes culturales*, Portuguese *bens culturais*, Italian *beni culturali*, German *Kulturgüter*, Dutch *cultuurgoederen*, and Russian *культурных ценностей*.

The development of the international cultural goods' protection law has been reflected at a European level. The Council of Europe has drawn up a number of documents with a similar thrust. Being of particular importance for the present topic, the centrepiece of this body of law constitutes the European Cultural Convention of 1954, which obliges the contracting parties to take appropriate measures to safeguard and to encourage the development of their national contribution to the common cultural heritage of Europe (Article 1). The States shall regard the objects of European cultural value placed under their control as integral parts of the common cultural heritage of Europe. They are specifically required to take appropriate measures to safeguard these objects and shall ensure reasonable access to them (Article 5). These general rules have meanwhile been flanked by particular requirements embodied in the Convention for the Protection of the Architectural Heritage of 1985 and the Convention for the Protection of the Archaeological Heritage of 1992. In 2005, the Council of Europe eventually adopted the Framework Convention on the Value of Cultural Heritage for Society, which takes a particular approach to cultural goods' protection. Preserving cultural heritage is no longer conceived exclusively as being a public policy but is also conceived as a task of the States performed in an individual's interest. Accordingly, the parties to the Framework Convention recognise that rights relating to cultural heritage are inherent in the right to participate in cultural life, as defined in the Universal Declaration of Human Rights (Article 1 lit. a). Moreover, the conservation of cultural heritage and its

[2]Cf. Prott and O'Keefe (1992), pp. 307–320.

[3]Similarly, the Spanish (*bienes culturales—patrimonio mundial*) and the Russian (*культурных ценностей—культурное наследие*).

[4]'Property'. In Merriam-Webster.com (21 March 2017).

sustainable use have human development as their goal (Article 1 lit. c). Couching cultural goods' protection in terms of individual rights, problematic as it may be from a theoretical viewpoint,[5] puts a special emphasis on the matter, especially when it comes to collisions with other individual positions, above all with property rights. On the other side of the coin, the Framework Convention stresses the individual and collective responsibility towards cultural heritage (Article 1 lit. b). The Convention thus takes a twofold approach: everyone, alone and collectively, has the right to benefit from cultural heritage and to contribute towards its enrichment, but he or she also has the responsibility to respect his or her own cultural heritage as much as that of others and consequently the common heritage of Europe (Article 4).

2.2 *Right to Property*

The provision of the right to property in Article 1 P1 reads as follows:

> Every natural or legal person is entitled to the peaceful enjoyment of his possessions. No one shall be deprived of his possessions except in the public interest and subject to the conditions provided for by law and by the general principles of international law.
>
> The preceding provisions shall not, however, in any way impair the right of a state to enforce such laws at it deems necessary to control the use of property in accordance with the general interest or to secure the payment of taxes or other contributions or penalties.

The Court has clarified the meaning of this provision during longstanding jurisprudential practice. In summary, Article 1 P1 contains three distinct, yet interrelated, rules concerning the right to property. The first rule enshrined in the first sentence of the first paragraph enunciates the general principle of peaceful enjoyment of property. The second rule concerns deprivations of property, which are allowed, according to the second sentence of the first paragraph, only in the public interest and are subject to the conditions provided for by law and by the general principles of international law. The third rule expressed in the second paragraph allows for regulations of the use of property in accordance with the general interest (or to secure the payment of taxes or other contributions or penalties).

Corresponding to its three-rule doctrine, the Court has developed three categories of interferences with the right to property: deprivations of property, measures controlling the use of property, and other interferences with the right to property. Every limitation of property must be seen in the light of the first rule, i.e. the general principle of property protection. This is why the conditions under which interferences are considered justified have largely converged. These must rely on a legal basis in domestic law, pursue a goal within the public interest, and strike a fair balance between the public and the individual interests at stake. The latter requirement boils down to a proportionality test, which is handled more or less strictly by

[5]For a pronounced critique of the language of rights, or 'rights talk', see Glendon (1991).

the Court, and is open to the acknowledgment of a certain margin of appreciation that the State may enjoy in the individual case. In addition to the States' negative obligations not to interfere with the right to property, the Court has recognised positive obligations incumbent on the States, aiming at the protection and promotion of individual property interests.[6]

3 Case Law

In the following, I shall give an outline of the Court's case law relating to the protection of cultural goods. The compilation, which is not intended to be exhaustive,[7] provides an ample overview of the range of legal problems that are presented within the present field of interest and allows a critical appraisal of the Court's jurisprudence.

3.1 Beyeler v. Italy *(2000)*

The Court was first confronted with a matter of cultural goods' protection at a time when its property doctrine had already been widely elaborated upon. The Grand Chamber judgment in *Beyeler v. Italy*[8] counts as a leading case on the protection of cultural goods under ECHR law and has thus received a considerable spectrum of scholarly attention.[9]

The rather complicated facts of the case can be summarised as follows. The applicant was a Swiss national and collector of art. In 1977, he bought Van Gogh's painting *Portrait of a Young Peasant* from an Italian collector through an intermediary for the equivalent of approximately EUR 600,000. Some 20 years before, the Italian Ministry of Culture had classified the painting as being a work of historical and artistic interest within the meaning of national legislation pertaining to cultural goods. The seller notified the Ministry of the purchase but named only the intermediary, not the applicant, as the buyer. The Ministry did not exercise its preemptive right within the 2-month deadline provided for by the pertinent statute. Six years later, in 1983, the intermediary revealed the actual parties of the purchase and together with the applicant informed the Ministry of the intention to sell the painting

[6]For a detailed account of the Court's property doctrine see Grabenwarter (2014), pp. 365–387.

[7]See also *Debelianovi v. Bulgaria*, no. 61951/00, 28 November 2008; *Kozacıoğlu v. Turkey* [GC], no. 2334/03, 2 July 2009; *Valette and Doherier v. France* (dec.), no. 6054/10, 29 November 2011; *Bogdel v. Lithuania*, no. 41248/06, 26 November 2013.

[8]*Beyeler v. Italy* [GC], no. 33202/96, ECHR 2000-I.

[9]Rudolf (2000), pp. 736–740; Zihler (2001), pp. 731–752; Rees (2005), pp. 505–513; Hoffmann (2006), p. 192; Conforti (2007), p. 174.

to the Peggy Guggenheim Collection in Venice for some EUR 2.5 million. They asked the Ministry to indicate whether the State's right of preemption would be exercised on the sale. A bureaucratic struggle ensued, concerning whether the notification of the purchase had been correctly made in the first place. After he had offered the painting to the Italian State without any success, the applicant sold it for approximately EUR 8 million to the Guggenheim Collection in 1988 and made proper notification of the transaction. Thereupon, the Ministry exercised its preemptive right, yet not regarding the 1988 sale but referring to the first transaction in 1977, thus stipulating a purchase price of EUR 600,000 instead of EUR 8 million. They argued that due to the incorrect declaration in 1977, the Ministry's preemptive right had subsisted. The acquisition of the State was justified by the fact that the painting was supposed to have been sold to a foreign national taking account of the dearth of works by Van Gogh in Italian museums. Legal proceedings before the Italian courts initiated by the applicant ultimately upheld the Ministry's decision.

The Court held that Article 1 P1 was applicable as Italian law recognised the legal position of the buyer, even if this position was revocable under certain conditions, that is to say, encumbered with the State's preemptive right. Hence, the applicant's interest in acquiring the painting, in the Court's view, constituted a possession within the meaning of Article 1 P1.[10] Consistently, the Court found that the exercise of the preemptive right amounted to an interference with the applicant's property right.[11] Neither the legality[12] nor the legitimate aim of the measure was seriously called into question. The Court noted in this respect that the control by the State of the market in works of art was a legitimate aim for the purposes of protecting a country's cultural and artistic heritage. In support of this statement, the Court referred to the UNESCO Convention of 1970, which accords, within certain limits, priority to the ties between works of art and their country of origin. To be sure, there was no such link between Italy and the *Portrait of a Young Peasant*, which Van Gogh had painted in France. Yet the Court recognised that it was legitimate for a State to facilitate, in the most effective way, wide public access to works of art lawfully on its territory and belonging to the cultural heritage of all nations.[13]

Up until this point, the Court had displayed generosity towards the national authorities in the field of cultural goods' protection. This lenient approach ended abruptly when it came to assessing the proportionality of the measure. The Court took particular issue with the fact that it had taken the Ministry 5 years, from 1983 to 1988, to exercise its preemptive right. During this period, it argued, the authorities' attitude towards the applicant had been oscillating between ambivalence and assent, and they had often treated him de facto as the legitimate title holder under the 1977

[10] *Beyeler v. Italy* [GC], no. 33202/96, §§ 98–105, ECHR 2000-I.

[11] *Beyeler v. Italy* [GC], no. 33202/96, § 106–107, ECHR 2000-I. It was explicitly left open whether the interference had to be classified as deprivation or as other interference as the complexity of the factual and legal position prevents its being classified in a precise category.

[12] *Beyeler v. Italy* [GC], no. 33202/96, §§ 108–110, ECHR 2000-I.

[13] *Beyeler v. Italy* [GC], no. 33202/96, §§ 111–113, ECHR 2000-I.

sale. Thus, by stalling the exercise of their preemptive right, the authorities had derived, according to the Court, an unjust enrichment from the uncertainty to which they had largely contributed themselves. Such an enrichment was incompatible with the requirement of a 'fair balance' and imposed a disproportionate and excessive burden on the applicant, thereby violating Article 1 P1.[14]

3.2 SCEA Ferme de Fresnoy v. France *(2005)*

While *Beyeler* concerned the protection of movable cultural goods, the case of *SCEA Ferme de Fresnoy v. France* relates to measures protecting a country's architectural cultural heritage.[15] The applicant was a farm company whose farmstead consisted of various buildings, including a chapel and a chapter house dating from the twelfth and thirteenth centuries and being the remains of a commandry of the Knights Templar. In 1992, the two mediaeval buildings were listed following the pertinent French Historic Monuments Act. As a consequence of the listing decision, the applicant company was obliged to seek the approval of the national heritage architect before proceeding with any building, demolition, or alteration work within the vicinity of the listed monuments. The *Conseil d'État* dismissed the company's appeal against the listing decision, having found that the buildings constituted a rare example of Templar architecture, the preservation of which was in the public interest. In the following years, the company applied for six different building or demolition permits, two of which were rejected, while the remainder was granted with moderate conditions regarding preservation requirements.

The application lodged with the Court did not concern the listing decision as such but instead the applicant company's inability to modify the area surrounding the listed buildings according to its wishes. In dispute were thus the statutory easements resulting from the listing decision. It was uncontested before the Court that these easements interfered with the right to property. The Court considered them as measures to control the use of property within the meaning of the second paragraph of Article 1 P1, the legality of which was out of question. The aim of ensuring the quality of the environment surrounding protected national heritage structures was held legitimate, also taking into account the margin of appreciation that national authorities enjoyed in determining what is in the general interest of the community. In this connection, the Court referred to the 2005 Framework Convention's commitment to the conservation of cultural heritage and its sustainable use as having human development as their goal. In contrast to the *Beyeler* case, the Court did not have serious doubts about the proportionality of the conservation measure. In accordance with its consistent case law on property, the Court recognised that the State enjoyed a wide margin of appreciation with regard both to choosing the means

[14] *Beyeler v. Italy* [GC], no. 33202/96, §§ 114–122, ECHR 2000-I.

[15] *SCEA Ferme de Fresnoy v. France* (dec.), no. 61093/00, ECHR 2005-XIII.

of enforcement and to ascertaining whether the consequences of enforcement were justified in the general interest for the purpose of achieving the object of the law in question. In the present case, it held that the restriction of the applicant company's right to property was not open to criticism *per se* as the company was simply obliged to seek the approval of the national heritage architect before engaging in any construction works. The Court considered that, in the specific case, out of six applications for building and demolition permits, only two had eventually been refused and had not been tested before the courts and that the conditions attached to the remainder had not been excessively restrictive. Moreover, the competent authorities had often sought to reconcile individual and public interests by way of compromise. These proposals, the Court noted, had, however, altogether been declined by the applicant company. All things considered, the Court was not convinced that an excessive and thus disproportionate burden had been placed on the applicant company.

3.3 Potomska and Potomski v. Poland *(2011)*

The *Potomska and Potomski* case takes us from France to the shores of the Baltic.[16] The applicants, a married couple, bought a plot of farmland from the Polish State back in 1974, on which they intended to build a house and a workshop. What they allegedly did not know was the fact that until its closure in 1970, the land had been used as a Jewish cemetery. In 1987, the cemetery was listed as a historic monument, being one of the few remnants of Jewish culture in the region. Linked up with the listing decision was a prohibition of any building activity on the plot unless the owners obtained exceptional authorisation by the competent authority. Instead, the applicants sought a way to exchange their plot for another on which they could realise their building plans. Alternatively, they asked the authorities to expropriate their land and compensate them so that they would receive the funds necessary to buy a parcel elsewhere. With these proposals, they ran from pillar to post. Yet almost 20 years elapsed without the problem being solved. Under Polish law, the applicants had no legal remedy to coerce the State into either substituting or expropriating the plot. Thus, they were dependent on the goodwill of the authorities, which lacked, at one time, suitable land for exchange and, at another, the funds to award compensation in the event of an expropriation.

The Court noted that the 1987 listing decision could have been regarded as a measure to control the use of property similar to that in *SCEA Ferme de Fresnoy*. However, the applicants had specifically complained about the authorities' prolonged failure to either expropriate the property or provide them with an alternative plot. Hence, the Court preferred to examine the application under the general principle of property protection, not as a measure within the meaning of the second

[16] *Potomska and Potomski v. Poland*, no. 33949/05, 29 March 2011.

paragraph of Article 1 P1.[17] In the Court's view, the listing decision as such had been legally adopted and had pursued a legitimate aim, namely the protection of the country's national heritage. It was emphasised that the preservation of the historical, cultural and artistic roots of a region and its inhabitants constituted an 'essential value', the protection and promotion of which are incumbent on the public authorities. In this connection, the Court referred to the Convention for the Protection of the Cultural Heritage of Europe.[18]

The Court reiterated its consistent jurisprudence on the requirements that the principle of proportionality imposes on measures restricting the right to property. In particular, it highlighted that Convention rights must be 'practical and effective' and that, if needed, the Court would 'look behind appearances and investigate the situation complained of'. In doing so, the conduct of the parties, including the means employed by the State and their implementation, was to be considered. Uncertainty arising from legislative or administrative decisions and practices, the Court stressed, was also a factor to be taken into account in assessing the State's conduct. In line with the *Beyeler* judgment, the Court held that where an issue in the general interest was at stake, it was incumbent on the public authorities to act in good time and in an appropriate as well as in a consistent manner.[19] Of course, the Court also acknowledged the State's margin of appreciation and underlined the 'social function' of property, which had to be put into the equation to determine whether a 'fair balance' had been struck.[20] For the Court, the main issue in the case of *Potomska and Potomski* concerned the legal effects of the listing decision, which prevented the applicants from developing their property as they had originally intended.[21] The Court noted that in the circumstances of the case, the most fitting measure would have been expropriation with payment of compensation or the offer of a suitable alternative property.[22] It took issue with the fact that the applicants had lacked any remedy whatsoever to compel the authorities to initiate expropriation proceedings or exchange the plot for another.[23] The Polish State was considered under the positive obligation to provide for such judicial mechanisms for settling effectively property disputes, especially when it is the State itself that is in dispute with an individual.[24] Also taking into account that the authorities had put the applicants off over decades, thereby creating an intolerable state of uncertainty, the Court concluded that the Polish State had failed to strike a fair balance and had thus imposed an excessive burden on the applicants, which was incompatible with Article 1 P1.

---

[17] *Potomska and Potomski v. Poland*, no. 33949/05, § 63, 29 March 2011.

[18] *Potomska and Potomski v. Poland*, no. 33949/05, § 64, 29 March 2011.

[19] *Potomska and Potomski v. Poland*, no. 33949/05, § 66, 29 March 2011.

[20] *Potomska and Potomski v. Poland*, no. 33949/05, § 67, 29 March 2011.

[21] *Potomska and Potomski v. Poland*, no. 33949/05, §§ 69–70, 29 March 2011.

[22] *Potomska and Potomski v. Poland*, no. 33949/05, § 71, 29 March 2011.

[23] *Potomska and Potomski v. Poland*, no. 33949/05, §§ 74–79, 29 March 2011.

[24] *Potomska and Potomski v. Poland*, no. 33949/05, § 74, 29 March 2011.

3.4 Fürst von Thurn und Taxis v. Germany *(2013)*

The facts of the *Fürst von Thurn und Taxis* case[25] can be traced back to the dissolution of family trusts in Germany. Over centuries, these funds had widely been used among noble families to keep their assets together and prevent the respective head of family from bargaining them away. In 1939, the family funds were dissolved by law, and the property contained in them was converted into 'normal' private property. In the course of this, the authorities were allowed to impose certain protective and security measures with respect to objects of particular artistic, scientific, historical or patrimonial value.

The applicant is the head of the Princely Family of Thurn und Taxis. By succession, he had acquired a court library and archives dating back to the fifteenth century. In 1943, the competent court had placed different parts of the library and archives, which until 1939 had formed part of a dissolved family trust, under public supervision. The respective owners had been ordered to obtain authorisation before changing, displacing or disposing the library or the archives or parts thereof. Furthermore, library and archives had to be maintained in an 'orderly condition'. In 2002, the applicant requested that the restrictions on his property be lifted by the competent domestic court arguing that they deprived him of making use of his property in any reasonable way. He had to bear considerable expenses to maintain the library and archives while being denied any possibility of profiting from his property. The total expenses estimated for the year 2002 amounted to EUR 295,000. His request was denied by the court of first instance on the ground of the exceptional cultural value of the library and archives. Despite conceding that the expenses were considerable, it pointed to the fact that there was no indication that the increase they had seen since 1943 was not merely due to general inflation. This decision was upheld by the appellate court, which added that the need to protect the cultural goods embodied in library and archives had persisted since 1943 and that at that time economic interests did not play a decisive role. Accordingly, the general change of the economic context did not justify the measures to be lifted. The high court supported its reasoning by referring to the 'historical and social circumstances under which the property was acquired' in the first place. It thereby alluded to the prominent role that the princely family had played in German history as holder of the monopoly on mail services in the Holy Roman Empire. The acquisition of the applicant's property could thus not be compared to the circumstances under which 'civil' property was acquired.

The Court examined the case in light of both Article 1 P1 and Article 14 ECHR (prohibition of discrimination). The decisions taken back in 1943 were classified as constituting an ongoing control of the use of property, which had to comply with the second paragraph of Article 1 P1.[26] In the Court's opinion, the measures relied on a

[25] *Fürst von Thurn und Taxis v. Germany* (dec.), no. 26367/10, 14 May 2013; for an in-depth analysis see Michl (2015), pp. 370–374.

[26] *Fürst von Thurn und Taxis v. Germany* (dec.), no. 26367/10, § 20, 14 May 2013.

sufficient legal basis in national law and pursued a legitimate aim, namely the protection of the country's cultural heritage.[27] With regard to the proportionality principle,[28] the Court observed that placing cultural goods under public supervision was not contestable *per se*, nor was there any indication in the concrete case that the authorities had exercised their powers of supervision in a disproportionate manner. What is more, the restrictions had already been incumbent on the property by the time the applicant had acquired ownership by way of succession. The Court deduced from this that the applicant must have been informed about the impugned measures. Besides, it was not possible to establish that the applicant was completely deprived of making use of his property as he had not submitted before the Court that he had sought and been denied authorisation for any specific transaction. He had had the possibility to challenge the necessity of the restrictions before the domestic courts and had done so, albeit without success. Regarding the maintenance costs, the Court noted that these were considerable. It argued, however, that it had to be taken into account that these expenses were also necessary to preserve the value of the applicant's property. Consequently, the Court rejected the applicant's complaint based on Article 1 P1 as manifestly ill-founded.

In view of Article 14 ECHR, which the applicant had invoked arguing that he had been discriminated against on grounds of his noble birth, the Court noted that it was not competent *ratione temporis* to examine whether the decisions of 1943 were of a discriminatory nature. The 2002 decision not to lift the restrictions, though subject to the Court's review, was not held problematic under Article 14 ECHR as the Court, following the domestic courts' findings, accepted that the applicant's property had been acquired under privileged conditions, which differed relevantly from the conditions under which ordinary property is acquired.[29]

3.5 Matas v. Croatia *(2016)*

The last case of this survey originated in the Dalmatian city of Split, where the applicant owned a commercial building that he used as a car repair workshop.[30] In 2003, the competent authority ordered a measure of preventive protection under Croatian cultural heritage protection law based on the assumption that the building constituted a rare example of early industrial architecture in Split. Pending the final evaluation of the cultural value, the order imposed certain obligations on the owner, bringing about specific restrictions of use and transfer and creating a preemptive right to the State's benefit. In case of compliance, the owner was awarded a claim to compensation. At first, the measure was ordered for 3 years. In 2006, it was

[27] *Fürst von Thurn und Taxis v. Germany* (dec.), no. 26367/10, § 21, 14 May 2013.
[28] *Fürst von Thurn und Taxis v. Germany* (dec.), no. 26367/10, §§ 22–29, 14 May 2013.
[29] *Fürst von Thurn und Taxis v. Germany* (dec.), no. 26367/10, §§ 31–33, 14 May 2013.
[30] *Matas v. Croatia*, no. 40581/12, 4 October 2016.

prolonged for another 3-year period. The applicant who had not been officially informed of the extension challenged it unsuccessfully before the domestic courts. During these proceedings, the authorities argued that they needed time for further investigations and that during the first 3 years, it had not been possible to obtain an excerpt from the land registry. In 2010, it was decided that the applicant's building should not be registered as an object of cultural heritage as the initial assumption, despite solid evidence, had not been corroborated in the event. During the proceedings before the domestic courts, the applicant submitted significant limitations on his use of property, in particular with respect to several failed attempts to sell the building. He also asked to be awarded EUR 200,000 to compensate for the damage he had sustained as a result of the authorities' conduct.

The Court categorised the preventive measure as being a measure to control the use of property.[31] It assumed that the measure and its prolonging were based on domestic law, leaving it to the national courts to interpret national legal provisions.[32] In line with the pertinent precedents, the Court accepted the conservation of cultural heritage as a legitimate aim of a measure limiting property rights.[33] Once again, the case was decided by a rather detailed proportionality scrutiny.[34] First, the Court emphasised that there had been no indication that measures of cultural heritage protection could be applied in respect to the building at the time the applicant purchased it. By explicit reference, the case was contrasted with the situation of the applicant in *Fürst von Thurn und Taxis*, who had known the restrictions on the property by the time he had acquired it. The Court further noted the 'significant restrictions on the applicant's use of property' and the adverse effect of these restrictions on the applicant's commercial projects. Referring to the analogous *SCEA Ferme de Fresnoy* case, the Court held that the measure was not open to criticism *per se*, having regard to the legitimate aim pursued and the wide margin of appreciations that the State enjoyed where cultural heritage issues were concerned. However, the Court found fault with two aspects of the Croatian authorities' conduct in the applicant's case. Firstly, it passed criticism on the duration of the measure, noting that there was no indication for any investigations of the authorities except for the alleged attempt to obtain a land registry excerpt. Given that land registry data were public information—'readily obtainable by other means, including via the internet'—the Court remarked almost sardonically, and that it was not proven that the authority had actually made a serious attempt to obtain this information, this was not an acceptable justification for applying the lengthy measure. The Court considered that 'the applicant should not have to bear any adverse consequences as a result of the alleged impossibility of the competent State bodies to coordinate their relevant actions in deciding on the matters affecting his property rights'. In this connection, the particular importance of the principle of good governance was invoked, which,

[31] *Matas v. Croatia*, no. 40581/12, § 32, 4 October 2016.

[32] *Matas v. Croatia*, no. 40581/12, §§ 33–34, 4 October 2016.

[33] *Matas v. Croatia*, no. 40581/12, § 35, 4 October 2016.

[34] *Matas v. Croatia*, no. 40581/12, §§ 36–47, 4 October 2016.

according to the Court's understanding, required that public authorities, when interfering with fundamental rights, must act in good time and in an appropriate and, above all, in a consistent manner. Secondly, the Court reproached the Croatian authorities with 'several procedural omissions' in the applicant's case. It emphasised that Article 1 P1 required that the individual must be afforded a reasonable opportunity to put his or her case to the relevant authorities for the purpose of effectively challenging interferences with his or her property rights. Contrary to this requirement, either the applicant had not been informed of the necessity of the measures or the authority had not transmitted its decisions to him. In addition, the domestic administrative court, when ruling on the legality of the measures, had merely taken into consideration the cultural value of the building but not considered the possible disproportionate effects of the protracted application, as well as the authorities' passivity with regard to finally resolving the matter. In view of this, the Court found that the domestic authorities' interference with the applicant's right to property fell short of the requirements of property protection under the Convention.[35]

4 Critical Analysis

Under closer scrutiny, the Court's case law on cultural goods and property deserves both praise and blame.

4.1 Cultural Goods' Protection as a Legitimate Aim

It is doubtlessly commendable that the Court takes a resolute stance in favour of cultural goods protection. Never has it once called into question the legitimate aim that States pursue when protecting goods of cultural value for any region, any country, Europe or the world. The Court thereby follows the overall directions set by international and European law, as can be observed by the references to the relevant legal documents in its reasoning. It is obvious that the Court has a genuine appreciation of the importance of protecting cultural goods on both a national and an international level. This is all the more remarkable as the Court could have put a stronger emphasis on its 'proper' law, namely the right to property pursuant Article 1 P1, and thus could have assumed a considerably more critical position towards the disputed State measures. As early as in the *Beyeler* judgment, it has, however, shown little inclination to quibble over the legitimacy of a measure, although this very case would have given occasion to a more severe scrutiny. Italy was, after all, not able to submit that there was any link between Van Gogh's painting and the country's cultural heritage. The only substantial argument for acquiring the painting was the

[35]*Matas v. Croatia*, no. 40581/12, § 48, 4 October 2016.

dearth of works by Van Gogh in Italian museums—an argument of tenuous persuasiveness considering that the painting should have been sold into a Venice-based art collection. On the Court's reading, this argument could not be based on the 1970 UNESCO Anti-Trafficking Convention since, from the Italian perspective, Van Gough was a foreign artist and the portrait had been painted in France.[36] The Court recognised, however, that in relation to works of art lawfully on its territory and belonging to the cultural heritage of all nations, it is legitimate for a State to take measures designed to facilitate in the most effective way wide public access to them, in the general interest of universal culture.[37] It thus transcended the scope of international cultural heritage law and conceded the States a broad margin in deciding which protection measure was in the general interest and therefore a legitimate aim under Article 1 P1. This generous approach fits neatly into the Court's overall jurisprudence on the right to property and thus does not give rise to any criticism. The same holds true for the application of the margin of appreciation doctrine. It is distinctive of the Court's property doctrine that national authorities are principally better placed than the international judge to appreciate what is in the public interest, all the more so as property legislation commonly involves consideration of political, economic and social issues, and the Court considers it therefore to be 'natural' that national legislatures enjoy a wide margin of appreciation in this field.[38] There is no discernible reason to hold otherwise in matters of cultural goods' protection.

4.2 *Biases in the Court's Reasoning*

While the Court's general commitment to the importance of protecting cultural goods appears to be appropriate, some aspects of its justification scrutiny are objectionable. On an admittedly unfavourable reading of the case law, one can even identify two biases that govern the Court's decisions: the 'applicant bias' and the 'State bias', which are closely interconnected. Both become particularly visible when comparing the two recent rulings, namely *Fürst von Thurn und Taxis* and *Matas*. As is recalled, the application in the former was rejected as manifestly ill-founded (Article 35 § 3 (a) ECHR), while in the latter the Court found a violation of Article 1 P1. The diverging decisions may be explained by the different facts upon which the Court had to rule. Yet, when looking more closely, there are also some indications for a biased appreciation of these facts by the Strasbourg judges.

---

[36] The Court did, however, not consider whether the painting had been sold to Italy legally and with the consent of the French authorities and thus had become part of the cultural heritage of Italy pursuant Article 4 (e) of the 1970 Convention.

[37] *Beyeler v. Italy* [GC], no. 33202/96, § 113, ECHR 2000-I.

[38] Cf. *Jahn v. Germany* [GC], no. 46720/99, 72203/01 and 72552/01, § 91, ECHR 2005-VI.

4.2.1 The 'Applicant Bias'

The first bias that I believe needs to be identified concerns the person of the applicant in the respective cases. In *Fürst von Thurn und Taxis*, the application was lodged by a nobleman who had acquired his property by way of succession from his equally noble ancestors. The aristocratic family under discussion is not a form of 'landed gentry' but ranks a Princely House of the Holy Roman Empire among the European high nobility. Of equally high rank is their fortune consisting not only of the cultural goods in question but also of vast real estate and capital assets.[39] The contrast to the applicant in *Matas*, a Dalmatian car shop owner, could hardly be starker. One cannot evade the impression that this contrast has left its mark on the Court's reasoning. In the *Fürst von Thurn und Taxis* case, the Court showed little understanding towards the applicant's grievances. On the contrary, it transformed arguments that would have spoken in favour of the applicant into their exact opposite. For example, the applicant had submitted that the maintenance costs he had to bear amounted to an excessive burden in view of the fact that he could not dispose of the property as he pleased. Though appreciating the considerable expenses, the Court argued that the costs of maintenance were also necessary to preserve the value of the applicant's property. This argument is manifestly flawed as it entirely neglects that property one cannot dispose of is not worth a penny. One could even claim that a measure controlling the use of property that imposes the maintenance costs on the owner is a more intensive interference with the right to property than an expropriation accompanied by just compensation. Equally astonishing is the Court's observation that the applicant must have been aware of the impugned restrictions by the time he acquired ownership by way of succession. It is by no means clear how the applicant's epistemic mental state was able to influence the standards of justification. In the Court's argument, we might hear the principle of *caveat emptor* resound, a principle that may very well govern cases in which property is acquired by sale. We may confront a buyer with the fact that he had known (or should have known) what he bought and therefore could not complain about restrictions incumbent on the good he had acquired. However, there is no room for this argument when it comes to acquisition by inheritance. For an heir, renouncing the inheritance is rarely an option. So why should it matter from the viewpoint of Article 1 P1 that he had known what he acquired? To be sure, the Court's decision in *Fürst von Thurn und Taxis* does not seem objectionable in the outcome, bearing in mind that the applicant's submissions as to the actual detriments he suffered were obviously poorly drafted. He was not able to indicate one occasion on which permission by the supervising authority had been denied, so the Court rightly saw no reason to intervene. However, the fact that the Court had little ambition to go into the details and take the applicant's complaints seriously has left a bitter aftertaste.

[39]In 2013, the applicant ranked on position 974 in the Forbes World's Billionares List; see https://www.forbes.com/profile/albert-von-thurn-und-taxis/ (21 March 2017).

This impression intensifies when matching *Fürst von Thurn und Taxis* with *Matas*. Contrary to the German prince, the Croatian car mechanic could be reassured of the sympathy of the Court's majority. This bias gave rise to severe criticism put forward by Judges *Lemmens* and *Ravarani* in their joint dissenting opinion. Besides expressing procedural objections, they reproached the majority with having sloppily appreciated the facts of the case. In particular, they found fault with the majority's view that the applicant had suffered under adverse effects of the preventive protection measure. In their view, the applicant's submissions did not permit to establish concrete effects on the applicant. He had, for instance, not submitted that he had sought and been denied authorisation for any specific transaction or activity relating to his property. The dissenters explicitly referred to *SCEA Ferme de Fresnoy* and *Fürst von Thurn und Taxis* as examples of the necessity for such submission. Besides, the applicant in *Matas* had not submitted that he had actually had to bear any expenses for the protection and preservation of the property. The only adverse effect, the judges noted, was the State's preemptive right, which was not addressed by the majority at all. The applicant's submission that the measure had discouraged prospective buyers had been countered by a substantial argument of the Government, in response to which the applicant had remained very vague. He was not able to prove that any business plan of his had been thwarted. Yet the majority had contented itself with the applicant's cursory arguments and had established the restrictions he had allegedly suffered in a rather abstract way. The dissenters noted sardonically in this connection:

> In general, we find it difficult to assess the proportionality of concrete measures by way of essentially abstract reasoning. Measures that have only theoretical effects, that are not really 'felt' by the subject, should in our view not be taken into account for the purposes of the proportionality test.

In addition, they emphasised that the Croatian Cultural Heritage Act had provided for compensation for the restriction of property rights, but the applicant had not seriously claimed compensation before the domestic courts. For them, this observation should have influenced the Court's reasoning in two respects. Firstly, compensation is a means by which the State is able to strike a fair balance between the owner's individual rights and the general interest pursued by the restrictive measure. Thus, the fact that the applicant would have been entitled to compensation cannot remain unconsidered when assessing the proportionality of the measure. Secondly, the applicant's omission to claim compensation before the domestic courts may very well justify declaring his application inadmissible due to non-exhaustion of domestic remedies. The dissenters have a point. Especially if one considers the rigid stance the Court took towards the applicant in the *Fürst von Thurn und Taxis* case, the majority's leniency towards the applicant in *Matas* comes as a surprise. It seems not too far-fetched to suspect that the relative social and economic situation of the applicants may have influenced the Court's sympathy and thus lead to a negative or positive bias, respectively. It is noted that this bias need not be a conscious one. Rarely will judges be free from any emotional attitude towards the parties of the case. Yet a bias, once disclosed, necessarily gives reason for criticising their reasoning which ideally abstains from personal preferences.

4.2.2 The 'State Bias'

The two cases discussed above display not only the 'applicant bias' of the Court but also a bias that is related to the respective State as the applicant's antagonist. In *Fürst von Thurn und Taxis*, the Court accepted the German authorities' measures altogether. There was no closer scrutiny of the authorities' conduct. By stark contrast, the Croatian authorities' (in-)activity in *Matas* was meticulously reviewed. To some extent, one gains the impression that the Court's majority was intent on teaching Croatia a lesson in good governance—a principle prominently invoked in the judgment—rather than assessing the case in light of Article 1 P1. Certainly, it emerges from the Court's consistent case law that measures interfering with property rights are required to meet certain standards of good administration. However, the Court has broad discretion in applying these standards in the concrete case. In *Matas*, it chose to adopt a scrutiny that was as so very particular about the standards of good governance as to bring up points that had not even been submitted by the applicant. The Court has, it is recalled, criticised the national authorities for not acting swiftly to obtain certain items of information that were, according to the Court's majority, publicly available. The dissenters found this 'a somewhat unfair way of treating the authorities', for the applicant had not raised the issue of public availability in his submissions. The Court's majority had, so to speak, unearthed this argument from the depths of the files without giving the Government any opportunity to state its view on the matter. It is remarkable that, contrary to the Court's majority, the dissenters understood a plausible explanation for the duration of the preventive measure. According to them, the Government had described in detail the complex nature of the process of determining cultural objects and mentioned the specific obstacles encountered during the large-scale operation carried out in respect of the industrial heritage in Split. The dissenting judges concluded:

> While that explanation seems plausible to us, the majority does not consider it worth even mentioning it when seeking to ascertain whether there was any justification for the application of the measure of preventive protection for six years.

And again, here they have a point. It is entirely incomprehensible why this explanation for the prolonging of the measure went by the board in the majority's reasoning. One may attribute this, which would be serious enough, to 'mere' sloppiness. Another plausible explanation could be a negative bias on the part of the Court's majority towards the Croatian authorities. Obviously, they had been somewhat over-challenged with the task they had to fulfil. Otherwise, it is hardly explicable why the preventive measure had been upheld over a 6 year-period. As their submissions before the Court prove, the Croatian authorities' conduct did not appear to be very professional. Their arguments were partly superficial, partly even contradictory. Appearances as such do, however, not warrant a judgment against a State. One would expect from a court to look into further details and appreciate all the relevant facts of a case, as the Strasbourg Court does when individual interests are at stake. While the famously thorough German authorities in *Fürst von Thurn und Taxis*, as well as the French authorities in *SCEA Ferme de Fresnoy*, received understanding and even sympathetic treatment by the Court, their Croatian colleagues came off badly. This was mainly their fault, but one can speculate that the Court's reasoning was also influenced by a certain 'State bias'.

4.3 Qualifying the Critique

The criticism put forward in the above demands some qualification. Firstly, it is noted that the Court necessarily decides individual cases. The Strasbourg Court is neither a supreme court that is responsible for a coherent legal order, such as the European Court of Justice or the US Supreme Court, nor is it as deeply embedded in a specific legal system as national constitutional courts are. In adjudicating, Strasbourg judges are not so much focussed on coherence and consistency in their jurisprudence but rather are focussed on doing justice to the individual who invokes the Court's help by its application. Therefore, cases such as those presented in this chapter need to be seen as singular instances above all. Despite the scholarly appeal of a coherent doctrine, for example on matters of property and cultural goods protection, Convention law by its very nature is characterised by flexibility and a certain degree of unpredictability. The criticism I have passed on the recent case law thus comes close to complaining about 'First World problems'. Secondly, the biases I have tried to identify in the Court's case law can never be proven beyond doubt. They are suspicions suggested by the facts of the cases considered and the diverging standards of legal reasoning displayed by the Court. As the question of whether a State measure protecting cultural goods violates Article 1 P1 can be reduced to a more or less indistinct weighing and balancing, one can hardly say what aspect exactly turned the scales. That its case law gives, however, rise to such suspicions should be a warning signal for the Court, for, in the long run, the acceptance of its judgments depends on the general assumption that its judges try hard to rid themselves of any preconception.

5 Conclusion

It has emerged that the Court accords the States a considerable leeway in deciding how cultural goods should be protected. If the Court has established violations of Article 1 P1, it was not due to illegitimate aims the States had pursued, but to inappropriate ways in which they had sought to achieve these goals. In assessing the appropriateness of State measures, one would, however, expect a more balanced approach of the Court, free from (the suspicion of) bias towards applicants and States. To summarise, the right to property under the ECHR draws certain boundaries for the protection of cultural goods, but does not pose an insurmountable obstacle for the national authorities fulfilling this task.

References

Conforti B (2007) Quelques réflexions sur la jurisprudence de la Cour Européenne des Droits de l'Homme en matière de propriété. In: Kohen MG (ed) Promoting justice, human rights and conflict resolution through international law. Liber Amicorum Lucius Calfisch. Brill, Leiden, pp 171–178

Glendon MA (1991) Rights talk. The impoverishment of political discourse. The Free Press, New York

Grabenwarter C (2014) European Convention on Human Rights. Commentary. Beck et al, Munich

Hoffmann BT (2006) European Union legislation pertaining to cultural goods. In: Hoffmann BT (ed) Art and cultural heritage. Law, policy and practice. CUP, Cambridge, pp 191–193

MacCormick N (2007) Institutions of law. An essay in legal theory. OUP, Oxford

Michl F (2015) Noblesse oblige? – Die Thurn-und-Taxis-Entscheidung des Europäischen Gerichtshofs für Menschenrechte. Bayerische Verwaltungsblätter 146:370–374

Prott LV, O'Keefe PJ (1992) 'Cultural heritage' or 'cultural property'? Int J Cult Prop 1:307–320

Rees G (2005) Kulturgüterschutz und EMRK. In: Grupp K, Hufeld U (eds) Recht – Kultur – Finanzen. Festschrift für Reinhard Mußgnung zum 70. Geburtstag am 26. Oktober 2005. Müller, Heidelberg, pp 499–516

Rudolf B (2000) Beyeler v. Italy, application no. 33202/96. Am J Int Law 94:736–740

Zihler F (2001) Eine Besprechung des Urteils Ernst Beyeler gegen den Staat Italien des Europäischen Gerichtshofs für Menschenrechte. ZEuS 3:731–752

Diversité et patrimoine culturels: Réflexions autour de la mise en œuvre de la Convention du patrimoine mondial

Claire Sainte-Beuve

Abstract Si en 1945, il était évident pour les États membres de l'UNESCO que la culture fasse l'objet d'une coopération interétatique, il n'a jamais été simple, pour eux, d'adopter une définition commune de la culture. L'étude de la mise en œuvre de la Convention du patrimoine mondial de 1972 s'inscrit dans cette réflexion et en révèle les enjeux. En effet, cet instrument a d'abord consacré une définition de la culture largement répandue sur le continent européen. Cette définition n'étant pas acceptée par les nouveaux États parties à la Convention, le système de 1972 a dû s'ouvrir à une conception plus large de la culture, mieux à même de protéger la diversité culturelle. La capacité d'adaptation du système de la Convention, ainsi que sa réussite quant à l'instauration d'une protection effective du patrimoine concerné, a influencé la politique culturelle des États tant au sein de l'UNESCO qu'en dehors. Pour autant, le système de 1972 n'est pas parvenu à répondre de manière satisfaisante à l'exigence croissante de protection de la diversité culturelle. Sa place de modèle est, dès lors, remise en question.

1 Introduction

> « Les arts et les sciences forment depuis longtemps en Europe une république, dont les membres, liés entre eux par l'amour et la recherche du beau et du vrai qui sont leur pacte social, tendent beaucoup moins à s'isoler de leurs patries respectives, qu'à en rapprocher les intérêts sous le point de vue si précieux d'une fraternité universelle. (...) qu'en faisant abstraction de ce faux intérêt de pays, qui est le partage des ignorans et des fripons: ce sera comme membre de cette république générale des arts et des sciences, et non habitant de telle ou telle nation, que je discuterai de cet intérêt que toutes les parties ont à la conservation du tout. Quel est-il cet intérêt ? C'est celui de la civilisation, du perfectionnement des moyens de bonheur et de plaisir, de l'avancement et des progrès de l'instruction et de la raison, de l'amélioration enfin de l'espèce humaine. Tout ce qui peut concourir à cette fin appartient à

C. Sainte-Beuve (✉)
Université de Picardie Jules Verne – Faculté de Droit et de Science politique, Pôle universitaire Cathédrale, Amiens Cedex 1, France
e-mail: claire.sainte-beuve@etud.u-picardie.fr

© Springer International Publishing AG, part of Springer Nature 2018

E. Lagrange et al. (eds.), *Cultural Heritage and International Law*,
https://doi.org/10.1007/978-3-319-78789-3_7

tous les peuples; nul n'a le droit de se l'approprier ou d'en disposer arbitrairement » (Quatremère de Quincy)[1].

« Vous êtes complètement différents de moi, mais je vous pardonne » (Geza Roheim)[2].

Au prisme de la notion de culture et des débats dont elle est l'objet, la notion de diversité culturelle entretient nécessairement des liens particuliers avec celle de patrimoine culturel. La Convention du patrimoine mondial de 1972[3] démontre à ce titre, notamment dans ses modalités d'application et son influence, les implications pratiques d'un tel rapport. En effet, la diversité culturelle se présente alors comme un élément cardinal de la politique culturelle des États parties à cette Convention, tout en étant l'une des sources principales de ses écueils faute d'une appréhension universellement partagée. Afin d'étudier ces liens entre diversité et patrimoine culturels, il conviendra avant toute chose de revenir plus en détail sur cette notion de diversité culturelle.

Cette notion serait apparue en droit international positif dans la Convention sur la protection et la promotion de la diversité des expressions culturelles, adoptée en 2005 au sein de l'UNESCO[4]. Elle y est définie de la manière suivante:

> « 'Diversité culturelle' renvoie à la multiplicité des formes par lesquelles les cultures des groupes et des sociétés trouvent leur expression. Ces expressions se transmettent au sein des groupes et des sociétés et entre eux »[5].

La composante culturelle de cette notion[6] est ici caractérisée d'un point de vue anthropologique, conformément à la définition « canonique »[7] posée en 1871 par

[1]Antoine Chrysostome Quatremère dit « Quatremère de Quincy » (1755-1849) est un archéologue et un homme politique. Ces phrases sont extraites de ses *Lettres sur le préjudice qu'occasionneroient aux Arts et à la Science, le déplacement des monuments de l'art de l'Italie, le démembrement de ses Écoles, et la spoliation de ses Collections, Galeries, Musées, etc.* (Rome, 1815).

[2]Propos de G. Roheim renvoyant à certaines tendances qualifiées de « différentialistes » selon lesquelles les différences entre cultures sont exacerbées, la tendance ethnocentriste des êtres humains étant exagérée au détriment d'une véritable analyse anthropologique de la culture (Roheim (1967)).

[3]La « Convention du patrimoine mondial » est le nom usuel pour la « Convention concernant la protection du patrimoine mondial, culturel et naturel », adoptée par la Conférence générale de l'Organisation des Nations Unies pour l'éducation, la science et la culture (UNESCO) lors de sa 17 ème session, Paris, le 16 novembre 1972.

[4]Cette convention fut adoptée par la Conférence générale de cette organisation lors de sa 33e session, Paris, le 20 octobre 2005 (ci-après « Convention de 2005 »). Affirmant dans cette convention la double nature culturelle et économique des biens et services culturels (alinéa 18, du préambule), les États parties s'engagent, dans le cadre de leurs politiques culturelles nationales, à favoriser la manifestation d'une pluralité d'expressions culturelles. Cela se traduit notamment en matière commerciale. L'ensemble des instruments normatifs de l'UNESCO sont disponibles sur son site internet: http://fr.unesco.org.

[5]Article 4, paragraphe 1, al. 1er, de la Convention sur la protection et la promotion de la diversité des expressions culturelles.

[6]Sur les liens entretenus entre les notions de culture et de diversité culturelle dans la Convention de 2005, voir not. Turp (2013), pp. 354-372.

[7]Journet (2002), p. 1.

Edward B. Tylor. Selon cet auteur, la culture est constituée de « la totalité des connaissances, des croyances, des arts, des valeurs, lois, coutumes et toutes les autres capacités et habitudes acquises par l'homme en tant que membre de la société »[8]. Autrement dit, la culture renvoie à l'ensemble des caractéristiques de l'*identité* d'un groupe ou d'un individu en tant que membre dudit groupe. Cette conception de la culture consacre l'évolution de cette notion dans le débat international relatif à la question culturelle. En effet, après 1945, la culture était envisagée essentiellement sous l'angle de la production artistique[9]. Toutefois, cette conception élitiste et eurocentrée fut vivement critiquée[10]. Aussi, pour remédier à cette difficulté, une définition anthropologique de la culture[11] a-t-elle été adoptée dans le cadre des réflexions sur la pertinence de l'action de l'UNESCO

---

[8]*Ibid.*

[9]Par exemple, en 1947, le Directeur général de l'UNESCO, Julian Huxley écrit que le mandat culturel de l'organisation « s'applique en premier lieu à tous les arts de la création, y compris la littérature et l'architecture, la musique et la danse, la peinture et les autres arts plastiques (...). Il peut s'appliquer à la culture même de l'esprit – culture tendant à développer les goûts et les facultés de l'homme, à lui faire connaître les œuvres intellectuelles et artistiques de notre temps et du temps passé, (...) à le doter d'une certaine dose de jugement, de sens critique et de personnalité. C'est dans ce sens que l'on peut parler du niveau de culture plus ou moins élevé d'une collectivité » (UNESCO, Commission préparatoire de l'Organisation des Nations Unies pour l'éducation, la science et la culture (1946) L'UNESCO: ses buts et sa philosophie par Julian Huxley, pp. 28-29. S'il mentionne l'acceptation anthropologique de la culture, c'est pour la relier aux activités de l'organisation en faveur des sciences sociales.

[10]L'idée de culture défendue par Huxley se rapproche de celle héritée des Lumières selon laquelle la culture « se réfère [...] au développement des fonctions spirituelles par des études et des exercices prolongés, ainsi qu'à l'acquis résultant du travail intellectuel » (Rivière (1990), p. 529). Si cette notion de culture défendue dès le XVIIIème siècle a quelque peu évolué pour prendre un sens collectif (en France, on parlera alors de « civilisation » alors qu'en Allemagne, sera consacré le terme de *Kultur*, *Bildung* renvoyant aux connaissances d'un individu), l'idée de l'homme « cultivé » perdure encore. Ce n'est qu'au XXème siècle, que la culture – envisagée par l'anthropologie, et particulièrement dans l'œuvre de Claude Lévi-Strauss – sera aussi comprise comme un phénomène globalisant et identitaire indépendamment de l'idée de progrès.

[11]« Dans son sens le plus large, la culture peut aujourd'hui être considérée comme l'ensemble des traits distinctifs, spirituels et matériels, intellectuels et affectifs, qui caractérisent une société ou un groupe social. Elle englobe, outre les arts et les lettres, les modes de vie, les droits fondamentaux de l'être humain, les systèmes de valeurs, les traditions et les croyances », préambule de la Déclaration de Mexico sur les politiques culturelles par la Conférence mondiale sur les politiques culturelles, Mexico City, 26 juillet – 6 août 1982. L'utilisation de cette définition a été consacrée à l'al. 5, du préambule, de la Déclaration universelle de l'UNESCO sur la diversité culturelle adoptée par la Conférence générale de l'UNESCO à sa 31ème session, Paris, le 2 novembre 2001 et à l'al. 7, du préambule de la Convention de 2005. Cette définition a aussi été précisée dans la Déclaration de Fribourg sur les droits culturels adoptée le 7 mai 2007 par un groupe de travail coordonné par l'Institut interdisciplinaire d'éthique et des droits de l'homme de l'Université de Fribourg dont le but était d'opérer une « clarification » nécessaire « pour démontrer l'importance cruciale de ces droits culturels ainsi que des dimensions culturelles des autres droits de l'homme ». Au sens de l'art. 2, par. a, de la Déclaration, le terme « culture » recouvre les « valeurs, les croyances, les convictions, les langues, les savoirs et les arts, les traditions, institutions et modes de vie par lesquels une personne ou un groupe exprime son humanité et les significations qu'il donne à son existence et à son développement ».

en matière de politiques culturelles. De même, il a été reconnu que les cultures se construisaient et s'enrichissaient au contact les unes des autres, ouvrant ainsi la voie à l'interculturalité[12]. Cristallisant ainsi les évolutions conceptuelles relatives à la culture au niveau international, la définition de la diversité culturelle posée par la Convention de 2005 renvoie bien à l'idée de la pluralité des *identités* coexistant dans le monde. Cette pluralité qui s'exprime tant sur le fond – par l'existence d'identités culturelles différentes – que sur la forme – cette hétérogénéité se manifestant à travers une pluralité de phénomènes.

Par ailleurs, il est précisé à l'article 4 de la Convention de 2005 que ces « expressions se transmettent au sein des groupes et des sociétés ». Or, d'un point de vue juridique, cette transmission est assurée à travers la protection du patrimoine culturel. La notion de patrimoine culturel, héritée du droit public européen, est généralement définie comme un ensemble de biens, monuments, ensembles ou phénomènes culturels qui sont protégés afin d'être transmis aux générations futures. Afin d'assurer l'effectivité de la protection juridique, seuls certains éléments du patrimoine – les plus « importants » pour l'identité du groupe – sont sauvegardés. Pour bénéficier de cette protection, ces éléments doivent donc être préalablement identifiés comme faisant partie du patrimoine par l'État qui octroie cette protection. La « mise en patrimoine » s'effectue en appréciant, classiquement, la *valeur* historique, artistique, en soi, *culturelle* du bien pour l'identité du groupe (qui est d'abord ici, le groupe culturel sur lequel repose l'autorité de l'État). Par conséquent, il était cohérent qu'à la suite de la définition de la diversité culturelle posée dans la Convention de 2005, un lien soit opéré avec le patrimoine culturel. Cela est d'autant plus logique que le patrimoine culturel a fait l'objet, depuis les débuts de l'UNESCO, d'une activité normative prolifique. Cette relation entre diversité et patrimoine culturels se matérialise dès lors comme suit:

> « La diversité culturelle se manifeste non seulement dans les formes variées à travers lesquelles le patrimoine culturel de l'humanité est exprimé, enrichi et transmis grâce à la

---

[12]Les relations entre cultures ont commencé à faire l'objet d'études au sein de l'organisation à partir de la fin des années 1970. Sur cette question, voir UNESCO Division des politiques culturelles et du dialogue interculturel (2007) L'UNESCO et la question de la diversité culturelle 1946-2007 Bilan et stratégies. Étude réalisée à partir d'un choix de documents officiels. http://unesdoc.unesco.org/images/0015/001543/154341mo.pdf, p. 31. À noter toutefois que dans la Déclaration des principes de la coopération culturelle internationale adoptée par la Conférence générale de l'UNESCO lors de sa 14ème session, Paris, le 4 novembre 1966, « l'influence réciproque » que les cultures « exercent les unes sur les autres » avait été soulignée (art. 1er, par. 3). La Convention de 2005, à son art. 4, par. 8, définit l'interculturalité comme « l'existence et l'interaction équitable de diverses culturels ainsi qu'à la possibilité de générer des expressions culturelles partagées par le dialogue et le respect mutuel ». Cette définition a pour particularité de comprendre ce phénomène comme quelque chose de positif, de bénéfique pour la compréhension mutuelle conformément aux buts assignés à l'organisation onusienne. Toutefois, il faut garder à l'esprit que les contacts entre cultures sont plus souvent des enjeux de domination que d'échanges pacifiques.

> variété des expressions culturelles, mais aussi à travers divers modes de création artistique, de production, de diffusion, de distribution et de jouissance des expressions culturelles, quels que soient les moyens et les technologies utilisées. »[13]

Paradoxalement, après avoir affirmé une définition large, *identitaire*, de la culture, il est précisé que la diversité culturelle se manifeste à travers deux types de phénomènes: le patrimoine culturel et les « divers modes de création artistique, de production, de diffusion, de distribution et de jouissance des expressions culturelles, quels que soient les moyens et les technologies ». Par conséquent, la diversité culturelle n'est entendue que par le biais de deux *manifestations* de l'identité culturelle: le patrimoine culturel *matériel* ou *immatériel*[14] et les modes d'expressions qui renvoient aux biens et services culturels dont la diversité doit être encouragée lors des relations commerciales. En somme, est davantage protégé un *produit* de l'identité culturelle que le *droit* d'exprimer les particularismes d'une identité. Dès lors, ces identités culturelles ne sont pas protégées dans leur globalité mais de façon sectorielle, on ne protège qu'« une partie » de celles-ci. Cette première analyse permet de mettre au jour les paradoxes existant entre l'évolution de la définition internationale de la culture, plus proche de son acceptation anthropologique, et la difficulté de ne pas envisager une protection *sectorielle* du phénomène culturel – sectorisation qui semble être certes un gage d'effectivité de la norme juridique mais aussi le lit de Procuste de la culture. Plus généralement, il est notable que dans l'élaboration du droit international de la culture, les sujets ont été confrontés à une double difficulté tant pour définir que retranscrire ce concept de culture en droit positif.

L'inscription dans le droit international positif de la notion de diversité culturelle associe indéniablement – et ce, même si le patrimoine n'est pas l'objet de la Convention de 2005 – diversité et patrimoine culturels. Néanmoins, il ne faut pas en déduire que l'idée de diversité des cultures a émergé à travers la réflexion ayant abouti à l'adoption de cette convention. En 1945, l'Acte constitutif de l'UNESCO précisait que l'organisation, dans la réalisation de ses buts, assure à ses États membres « l'intégrité et la féconde diversité de leurs cultures »[15]. D'ailleurs, c'est avec la protection internationale du patrimoine culturel que l'impératif de préservation d'une certaine diversité s'est renforcé. Par exemple, le premier instrument

---

[13]Art. 4, par. 1, al. 2, de la Convention de 2005.

[14]À la lumière de l'ensemble des instruments normatifs de l'UNESCO en matière de patrimoine culturel – et, pour ne prendre que les exemples de ses instruments conventionnels –, il est possible de considérer que le patrimoine culturel est protégé tant dans son aspect matériel (Convention pour la protection des biens culturels en cas de conflit armé, La Haye, 14 mai 1954; Convention concernant les mesures à prendre pour interdire et empêcher l'importation, l'exportation et le transfert de propriété illicites des biens culturels, Paris, le 14 novembre 1970; Convention concernant la protection du patrimoine mondial, culturel et naturel, Convention sur la protection du patrimoine culturel subaquatique, Paris, le 2 novembre 2001) qu'immatériel (Convention pour la sauvegarde du patrimoine culturel immatériel, Paris, le 17 octobre 2003).

[15]Art. 1er, par. 3 de l'Acte constitutif de l'UNESCO, Londres, 16 novembre 1945.

contraignant de l'UNESCO en matière de protection des biens culturels[16] dispose que « les atteintes portées aux biens culturels, *à quelque peuple qu'ils appartiennent*, constituent des atteintes au patrimoine culturel de l'humanité entière, étant donné que *chaque peuple* apporte sa contribution à la culture mondiale »[17]. Puisqu'il s'agit de préserver le patrimoine « de chaque peuple », le caractère pluriel du patrimoine est reconnu, c'est-à-dire que celui-ci peut être différent en fonction de chacun de ces groupes. De plus, une grande variété de biens culturels est protégée: des biens meubles ou immeubles, des édifices ou centres monumentaux abritant des biens meubles ou encore des immeubles[18]. En réalité, l'idée contemporaine de diversité culturelle est déjà présente en 1954 dans la mesure où cet instrument a pour objet de protéger tant une pluralité de patrimoines, d'identités que plusieurs types de biens. La Convention de 1954 ne révolutionne pas le droit international du patrimoine culturel qui existait avant 1945 dans la mesure où elle vise à protéger certains biens dits « culturels » des destructions pouvant être commises en cas de conflit armé[19]. La Convention pour la protection du patrimoine mondial, culturel et naturel adoptée en 1972 innove davantage dans ce domaine. Pour la première fois, un instrument contraignant est adopté afin de protéger, en temps de paix, des biens culturels (et naturels) de menaces structurelles telles que « l'évolution de la vie sociale et économique »[20] en instaurant « un système efficace de protection collective du patrimoine culturel et naturel de valeur universelle exceptionnelle organisé d'une façon permanente et selon des méthodes scientifiques et modernes »[21]. Cette protection collective se matérialise de manière originale par l'instauration de mécanismes d'assistance financière et technique. Elle est également octroyée à un nombre limité de biens, reconnus par un organe intergouvernemental – le Comité du patrimoine mondial[22] – pour leur valeur « mondiale ». Cet instrument a pris une place particulière dans la politique culturelle internationale des États dans la mesure où c'est l'une des rares conventions culturelles qui soit devenue rapidement universelle et qui a notamment servi de modèle pour les instruments régionaux en

---

[16] La Convention pour la protection des biens culturels en cas de conflit armé.

[17] Al. 2, du préambule, de la Convention de 1954. Italiques rajoutées.

[18] Art. 1er, *ibid.*

[19] Historiquement, le droit international du patrimoine culturel est né en droit de la guerre. La protection de biens pour leur nature « culturelle », indépendamment de leur caractère civil en temps de conflit armé, a notamment été prévue par l'article 27 du Règlement concernant les lois et coutumes de la guerre sur terre, Convention concernant les lois et coutumes de la guerre sur terre, La Haye, le 18 octobre 1907 (disponible en ligne sur le site du Comité international de la Croix-Rouge, https://www.icrc.org/fr) et le Traité concernant la protection des institutions artistiques et scientifiques et des monuments historiques (Pacte Roerich) adopté dans le cadre de l'Union panaméricaine, Washington, le 15 avril 1935 (Recueil des Traités de la Société des Nations (1936), vol. 167). Sur cette question, voir not. Bugnion (2004), pp. 313-324.

[20] Al. 1er, du préambule, de la Convention du patrimoine mondial.

[21] Al. 8, *ibid.*

[22] Nom usuel du Comité intergouvernemental de la protection du patrimoine mondial culturel et naturel.

la matière. D'ailleurs, l'influence de son régime juridique s'est également exercée sur les autres conventions culturelles de l'organisation. Le développement inédit de son Secrétariat dans le fonctionnement interne de l'UNESCO et la notoriété de la Convention aux yeux du grand public sont aussi des éléments qui témoignent de l'importance de cet instrument[23].

Cette prédominance de la Convention du patrimoine mondial en fait un objet d'étude privilégié de l'action internationale en matière culturelle. En 1972, la Convention est adoptée afin de préserver les différents patrimoines culturels existant dans le monde, qui sont autant de manifestations des diverses identités culturelles. Durant la mise en œuvre de la Convention, les États parties ont été confrontés à la difficulté de protéger des biens représentatifs de cette diversité. Dès lors, pour tenter de surmonter cette difficulté, le système de la Convention[24] a reconnu une définition plus anthropologique de la culture, plus à même d'accueillir la reconnaissance de nouvelles manifestations de l'identité culturelle des peuples. Ce traitement de la diversité culturelle au sein du système de la Convention aura des incidences tant sur la protection internationale du patrimoine culturel que sur le débat plus général concernant la question culturelle. Ainsi, l'étude de l'évolution du système conventionnel de 1972 va permettre de mettre au jour à la fois les mutations de la notion de culture et de diversité culturelle au niveau international et de produire une analyse critique du droit international du patrimoine culturel à l'aune des exigences récentes de diversité. L'enjeu est alors de montrer les interdépendances et les tensions qui existent entre les notions de diversité et patrimoine culturels. Il s'agira dans cette optique d'étudier, d'une part, la manière dont la notion de diversité culturelle a émergé au sein de la Convention et de son système (Sect. 2). Il faut également souligner, d'autre part, que le traitement de la diversité des cultures par la Convention de 1972 a influencé la politique culturelle des États tant au sein de l'UNESCO qu'en dehors (Sect. 3) avant de mettre en perspective les conséquences de cette influence (Sect. 4).

2 L'importance de la notion de diversité culturelle au sein du système de la Convention de 1972

Dans le texte de la Convention de 1972, la notion de diversité culturelle telle qu'avancée en 2005 n'apparaît pas expressément[25]. Toutefois, l'étude de l'objet, des buts et des modalités de mise en œuvre de cet instrument, à la lumière du

[23]Voir *infra.* Pour une description précise des particularités du fonctionnement des organes de la Convention, voir not. Bories (2010), pp. 139-165.

[24]Le terme de « système » renvoie ici tant aux mécanismes de protection mis en place au sein de la Convention pour la protection du patrimoine mondial qu'à son organisation institutionnelle.

[25]Il est seulement mentionné que l'élection des membres du Comité du patrimoine mondial doit « assurer une représentation équitable des différentes régions et cultures du monde » (art. 8, par. 2).

contexte de son adoption révèle que ses rédacteurs avaient le souci de préserver cette diversité (2.1). Par ailleurs, l'examen de l'évolution du système de la Convention montre que celui-ci s'est adapté au fil des ans à une définition plus large du phénomène culturel, plus à même de prendre en compte la diversité des cultures (2.2).

2.1 *Un système conventionnel élaboré pour la protection de la diversité culturelle*

Eu égard à l'idéologie prônée durant les premières années d'existence de l'UNESCO, l'impératif de préservation d'une certaine diversité des cultures se manifeste en premier lieu dans le concept même de patrimoine mondial, dont la protection constitue l'objet de la Convention de 1972 (2.1.1). En second lieu, l'objet même de cette convention a en réalité permis d'instaurer un régime juridique protecteur de la diversité au travers d'une pluralité de patrimoines visés (2.1.2).

2.1.1 Un objet entre universalisme et préservation des différences

La Convention de 1972 a pour objet la protection de biens culturels et naturels possédant une « valeur universelle exceptionnelle »[26]. Les rédacteurs de cet instrument sont partis du postulat selon lequel « la dégradation ou la disparition d'un bien du patrimoine culturel et naturel constitue un appauvrissement néfaste du patrimoine de tous les peuples du monde »[27]. Postulat qui découle du syllogisme suivant: tous les peuples font partie de la même communauté humaine, tous les peuples ont un patrimoine culturel, donc le patrimoine de ces peuples est important pour tous ces groupes. Ce syllogisme illustre le mouvement opéré par les rédacteurs du particulier vers l'universel – glissement qui permet de justifier l'action internationale en la matière: c'est parce que ces biens sont importants pour *nous tous*, que nous devons *tous* nous engager à les protéger. Ainsi, en ce que ce patrimoine est composé de l'ensemble des patrimoines des peuples, les rédacteurs ont pris en compte la pluralité des cultures dans lesquelles il se manifeste. Considérer les « peuples » comme les

---

Cette règle se retrouve notamment dans la Charte des Nations Unies dans laquelle il est précisé à son article 23 que les membres non permanents du Conseil de sécurité sont élus sur la base de leur participation au maintien de la paix et d'« une répartition géographique équitable ». Cette règle permet dès lors, dans des organes internationaux dans lesquels chaque État ne peut pas être représenté, d'assurer une représentation certaine des différentes régions du monde (et de manière implicite, un équilibre des intérêts en présence). Au sein de la Convention de 1972, l'adjonction du terme de « cultures » permet de reconnaître qu'il existe ce que l'on pourrait appeler des « espaces culturels » transnationaux, transétatiques voire transcontinentaux.

[26]Art. 1 et 2, de la Convention du patrimoine mondial.

[27]Al. 2, du préambule, de la Convention du patrimoine mondial.

titulaires de ce patrimoine permet à la fois d'atténuer une conception statocentrée de la culture (on ne parle pas ici de patrimoine étatique) logique dans le cadre de relations interétatiques tout en considérant que celle-ci ne peut néanmoins s'épanouir qu'au sein de l'État. Ce glissement du particulier vers l'universel n'est pourtant pas l'apanage de la Convention du patrimoine mondial ni même celui des instruments normatifs en matière de patrimoine culturel adoptés après 1945[28]. Il est précisé en 1972 que parmi ces patrimoines culturels, il existe également des biens qui « présentent un intérêt exceptionnel qui nécessite leur préservation en tant qu'élément du patrimoine mondial de l'humanité tout entière »[29]. Par conséquent, même si le patrimoine culturel des peuples est important car il est constitutif de leurs identités, certains biens sont d'*égale importance* pour l'ensemble des êtres humains. Il existerait donc des biens qui auraient une valeur particulière pour l'*identité de tous*, qui constitueraient ce patrimoine « mondial ». Ces premiers constats amènent à la question suivante: pourquoi a-t-on jugé nécessaire de reconnaître l'existence d'un patrimoine « mondial », une sorte de « super-patrimoine », de « patrimoine de patrimoine » ? Cette interrogation est d'autant plus nécessaire que cette notion apparaît principalement au sein de cet instrument[30]. Plusieurs éléments de réponse peuvent être apportés à ce sujet.

En premier lieu, il s'agissait en 1972 d'adopter un instrument qui puisse être l'outil d'une protection *effective* des éléments du patrimoine. Cette effectivité passait par les moyens qui pouvaient être mobilisés par les États parties à la Convention pour la protection du patrimoine. Cette volonté est née surtout de la campagne lancée en 1960, à l'appel du ministre égyptien de la Culture et sous la coordination de l'UNESCO, pour le sauvetage de monuments menacés par la construction du barrage d'Assouan et donc par le développement économique également souhaité par l'État égyptien[31]. Cette campagne qui durera près de 20 ans a prouvé à la communauté internationale que, pour protéger ces monuments, une coopération technique et financière était indispensable car certains États n'étaient pas à même de protéger des biens dont la valeur est reconnue en dehors de ces frontières. Ainsi, pour mettre en place cette coopération, les concepts de patrimoine mondial et de valeur universelle exceptionnelle permettent avant tout de limiter les biens éligibles à

[28]Il est précisé dans le préambule du Pacte de Roerich de 1935 que ce traité a vocation à « préserver (...) en temps de danger tous les monuments immeubles, qu'ils soient de propriété nationale ou privée, qui constituent le *patrimoine de la culture des peuples* » (italiques rajoutées).

[29]Al. 6, du préambule, de la Convention du patrimoine mondial.

[30]Si la plupart des instruments en matière de patrimoine culturel ont affirmé l'appartenance des biens ou phénomènes protégés au « patrimoine culturel de l'humanité » (par exemple: al. 2, du préambule de la Convention de 1954; al. 5, du préambule de la Convention pour la sauvegarde du patrimoine culturel immatériel de 2003), aucun instrument n'a été aussi loin d'un point de vue conceptuel en accordant une protection à un nombre de biens limités pour leur valeur « universelle ». En effet, dans les autres instruments, le patrimoine culturel ne doit pas avoir une valeur « universelle », c'est uniquement sa protection qui est d'intérêt commun. Toutefois, l'exemple de la Convention de 2003 est un peu particulier, voir Sect. 3.1.1.

[31]Voir not. Save-Soderbergh (1992).

une protection par la Convention car une protection effective et exhaustive est matériellement impossible.

En deuxième lieu, le caractère « mondial » du patrimoine protégé dans le texte de 1972 révèle les oscillations conceptuelles de l'UNESCO à ses débuts entre universalisme et affirmation des différences sur la question culturelle. L'UNESCO en tant qu'héritière de l'Organisation de la coopération intellectuelle (OCI) de la Société des Nations (SDN) créée en 1922 possède un mandat culturel afin de contribuer à la compréhension mutuelle et ainsi au maintien de la paix. Or, cette mission présuppose l'affirmation d'une « philosophie » particulière. En 1920, Paul Appell, recteur de l'Université de Paris et président du comité exécutif de l'Association française pour la SDN écrit à Éric Drummond, secrétaire général de l'organisation que « *l'unité morale des cœurs et des consciences* doit précéder et préparer la réconciliation des intérêts, le règlement juridique des conflits et l'organisation politique de la Paix »[32]. Ce désir de favoriser le non-recours à la force, non plus uniquement de manière juridique mais également *culturelle*, se retrouve dans le préambule de l'Acte constitutif de l'UNESCO dans la phrase désormais célèbre « les guerres prenant naissance dans l'esprit des hommes, c'est dans l'esprit des hommes que doivent être élevées les défenses de la paix »[33]. Dans ce sens, la nécessité de l'instauration d'une morale « universelle » est ensuite précisée lorsqu'il est dit que « cette paix doit être établie sur le fondement de la solidarité intellectuelle et morale de l'humanité »[34]. Plus encore, certains pensaient que pour instaurer cette morale universelle, il fallait défendre une « culture mondiale unique » dont l'instauration serait la première étape vers un « gouvernement mondial »[35]. Des partisans de cette politique au sein de la SDN ont travaillé à la création de l'UNESCO, par exemple, Julian Huxley, qui en sera le premier Directeur général. Néanmoins, cette idée de culture mondiale unique a très vite été critiquée. Les pays de l'Ouest considéraient en effet ce mouvement d'universalisation comme réducteur de la diversité humaine. Quant aux pays de l'Est, ils y voyaient un signe évident d'impérialisme culturel. C'est ainsi qu'en 1948, le Directeur général de l'époque, Torres Bodet, nia l'idée que l'UNESCO visât à « devenir un organisme de propagande au service d'une opinion unique » et rajouta un an plus tard qu'« harmonie ne veut pas dire uniformité. Loin de moi le désir de préconiser un univers monotone formé d'individus et de peuples aussi interchangeables que les pièces d'une machine fabriquées à la chaîne. Ce qui caractérise la vie, c'est la *diversité* »[36]. Cette première apparition du terme de diversité dans un discours d'un Directeur général de l'UNESCO est d'importance dans la mesure où cela va marquer un tournant conceptuel non négligeable dans l'histoire de l'organisation. En effet, ce dernier montre la prise en compte des *différences* de culture dans l'optique de l'action

[32]Cité in: Renoliet (1999), p. 20. Italiques rajoutées.

[33]Al. 1er, du préambule de l'Acte constitutif de l'UNESCO.

[34]Al. 5, du préambule, de l'Acte constitutif de l'UNESCO.

[35]Voir not., Maurel (2010).

[36]Italiques dans le texte. Cité par Maurel, *ibid.*, p. 17.

commune des États au sein de l'organisation. En somme, on assiste après ce discours à un changement de paradigme. À la création de l'UNESCO, on pensait que l'« harmonie » serait atteinte par l'affirmation d'une morale universelle, uniforme, phase ultime de l'idéal de progrès défendu au XVIIIème siècle par les Lumières. En revanche, dès 1948, l'universalisation devant conduire à la compréhension mutuelle résidait dans la commune croyance en la diversité. À partir de ces constats, on remarque que la Convention du patrimoine mondial est née dans un contexte particulier – contexte qui déterminera les valeurs choisies par ses rédacteurs. D'un côté, le caractère mondial du patrimoine est proche de l'universalisme originel de l'organisation, car l'importance des biens de ce patrimoine est égale pour tous, fait partie d'une identité *commune*. De l'autre côté, comme ce patrimoine est avant tout le patrimoine *de chaque peuple*, l'idée d'un universalisme s'épanouissant dans la diversité est également reconnue[37]. Dès lors, on peut dire que la notion de patrimoine mondial s'inscrit à mi-chemin des deux acceptions de l'universalisme prônées au sein de l'UNESCO à ses débuts. Le patrimoine mondial a donc vocation à justifier un intérêt commun renforcé à la protection de ces biens, intérêt qui se matérialise par le régime juridique mis en place dans la Convention.

2.1.2 Le régime juridique du patrimoine mondial, protecteur de la diversité

Eu égard aux considérations relatives à l'esprit et à l'objet de la Convention, l'objectif de protection du patrimoine mondial se traduit de deux manières. D'une part, afin de bénéficier de la protection accordée par la Convention, les États doivent *demander* l'inscription du bien sur les Listes du patrimoine mondial[38]. L'inscription est octroyée ou non par le Comité du patrimoine mondial composé de représentants des États parties élus par l'Assemblée générale des États parties à la Convention[39] s'il est considéré que le bien en question possède une « valeur universelle exceptionnelle ». Une fois le bien inscrit sur les Listes du patrimoine mondial, l'État partie s'engage à mettre en place l'ensemble des mesures légales et techniques nécessaires à la conservation[40] et en informe le Comité par l'envoi régulier de rapports[41]. En contrepartie, si l'État n'est pas en mesure d'assurer la conservation du bien listé, il peut demander au Comité la

[37] De plus, le patrimoine mondial étant issu du patrimoine « des peuples », il est également reconnu dans la Convention une diversité « interne » à la structure de l'État, diversité admise par l'UNESCO suite aux mouvements de décolonisation. Voir UNESCO Division des politiques culturelles et du dialogue interculturel (2007), *op.cit.*, p. 31.

[38] Art. 11, par.3, de la Convention. Il existe deux listes: la Liste du patrimoine mondial et la Liste du patrimoine mondial en péril qui répertorient les biens d'une valeur universelle exceptionnelle qui sont particulièrement menacés (voir art.11, par. 4, de la Convention).

[39] Art. 8, par. 1 et 2, de la Convention.

[40] Art. 5, de la Convention.

[41] Art. 29, de la Convention.

fourniture d'une assistance technique et/ou financière[42]. Cette assistance est fournie grâce au Fonds du patrimoine mondial qui est notamment alimenté par les contributions obligatoires et volontaires des États parties à la Convention[43]. Ainsi, une fois parties à la Convention, les États s'engagent juridiquement à conserver le patrimoine de valeur universelle situé sur leur territoire et conserver les autres biens d'égale importance sur le territoire des États ne pouvant pas protéger par eux-mêmes leur patrimoine[44]. La véritable innovation de ce régime juridique est l'existence de véritables mécanismes internationaux (Fonds, assistance technique/financière) qui permettent une protection efficace dudit patrimoine. Or, ces mécanismes permettent de protéger la diversité des patrimoines puisqu'ils ont pour but de donner à *tous* les États parties les moyens techniques et/ou financiers qui leur font parfois défaut pour protéger leur patrimoine.

Outre cette coopération renforcée, le plus remarquable dans le système conventionnel de 1972 est que l'identification des biens appartenant au patrimoine mondial repose sur un processus interétatique – processus qui, par sa nature, permettra l'inscription de biens issus d'une pluralité de patrimoines. L'identification des biens du patrimoine mondial se déroule en deux étapes. Dans un premier temps, les États, sur la base des inventaires des biens susceptibles d'être inscrits sur les Listes du patrimoine mondial[45] se trouvant sur leur territoire, soumettent un dossier d'inscription. Dans un second temps, c'est le Comité du patrimoine mondial qui décide si le bien est inscrit sur les Listes entre dans la définition du patrimoine mondial posée aux articles 1 et 2, de la Convention et possède une valeur universelle exceptionnelle. La typologie des biens protégés et la valeur universelle exceptionnelle sont définies de façon très floue dans le corps de la Convention. Ces concepts ont donc fait l'objet de précisions ultérieures dans les Orientations devant guider la mise en œuvre de la Convention du patrimoine mondial[46] adoptées par le Comité. L'appréciation de l'importance des biens repose alors sur un faisceau d'indices, de *valeurs* issues d'un consensus né au sein du Comité pour inscrire les biens sur la Liste. De plus, ce consensus se fondra nécessairement sur la pluralité des cultures dont les États sont les représentants et cette prise en compte de la diversité culturelle se retrouvera, en raison de cette identification interétatique, dans les Listes du patrimoine mondial. Autrement dit, chaque État partie défendant des « intérêts culturels » particuliers, ce mécanisme d'identification permettra forcément de protéger une diversité de patrimoines. Par ailleurs, si le flou qui entoure cette identification peut rendre hasardeuse, pour le juriste, l'application de ce texte, il n'en demeure pas moins que cette indétermination a contribué à faire perdurer la Convention dans le temps. Cet instrument « souple » a pu effectivement évoluer face aux difficultés rencontrées durant la mise en œuvre de la Convention et

[42]Art. 19 et s., de la Convention.

[43]Art. 15, de la Convention.

[44]Sans que soit porté atteinte à la souveraineté des États, voir l'art. 6, de la Convention.

[45]Art. 11, de la Convention.

[46]Ci-après les « Orientations ».

s'adapter aux changements conceptuels, notamment en matière de protection de la diversité culturelle.

2.2 *Un système conventionnel adapté aux mutations de la diversité culturelle*

L'adaptation du système conventionnel de 1972 a été permise par le flou entourant les définitions des biens pouvant être inscrits sur les Listes du patrimoine mondial dans le corps de la Convention – flou qui devait être surmonté pour que la Convention soit mise en œuvre (2.2.1). Le Comité a par la suite ouvert le concept de patrimoine mondial à une acception plus large de la culture afin de rendre les Listes du patrimoine mondial plus représentatives de la diversité culturelle (2.2.2).

2.2.1 Une précision inévitable des critères

On retrouve aux articles 1 et 2, de la Convention de 1972 la définition des biens susceptibles d'être inscrits sur les Listes du patrimoine mondial. L'article premier de la Convention concerne plus particulièrement le patrimoine culturel mondial – patrimoine qui est défini de la façon suivante:

> « Aux fins de la présente Convention sont considérés comme 'patrimoine culturel':
>
> les monuments: œuvres architecturales, de sculpture ou de peinture monumentales, éléments ou structures de caractère archéologique, inscriptions, grottes et groupes d'éléments, qui ont une valeur universelle exceptionnelle du point de vue de l'histoire, de l'art ou de la science,
>
> les ensembles: groupes de constructions isolées ou réunies, qui, en raison de leur architecture, de leur unité, ou de leur intégration dans le paysage, ont une valeur universelle exceptionnelle du point de vue de l'histoire, de l'art ou de la science,
>
> les sites: œuvres de l'homme ou œuvres conjuguées de l'homme et de la nature, et zones incluant des sites archéologiques, qui ont une valeur universelle exceptionnelle du point de vue historique, esthétique, ethnologique ou anthropologique. »

Si la typologie des biens semble aisément identifiable (monument-ensemble-site), l'appréciation des caractéristiques intrinsèques de ces derniers (intérêts historiques, artistiques, esthétiques, anthropologiques, etc.) et de leur valeur universelle exceptionnelle l'est beaucoup moins. En conséquence, le Comité du patrimoine mondial, dès sa première session[47], a eu à les préciser pour que la Convention puisse

[47] La 1ère session du Comité s'est déroulée à Paris, du 27 juin au 1er juillet 1977. Voir par. 17 et s. du Rapport final de cette réunion (UNESCO, Comité du patrimoine mondial (1977) Rapport final CC-77/CONF.001/9). L'ensemble des décisions du Comité sont disponibles sur le site du Centre du patrimoine mondial, le Secrétariat de la Convention à l'adresse suivante: http://whc.unesco.org/fr/decisions/.

être appliquée. À travers cette réflexion, la question de la préservation des particularismes a tout de suite été posée. En effet, il fallait que les critères formulés par le Comité puissent permettre à l'ensemble des États parties à la Convention de pouvoir inscrire des biens se trouvant sur leur territoire afin que les Listes révèlent « un juste équilibre tant sur le plan géographique qu'entre les biens culturels et naturels »[48]. Cette volonté d'inscrire des biens issus d'une pluralité d'identités culturelles peut s'expliquer de deux manières. D'une part, elle permet de rendre la Liste plus crédible et « légitime »: en effet, si une région (ou un espace culturel)[49] est surreprésentée, cela équivaudrait à reconnaître qu'elle a plus d'influence sur la « culture mondiale » – ce qui rendrait malaisée la compréhension mutuelle. Dès lors, l'objectif de la Convention ne serait pas atteint. D'autre part, reconnaître implicitement toutes les « cultures » encourage les États à ratifier la Convention. Toutefois, en raison des valeurs véhiculées par le concept de patrimoine, la tâche du Comité n'est pas aisée.

La première difficulté pour le Comité a été le caractère culturellement localisé du concept de patrimoine, tel qu'esquissé dans la Convention. À ce titre, le Conseil International des Monuments et des Sites (ICOMOS), l'organisation consultative compétente en matière culturelle qui assiste le Comité[50], affirme qu'il est difficile de formuler des critères « universels » en raison tant du « caractère variable et subjectif de l'évaluation des qualités » des biens que de « l'influence de la pensée occidentale » et qu'il est malaisé de rendre compte des « différence(s) entre les perceptions à l'intérieur d'une culture donnée et à l'extérieur de celle-ci »[51]. En effet, comme cela a été souligné auparavant, la protection du patrimoine culturel matériel, monumental, est apparue sur le continent européen. Or, en dehors de cet espace géographique, bon nombre de groupes culturels transmettent surtout des traditions, des valeurs, des croyances – des phénomènes culturels en soi, dénués de matérialité. Aussi, dans l'optique d'assurer à la Liste plus de crédibilité, le Comité a-t-il élargi la définition du patrimoine mondial en reconnaissant de nouvelles formes patrimoniales pour tenter de dépasser l'ethnocentrisme originel de cette notion.

---

[48]Par. 18, p. 3, du Rapport final de la 1ère session du Comité, *ibid.*

[49]La représentation des biens listés au sein des cinq régions admises au sein de l'UNESCO (Afrique, États arabes, Asie et Pacifique, Europe et Amérique du Nord, Amérique latine et Caraïbes) fait l'objet de statistiques sur le site du Centre du patrimoine mondial à l'adresse suivante: http://whc.unesco.org/fr/list/stat. Toutefois, deux biens peuvent être classés dans plusieurs régions (« Uvs Nuur Bassin » et « L'œuvre architecturale de Le Corbusier, une contribution au Mouvement Moderne »). Il faut aussi noter que dans son appréciation des critères, les groupes culturels envisagés ne sont pas les régions de l'UNESCO, d'où l'ajout d'« espaces culturels » pour éviter les confusions.

[50]Voir not. sur la question de la participation des organisations consultatives, les art. 8, par. 3 et 13, par. 7, de la Convention.

[51]Par. 19, du Rapport final de la 1ère session du Comité, *op. cit.*

2.2.2 Un élargissement de la notion de patrimoine mondial motivé par le respect de la diversité des cultures

Afin de pouvoir protéger une plus grande pluralité de patrimoines au sein de Listes du patrimoine mondial, le Comité a adapté le concept de patrimoine mondial à une définition anthropologique de la culture. En effet, cette acceptation du phénomène culturel étant plus large, elle permet d'englober plus de cultures différentes. Cette ouverture conceptuelle se matérialise à la fois par la reconnaissance des relations entre les cultures et par la dimension immatérielle du patrimoine.

Dans un premier temps, la définition du patrimoine mondial s'est ouverte à l'interculturalité. Dès 1980[52], il a été possible d'inscrire des biens culturels en série, c'est-à-dire des biens séparés géographiquement mais reliés entre eux car appartenant soit « à un même groupe historico-culturel », soit à « un même type de bien caractéristique de la zone géographique ». Ces biens en série peuvent être soit nationaux, soit transnationaux, voire transcontinentaux. De plus, à partir des années 1990[53], deux autres types de biens ont été pris en compte; ils sont spécifiques en raison de leur étendue: les canaux[54] et les routes ou itinéraires culturels[55]. Un canal est « une voie navigable construite par l'homme »[56] dont l'importance « peut être étudiée selon des facteurs technologiques, économiques, sociaux et paysagers »[57]. Est par exemple prise en compte l'existence « des mouvements de population et [d'] une interaction des groupes culturels »[58]. Une route du patrimoine (ou « itinéraire culturel ») est quant à elle « composée d'éléments matériels qui doivent leur valeur culturelle aux échanges et à un dialogue multidimensionnel entre les pays ou régions, et qui illustrent l'interaction du mouvement, tout au long de la route, dans l'espace et le temps »[59]. Ces trois nouveaux types de biens mettent en valeur les interactions entre groupes culturels tant au sein d'un État (biens en série nationaux, canaux, routes) que dans des zones géographiques plus larges (biens en série transnationaux ou transcontinentaux, canaux, routes) et les relations culturelles entre ces groupes dans le temps[60]. Cela démontre qu'a été intégré, dans l'appréciation du concept de

---

[52]UNESCO, Comité du patrimoine mondial (1980) Orientations devant guider la mise en œuvre de la Convention du patrimoine mondial WHC 2/Révisé, par. 14, p. 4. Les différentes versions des Orientations sont disponibles en ligne à l'adresse suivante: http://whc.unesco.org/fr/orientations/.

[53]Ces notions ont été discutées à partir de la 19ème session du Comité (Berlin, 1995) (UNESCO, Comité du patrimoine mondial (1995) Rapport final WHC-95/CONF.203/16).

[54]UNESCO, Comité du patrimoine mondial (2016) Orientations devant guider la mise en œuvre de la Convention du patrimoine mondial WHC.16/01, annexe 3, par. 6-20, pp. 81-82. Ci-après « Orientations 2016 ».

[55]Orientations 2016, annexe 3, par. 21-24, pp. 82-83.

[56]Orientations 2016, annexe 3, par. 17, p. 81.

[57]Orientations 2016, annexe 3, par. 20, p. 81.

[58]Orientations 2016, annexe 3, par. 20, (iii), b), p. 82.

[59]Orientations 2016, annexe 3, par. 23, p. 82.

[60]À titre d'exemple, il est précisé au sein des Orientations que le concept de routes du patrimoine « est fondé sur la dynamique du mouvement et l'idée d'échanges, avec continuité dans l'espace et le temps » (Orientations 2016, annexe 3, par. 24, p. 82).

patrimoine mondial, le caractère dynamique du phénomène culturel qui se construit à la fois sur les relations entre les groupes et qui est issu d'un processus historique complexe et multidimensionnel. De surcroît, le Comité a considéré tant la diversité culturelle « interne » à l'État que la diversité « externe » des cultures conformément à la politique culturelle défendue au sein de l'organisation[61]. Cette ouverture à l'interculturalité du patrimoine a également abouti à ce que depuis 1988[62], le Comité demande aux États, pour justifier de la valeur universelle exceptionnelle d'un bien, de procéder à une analyse comparative des biens similaires pouvant exister dans d'autres pays. On est alors loin de la conception originelle du Comité en 1977, qui prônait la détermination de la valeur culturelle du bien en fonction d'une culture donnée[63]. Ces premiers pas vers l'interculturalité, dont la manifestation reste le plus souvent intangible, ouvrent la voie à la reconnaissance du caractère immatériel du patrimoine.

Le Comité a reconnu, dans un deuxième temps, des biens dont la valeur résidait non plus uniquement dans leurs qualités matérielles mais davantage dans la symbolique du lieu: les « paysages culturels ». En 1992[64], le Comité a défini cette nouvelle catégorie de la manière suivante:

> « Les paysages culturels sont des biens culturels et représentent les 'œuvres conjuguées de l'homme et de la nature' mentionnées à l'article 1 de la *Convention*. Ils illustrent l'évolution de la société humaine et son établissement au cours du temps, sous l'influence des contraintes physiques et/ou des possibilités présentées par leur environnement naturel et des forces sociales, économiques et culturelles successives, externes aussi bien qu'internes »[65].

Ces paysages permettent de reconnaître que le patrimoine mondial peut trouver sa valeur dans sa dimension immatérielle, plus importante dans certaines cultures, et ainsi dépasser l'ethnocentrisme originel du concept de patrimoine mondial. Toutefois, force est de constater que cette ouverture conceptuelle est très limitée dans la mesure où elle repose sur une conception dualiste du monde, opposant nature et culture – conception, elle-même ethnocentrée. En effet, ces paysages culturels puisent leur valeur dans la relation qu'a tissée l'homme avec la nature. Dans cette catégorie, culture et nature semblent donc indissociables. Concept novateur par rapport à la politique patrimoniale classique occidentale – tout en allant dans le sens de la protection conjointe des patrimoines culturel et naturel conformément au double objet novateur de la Convention[66] –, il peut apparaître pour d'autres comme

---

[61]Voir *supra*.

[62]UNESCO, Comité du patrimoine mondial (1988) Orientations devant guider la mise en œuvre de la Convention du patrimoine mondial WHC/2 Révisé, par. 9, p. 8.

[63]UNESCO, Comité du patrimoine mondial (1988) Orientations devant guider la mise en œuvre de la Convention du patrimoine mondial CC-77/CONF.001/8, par. 7, p. 4.

[64]UNESCO, Comité du patrimoine mondial (1992) Rapport final WHC-92/CONF.002/12.

[65]Orientations 2016, par. 47, p. 12.

[66]Sans revenir sur la genèse de l'adoption de la Convention dans ses détails, il faut rappeler que ce texte est né de la fusion de deux projets: l'un en matière de patrimoine culturel porté par l'UNESCO et l'autre sur le patrimoine naturel soutenu par l'Union internationale pour la conservation de la nature (UICN). Michel Batisse, qui fut sous-Directeur du secteur des sciences de 1972 à 1984, a œuvré pour cette « réconciliation » nature-culture, même s'il la considère d'abord comme

un truisme. En effet, la distinction culture-nature est née en Occident mais n'est pas universellement reconnue surtout dans des sociétés ayant une vision holistique du monde[67]. De surcroît, même si la conception dualiste tente d'être dépassée, les trois « catégories majeures » de paysages culturels décrites dans les Orientations révèlent que ces paysages ne sont envisagés autrement que par la même dichotomie discutée culture-nature. En effet, il est précisé que:

> « Les paysages culturels reflètent souvent des techniques spécifiques d'utilisation viable des terres, prenant en considération les caractéristiques et les limites de l'environnement naturel dans lequel ils sont établis ainsi qu'une relation spirituelle spécifique avec la nature (...) »[68].

Avant que ne soient définies les trois catégories « majeures » de paysages culturels:

> « Les paysages culturels se divisent en trois catégories majeures:
>
> Le plus facilement identifiable est le paysage clairement défini, conçu et créée intentionnellement par l'homme, ce qui comprend les paysages de jardins et de parcs créés pour des raisons esthétiques qui sont souvent (mais pas toujours) associés à des constructions ou des ensembles religieux.

« symbolique » durant l'adoption de la Convention: « nul peut-être n'a mieux exprimé ce sentiment que René Maheu lui-même dans son allocution devant la Conférence de Stockholm: « Longtemps objets d'investigations et de dévotions distinctes voire rivales, voici que nature et culture apparaissent dans le même temps menacées l'une et l'autre, et avec elles l'homme lui-même qui n'existe qu'en leur conjonction ». Pouvait-on mieux proclamer l'impérieuse nécessité de cette réconciliation trop longtemps différée des deux fondements de l'aventure humaine, dont la Convention du Patrimoine mondial apparaît alors comme le premier pas, un pas symbolique peut-être, mais clairement engagé dans la direction de l'avenir » (Batisse, Bolla (2003), pp. 41-42).

[67]Par exemple, l'anthropologue Philippe Descola a remis en cause cette dichotomie à partir de son expérience ethnographique auprès des Achuar en Amazonie équatorienne. Il affirme que « les catégories dont nous disposons pour décrire l'univers achuar sont figées depuis le « miracle grec » dans un même face-à-face conceptuel. Or, l'idée que la nature est le champ des phénomènes qui se réalise indépendamment de l'homme est évidemment complètement étrangère aux Achuar. Pour ceux-ci, la nature n'a pas plus d'existence que la surnature, la vieille distinction lucrécienne entre le réel et la chimère ne pouvant se concevoir que comme le reflet de l'autre. Malheureusement, les concepts que nous a légués la tradition sont marqués d'un naturalisme implicite qui incite toujours à voir dans la nature une réalité extérieure à l'homme que celui-ci ordonne, transforme et transfigure. Habitués à penser les catégories reçues en héritage, il nous est particulièrement difficile d'échapper à un dualisme aussi profondément enraciné. C'est pourtant ce qu'il faudra tenter pour rendre compte du continuum postulé par les Achuar entre les êtres humains et les êtres de la nature » (Descola (1986), p. 119). Il conclut son étude en rejetant ce dualisme de la manière suivante: « pourquoi parler de nature domestique, puisqu'on aura maintenant deviné qu'à travers ces termes c'est ce que les Achuar conçoivent comme la culture que nous désignons ? Au risque assumé d'une possible équivoque, nous avons employé cette expression comme un artifice rhétorique afin de bien souligner que la part de matérialité qui n'a pas été directement engendrée par l'homme et que nous appelons ordinairement nature peut être représentée dans certaines sociétés comme un élément constitutif de culture » (p. 401). Pour plus de précisions sur le dépassement de cette distinction, voir également Descola (2001).

[68]Orientations 2016, annexe 3, par. 9, p. 78.

La deuxième catégorie est le paysage essentiellement évolutif. Il résulte d'une exigence à l'origine sociale, économique, administrative et/ou religieuse et a atteint sa forme actuelle par association et en réponse à son environnement naturel. Ces paysages reflètent ce processus évolutif dans leur forme et leur composition. (...)

La dernière catégorie comprend le paysage culturel associatif. L'inscription de ces paysages sur la Liste du patrimoine mondial se justifie par la force d'association des phénomènes religieux, artistiques ou culturels de l'élément naturel plutôt que par des traces culturelles matérielles, qui peuvent être insignifiantes ou mêmes inexistantes »[69].

Ainsi, ces paysages culturels sont définis soit par l'influence de la nature sur le phénomène culturel (paysage essentiellement évolutif (ii)), soit par la valeur donnée par le phénomène culturel à la nature (paysage clairement défini (i); paysage culturel associatif (iii)). À noter toutefois que les paysages culturels associatifs ont pour particularité de pouvoir être reconnus sans existence de « traces culturelles matérielles ». Par conséquent, on peut affirmer qu'est ici reconnue une vision plus holistique des interactions entre l'homme et son environnement, qui montre le dépassement de la conception matérialiste du patrimoine. Toutefois, cela peut être relativisé dans la mesure où l'inscription de ces paysages se justifie par l'opposition culture-nature, leurs valeurs résidant dans « la force d'association des phénomènes religieux, artistiques ou culturels de l'élément naturel »[70]. De plus, même si pendant longtemps, l'anthropologie a raisonné en termes dualistes en raison de l'histoire de cette discipline, cette approche ne permet pas de reconnaître que, pour certains, la distinction culture-nature n'a pas lieu d'être. Les relations nature-culture sont en effet avant toute chose, un phénomène que l'on peut qualifier de « culturel ». Par ailleurs, il faut noter que les canaux du patrimoine ont été considérés comme une nouvelle sous-division de la catégorie des paysages culturels. Si les mêmes constats relatifs aux écueils du traitement des rapports nature-culture peuvent donc être opposés au concept de canal, une autre observation peut être formulée. On peut dire effectivement que le Comité est confronté à des difficultés quant à la prise en compte de la complexité du phénomène culturel au sein d'un groupe à cause de cette approche dualiste concernant les paysages culturels. Or, étendre la catégorie des paysages culturels à des ensembles plus larges – à plusieurs groupes culturels – accroît la difficulté et accentue le caractère *artificiel* de cette forme patrimoniale. *A contrario*, et à l'instar des routes du patrimoine, la catégorie des canaux a toutefois pour avantage non négligeable de favoriser une coopération interétatique accrue (car la soumission du dossier d'inscription suppose une concertation et l'accord des États concernés) et ainsi, de favoriser d'autant plus la compréhension mutuelle[71]. En

[69]Orientations 2016, annexe 3, par. 10, p. 78.

[70]Orientations 2016, annexe 3, par.10, iii), p. 78.

[71]À ce titre, il est précisé au par. 22, de l'annexe 3, p. 82 des Orientations de 2016 que le concept de routes « offre un cadre privilégié dans lequel peuvent se développer une compréhension mutuelle, une approche plurielle de l'histoire, et la culture de la paix ». Ces routes du patrimoine sont l'application en matière patrimoniale des « projets interculturels » lancés par l'UNESCO dans le cadre de la Décennie mondiale du développement culturel lancée en 1988 (voir UNESCO Division des politiques culturelles et du dialogue interculturel (2007), *op. cit.*, p. 37). Par exemple, des études

conséquence, les effets de cette ouverture conceptuelle sur la préservation de la diversité culturelle seront sans doute limités car l'ethnocentrisme de la notion de patrimoine mondial ne semble pas être surpassé.

Par ailleurs, la reconnaissance de la conception plus globalisante du phénomène culturel se retrouve également au stade de l'évaluation de la conservation du bien. Outre les conditions posées par les articles 1 et 2 de la Convention et les critères d'évaluation de la valeur universelle exceptionnelle, les biens proposés doivent pour être inscrits remplir les conditions d'intégrité et d'authenticité[72]. Pendant longtemps, pour être authentique, un bien culturel devait être conservé autant que possible pour rester dans son état originel[73]. Cette prescription de l'anastylose, inspirée par la politique patrimoniale occidentale, a été remise en cause par certains États dont la culture ne reconnaît pas pareillement la valeur du patrimoine tant parce que les matériaux de construction ne le permettraient pas (adobe, bois, terre, etc.) que parce que la « tradition » n'en fait pas un impératif. Suite à la soumission par le Japon du Hôriy-ji, ensemble de temples en bois qui avaient subi de nombreuses rénovations au fil des siècles, certains experts ont affirmé que les temples ne remplissaient pas la condition d'authenticité au sens des Orientations. En effet, dans la culture japonaise, la reconstruction de ces temples était effectuée régulièrement selon des rites ancestraux. Autrement dit, la valeur patrimoniale de ces temples résidait davantage dans la transmission de ces rites ancestraux que dans les temples en eux-mêmes. Face à ces nouveaux enjeux, une large discussion a été lancée au sein des organes de la Convention[74] et a abouti à l'adoption de la Déclaration de Nara sur l'authenticité lors de la 18ème session du Comité[75] dans laquelle celle-ci s'évalue selon les critères reconnus comme pertinents dans la culture concernée[76]. À cette occasion, il est également reconnu officiellement que « les cultures et les sociétés s'expriment dans des formes et des modalités d'expression, tant tangibles que non tangibles, qui constituent leur patrimoine. Ces formes et modalités doivent être respectées »[77].

Par conséquent, le Comité, par la révision des Orientations, a tenté d'ouvrir la notion de patrimoine mondial à d'autres visions de la transmission, moins «

---

ont été produites dans ce cadre sur la Route de la Soie durant cette période (et l'inscription du bien « Routes de la Soie: le réseau de routes du corridor de Chang'an-Tian-shan » sera effectuée par le Comité à sa 38ème session (Qatar, 2014) (UNESCO, Comité du patrimoine mondial (2014) décision 38 COM 8B.24 Rapport final WHC-14/38.COM/16)).

[72]Les biens qui remplissent les critères dits « naturels » n'ont pas à remplir la condition d'authenticité (Orientations 2016, par. 78 et s.).

[73]Voir not. sur cette question: Prott (1998), p. 247.

[74]Elle fait notamment suite à une étude réalisée par l'ICOMOS à la demande du Comité qui a montré la surreprésentation de biens répondant aux canons du patrimoine monumental à l'occidental. Voir UNESCO, Comité du patrimoine mondial (1994) Compte-rendu et recommandations de la réunion d'experts sur la « Stratégie globale » pour assurer la représentativité de la Liste du patrimoine mondial (Siège de l'UNESCO, 20-22 juin 1994) WHC-94/CONF.003/INF.6. http://whc.unesco.org/archive/1994/whc-94-conf003-inf6f.pdf, p. 3.

[75]UNESCO, Comité du patrimoine mondial (1994) Rapport final WHC-94/CONF.003/16.

[76]Voir not. Orientations 2016, annexe 4, par.11 du préambule de la Déclaration, p. 86.

[77]Orientations 2016, annexe 4, par.7 du préambule de la Déclaration de Nara, p. 86.

européennes ». Cette ouverture conceptuelle avait vocation tant à rendre les Listes du patrimoine mondial plus crédibles qu'à s'adapter, *de facto*, à une définition plus englobante de la culture et du patrimoine affirmée dans le débat international relatif à ces questions[78]. Néanmoins, force est de constater que d'un point de vue théorique, cette ouverture n'a pas permis de mettre fin à l'ethnocentrisme sous-jacent à la notion de patrimoine mondial car d'autres concepts tout aussi ethnocentrés ont été utilisés (à travers la catégorie des paysages culturels). De plus, cette ouverture n'est pas considérée suffisante. Par exemple, le préambule de la Convention pour la sauvegarde du patrimoine culturel immatériel dispose qu'« il n'existe à ce jour aucun instrument multilatéral à caractère contraignant visant la sauvegarde du patrimoine culturel immatériel »[79]. Le concept de patrimoine mondial ne recouvrait donc pas l'immatériel. Aussi, aujourd'hui encore, la moitié des biens listés se trouve-t-elle dans la région Europe et Amérique du Nord[80]. Ce système ne semble donc pas à même de respecter la diversité culturelle. Toutefois, malgré ces écueils, le système de la Convention de 1972 reste un instrument prépondérant au sein de la protection internationale du patrimoine.

3 L'influence du système de la Convention de 1972 sur la notion de diversité culturelle

Le système de la Convention du patrimoine mondial a influé sur les instruments conventionnels antérieurs relatifs au patrimoine culturel. Cette influence se retrouve à plusieurs échelles (internationales, régionales, etc.) et s'est exercée concernant tant les mécanismes de protection du patrimoine mondial que les concepts sur lesquels ils reposent. Ainsi, la Convention de 1972 a contribué à la standardisation des normes de protection du patrimoine culturel (3.1). Dans la mesure où, comme le rappelle à

[78]Conforme à la Déclaration de Mexico de 1982 dans laquelle il est précisé à son par. 23 que « le patrimoine culturel d'un peuple s'étend aux œuvres de l'artiste, de ses architectes, de ses musiciens, de ses écrivains, de ses savants, aussi bien qu'aux créations anonymes, surgies de l'âme populaire, et à l'ensemble des valeurs qui donnent un sens à la vie. Il comprend les œuvres matérielles et non matérielles qui expriment la créativité de ce peuple: langue, rites, croyances, lieux et monuments historiques, littérature, œuvres d'art, archives et bibliothèques ».

[79]La Convention de 2003 a pour objectif premier de sauvegarder le patrimoine culturel lorsque celui se manifeste *uniquement* de manière intangible (voir art. 2, de la Convention). Toutefois, le fait que le patrimoine immatériel ne fasse pas l'objet d'un instrument contraignant aurait pu être affirmé de façon moins catégorique, si on avait considéré que l'ouverture à l'immatérialité de la Convention de 1972 avait été suffisante.

[80]Durant la 18ème session du Comité, le Comité a adopté une « Stratégie globale pour une Liste du patrimoine mondial représentative, équilibrée et crédible ». En 1999, l'Assemblée générale des États parties adopte une résolution dans laquelle il est demandé aux États surreprésentés de limiter leur demande d'inscription (voir Orientations 2016, par. 54 et s., pp. 13 et s.). Les changements opérés au sein des Orientations et les stratégies visant à garantir la représentativité de la Liste, qui ont été nombreux depuis 1994, n'ont pas encore véritablement porté leurs fruits.

juste titre Vittorio Mainetti: « à travers la protection du patrimoine culturel, sous les diverses formes que ce dernier peut avoir, on protège aussi l'identité des peuples détenteurs et donc de la diversité culturelle »[81], l'impact de cette standardisation sur l'acceptation contemporaine de la diversité culturelle doit être souligné (3.2).

3.1 La contribution de la Convention de 1972 à la standardisation des normes internationales de protection du patrimoine culturel

Cette standardisation se remarque en premier lieu à l'intérieur des instruments normatifs de l'UNESCO (3.1.1). Outre cette influence, c'est au Conseil de l'Europe – organisation régionale qui s'est appropriée la question culturelle dès sa création – que l'on constate que la Convention du patrimoine mondial a été un modèle (3.1.2).

3.1.1 Un standard de protection pour les instruments culturels postérieurs de l'UNESCO

Les politiques culturelles de l'UNESCO ont été les premières influencées par la Convention de 1972[82]. Dans l'esprit des conventions antérieures de l'organisation, le glissement du particulier vers l'universel est opéré sans équivoque afin de justifier l'intérêt commun des États à la protection de nouveaux patrimoines. Par ailleurs, il est notable que le « flou » entourant la définition du concept de patrimoine mondial a été conservé dans les deux autres conventions en matière de patrimoine culturel. Les éléments protégés pour être transmis aux générations futures le sont parce qu'ils sont identifiés par l'État concerné et parce qu'ils sont d'importance par rapport à un certain nombre de valeurs. Ainsi, il convient de remarquer que sous l'influence de la Convention de 1972, le concept de patrimoine culturel a été étendu à d'autres formes patrimoniales. Toutefois, cette standardisation des normes de protection du patrimoine culturel à partir du modèle de 1972 ne semble pas avoir été totale. En effet, les concepts de « patrimoine mondial » et donc de « valeur universelle exceptionnelle » ont été abandonnés dans les instruments conventionnels soit parce qu'en raison des menaces contre lesquelles l'instrument entendait lutter, cela

[81]Mainetti (2013), p. 86.

[82]Cette influence se traduit en premier lieu par la place centrale qu'a acquise la Convention au sein de la politique culturelle de l'organisation. Par exemple, lorsque l'Assemblée générale des Nations Unies adopte une résolution (A/RES/56/8) faisant de l'année 2002 l'« Année des Nations Unies pour le patrimoine culturel », elle se « félicite » du succès particulier de la Convention de 1972 qui va fêter son 30ème anniversaire. Cet anniversaire amorcera également la réflexion concernant la Convention de 2003.

ne paraissait pas nécessaire[83], soit parce que cette valeur universelle était considérée comme un frein à la préservation du phénomène culturel et de sa diversité dans la Convention de 2003 relative au patrimoine immatériel. Cette exclusion du concept de valeur universelle exceptionnelle dans le cadre de la protection du patrimoine immatériel nécessite d'être étudiée plus amplement car elle n'est pas dénuée d'ambiguïté et révèle les écueils du modèle de 1972 relatifs à la protection de la diversité culturelle.

La réflexion relative à la préservation de ces phénomènes culturels est née au sein de l'Organisation mondiale de la propriété intellectuelle (OMPI) dans les années 1970 en raison des questions relatives aux droits d'auteur qu'elle sous-tend. Néanmoins, l'UNESCO, en tant qu'organisation « culturelle », est vite devenue partie à ce débat. L'action de l'UNESCO se traduira par l'adoption, en 1989, de la Recommandation sur la sauvegarde de la culture traditionnelle et populaire[84] puis par l'élaboration de deux programmes visant à promouvoir certains éléments du patrimoine immatériel: le programme des « Trésors humains vivants » en 1993 et celui des « Chefs d'œuvre du patrimoine oral et immatériel de l'humanité » en 1998. Ces trois initiatives ont pour particularité de reconnaître l'importance des phénomènes culturels pour le « patrimoine culturel de l'humanité » et la protection des « identités culturelles »[85]. De même, afin de sauvegarder ce patrimoine, les États doivent établir des inventaires et mettre en place des actions de sensibilisation des communautés à ce patrimoine[86]. Plus encore, c'est le système de listes, similaire à celui de la Convention de 1972 qui a été repris dans ces mécanismes: les États sont invités à soumettre l'inventaire de leur patrimoine immatériel en vue d'établir une liste « mondiale » des éléments les plus importants[87]. Dès lors, par ce double

[83]La Convention sur la protection du patrimoine culturel subaquatique vise la protection de « toutes les traces d'existence humaine présentant un caractère culturel, historique ou archéologique qui sont immergées, (…), depuis 100 ans au moins » (art. 1er). Ici, ces traces sont importantes non pas parce qu'elles sont uniques, qu'elles ont une valeur exceptionnelle: elles tirent leur valeur du fait qu'elles révèlent une activité humaine dans un environnement particulier. De plus, les États s'engagent à protéger un patrimoine qu'ils n'ont pas à identifier car une « limite d'âge » est imposée – l'identification aurait été en effet impossible à effectuer par un État en fonction de l'emplacement du bien considéré.

[84]Adoptée par la Conférence générale de l'UNESCO lors de sa 25ème session, Paris, le 15 novembre 1989.

[85]Voir not., al. 1er, du préambule et A. de la Recommandation de 1989, par. 2, de la Résolution du Conseil exécutif portant création à l'UNESCO d'un dispositif concernant les « biens culturels vivants » (trésors humains vivants) (142 EX/18 et 142 EX/48. http://unesdoc.unesco.org/images/0009/000958/095807F.pdf, pp. 20-21) et le préambule de la résolution de la Conférence générale adoptée en 1997 (Résolution adoptée sur le rapport de la Commission IV à la 27e séance plénière, le 12 novembre 1997, http://unesdoc.unesco.org/images//0011/001102/110220f.pdf, pp. 54-55).

[86]Voir par ex., B. et C. de la Recommandation de 1989.

[87]Dans la résolution portant création du programme « Trésors humains humains », le Conseil « exprime l'espoir que l'UNESCO pourra, si le système de la liste nationale est un succès, créer dans un deuxième temps une liste mondiale des « biens culturels vivants » » (par. 6). En 1998, il est précisé par les « chefs d'œuvres du patrimoine oral et immatériel de l'humanité » sont « proclamés » par le Directeur général sur recommandation d'un jury en raison de leur « valeur exceptionnelle »

niveau – national puis mondial – d'identification du patrimoine, on retrouve le concept de valeur universelle exceptionnelle. Le 30ème anniversaire de la Convention du patrimoine mondial et la priorité accordée à ce type de patrimoine immatériel et à la diversité culturelle par la Troisième réunion des ministres de la Culture tenue à Istanbul en 2002[88] ont mis au jour la nécessité d'adopter un instrument contraignant en la matière. Si la révision de la Convention de 1972 avait été un temps envisagée pour inclure ce nouveau patrimoine, elle a été vite abandonnée. Le principal obstacle résidait dans la définition posée du patrimoine mondial, jugée trop « eurocentrée »[89] et dont la valeur universelle exceptionnelle était, malgré les précisions apportées par le Comité, trop floue. Aussi, la valeur universelle était considérée comme inappropriée au patrimoine immatériel car « la création d'une sorte de hiérarchie entre éléments du patrimoine immatériel est apparue incompatible avec la nature de ce patrimoine, le nombre presque infini de ses éléments et la composante sociale de ses manifestations »[90]. Toutefois, cela n'a pas empêché les négociateurs de la Convention de 2003 de calquer le fonctionnement et la protection accordée au patrimoine de l'instrument de 1972: un Comité intergouvernemental est chargé de dresser les Listes représentatives du patrimoine culturel immatériel de l'humanité, d'accorder une assistance financière et technique aux États qui en font la demande. Et les États sont soumis à des obligations similaires d'inventaire et de sauvegarde de ce patrimoine. Si les phénomènes culturels ne sont pas listés pour leur « valeur universelle exceptionnelle », ils le sont pour leur « représentativité » du patrimoine immatériel de l'humanité. De plus, ces listes sont établies afin d'« assurer une meilleure visibilité » de ce patrimoine[91]. Par conséquent, même si les rédacteurs de la Convention de 2003 rejettent l'idée d'une « hiérarchie » entre les éléments du patrimoine immatériel, celle-ci demeure *de facto* entre les éléments inscrits et ceux qui ne le sont pas. Ainsi, on retrouve dans la représentativité, un concept analogue à celui de la valeur universelle exceptionnelle mais il a l'avantage d'être plus « neutre »[92], moins péjoratif dans ce contexte.

(Rapport du Directeur général sur les critères précis de choix des espaces culturels ou des formes d'expression culturelle qui méritent d'être proclamés par l'UNESCO chefs-d'œuvre du patrimoine oral et immatériel de l'humanité, 155EX/15 et Add. et Corr. 155EX/56. http://unesdoc.unesco.org/images//0011/001142/114238f.pdf, p. 13).

[88]Elle s'est tenue du 16 au 17 septembre 2002 et avait pour thème « Le patrimoine culturel immatériel, miroir de la diversité culturelle ». Elle a abouti à l'adoption de la Déclaration d'Istanbul (http://portal.unesco.org/fr/files/6209/10328673500Communiqu%E9Final-F-17sept.pdf/Communiqu%E9Final-F-17sept.pdf).

[89]Voir Blake (2002), pp. 80-81.

[90]Scovazzi (2008), p. 102.

[91]Art. 16, par. 1, de la Convention de 2003.

[92]Ce changement terminologique serait peut-être motivé par une critique du système de la Convention de 1972. En effet, le concept de valeur universelle exceptionnelle semble tendre davantage vers cette idée de représentativité dans la mesure où 1073 biens sont inscrits sur les Listes du patrimoine mondial (suite à la 41ème session du Comité qui s'est déroulée à Cracovie du 2 au 12 juillet 2017).

En somme, le concept de patrimoine immatériel s'est ouvert au caractère dynamique et englobant de la culture depuis les années 1990. En revanche, la consécration dans un instrument contraignant de sa protection a eu pour conséquence de faire perdurer les concepts et mécanismes classiques de protection du patrimoine alors que ces derniers ne sont parvenus à protéger ni la diversité des identités, ni l'hétérogénéité des phénomènes culturels dans le système de 1972. Autrement dit, l'influence de la Convention de 1972 se mesure tant positivement (en ce que ces mécanismes de protection se retrouvent dans d'autres instruments de l'UNESCO relatifs à de nouvelles formes patrimoniales) que négativement (en ce que ces instruments ont parfois pris de la distance sur le concept de patrimoine mondial dans l'objectif de préserver la diversité culturelle). Le rayonnement de la Convention du patrimoine mondial s'observe également au sein d'organisations internationales à vocation régionale notamment européennes. Or, l'étude de ces exemples régionaux sera intéressante pour confirmer ou non les faiblesses du modèle de 1972 concernant la préservation de la diversité des cultures.

3.1.2 Un standard de protection pour les instruments culturels européens

Le système de la Convention de 1972 a aussi particulièrement influencé la politique culturelle des États européens. À première vue, l'exemple de l'Europe semble peu pertinent pour l'analyse des rapports entre patrimoine et diversité culturels. En effet, comme souligné précédemment, les premières critiques formulées concernant ces relations sont nées du fait que le patrimoine mondial a transcrit un concept de transmission eurocentré qui n'a pas pu malgré ces évolutions répondre à l'impératif de diversité culturelle. Dès lors, on pourrait croire que si le système a influencé la politique culturelle européenne, cette influence n'a pu être que positive, respectueuse de la conception de la culture et de la diversité de cet espace culturel. Cependant, cela ne se révèle pas si évident.

L'institutionnalisation de la coopération en Europe n'est pas récente et son évolution a nécessairement amené les institutions à se saisir de la question culturelle. Et c'est au sein du Conseil de l'Europe que l'on peut remarquer la plus grande activité en la matière[93]. D'une part, l'influence de l'UNESCO au sein de cette organisation se mesure d'un point de vue politique. En effet, a été conclue sous l'auspice du Conseil de l'Europe une série d'instruments s'inscrivant dans la lignée de l'institution onusienne dès les années 1960: la Convention de 1969 relative au patrimoine archéologique[94] et celle de 1985 sur les infractions visant des biens

[93]En raison de la brièveté de cette étude, un seul exemple régional a été choisi. Le cas du Conseil de l'Europe est particulièrement instructif car le Conseil est la seule organisation régionale à avoir une activité normative presque aussi dense que l'UNESCO en matière de protection du patrimoine culturel.

[94]STE (066), Londres le 6 mai 1969. Elle a été révisée en 1992 (STE (143), La Valette, 16 janvier 1992).

culturels[95], deux domaines déjà encadrés par l'UNESCO en 1956[96], en 1964[97] et en 1970[98]. On voit donc que l'action de l'UNESCO a fortement conditionné la mise à l'agenda du Conseil de l'Europe de problématiques relatives à la préservation des biens culturels et montre par la même occasion sa volonté d'adopter une politique analogue. Cette action avait été rendue nécessaire dès 1954, par l'adoption de la Convention culturelle européenne dans laquelle les États membres avaient opéré le même lien entre culture et compréhension mutuelle, vecteur d'une Europe unie derrière une culture commune. D'autre part, c'est l'incidence, beaucoup plus marquée, de la Convention de 1972 sur des instruments conventionnels postérieurs adoptés au sein du Conseil de l'Europe qui est la plus significative. Par exemple, la Convention pour la sauvegarde du patrimoine architecturale de l'Europe de 1985[99] et la Convention européenne du paysage de 2000[100] opèrent un renvoi à la Convention de 1972, affirmant ainsi qu'elles s'inscrivent dans sa lignée sans pour autant porter atteinte à son application. Il est d'ailleurs frappant de remarquer que même si ces instruments n'instaurent pas littéralement des mécanismes de protection similaires (assistance financière, liste de biens de valeur exceptionnelle, etc.), on y retrouve néanmoins des concepts clés du système de 1972. Par exemple, la Convention concernant le patrimoine architectural de l'Europe définit le patrimoine protégé par le même triptyque « monument-ensemble-site ». Cette similarité s'explique à la lecture des rapports explicatifs[101] de ces deux conventions qui se sont attachés à montrer les différences et les similitudes avec la Convention de 1972. Ces rapports mettent en avant le caractère complémentaire des instruments régionaux avec la Convention tout en précisant l'importance de prendre en compte, sur des objets similaires (patrimoine architectural, paysage), les particularismes européens[102]. Aussi, ces objets sont protégés en raison de leur importance pour « le patrimoine

[95]STE (119), Delphes, le 23 juin 1985.

[96]Recommandation définissant les principes internationaux à appliquer en matière de fouilles archéologiques adoptée par la Conférence générale de l'UNESCO lors de 9ème session, New Delhi, le 5 décembre 1956.

[97]Recommandation concernant les mesures à prendre pour interdire et empêcher l'exportation, l'importation et le transfert de propriété illicites des biens culturels adoptée par la Conférence générale de l'UNESCO lors de sa 13ème session, Paris, le 19 novembre 1964.

[98]Convention concernant les mesures à prendre pour interdire et empêcher l'importation, l'exportation et le transfert de propriétés illicites des biens culturels.

[99]STE (121), Grenade, le 3 octobre 1985. L'ensemble des instruments normatifs du Conseil de l'Europe et leurs rapports explicatifs sont disponibles à l'adresse suivante: http://www.coe.int/fr/web/conventions/full-list.

[100]STE (176), Florence, le 20 octobre 2000.

[101]Conseil de l'Europe. Rapport explicatif de la Convention pour la sauvegarde du patrimoine architectural de l'Europe, STE (121); Conseil de l'Europe. Rapport explicatif de la Convention européenne du paysage, STE (176).

[102]À ce titre, il est précisé dans le rapport explicatif de la Convention pour la sauvegarde du patrimoine architectural de l'Europe que le texte du Conseil de l'Europe « présente un ensemble de dispositions conçues et adaptées à l'échelon européen » (p. 11).

culturel de l'Europe », qui est un « bien commun à tous les Européens »[103], fondement d'une identité commune européenne. Dès lors, on comprend que l'insuffisance de la prise en compte de la diversité culturelle dans la Convention de 1972 rendait nécessaire une action au niveau régional. En somme, l'exemple de la politique culturelle du Conseil (comme celle de l'UNESCO après 1972) témoigne de l'influence de la Convention de 1972 sur la standardisation des normes de protection du patrimoine culturel – standardisation qui, même en étant constante, semble être contestée pour son incapacité à protéger la diversité culturelle.

3.2 La remise en cause de cette contribution face à l'acceptation contemporaine de la diversité culturelle

La diversité culturelle consacrée en 2005 renvoie tant à la pluralité des identités culturelles qu'à l'hétérogénéité des phénomènes qui se manifestent à travers ces identités. Corrélativement, la standardisation des normes de protection du patrimoine culturel, sous l'influence du système de la Convention de 1972, entre dès lors en conflit avec cette acceptation contemporaine hétérogène de la diversité culturelle.

L'étude de la mise en œuvre de la Convention du patrimoine mondial laisse apparaître que son système n'a pas réussi à protéger la diversité des cultures dans la pratique. Tout d'abord, l'ouverture conceptuelle opérée par le Comité afin d'intégrer une conception plus large du phénomène culturel n'a pas suffi à protéger la pluralité des identités culturelles existant dans le monde dans la mesure où un espace culturel (la région Europe et Amérique du Nord) demeure surreprésenté au sein des Listes du patrimoine mondial. De plus, s'il est tenté avec la Convention pour la sauvegarde du patrimoine culturel immatériel de remédier à ce déséquilibre en protégeant un patrimoine davantage présent dans les pays du Sud, c'est de nouveau un échec. Celui-ci se mesure effectivement par le fait que certains États, déjà surreprésentés dans les Listes du patrimoine mondial, le sont également dans les Listes de la Convention de 2003[104]. Ensuite, force est de constater que, par l'établissement

---

[103]Al. 2, du préambule de la Convention pour la sauvegarde du patrimoine architecturale de l'Europe, al. 2, du préambule de la Convention européenne sur les infractions visant des biens culturels. Dans le même sens, la Convention européenne pour la protection du patrimoine archéologique (révisée, La Valette, 16 janvier 1992) mentionne l'existence « d'un patrimoine archéologique européen » (al. 8, du préambule). Plus encore, le paysage est protégé dans la Convention de 2000 en tant que « composante fondamentale du patrimoine culturel et naturel de l'Europe » dans le but de consolider « l'identité européenne » et il est prévu à l'article 3 de la Convention-cadre du Conseil de l'Europe sur la valeur du patrimoine culturel pour la société (STE (199), Faro, 27 octobre 2005) que « les Parties conviennent de promouvoir une reconnaissance du patrimoine commun de l'Europe ».

[104]Par exemple, la France et l'Espagne qui font partie des cinq pays ayant le nombre le plus important de biens inscrits sur les Listes du patrimoine mondial sont aussi respectivement les 3ème et 4ème États parties à la Convention de 2003 qui ont le plus d'éléments du patrimoine immatériel inscrits sur les Listes de cet instrument (voir les statistiques élaborées par les Secrétariats des Conventions: pour la

d'une politique culturelle analogue au niveau européen, le système de la Convention n'est pas parvenu à prendre en compte de manière satisfaisante une identité culturelle particulière, propre à ce continent: l'identité européenne[105]. Enfin, c'est au sein du Conseil de l'Europe que les critiques les plus sévères ont été formulées à l'encontre du système de 1972 – critiques qui ont contribué à l'adoption de la Convention-cadre du Conseil de l'Europe sur la valeur du patrimoine culturel pour la société en 2005 à Faro[106]. Dans cette dernière, il est question de mettre en lumière la valeur du patrimoine culturel pour la société dans sa globalité: le patrimoine n'est plus perçu comme la manifestation de certains phénomènes culturels mais comme un phénomène global qui permet de mieux prendre en compte la diversité des cultures, tant dans ses formes que ses origines. Ce droit au patrimoine culturel est ainsi « inhérent au droit de participer à la vie culturelle »[107]. Aussi, il est précisé dans son rapport explicatif que la Convention-cadre se démarque de la Convention de 1972 car « le travail à l'échelon mondial de l'UNESCO continue d'adopter une démarche de protection sectorielle par l'établissement d'une liste des biens majeurs considérés comme patrimoine mondial, tandis que la Convention [de Faro] traite des patrimoines culturels dans leur globalité ». Ainsi, en 2005, le Conseil de l'Europe tente davantage de surmonter les écueils de l'action internationale que d'en assurer la complémentarité sur le plan européen.

Pourquoi ce modèle de 1972, tant critiqué, n'a-t-il pas été abandonné ? Plusieurs éléments de réponse peuvent être apportés. D'un côté, l'approche sectorielle qui est contestée lors de la Convention de Faro a permis l'instauration d'une protection effective de certains biens. En effet, si la culture est entendue largement, dans un sens anthropologique, elle comprend des phénomènes que le droit protège déjà dans d'autres domaines (droits d'auteur, etc.) ou qu'il n'a pas vocation traditionnellement à sauvegarder en tant que tel (« folklore », etc.). Cette concurrence normative entre ces différents objets rend particulièrement complexe l'élaboration d'une norme commune de protection. D'un autre côté, la visibilité des biens du patrimoine mondial acquise lors de leurs inscriptions sur les Listes de la Convention de 1972 fait naître de nouveaux enjeux. Le classement international sur ces listes devient tant un facteur de développement économique en raison de l'activité touristique qu'il suscite qu'un instrument de la diplomatie culturelle des États[108]. Par ailleurs, d'un

---

Convention de 1972 (http://whc.unesco.org/fr/list/stat#s2); pour la Convention de 2003 (http://www.unesco.org/culture/ich/fr/listes?multinational=3&display1=inscriptionID&display=maps#tabs)). On constate alors que la protection de nouvelles formes patrimoniales au lieu de favoriser la diversité culturelle a surtout profité aux États ayant une politique importante en la matière.

[105]Telle qu'affirmée dans les instruments du Conseil de l'Europe.

[106]Pour une présentation détaillée de cette convention et de ses enjeux, voir not. Négri (2016).

[107]Art. 1er, par. 1, de la Convention-cadre du Conseil de l'Europe sur la valeur du patrimoine culturel pour la société.

[108]Or, ces enjeux compromettent fortement l'objectif initial de l'organisation et de la Convention qui est de favoriser la compréhension mutuelle. En effet, comme le rappelle V. Citot: « croire que les questions culturelles peuvent être parfaitement indépendantes des enjeux politiques et géopolitiques, c'est faire preuve d'idéalisme, puisque c'est ignorer le lien essentiel qui relie la

point de vue théorique, « le patrimoine matériel n'a de valeur que par sa dimension immatérielle »[109]. En effet, l'octroi d'une protection juridique à un bien ou à un phénomène lui confère une importance qui justifie sa transmission aux générations futures. La reconnaissance de cette importance par l'identification étatique et/ou internationale modifie la perception de l'élément patrimonial. Par exemple, le classement d'un monument religieux enlève une partie de la sacralité du lieu, l'édifice n'est plus considéré seulement comme un lieu de culte mais également comme un lieu de patrimoine car sa dimension religieuse n'est pas partagée par tous. De manière plus générale, l'identification n'est pas neutre car selon Marcel Mauss « l'homme s'identifie aux choses et identifie les choses à lui-même en ayant à la fois le sens des différences et des ressemblances qu'il établit »[110]. On assiste alors à une acculturation juridique, à une modification du phénomène culturel dont on souhaitait – en adoptant la norme – préserver l'intégrité. Il pourrait donc être envisagé, pour protéger de manière plus efficace la diversité culturelle, de substituer à l'instar de la Convention de Faro, un droit *au* patrimoine culturel à un droit *du* patrimoine culturel comportant des obligations positives pour les États de permettre aux individus de préserver leur identité culturelle dans le temps selon les modalités qu'ils souhaitent. Cette approche véhiculerait dès lors une plus grande diversité, plus respectueuse de la définition anthropologique de la culture même si un instrument plus global perdrait en efficacité[111]. Ainsi, cela réduirait les paradoxes contemporains existant entre l'affirmation d'une définition large de la culture et la protection d'une diversité envisagée de manière sectorielle.

4 Conclusion

Si la Convention du patrimoine mondial et le concept même de patrimoine culturel semblent inopérants face à l'exigence croissante de protection de la diversité culturelle, comment assurer juridiquement la transmission de certains biens et/ou phénomènes pour les générations futures ? La réflexion menée par Alexandre Kiss concernant le « droit des générations futures » peut donner une ébauche de réponse à cette question. En 1998, cet auteur[112] remarquait qu'il existe au sein du droit international un « droit des générations futures » car certains instruments normatifs sont constitués d'« une volonté de créer par [leurs] règles une irréversibilité juridique

culture et les cultures aux « infrastructures » sociales, aux sociétés dans leur diversité. Mais c'est aussi faire preuve d'angélisme, car c'est refuser de voir que la culture est l'enjeu de lutte de pouvoir, que la domination culturelle est bel et bien une forme de domination, aux conséquences économiques et politiques » (Citot (2008), pp. 177-190).

[109]Benhamou (2010), p. 121.

[110]Mauss (1974), p. 130.

[111]Voir not. Cornu (2005), p. 254.

[112]Kiss (1998), pp. 49-57.

en faveur des futures bénéficiaires »[113]. Ce nouveau droit aurait été construit afin de transmettre des ressources naturelles ou un patrimoine culturel de l'humanité (dont le patrimoine mondial fait partie) car leur perte est aussi irréversible qu'imminente en raison de la mondialisation[114]. Partant de ce constat, il se demande quelle doit être la protection accordée à ces éléments. Convient-il de tout protéger ? Faut-il protéger seulement une partie de ces ressources pour réussir à en protéger l'essentiel ? Plus largement, il considère que s'interroger sur ces modalités de protection est fondamentale dans la mesure où:

> « ... tout droit repose sur un système de valeurs et que ce système ne sera pas nécessairement le même au terme de plusieurs générations. Maintenir les options signifie les options fondamentales, mais, précisément, nous déterminons ce qui est important en fonction de notre système de valeurs. Donc le contenu du droit des générations futures peut changer dans le temps, alors que des générations ultérieures pourraient préférer revenir en arrière, sans en avoir la faculté »[115].

La protection du patrimoine culturel s'inscrit indéniablement dans ce droit des générations futures car elle concerne des biens ou phénomènes menacés par la globalisation qui uniformise les cultures et dont la perte est par définition irréversible. Toutefois, cette protection s'organise autour de concepts, de valeurs issues de l'héritage européen. Les modalités de la transmission, sur le fondement des concepts de patrimoine et de patrimoine mondial, ne protègent que quelques éléments de l'identité des cultures afin d'assurer la transmission d'une certaine diversité culturelle. Cela aboutit, en raison du phénomène d'acculturation consécutif à la protection, à la création au niveau international d'une historiographie universelle. Cette dernière, si elle peut être critiquée sur de nombreux points est toutefois défendable en ce qu'elle semble être un des derniers remparts juridiques contre l'uniformisation des cultures causée par la mondialisation. Toutefois, comment faire pour permettre aux générations futures d'avoir accès à ce patrimoine sans pour autant leur imposer des valeurs ethnocentrées et propres à notre époque ? Kiss propose, pour surmonter cette contingence de valeurs, de rechercher ce qui caractérise l'humanité de manière *permanente*[116]. Concernant les ressources naturelles, il affirme que ce qui doit être protégé est ce qui permet de répondre aux besoins vitaux de l'homme. Du point de vue du patrimoine culturel, la transmission d'éléments de l'identité culturelle d'un groupe aux générations suivantes est-elle un élément partagé par tous et de tout temps ? À cette question, les anthropologues répondent par l'affirmative[117], chaque société se caractérisant par la transmission d'objets et de phénomènes qui permettent de témoigner de l'identité du groupe et de

---

[113]Kiss (1998), p. 51.

[114]Kiss (1998), p. 50.

[115]Kiss (1998), p. 52.

[116]Kiss (1998), p. 53.

[117]Par exemple, Maurice Godelier affirme que chaque société possède des « choses qu'on donne, des choses qu'on vend » et des choses « qu'il ne faut ni donner ni vendre, qu'il faut garder » (Godelier (1996), p. 49).

sa continuité dans le temps. C'est donc dans la transmission que l'on trouve l'élément permanent sur lequel il faut se focaliser selon Kiss. Néanmoins, les modalités de cette transmission sont propres à chaque groupe. Par conséquent, pour protéger la diversité des identités culturelles de manière plus pertinente pour les générations futures, ne faudrait-il pas davantage consacrer un droit à cette identité qu'un droit protégeant difficilement des manifestations de ces identités ? Force est de constater qu'il serait malaisé de mettre en œuvre cette approche plus globale. D'une part, la brève analyse de la mise en œuvre de la Convention du patrimoine mondial et de son influence montre notamment qu'une protection sectorielle du patrimoine culturel a l'avantage de pouvoir être effective. D'autre part, elle a aussi révélé que ce genre de protection était appréciée par les États pour les enjeux politiques et économiques qu'elle sous-tend. En effet, d'un point de vue politique, il semble peu envisageable que les États abandonnent ces mécanismes. Ainsi, pour envisager la préservation effective des identités culturelles en droit international, il faudrait surtout que la diversité des cultures soit véritablement une valeur partagée et assumée dans la politique juridique extérieure des États.

Références

Batisse M, Bolla G (2003) L'invention du « patrimoine mondial ». Association des anciens fonctionnaires de l'UNESCO, Paris

Benhamou F (2010) L'inscription au patrimoine mondial de l'humanité. La force d'un langage à l'appui d'une promesse de développement. In: Revue Tiers Monde 2(202), Armand Colin, Malakoff, pp. 113-130

Blake J (2002) Élaboration d'un nouvel instrument normatif pour la sauvegarde du patrimoine culturel immatériel: éléments de réflexion. UNESCO, CLT-2001/WS/8 Rev

Bories C (2010) La Convention du patrimoine mondial, à l'aube de son 40e anniversaire: un colosse aux pieds d'argile ? In: Annuaire français de droit international, CNRS Éditions, Paris, pp. 139-165

Bugnion F (2004) La genèse de la protection juridique des biens culturels en cas de conflit armé. In: Revue internationale de la Croix-Rouge 86(854) ou Comité international de la Croix-Rouge, https://www.icrc.org/fr/international-review

Citot V (2008) Du juste équilibre entre technocratie et démocratie dans une organisation internationale. L'exemple de l'Unesco. Le Philosophoire 2(30), Éditions Vrin, Paris, pp. 177-190

Cornu M (2005) L'émergence du principe de diversité culturelle. In: Labouz M-F, Wise M (dir.) La diversité culturelle en question(s). Bruylant, Bruxelles, pp. 251-259

Descola P (1986) La nature domestique: symbolisme et praxis dans l'écologie des Achuar. Éditions de la Maison des Sciences de l'Homme (avec l'aide de la Fondation Singer-Polignac), Paris

Descola P (2001) Par-delà la nature et la culture. In: Le Débat 2(114), Gallimard, Paris, pp. 86-101

Mainetti V (2013) La diversité culturelle à l'UNESCO: ombres et lumières. In: Foblets M-C, Yassari N (dir.) Approches juridiques de la diversité culturelle. Martinus Nijhoff Publishers/Brill, Leiden/Boston, pp. 59-107

Mauss M (1974) OEuvres (2). Éditions De Minuit, Paris

Francioni F, Lenzerini F (eds) (2008) The 1972 World Heritage Convention: a Commentary. Oxford University Press, Oxford

Godelier M (1996) L'énigme du don. Flammarion/Champs essai, Paris

Journet N (dir.) (2002) La culture. De l'universel au particulier. Sciences humaines éditions, Auxerre

Kiss A (1998) L'irréversibilité et le droit des générations futures. In: Revue juridique de l'Environnement 23(1), Éditions Lavoisier, Cachan, pp. 49-57

Maurel C (2010) Le rêve d'un « gouvernement mondial » des années 1920 aux années 1950. L'exemple de l'Unesco. In: Histoire@Politique. Politique, culture, société, (10), Revue électronique du Centre d'histoire de Sciences po, https://www.histoire-politique.fr

Scovazzi T (2008) La notion de patrimoine culturel de l'humanité dans les instruments internationaux. In: Nafziger J, Scovazzi T (dir.) Le patrimoine culturel de l'humanité. Martinus Nijhoff Publishers/Brill, Leiden/Boston, pp. 3-144

Négri V (2016) Dynamiques de la diversité dans la Convention-cadre du Conseil de l'Europe sur la valeur du patrimoine culturel pour la société. In: Négri V (dir.) La diversité dans la gouvernance internationale. Perspectives culturelles, écologiques et juridiques. Bruylant, Bruxelles, pp. 55-71

Prott L V (1998) Les normes internationales relatives au patrimoine culturel. In: UNESCO Rapport mondial sur la culture: culture, créativités et marchés. UNESCO, Paris, pp. 247-257

Renoliet J-J (1999) L'UNESCO oubliée. La Société des Nations et la coopération intellectuelle (1919-1946). Publications de la Sorbonne, Paris

Rivière C (1990) Entrée « Culture ». In: Auroux S (dir) Encyclopédie philosophique universelle: les notions philosophiques A-L (2). PUF, Paris, p. 529

Roheim G (1967) Psychanalyse et Anthropologie. Gallimard, Paris

Save-Soderbergh T (1992) Victoire en Nubie. La Campagne internationale de sauvegarde d'Abou Simbel, de Philae et d'autres trésors culturels. UNESCO, Paris. http://unesdoc.unesco.org/images/0009/000919/091978F.pdf. Consulté le 2 février 2017.

Turp D (2013) La contribution du droit international au maintien de la diversité culturelle. In: RCADI, t. 363, pp. 333-453

Part III
Protection in Times of War

Blue Helmets for Culture: Involving Communities in the Protection of Their Heritage

Gabriele D'amico Soggetti

Abstract The Memorandum regarding the Italian task force (ITF) in the framework of UNESCO's Global Coalition Unite4Heritage was formally entered into force on 16 February 2016. While congratulatory articles on and high expectations of the "Blue Helmets for Culture" (BHC) initiative, which was how the ITF came to be known, spread like wildfire, the task force remains nonoperative 18 months later. While the operational guideline negotiations are still underway, and as such also the concrete features of the ITF's operationalization, I argue that the BHC initiative's ultimate success will depend on reaching out and involving the local communities whose heritage they will attempt to protect. In line with diverse scholarship on cultural heritage management, as well as the guidelines and strategic objectives of the World Heritage Committee on the same, I argue that civil society's participation and engagement can mean the difference between success and failure in BHC's performance in protecting heritage. Furthermore, BHC can become an important site for operationalizing an exercise of local community involvement. The outcome of this exercise, I argue, would be providing states with a concrete set of examples in which local community involvement would be assessed as positive not only in theory but also in practice. This would help to curtail states' reservations, real or imagined, against concrete measures of implementing local communities' participation and involvement in protecting heritage.

1 Introduction

The Blue Helmets for Culture (BHC)[1] initiative was Italy's response to the international outcry that spread as wildfire in response to the ever-increasing destruction of cultural heritage throughout the world. Year 2015 was an "annus horribilis" of sorts

[1]I will refer to the Italian task force as 'BHC' or 'task force' interchangeably.

G. D'amico Soggetti (✉)
FU Berlin, Berlin, Germany
e-mail: gabrieledami@zedat.fu-berlin.de

© Springer International Publishing AG, part of Springer Nature 2018

E. Lagrange et al. (eds.), *Cultural Heritage and International Law*,
https://doi.org/10.1007/978-3-319-78789-3_8

regarding the protection of cultural heritage. Irina Bokova, the Director General of UNESCO, the UN agency that specializes, inter alia, in the promotion and safeguarding of culture in all its forms and expressions, referred to "cultural cleansing"[2] while describing the destruction of cultural heritage in Iraq and Syria. She went on to "commend the leadership shown by Italy in promoting new and ambitious strategies to cope with the unprecedented challenge of deliberate attacks on cultural heritage in conflict situations around the world."[3] This statement was made during the signing ceremony of the Memorandum of Understanding (hereafter "the Memorandum") on the Italian task force in the framework of the UNESCO Global Coalition Unite4Heritage. The Memorandum, which was concluded between UNESCO and the Italian government in 2016, was in line with the 2015 UNESCO Resolution C38/48, which invited UNESCO, in cooperation with member states, to define mechanisms of rapid mobilization of experts "for the protection of culture and the promotion of cultural pluralism in the event of armed conflict."

The proliferation of the term "BHC"[4] in reference to the Italian task force,[5] which was employed by the media, Italian officials, and ministerial statements alike, proved to be an "effective slogan"[6] in putting the importance of cultural heritage protection front and center. The term's allusion to cultural peacekeeping[7] entered the public consciousness virtually uncontested and was key in mobilizing public opinion on the issue of cultural heritage projection.

As per the Memorandum's text stipulations, the task force would be comprised of an array of civilian and military experts on heritage protection and the like, providing, inter alia, "technical supervision and training in order to assist national authorities and other *local actors* [emphasis mine] in implementing emergency preparedness and response measures for the protection and safeguarding of cultural and natural heritage." While a definition of local actors in the Memorandum's context is still pending, against the background of six UNESCO culture conventions and two additional protocols,[8] I argue for the inclusion of local communities in the

---

[2]UNESCO (2014), p. 5.

[3]Ibid.

[4]The proliferation of terms referring to the Italian task force of the Memorandum between the Italian government (Italian government (2016)) and UNESCO led to this confusion. UNESCO consistently referred to either the Italian task force in the framework of the Global Coalition Unite4Heritage or the Italian 'Unite4Heritage' task force. Italian officials and statements, however, used the term 'Italian task force', 'blue helmets for culture' (the most prominent one of all three), or 'Unite4Heritage task force', referring interchangeably to the task force as specified by the Memorandum and *an* Italian task force that is active nationwide and may in part or in whole become part of what the Memorandum envisions.

[5]How the latter is previewed to be referred as by the Memorandum.

[6]Foradori and Rosa (2017), p. 145.

[7]Foradori (2017a), p. 1.

[8]The 1954 Hague Convention for the Protection of Cultural Property in the Event of Armed Conflict; the Protocol 1954 to The Hague Convention for the Protection of Cultural Property in the Event of Armed Conflict 1956; the Second Protocol to the Hague Convention of 1954 for the Protection of Cultural Property in the Event of Armed Conflict 1999; the 1970 Convention on the

list of local actors that will receive training from the BHC experts. Arguably, the notion that local communities should be involved in the protection of *their* heritage has only relatively recently developed.[9] Notwithstanding, this notion is the result of rigorous research of scholars with a great variety of interests, ranging from how to incorporate the plurality of local interests and values into heritage management while promoting sustainable development of a heritage site and the local area[10] to the political dimension of cultural heritage's connection to identity,[11] including in the context of human rights and cultural pluralism.[12] Conversely, responding to attacks to cultural heritage with a task force, such as BHC, that seemingly carries a "blue helmet" mandate impressed upon the public that the gravity of the situation was fraught with the need for experts. Although the BHC initiative is a positive step toward promoting cultural heritage protection, I argue that its ultimate success will depend on involving the local communities whose heritage is under threat and provide the latter with a concrete space and role in which they could directly contribute to its protection. Participation of the local communities that developed/cared for or are concerned about the heritage in question is crucial: without participation, no matter the experts' inputs, states can only implement a limited set of protection provisions for cultural heritage.

2 BHC's Future: Smaller Expectations but Greater Potentials

The numerous and ever-growing deliberative attacks on cultural heritage were not mounted solely for the purpose of eradicating the bearers of certain lifestyles and ways of life; they meant to annihilate the culture under attack—eradicate any living proof and testament of its very existence.[13] This understanding entered the public conscious in a dramatic manner when the "iconoclastic fury of the Islamic State of

Means of Prohibiting and Preventing the Illicit Import, Export and Transfer of Ownership of Cultural Property; the 1972 Convention Concerning the Protection of the World Cultural and Natural Heritage; the 2001 Convention on the Protection of the Underwater Cultural Heritage; the 2003 Convention for the Safeguarding of the Intangible Cultural Heritage; and the 2005 Convention on the Protection and Promotion of the Diversity of Cultural Expressions.

[9]Art. 15 of the 2003 UNESCO Convention.

[10]Araoz (2011), Brattli (2009), Leask and Fyall (2006) and Winter (2011).

[11]Assi (2012), De Cesari (2010) and Scham and Yahya (2003).

[12]Ekern et al. (2012), Logan (2012), Shepherd (2006) and Sinding-Larsen (2012).

[13]The report of the "Heritage and Cultural Diversity at Risk in Iraq and Syria" international conference at UNESCO Headquarters on 3 December 2014 aptly pointed out the link between culture and conflict, inter alia, as 'the deliberate targeting of cultural heritage in an attempt to destroy the legitimacy of the other to exist as such, exemplifying the most violent forms of fanatic violence today'.

Iraq and Syria"[14] destroyed several sites in the ancient city of Palmyra, a UNESCO World Heritage Site. According to Giovanni Boccardi, Chief of UNESCO's Emergency Preparedness and Response Unit, protecting cultural heritage ceased to be handled as "addressing a secondary issue, a sort of luxury for antiquarians or art histories, but [as] contributing to peace, stability, security, and the future sustainable development of those populations affected by war."[15]

On the international level, these understandings and developments were addressed with historic resolutions 2199 (2015) and 2347 (2017) adopted by the United Nations (UN) Security Council, the first-ever to focus on cultural heritage and recognize the importance of heritage protection for peace and security.[16] Notwithstanding the importance of these steps for the advancement and implementation of international heritage law, I underline that all these international commitments will need to translate into concrete measures on the local level. I argue that the strategic advantage of the BHC initiative lies in how it is going to operate on the ground, especially regarding the potential involvement of the local communities whose heritage is under threat.

It is true that the aforementioned UN Security Council resolutions may herald "the engagement of a cultural component in UN peace-keeping missions."[17] Nonetheless, the mandate of BHC, as it is laid down by the Memorandum's text, mainly regards/concerns technical aspects to cultural heritage protection. Understandably, this may deflate the hopes that have been raised about preventing situations like the destruction of the ancient city of Palmyra—especially considering the very image of blue helmets on which the "slogan" of BHC capitalized. However, as the report on the Implementation of the Strategy for the Reinforcement of UNESCO's Action for the Protection of Culture and the Promotion of Cultural Pluralism in the Event of Armed Conflict (hereafter the "UNESCO Strategy") made explicit, "ensuring the physical protection of ... a heritage site or Museum" is categorically out of the picture.[18] In line with this understanding, the same applies to all deployment mechanisms, including BHC, which would be launched under the auspices of UNESCO. BHC's military experts therefore do not have a mandate to engage in battle to save antiquities—the enumerated functions of BHC stipulated in the Memorandum's text preclude this.

In part, this lack of clarification regarding the exact function of the task force is also due to the vast scope of BHC's mandate. In contrast to the UNESCO Strategy, it does not limit itself only to events of armed conflict; BHC experts may also be deployed—as long as the Italian state accepts the invitation of another UNESCO

[14]Foradori (2017a).

[15]As quoted in Ahmed (2015).

[16]UNESCO (2017).

[17]Foradori (2017b).

[18]UNESCO, Proposal for the Establishment and Maintenance of a Mechanism for the Rapid Intervention and Mobilization of National Experts (Roster "Unite4Heritage"), UNESCO Doc. UNESCO 201 EX/5 Part I (E) of 24 March 2017, Annex II, p. 1.

member state seeking help in situations of natural disaster and other kinds of crises in which experts would be able to provide their *technical* expertise regarding the protection of heritage. Despite not being anywhere close to a "UN peacekeeping force,"[19] as per the media's portrayal, BHC and its specialists' technical expertise are nonetheless critical for protecting heritage. Their roles have grown in importance, I argue, because in addition to the highly qualified experts Italy is providing through the Department of the Italian Carabinieri[20] for the Protection of Cultural Heritage, the Memorandum's text previews that training will be provided not only to national authorities but also to "local actors." If "heritage protection without community involvement and commitment is an invitation to failure,"[21] I argue that BHC constitutes a way for operationalizing an exercise of local community involvement.

3 Communities at the Heart of Heritage Protection: How Could BHC Enhance the Community Dimension of Heritage Preservation?

As prescribed by the text of the Memorandum, one of the functions of BHC consists in "providing technical supervision and training in order to assist national authorities and other local actors in implementing emergency preparedness and response measures for the protection and safeguarding of cultural and natural heritage." The Memorandum does not go on defining who comprises the "local actors" or what constitutes the operational guidelines that might shed some light on the matter. Notwithstanding the foregoing, by examining UNESCO conventions on heritage and culture, it does not require a far stretch of imagination to understand the "local actors" reference as including the communities relevant to the heritage in need of protection. The recognition and the elevation of the role of communities in regard to heritage—presently a matter of rigorous scholarship and formal recognition under international law—[22] was a concept that nonetheless evolved through time to reach its present status.

During the 2007 World Heritage Committee's 31st session, background information was given in an evaluation report assessing that "heritage protection without community involvement and commitment is invitation to failure." This understanding is the culmination of the significant development that the notion of cultural heritage has undergone during the twentieth century. The 1972 UNESCO Convention Concerning the Protection of the World Cultural and Natural Heritage, in line

[19]Florence Daily News (2017).

[20]The Carabinieri Corps have a dual role and ministerial affiliation as police and armed forces. Through its Commander General, they report on the Chief of Defense for military duties, whereas their public order and security duties fall within the Ministry of Internal Affairs.

[21]UNESCO (2007b), p. 2.

[22]Urbinati (2012).

with most national legislation concerned with the protection of cultural artifacts, understood heritage as material heritage. In the Convention, there were only three references to the notion of community, two of which referred to states as the "international community" bearing the obligation to both cooperate (Art. 6) and to participate in bearing the financial costs of world heritage protection (Art. 25). Only Article 5 of the 1972 Convention refers to the community as *heritage's stakeholders*, stating that to "ensure that effective and active measures are taken for the protection, conservation, and presentation of the cultural and natural heritage," states parties "shall endeavour, in so far as possible, and as appropriate for each country to adopt a general policy which aims to give the cultural and natural heritage a function in the life of the community."[23]

However, defining cultural heritage through the lens of materiality implied assuming a static definition of heritage: a material artifact, symbolic as a masterpiece of human creative genius or for the understanding of a certain stage of civilization, historical period, etc. That conversely meant that the process of measuring the value of a certain cultural heritage did not need to include anyone other than public bodies and experts. In so doing, the Convention was following the mainstream approach, which, embodied in the Venice Charter for the Conservation and Restoration of Monuments and Sites (1964), has been the object of significant reinterpretation and critical assessment.

It was the 1994 Nara Document on Authenticity[24] that revolutionized the concept of cultural heritage. This document anticipated crucial themes that UNESCO would bring on board in the decades to come (such as the value of cultural diversity) and contained four references to the notion of cultural communities. Specifically, in Article 8 of the document, it is stated:

> Responsibility for cultural heritage and the management of it belongs, in the first place, to the cultural community that has generated it, and subsequently to that which cares for it. However, in addition to these responsibilities, adherence to the international charters and conventions developed for conservation of cultural heritage also obliges consideration of the principles and responsibilities flowing from them. Balancing their own requirements with those of other cultural communities is, for each community, highly desirable, provided achieving this balance does not undermine their fundamental cultural values.

Cultural communities are, following the reasoning of the Nara Document, those having generated the (still materially defined) heritage and those caring for it at the same time.[25] The notion of heritage, and conversely the role of communities, has known its greatest evolution through the 2003 UNESCO Convention on intangible cultural heritage (hereafter "the Convention"), the first international legal document that defines heritage as encompassing the requisite of materiality and makes it explicit that communities are part of heritage as a living and intergenerational dynamic between people, matter, and values. The growing role of communities in the understanding of what heritage is about and how it should be managed is evident from the definition that the Convention adopts for intangible cultural heritage:

[23]UNESCO (2007a).

[24]UNESCO (1994).

[25]ICOMOS (2014).

> the practices, representations, expressions, knowledge, skills – as well as the instruments, objects, artefacts and cultural spaces associated therewith – that communities, groups and, in some cases, individuals recognize as part of their cultural heritage. This intangible cultural heritage, transmitted from generation to generation, is constantly recreated by communities and groups in response to their environment, their interaction with nature and their history, and provides them with a sense of identity and continuity, thus promoting respect for cultural diversity and human creativity. For the purposes of this Convention, consideration will be given solely to such intangible cultural heritage as is compatible with existing international human rights instruments, as well as with the requirements of mutual respect among communities, groups and individuals, and of sustainable development (Art. 2.1).[26]

Per this understanding, communities perform major tasks: production, transmission, recognition, and recreation. Who composes the community entitled to recognize heritage, and how is such recognition expected to take place? This is a question still awaiting an answer, as World Heritage Sites are meant to facilitate the exchange of international best practices to be applied by states to the entire sector of heritage management. As underlined by Urbinati, the ICH Committee does offer the possibility of communities, groups, and individuals to attend its meetings (2012). However, such participation is "solely on ad hoc basis and only with a consultative status."[27] Some space for communities' participation is provided by the Operational Guidelines (2011) to the Convention, which state that "only the States Parties to the Convention may submit nominations. They have an obligation to ensure the widest possible participation of the communities in elaborating the safeguarding measures. They must also obtain their free, prior and informed consent." In 2009, the Subsidiary Body of the Convention provided some important clarifications regarding communities' participation in the candidacy process. It stated that, first, states parties have to "[...] demonstrate the participation of [the] community [concerned] in the elaboration of the nomination and the safeguarding measures" and, second, that "[...] it [...] [is] crucial for the community to be involved not only in devising and implementing measures for safeguarding of its heritage, but also in taking key decisions."

Arguably, the operational guidelines are legally binding for the states parties to the Convention under Article 31(3)(b) of the Vienna Convention on the Law of Treaties; moreover, in contrast to human rights treaties, "the UNESCO Conventions do not have [...] independent monitoring bodies."[28] Ostensibly, the promotion of communities' involvement is prominent in all recent UNESCO conventions regarding culture,[29] yet states parties to the care not willing to relinquish control in regard to how they will be implemented and who will assess if they were correctly implemented. Practically, it all depends on the willingness of a particular state to implement and, especially, how it will choose to do so. It is in this particular context that I argue that the BHC initiative has great potential for contributing to the

[26]UNESCO (2012), p. 211.

[27]Urbinati (2012), p. 211.

[28]Donders (2015).

[29]Especially the 2003 Convention on Intangible Cultural Heritage and the 2005 Convention on the Promotion of the Diversity of Cultural Expressions.

involvement and participation of relevant communities in heritage protection and conservation. Training local communities in emergency preparedness measures for protecting their heritage has the advantage of assisting the states in reacting quickly to situations in crisis. Local communities in this respect would be like trained personnel who are always "on duty" due to their proximity to the area. The minimization of costs is also a benefit; in crisis situations where human lives are at stake, the prioritization of protecting heritage may not be either high in the list or rendered active in the first phase of the crisis situation—crucial in preventing damage from occurring. A crucial example could be the community volunteers of the Italian National Civil Service and its central role for placing mobile cultural properties into safe havens before buildings and churches damaged by natural disasters collapsed.[30] This example is a crucial one since, according to the Memorandum, BHC will also respond to UNESCO member states' requests for assistance in protecting their heritage also in natural disaster situations. It is especially in these kinds of scenarios—in which the "enemy" to heritage is not a destructive iconoclasm but the natural elements—that having trained local communities really makes the difference between success and failure in preventing damages to cultural and natural heritage.

Most importantly, the BHC would provide an international setting in which local communities' involvement in regard to their participation and training in protecting (their) heritage would be tested and best practices could be shared. BHC's deployment, per Memorandum stipulations, is undertaken only after a bilateral agreement between the parties involved has taken place. Instead of trying to convince states parties and the international community of the theoretical soundness of involving local communities in heritage protection, I argue that seeing is believing. BHC can provide the kind of small-scale paradigms and case studies—through multiple examples of successful bilateral cooperation—that demonstrate that there are many value-creating opportunities in involving local communities in protecting cultural heritage. Many a state perceives the involvement of local communities as a potential encroachment of its presently sole authority in decision making. As Donders (2015) pointed out regarding UNESCO conventions, "States prefer to keep the supervision of the treaty in their own hands, including the drafting and adoption of operational guidelines." This need not to be the case in the field of heritage protection. Often, the feelings of entitlement and ownership of local communities toward local cultural heritage, which states fear as potentially possible motivators for secession movements within their territories, could in fact be utilized by states to ensure the continuity of their cultural heritage.[31]

[30]Servizio Civile Nazionale (2014).

[31]Historic England (2015).

4 Conclusion

While "innocent folklore"[32] or heritage sites and museums are the kind of culture that, in theory, a state may easily vouch to protect, things get more complicated when it comes to involving the local communities in protecting their heritage as valid stakeholders. A way to untangle this knot, I argue, may have unwittingly presented itself through the Italian BHC initiative. Concluded by UNESCO and Italy, BHC is how the Italian task force in the framework of UNESCO's Global Coalition Unite4Heritage came to be widely known. It was this response to "the deliberate targeting of cultural heritage in an attempt to destroy the legitimacy of the other to exist as such, exemplifying the most violent forms of fanatic violence today"[33] that brought to the forefront the importance of heritage in relation to the local communities.

It was only recently that the protection of culture and heritage escaped the accusations of falling within the realm of concerns of connoisseurs and artistic minorities, at the expense of real people.[34] ISIS militants' destructive hate toward cultural heritage in Iraq and Syria easily fortified the view that these two types of destruction (of people and of heritage) more often than not go hand in hand. It was then that the "big guns" got called in to rectify the situation on the ground—namely, the destruction of heritage in monumental proportions worldwide. The UN Security Council adopted two historic resolutions acknowledging the relationship between heritage protection and peace and security. UNESCO launched a global coalition, adopted a resolution, and developed a strategy and a work-in-progress action plan in order to, inter alia, create a roster of experts and find mechanisms through which they could be quickly deployed on the ground so as to provide their expertise pre-, during, and postconflict in protecting heritage. And while in name, Blue Helmets for Culture—Italy's response to that quest—seemed to consist of a cultural peacekeeping unit of sorts, the reality is that this remains fiction presently. In spite of this, I argue that BHC's real potential lies in involving local communities in (their) heritage's protection and actively training them on how to go about it. This is very much in line with the BHC mandate as stipulated in the text of the Memorandum.

The real novelty in this approach is that this will provide the ground for operationalizing local communities' involvement in protecting heritage on a small scale. The BHC, per Memorandum stipulations, is largely a bilateral agreement. By having a set of case studies showcasing the positive outcomes of local community participation in protecting heritage, many a state's trepidations regarding its monopoly on decision making will be acquiesced.

[32]Stamatopoulou (2004).

[33]UNESCO (2014), p. 3.

[34]Ahmed (2015).

References

Ahmed B (2015) Time is of the essence to save ancient Syrian sites, and the UN is considering 'Monuments Men'. https://thinkprogress.org/time-is-of-the-essence-to-save-ancient-syrian-sites-and-the-un-is-considering-monuments-men-825b78b91b5c/. Accessed 6 Oct 2017

Araoz G (2011) Preserving heritage places under a new paradigm. J Cult Herit Manag Sustain Dev 1:55–60

Assi E (2012) World heritage sites, human rights and cultural heritage in Palestine. Int J Herit Stud 18:316–323

Brattli T (2009) Managing the archaeological world cultural heritage: consensus or rhetoric? Nor Archaeol Rev 42:24–39

De Cesari C (2010) Creative heritage: Palestinian heritage NGOs and defiant arts of government. Am Anthropol 112:625–637

Donders YM (2015) Cultural rights and the UNESCO convention: more than meets the eye? In: De Beukelaer C, Pyykkönen M, Singh JP (eds) Globalization, culture and development-the UNESCO convention on cultural diversity. Springer/Palgrave/MacMillian, pp 117–131

Ekern S, Logan W, Sauge B, Sinding-Larsen A (2012) Human rights and world heritage: preserving our common dignity through rights-based approaches to site management. Int J Herit Stud 18 (3):213–225

Florence Daily News (2017) UN culture's blue helmets were born in florence. Florence Daily News, 3 April. http://www.florencedailynews.com/2017/04/03/un-culture-blue-helmets-born/. Accessed 11 Nov 2017

Foradori P (2017a) Protecting cultural heritage during armed conflict: the Italian contribution to 'cultural peacekeeping'. Mod Italy 22(1):1–17

Foradori P (2017b) Blue helmets for culture. https://sustainablesecurity.org/2017/05/16/blue-helmets-for-culture/. Accessed 6 Oct 2017

Foradori P, Rosa P (2017) Expanding the peacekeeping agenda. The protection of cultural heritage in war-torn societies. Glob Chang Peace Secur 29(2):145–160

Historic England (2015) Pillars of the community. The transfer of local authority heritage assets. https://content.historicengland.org.uk/images-books/publications/pillars-of-the-community/heag032-pillars-of-community.pdf/. Accessed 7 Oct 2017

International Council on Monuments and Sites (2014) The Nara document on authenticity. International Charter for the Conservation and Restoration of Monuments and Sites. The Venice Charter. 1–6 November 1994, 20th anniversary/25 May 1964, 50th anniversary. ICOMOS, Firenze

Italian Government (2016) Memorandum of understanding between the government of the Italian Republic and UNESCO on the Italian National 'Task Force in the Framework of UNESCO's Global Coalition Unite4Heritage'. http://www.beniculturali.it/mibac/export/MiBAC/sito-MiBAC/Contenuti/MibacUnif/Comunicati/visualizza_asset.html_65556661.html. Accessed 7 Oct 2017

Leask A, Fyall A (2006) Managing world heritage sites. Elsevier Ltd, Amsterdam

Logan W (2012) Cultural diversity, cultural heritage and human rights: towards heritage management as human rights-based cultural practice. Int J Herit Stud 18:231–244

Scham S, Yahya A (2003) Heritage and reconciliation. J Soc Archaeol 3:399–416

Shepherd R (2006) UNESCO and the politics of cultural heritage in Tibet. J Contemp Asia 36:243–257

Sinding-Larsen A (2012) Lhasa community, world heritage and human rights. Int J Herit Stud 18:297–306

Stamatopoulou E (2004) Why cultural rights now? https://www.carnegiecouncil.org/studio/multimedia/20040923b-why-cultural-rights-now#2. Accessed 5 Oct 2017

Ufficio per il Ufficio Civile Nazionale (2014) FAQ. http://www.serviziocivile.gov.it/main/area-enti-hp/progetti-di-scn/faq/. Accessed 7 Oct 2017

UNESCO (1994) Convention concerning the protection of the world cultural and natural heritage, information note: Nara document on authenticity. Experts meeting, WHC-94-/CONF.003/INF.008, Phuket, Thailand. http://whc.unesco.org/archive/nara94.htm
UNESCO (2007a) Basic texts of the 1972 World Heritage Convention. UNESCO World Heritage Centre, Paris
UNESCO (2007b) Convention concerning the protection of the world cultural and natural heritage, item 13: evaluation of the results of the implementation of the committees strategic objectives. WHC-07-31.COM/13B. Paris, France, p 2. http://whc.unesco.org/archive/2007/whc07-31com-13be.pdf
UNESCO (2012) Basic texts of the 2003 convention for the safeguarding of the intangible cultural heritage. UNESCO, Paris
UNESCO (2014) Heritage and cultural diversity at risk in Iraq and Syria. http://unesdoc.unesco.org/images/0023/002325/232562e.pdf. Accessed 6 Oct 2017
UNESCO (2017) UN Security Council adopts historic resolution for the protection of heritage. http://whc.unesco.org/en/news/1648. Accessed 6 Oct 2017
Urbinati S (2012) The role for communities, groups and individuals under the convention for the safeguarding of the intangible cultural heritage. Cultural heritage, cultural rights, cultural diversity: new developments in international law, pp 201–221
Winter T (2011) The political economies of heritage. In: Anheier HK, Isar YR (eds) Cultures and globalization: heritage, memory and identity. Sage, London, pp 70–138

Managing Cultural Sustainability: Safe Haven, Cultural Property, and Sustainability in Best Practice

Martin Gerner

Abstract Armed conflicts, and crises of manifold origins and different in extent are urgently challenging the international community how to cope with what is considered the cultural essence of humankind. Precisely, in view of increasing global threats, how can cultural property be protected effectively? If required protective measures of source states are subject to fail, very often evacuation is the last resort in case of emergency. In order to keep retrieved cultural property preliminarily safe, so-called safe haven can be established and provided in accordance with international law. Respective options of how this is embodied in theory and practice will be scrutinized further. Having carefully examined legal considerations and taken into account respective comments shared by renowned experts,

- safe haven should be established individually at a bilateral basis and promoted globally,
- culture-bound secret safe haven should be envisaged in order to foster cultural sustainability,
- civil heritage protection should be enhanced, and
- military collaboration in the field of protecting cultural property should be considered and extended if applicable.

1 Introduction

Culture is considered to be the underlying dimension of sustainability. Cultural property or heritage may be interpreted as its essence. Hence, the cultural dimension of sustainability is often omitted, even though it is crucial to be comprehensively considered, at least since the United Nations Decade of Education for Sustainable

M. Gerner (✉)
Institut für Auslandsbeziehungen (ifa), Research Programme Culture and Foreign Policy, Stuttgart, Germany
e-mail: martin.gerner@tu-dresden.de

© Springer International Publishing AG, part of Springer Nature 2018

E. Lagrange et al. (eds.), *Cultural Heritage and International Law*,
https://doi.org/10.1007/978-3-319-78789-3_9

Development from 2005 to 2014.[1] Expressly since then, culture is regarded the source of sustainable behavior, originating from different cultural behaviors and industries. In this respect, safe havens are shining examples of how to apply the multidimensional concept of sustainability to cultural property and heritage.

Considerable paperwork has already been spent on various aspects of both sustainability and the protection of cultural property. Without any doubt, there are meaningful scientific contributions made by prominent scholars highlighting the importance of international conventions and legal frameworks in order to prevent cultural heritage from being damaged, looted, or destroyed. However, the gap between theory and practice is sometimes considerable. Explicitly addressing Sustainable Development Goals (SDGs) 9.1 and 11.4 on developing quality, reliable, sustainable, and resilient infrastructure, including regional and transborder infrastructure, and strengthening efforts to protect and safeguard the world's cultural and natural heritage, respectively,[2] this contribution aims at bridging this discrepancy by primarily focusing on the practical aspects of cultural sustainability and clearly favoring a hands-on and best-practice approach.

Increasing global threats to objects of cultural value caused by armed conflicts and crises of manifold provenance and scale lead to the prevalent question of how this cultural essence of utmost importance and significance for the entire mankind may be safeguarded effectively.

In order to preserve cultural property during times of conflict and war, states parties commit themselves through international conventions on a contractual basis. However, all efforts under international law are bound to fail if obligations are violated, warped, or not assumed at all. In these cases, cultural property and heritage are particularly fragile and vulnerable.

In the event of failed protective mechanisms contained by the source state, emergency evacuation regularly remains the solution of last resort in order to rescue cultural heritage within national borders or beyond. To this end, refuges, so-called *safe havens*, ought to be established and provided according to international law for their safekeeping. Based upon international legal standards, adequate requirements are to be taken into account in order to grant asylum to cultural property.

Since 2015, Switzerland has been at the cutting edge in terms of conceptualizing safe havens on a global scale, not only by adapting and updating its domestic legislation, but also by already providing refuges physically. With its fully-fledged revision of national legislation toward protecting cultural property in armed conflict, the Swiss state meets those aforementioned requirements in order to gradually render possible a unique safe-haven option for endangered cultural property threatened by war and conflicts. This provision is based upon agreements between contracting parties. Subsequently, the question arises whether and how this concept of safe havens should or might be applied in comparable situations. In this regard, France,

[1]Gerner (2013), pp. 157, 196.

[2]United Nations General Assembly, Transforming our world: the 2030 Agenda for Sustainable Development, 25 September 2015, UN Doc. A/RES/70/1, para. 59.

the United States of America, and Italy in the meantime have taken substantial attempts into a similar direction, too.[3]

2 Cultural Property in Trouble Spots

Cultural property is occasionally referred to as the "cultural essence"[4] since the fact of its mere existence unfolds its utmost significance for the entire mankind. It largely reflects an identity-shaping focal point of cross-cultural, communicative, and collective memory. Cultural property, both tangible and intangible, ought to be considered the traditional substance of our human existence. Due to that fact, there is need for shared responsibility of generations to come in order to preserve and safeguard those treasures of humankind. Of course, those patterns of responsible behaviors involve cross-border approaches since threats are often transnational in a globalized world.

In light of recent events in view of trouble spots around the globe, international efforts in cultural property protection are pivotal. It is deeply distressing to observe how the so-called and self-appointed Islamic State of Iraq and the Levant (IS/ISIL/Da'ish) plunders and destroys both modern settlements and ancient cultural heritage in Iraq and in Syria without any restraint.[5] Boko Haram terrorizes the northern part of Nigeria, and terrorist militant movements purposefully and visibly razed UNESCO world heritage sites in Mali to the ground in 2012.[6] In 2011, the world famous Egyptian Museum of Cairo was looted in the revolutionary aftermaths of the Arab Spring.[7] The 2003 Iraq war enabled an unprecedented raid through the National Library and Museum of Baghdad; huge amounts of national treasures had been stolen or pillaged in inconceivable dimension of self-acquisition.[8] Besides, there are crises of different origins in global dimension, too, that threaten cultural property irretrievably. Natural disasters like drought and desertification, severe weather and inundations, earthquakes, and tsunamis or volcanic eruptions, caused or favored by climate change, are of increasingly critical priority with respect to the

[3]This paper is based on an elaborated study entitled 'Safe Haven in Deutschland?—Handlungsoptionen für Bergungsorte bedrohter Kulturgüter' published within the scope of the Culture and Foreign Policy research programme of the Institut für Auslandsbeziehungen (ifa) with support of the Deutsches Archäologisches Institut (DAI) and financed through the Federal Foreign Office; Gerner (2017).

[4]Bundesamt für Bevölkerungsschutz (2004b), p. 10; Hipp (2000), p. 5.

[5]Schuler (2015), pp. 24, 26; World Heritage Committee (2015), p. 2; Hollande (2016b); Howard et al. (2015).

[6]Deutsches Archäologisches Institut (2014b), p. 11; Schuler (2015), p. 25; Spreckelsen (2015); Dutertre (2015); see also Hall, in this volume, sub 2, with regard to the Al Mahdi judgment of the ICC.

[7]De Caro (2015) and Hollande (2016a).

[8]Hilgert and Drost (2016) and Irmscher (2007).

preservation of cultural heritage in danger.[9] Impacts are equally drastic since resulting damage is usually regarded irreversible; all too often, total damage amounts to "cultural cleansing."[10]

Learning from the legal, humanitarian, and cultural failures of the twentieth century, the international community has been committing itself to the protection of cultural property in the event of armed conflict since at least the 1954 Hague Convention for the Protection of Cultural Property in the Event of Armed Conflict[11] (referred to as Hague Convention). That is considered a milestone of cultural property protection as integral part of international humanitarian law; for the first time, a legally binding means had been provided for that movable and immovable property that is of fundamental cultural value for mankind.[12] The Second Protocol to the Hague Convention of 1954 for the Protection of Cultural Property in the Event of Armed Conflict of March 1999 updates and renders more precise specific provisions of enhanced protection of cultural property in the event of severe or intentional violation throughout armed conflicts.

Those cases cover illegal acquisition, military abuse, malicious damage, or arbitrary demolition. These characteristics can currently be observed to a large extent.[13] This implicates that increasing rates of regional and ethnic conflicts involving militant movements and terrorist splinter groups come along with a loss of state authority that leads to enormous challenges with respect to safeguarding cultural property. In many cases, international obligations of protecting cultural property are violated without effective sanction mechanisms provided by the international community.[14]

Irrespective of implications taken into considerations by international scholars toward those violators, who are neither legally nor ethical-morally bound,[15] the question arises how to effectively deal with the cultural property itself in the event of such attacks. This is even more important given the rather reluctantly executed mandate of the International Criminal Court (ICC)—the only documented case being so far *Ahmad Al Faqi Al Mahdi* (ICC-CPI-20150926-PR1154).[16] What to do, Standing by and keeping watching, or acting courageously? No doubt, international conventions without respective supporting mechanisms of implementation and enforcement amount to *paper tigers* in the *de facto* sense.

---

[9]Schorlemer and Maus (2014).

[10]Schuler (2015), p. 24; Costa (2015).

[11]Convention of 14 May 1954, UNTS 249, p. 215.

[12]Lenzerini (2015); De Caro (2015); comprehensively Schorlemer (2017).

[13]Dutertre (2015) and Hilgert (2015).

[14]Neumann (2013), p. 89.

[15]Schmidt-Radefeldt (2007), pp. 407–408; Büchel and Hostettler (2002), p. 10; Schuler (2015), p. 26; Lenzerini (2015); Dutertre (2015).

[16]International Criminal Court (27.09.2016); Hilgert and Drost (2016); Hofmann (2015); Open Society Justice Initiative (2016a, b); Lenzerini (2015); see also Hall, in this volume, sub 2.

In comparably dramatic situations of supposed helplessness like these, a safe-haven concept might provide guidance in the most practical way. It enables a refuge option accommodating needs of threatened cultural property from abroad in order to be temporarily kept safe. In other words, that is to provide *asylum* to cultural property through combining intermediate store with long-term repository qualities. In that particular context, this provision automatically touches upon sentiments of reliance and credibility and of presumed restitution after all. Since the beginning of 2015, the Swiss model has been considered the first-mover blueprint achieving to provide a so far unique safe-haven option for respective states and corresponding cultural property in danger. This had been made possible by completely revising the legal basis of the federal law on protecting cultural property in the event of armed conflict, including several national provisions in legal, logistic, and financial perspective.

Based on related expertise, there are promising considerations to be made by carefully scrutinizing political-cultural aspects and legal implications of safe-haven provisions in respective domestic legislation. In this context, it is interesting to observe whether corresponding provisions already prevail *de lege lata* or whether they might be implemented alternatively *de lege ferenda* in the realm of protecting cultural property. In this regard, the 2008 *Guidelines for the Establishment and Conduct of Safe Havens for Cultural Material* der *International Law Association (ILA)* hold an important stake in this process. In terms of a continuing research agenda, it might be of common interest how these guidelines do influence national legislation effectively, although without any legally binding effect. The resulting scope of actions needs to be taken into account in a legal, organizational, logistic, and financial perspective. Best practices like the Swiss model ought to be shared accordingly; they might be inspiring and reasonable. An additional challenge is to openly question whether protecting cultural property in the *de facto* sense would not be more effectively serving the purpose of developing informal to clandestine channels to the end of providing discrete solutions in emergency situations. Such *secret safe havens* would prevent from public pressure; invaluable expert knowledge on the significance of cultural property would remain in safe hands; related business models of dealers and pot diggers would be blocked, and attractiveness subject to decline.

3 Theory and Practice of Protecting Cultural Property

3.1 Definitions

Cultural property comprises masterpieces created or investigated by men and is of fundamental importance to the cultural history. It represents the traceable component of cultural memory and heritage of human existence and skills.[17] Cultural property can be tangible—material—or intangible—immaterial—in nature.[18] Traditionally, legal provisions of cultural property protection make reference to the material dimension expressing the substantial and tangible character of both cultural and natural heritage.[19] Protective status for cultural property might be obtained on local, regional, national, and international levels. The most known institute of protection is the cultural heritage of mankind.[20] Awarded cultural property—movable or immovable—needs to be described,[21] registered (inventory), listed, and marked according to international legislation.[22] There is no common ground for a universally valid definition of cultural property[23]; however, there is a provisional approach of defining cultural property as physical objects, movable or immovable, single pieces or collections and ensembles that are created, modified, or shaped by men reflecting its cultural development, and which display a historic, artistic, scientific, architectural, archaeological, or different cultural value of diverse dimensions.[24] In Germany, cultural property is legally defined in a more focused way as any movable object or collection of artistic, historic, or archaeological importance or affiliated to another domain of cultural heritage, notably of paleontological, ethnographic, numismatic, or scientific significance.[25]

Trouble spots, either conflict or crises regions, can tremendously pressurize cultural property abruptly. Conflict-related threats—armed conflicts, civil war, secession, failed states, economic crises, etc.—lead to two different types of hazards. In the first place, there is direct military aggression through applying force of arms (armed conflict). In the second place, cultural property is increasingly threatened by more diffuse, terrorist activities, whose scaring attacks and shell fires approvingly accept or cause damage in a purposeful or collateral way.

Crises-related threats comprise different sources of natural or environmental catastrophes originating from natural or anthropogenic (man-made) sources.[26] Similar to the conflict terminology, respective threats can be divided into urgent and

[17] Article 1 of the 1954 Hague Convention; Gornig (2007); Rietschel (2009).

[18] Schorlemer (1992), Gornig (2007), Stachowiak (2009) and Schorlemer (2015).

[19] Schorlemer (1992), pp. 51–54; Fechner (1996), pp. 17–35; Hipp (2000), p. 67; Gornig (2007), pp. 24; Rietschel (2009), pp. 8–11; Bundesamt für Bevölkerungsschutz und Katastrophenhilfe (2012), p. 8; Engelhardt (2013), pp. 10–11.

[20] United Nations Organization for Education, Science and Culture (1972) Convention concerning the Protection of the World Cultural and Natural Heritage.

[21] Gornig (2007), p. 18; El-Bitar (2007), pp. 34–36.

[22] Schorlemer (1992), p. 308; Gornig (2007), pp. 22–24; Deutsche UNESCO-Kommission et al. (2009); Bundesamt für Bevölkerungsschutz und Katastrophenhilfe (2012), p. 8.

[23] Schorlemer (1992), p. 82; Bernsdorff and Kleine-Tebbe (1996), p. 11; Gornig (2007), p. 17; Engelhardt (2013), p. 8.

[24] Odendahl (2005), p. 671.

[25] § 2 para. 1 no. 10 Kulturgutschutzgesetz (BGBl. 2016 I S. 1914).

[26] Schorlemer (1992), p. 122; Schorlemer and Maus (2014); Beauftragte der Bundesregierung für Kultur und Medien and Bundesministerium des Inneren (2015), pp. 8–9; Schorlemer (2015), p. 523.

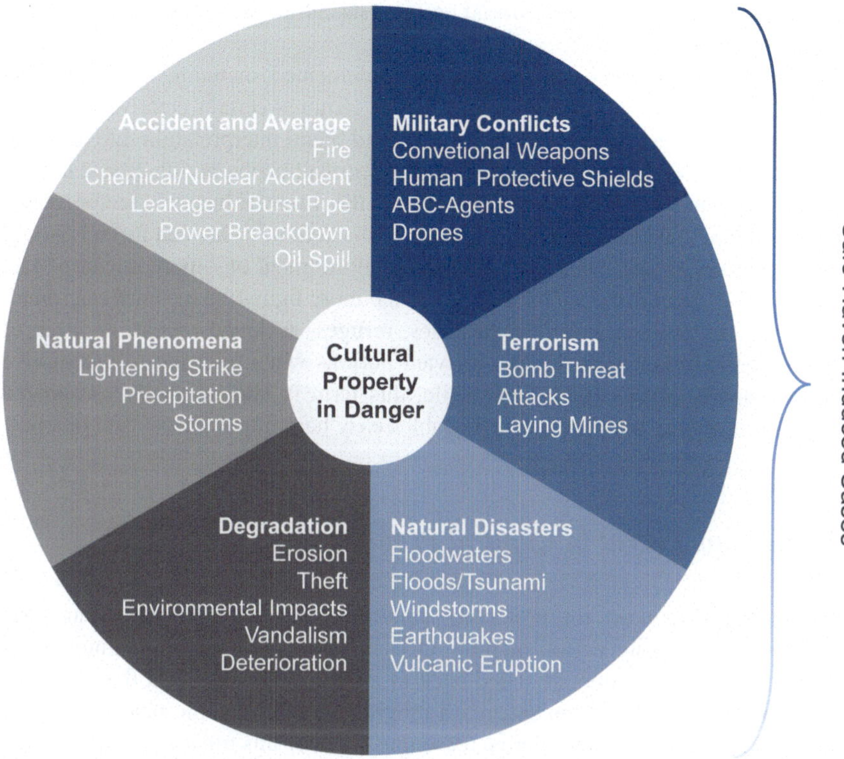

Fig. 1 Potential threats to cultural property and safe-haven-induced cases [Based on Friedrich (2007), p. 41; ICOM Deutschland e. V. (2014), pp. 25–68.]

latent ones. Due to its characteristics, immovable cultural property is more affected than movable one. From an epistemological point of view, there is hardly any distinction to be made which source different threats originate from. However, there is need to distinguish which means of control or prevention of cultural property devastation is eventually applied.[27] Preventive mechanisms and effective provisions are particularly required for urgent conflicts and crises; they essentially differ from cultural property protection in times of peace or nonconflict periods primarily aiming at mere preservation of substance (see Fig. 1).[28]

Cultural property protection concentrates on protective measures of states or the international community. It is considered to be the preemptive, reparative, and repressive safeguarding instance preventing cultural property from being violated

[27]Engelhardt (2013), p. 259.

[28]Fechner (1991); Schorlemer (1992); Schädler-Saub (2008); Konferenz nationaler Kultureinrichtungen (2012); Engelhardt (2013), p. 259; Lenzerini (2015).

in its substance, its sovereign-territorial ties, and its culture-unbound deterioration in cultural significance.[29]

Different means have been discussed and implemented, including the preemptive approach of safe havens. Defining safe havens requires certain creative potential. This already becomes obvious when trying to find literal interpretation into different linguistic contexts. On the one hand, there is the romanticizing notion of safe havens in movies; on the other hand, the term is used in the financial business sector related to resisting crises and ensuring certain levels of discretion.[30] One can further choose between notions of safe havens in a maritime environment or—more matter-of-fact but still wet—retention basin.[31] One reaches the more figurative meanings aground; safe havens are defined as safe sanctuaries, refuges, secluded retreat, or place of refuge. Those are the preferred and relevant notions when referring to preemptive cultural property protection.[32] Meanwhile, this term is internationally recognized and coined *terminus technicus*, which enables easy handling in theory and practice.

3.2 Lessons Learnt in Cultural Property Law

Understanding the need for protecting culturally significant property has been developing over a long period of time. Occasionally, the tentative beginnings of cultural property protection are dated back to antiquity already.[33] At that time, the primary objective had been to safeguard religious sites and cultic places.[34] In this respect, there is cause for speculative reasoning whether this truly used to be serious commitment or just wishful thinking when taking a look back in history. However, it is proven that looting, (armed) robbery, and devastation of cultural property has always been regarded an appropriate means of warfare that has enjoyed some kind of unscrupulous fascination in tactic-strategic terms.[35]

In the aftermaths, until the late medieval period, the first approaches of lawfully claiming cultural treasures in times of war or conflict evolved. Considered originally as rights for spoils of war, these claims have gradually been transformed and integrated into protective provisions for cultural property within the law of armed conflict. This particularly happened in the course of growing, better equipped, and technically advanced military disputes.[36]

---

[29] Odendahl (2005), p. 671; Kila (2008), pp. 219 et seq.

[30] Adler and Cerutti (2015).

[31] Engelhardt (2013), p. 201.

[32] Bundesamt für Bevölkerungsschutz und Katastrophenhilfe (2012), pp. 8, 10; Schweizerische Bundeskanzlei (2013), p. 8988.

[33] Engelhardt (2013), p. 203.

[34] Ibid.

[35] Gornig (2007), p. 32; Schmidt-Radefeldt (2007), pp. 401–402; Engelhardt (2013), pp. 203–204.

[36] Odendahl (2005), p. 107; Gornig (2007), p. 32; Engelhardt (2013), p. 203.

Toward the end of the Middle Ages, considerations gained momentum on how to protect cultural property in nonconflict situations. Beyond battlefields, issues of protective preservation got successively important. Resulting provisions of protecting cultural property legally in times of peace can be acknowledged as remarkable milestone in civilization.[37] A noteworthy international dimension of systematically protecting cultural property had only been achieved in the twentieth century. As a matter of fact, this was primarily due to the historical breaks and political turning points, drastically and dynamically driven by the consequences of World War II, in particular.[38]

Due to massive violations of rights to artistic and cultural property, in the postwar period, their protection has consequently been interpreted as a matter of the international community. In addition, the ranks of those who advocate cultural property protection to form an integral part of international humanitarian law were constantly swelling.[39] With the invasion of Iraq by troops of the United States of America in 2003, this paradigmatic shift became manifest at the latest.[40] In recent times, intentional destruction of cultural property bluntly amounts to war crimes without any diplomatic restraint.[41] In doing so, the reference framework for potential threats to cultural property is escalated. At first, clearly definable and classifiable criteria were required for tangible and movable cultural property threatened by armed conflict. Meanwhile, there is a corresponding tendency of claiming the provisions and related actions materialized in international law *expressis verbis* for crises-related situations of hazard. These apply to natural catastrophes, above all, and include affected intangible and immovable cultural property, too.[42] Though differing in origins, this extended notion can be evaluated similarly in terms of protection requirements, whose central points of regulating efforts in both martial law and peace law are the protection from looting and destruction, the protection from illegal displacement, and the protection of substance of cultural property.[43]

In order to accommodate these claims effectively in situations of conflicts and crises, novel concepts and more powerful means of international cultural heritage protection must be implemented. Conceptually sophisticated, however hardly ever applied in practice, is the aforementioned safe-haven approach[44]: by the beginning of the twenty-first century, there was hardly any sign of safekeeping cultural

[37]Odendahl (2005), pp. 107 et seq.; Engelhardt (2013), pp. 203–204.

[38]Hipp (2000), p. 47; Jakubowski (2015).

[39]Schorlemer (1992), p. 560; Büchel and Hostettler (2002), pp. 9–10; Turner and Fiedler (2003); Engelhardt (2013), p. 204.

[40]Hensel (2005); Irmscher (2007); Schmidt-Radefeldt (2007), p. 401.

[41]Büchel and Hostettler (2002), p. 10; Article 8 (2) (b) (ix) and (e) (iv) United Nations (2002) Rome Statute of the International Criminal Court: A/CONF.183/9; International Committee of the Red Cross (2008), pp. 7–8; Oehlen (2015); Lenzerini (2015); Dutertre (2015); Hilgert (2015).

[42]Schorlemer and Maus (2014).

[43]Engelhardt (2013), p. 204; International Committee of the Red Cross (2004), pp. 4 et seq.

[44]Engelhardt (2013), pp. 208–212.

property until its moment of restitution to authorized beneficiaries. Hence, such provision expressing the notion of refuge or safe haven did not exist.[45]

However, the 1954 Hague Convention[46] and the Regulations for the Execution of the 1954 Hague Convention[47] already refer to the concept of refuge even though no mention is made of refuge in third states. The Guidelines for the Implementation of the 1999 Second Protocol to the Hague Convention of 1954 for the Protection of Cultural Property in the Event of Armed Conflict list the "[e]stablishment of refuges for movable cultural property under enhanced protection for its temporary protection" as a possible emergency measure.[48] Those emergency measures are taken during an armed conflict in principle. They shall ensure the adequate protection of the cultural property concerned and prevent its deterioration, destruction, or looting.[49]

Furthermore, it is solely provided for property of outstanding cultural importance for humankind. According to the Guidelines for the Implementation of the 1999 Second Protocol, such significance may be deduced, inter alia, from the following criteria:

- it is an exceptional cultural property bearing testimony to one or more periods of the development of humankind at the national, regional or global level;
- it represents a masterpiece of human creativity;
- it bears an exceptional testimony to a cultural tradition or to a civilization which is living or which has disappeared (...)[50]

The safe-haven principle is intuitive: endangered or threatened cultural property is transferred from the *source state*[51] to a *safe haven state*[52] agreed upon beforehand; it is stored and kept safe on-site in order to return it to the source state once the threatening situation is over.[53]

[45]Engelhardt (2013), p. 204.

[46]Article 1 lit. b, Article 8 paras. 1 and 2, Article 17 para. 1 lit c.

[47]UNTS 249, 270, Articles 11, 13, 19.

[48]United Nations Organization for Education, Science and Culture (2012) Guidelines for the Implementation of the 1999 Second Protocol to the Hague Convention of 1954 for the Protection of Cultural Property in the Event of Armed Conflict: CLT-09/CONF/219/3 REV. 4, p. 50; see also van Woudenberg (2008), pp. 172 et seq.

[49]Guidelines (n 46), para. 118; see also Kila (2008), pp. 214 et seq; Liston (1993), p. 12; Buhse (1959), p. 77.

[50]Guidelines (n 46), para. 33; see also Odendahl (2009); Engelhardt (2013), p. 209; Schorlemer (2015), p. 520.

[51]International Law Association (2008a), p. 2; Engelhardt (2013), p. 259.

[52]Engelhardt (2013), p. 209.

[53]Ibid.

3.3 Limits of Cultural Property Protection

Globally protecting cultural property encompasses two fundamental, sometimes conflicting dicta that need to be carefully evaluated from case to case. On the one hand, there is the principle of locally rooted (*ratione loci*) and issue-related (*ratione materiae*) responsibility when dealing with cultural property.[54] Thus, to export or displace cultural property abroad ought to be considered a subordinated solution.[55] On the other hand, at international scale, the protection of cultural property is perceived as a concern shared by the international community.[56] Hence, there is a shift of cultural property protection from a territorial to a humanitarian notion.[57] The fiduciary principle is prominently listed in importance.[58] It reflects upon the evolution of international law from the *common heritage of mankind* approach[59] to the *erga omnes* approach with equally balanced state-party accountability.[60] Both principles lead to nationally or internationally differentiated responsibilities with obligations or guidelines for implementation.[61]

The background for those considerations is the increase of multiple types of threatening situations that challenge or render impossible the culture-bound *in situ* responsibility (*ratione loci*).[62] By thinking from the cultural property itself, this theoretical reasoning—which is thoroughly justified for classifying and scientifically evaluating—is suddenly losing importance. This applies to both the frequently cited reference to obligations imposed on conflicting parties by international law[63] and devastations condemned as *war crimes*[64]: "Recalling that intentional attacks against buildings dedicated to religion, education, art, science or charitable purposes and historic monuments may amount to war crimes."[65] Such a theory-driven point of view is usually too shortsighted in practice since it hardly provides any constructive option for action with yielding results.

Without questioning, discrediting, or disregarding existing legal provisions, it seems as if the political-pragmatic dimension takes the leading role in situations of conflict and crises, which would be the analog to evacuation scenarios in emergency

---

[54]Schorlemer (1992), p. 563.

[55]Article 4 lit. ii European Convention on the Protection of the Archaeological Heritage of 6 May 1969, European Treaty Series No. 66.

[56]Engelhardt (2013), p. 216; Schorlemer (1992), p. 566.

[57]Fiedler (1996); Dutli (2002), pp. 23–24; Zimmermann (2010).

[58]Schorlemer (1992), pp. 564 et seq.; Engelhardt (2013), pp. 213 et seq.

[59]Engelhardt (2013), p. 216; Schorlemer (1992), p. 566.

[60]Schorlemer (1992), pp. 565, 576; Francioni and Lenzerini (2003).

[61]No. 1 Stiftung Preußischer Kulturbesitz (2003).

[62]Brockschmidt (2015); Cunliffe et al. (2016), p. 18; Hollande (2016b).

[63]Deutscher Reichstag (1907) Abkommen betreffend die Gesetze und Gebräuche des Landkriegs: Haager Landkriegsordnung, (RGBl 1907 Jg. 1910 S. 107–151).

[64]Dutertre (2015).

[65]No. 6 World Heritage Committee (2015).

relief. This is because even though states parties are obliged to provide comprehensive protective measures vis-à-vis cultural property, it helps little if conventions are not honored accordingly by combatants both due to the prevailing lack of respect for different cultures and—just as in the antiquity—through devastating cultural sites intended to hit and injure the opponent or enemy the most.[66]

To sum up, much more significance of cultural property protection is lying in the factual, the real-tangible action. This attempt requires—not exclusively in the context of safe havens—a pronounced focus on specifically designed propositions that go along with operational concepts to safeguard and rescue cultural property in danger. Therefore, calling upon to outlaw acts of extermination as war crimes is honorable; still, de facto enforcement is deemed to thwart since the Hague Convention already provides well-established handling toward the destruction of cultural property—however, those international agreements are consequently ignored and violated by IS/ISIL/Da'ish...[67]

The frequently raised request of UN-mandated rapid deployment forces of so-called *Blue Helmets* dedicated to culture—"the possibility of introducing a specific dimension of heritage protection in the mandates of peacekeeping missions"[68]—appears to be creative, charming, and certainly desirable; however, such commitment in practice seems barely imaginable at the moment.[69] Little seems to have changed the record that to date, at international scale there is not a quarter as adequate, comprehensive protection system. At present, intentional devastation of places of discovery cannot even be impeded if the sovereign state on which the site is located behaves indifferently toward deterioration or is incapable of doing so because of own weakness.[70]

3.4 Guidelines for the Establishment and Conduct of Safe Havens for Cultural Material

Both the 2008 *Guidelines for the Establishment and Conduct of Safe Havens for Cultural Material of the International Law Association*[71] and the implementation guidelines of the Second Protocol to the 1954 Hague Convention[72] explicitly refer to

---

[66]Gornig (2007), p. 62.

[67]Schuler (2015), p. 26; Kila (2008), pp. 214 et seq.

[68]No. 23 World Heritage Committee (2015), p. 3.

[69]Schuler (2015), p. 26; No. 23 World Heritage Committee (2015), p. 3; Lenzerini (2015); Scammell (2015); see also D'amico, in this volume.

[70]Fechner (1991), p. 124; van Beuren (2008).

[71]International Law Association (2008a).

[72]N 48; No. 22 World Heritage Committee (2015), p. 3.

the refuge concept included in the Hague Convention.[73] In contrast to the latter, causalities or circumstances of violating cultural property are of subordinate or minor relevance with respect to the ILA guidelines. That is because the driving factor is no longer causality or reason for a threatening situation but rather its potential impact on cultural property in need of protection. Hence, those ILA guidelines do not comply with the distinction between means of protecting cultural property in peace times and those linked to law of armed conflict.[74]

The sole precondition is hazardous circumstances threatening cultural property at the place where it is commonly kept in terms of damage, loss, or devastation.[75] In this respect, these guidelines accommodate the rather universal approach of emphasizing the potential vulnerability of cultural material instead of focusing on the commonly used, differentiating taxonomy of hazardous sources. Without any doubt, this amounts to a completely novel quality of dealing with local value and handling of cultural property:

> Safe havens are facilities created in order to care for cultural material that has been endangered by armed conflict, natural disasters, illegal excavation, or other insecurity and has therefore been removed for safekeeping and preservation from the territory of the source state to the territory of another state or to a place of safety in the source state.[76]

Constituting elements of safe havens are mentioned *in extenso*; they can be considered as quasi-legal definition:

- Facilities created for the purpose of taking care of cultural material;
- Which is threatened by armed conflict, natural disasters, illicit excavations, or other imponderables;
- And thus for reasons of safekeeping and preservation being displaced;
- From the sovereign territory of a source state either at the sovereign territory of another state or at a protected place (refuge) within the source state itself.

These guidelines are primarily intended to convince state authorities of safekeeping and safeguarding cultural material. This includes restitution within or beyond the source state as the consequence of preliminary displacement, too.[77] This ambitious endeavor can only succeed through participation, active reference, and commitment on a voluntary basis since neither resolutions taken by the International Law Association nor guidelines are legally binding on international or domestic level. In fact, they are to be recognized as invitation and encouragement directed to the international community of states to establish safe-haven facilities for the protection

[73]Chapter I Article 1 b), No. 1 and 2, and Article 17 No. 1 lit. c); Chapter II Articles 11, 13 and 19 United Nations Organization for Education, Science and Culture (1954) Final Act of the Intergovernmental Conference on the Protection of Cultural Property in the Event of Armed Conflict, The Hague, 1954.

[74]Engelhardt (2010), p. 61; Engelhardt (2013), p. 259; Goes (2015), p. 50.

[75]Engelhardt (2010), p. 60.

[76]International Law Association (2008a), p. 3.

[77]International Law Association (2008a, b) and Siehr and Bauer (2009).

Table 1 Obligations by safe-haven state[a]

Criteria	Scope
Fiduciary diligence	• Taking responsibility for safekeeping and preserving entrusted cultural material, even in the particular case of unknown provenance • Considering means of highest protective standards in order to prevent cultural material from hazards or devastation
Applicable law	• Applying the legislation of the state in which the cultural material is kept (safe-haven state) • Respecting legislation and legal traditions of the source state
Export regulations	• Refusing acceptance of such cultural material being displaced under violation of official export regulations • Making exceptions in cases of secured state of knowledge for approving conditions for displacement that justify issuing certificates of export
Inventory	• Inducing to provide an inventory of commissioned deposited cultural material • Guaranteeing public access to information of the inventory
Exposition	• Providing opportunities to exhibit deposited cultural material if not opposed to regulations and traditions of the source state • Ensuring that cultural artifacts are properly indicated as salvage
Lending	• Lending salvage only with explicit consent of the source state through its legal entities
Revenues	• Devoting resources from revenues of exhibiting or lending for preserving and safekeeping of cultural material exclusively
Integrity	• Avoiding any measures undertaken by the safe-haven state suited to promote illicit trade with cultural material or to expose it to alternative risks
Restitution	• Enabling the restitution of cultural material (cultural property) as soon as the legitimate owner or legal entity disposes of (integrity) • Examining pondering conditions for preserving and safekeeping cultural material of the source state through its legal entities
Place of jurisdiction	• Taking note of the competent jurisdiction, notably when concurrent • Recognizing decisions made by competent courts of the safe-haven state in view of how to deal with salvage

[a]The synopsis is based on 4. Obligations of Safe Havens lit. a) to lit. j) International Law Association (2008a), pp. 3–4; Engelhardt (2010), pp. 58 et seq; Engelhardt (2013), pp. 230 et seq

of cultural property. For that matter, they ought to be considered as legally nonbinding instructions for domestic implementation of safe havens.[78]

That is the underlying assumption when formulating single provisions and *obligatory* specifications of implementing safe havens for threatened cultural property (see Tables 1 and 2).

Duties by far outweigh rights; both are mainly on the part of the safe-haven state which is due to the fiduciary nature—safekeeping third-party cultural property based on trust—of safe havens. The basic declaratory principles can be described as follows[79]: the duty to take care (*due diligence*) is pivotal, particularly complying

[78]Engelhardt (2013), p. 255.

[79]Engelhardt (2013), pp. 259 et seq.

Table 2 Obligations by source state[a]

Criteria	Scope
Information	• Providing all information required in order to enable the safe-haven state to meet its obligations
Financing	• Remunerating the safe-haven state for expenses of preserving, safekeeping, and returning back cultural material in reasonable extent
Guarantees	• Ensuring preserving and safekeeping cultural material requested for restitution after accomplished taking back

[a]The synopsis is based on 5. Obligations of Source States or Entities lit. a) to lit. c) International Law Association (2008a), pp. 3–4; Engelhardt (2010), pp. 60 et seq.; Engelhardt (2013), pp. 230 et seq

with cultural customs and traditions in the course of safekeeping.[80] Furthermore, it is required to prevent recovered and safeguarded cultural property from illicit trade.[81] That is why salvage of unknown provenance must be rejected for safe-haven cases. In order to avoid camouflaged market areas and to prevent cultural property from both robbery, and the crime of receiving and disposing, acquiring illicitly exported cultural property must be prohibited; export regulations must strictly be abided by.[82] The same applies to providing inventories and comprehensive obligations with respect to information and labeling.[83] Interestingly enough, there are well-defined cases of commercially marketing or officially utilizing of cultural material. At first glance, this might appear unusual but ought to be conceded for the sake of the cultural property only.[84] Managing the complex restitution issue sounds plausible according to the principle of good faith; however, its handling in practice is legally difficult and might require certain restitution guarantees in most of the cases.[85]

In addition to the aforementioned guidelines, there are a number of optional declarations of negotiated agreements. These are by and large based on the safe-haven concept along the lines of the *International Law Association*.[86] In the exhibition context, two designated declarations can be mentioned: the *Berliner Resolution*[87] and the *ICOM Code of Ethics for Museums* with its *Repositories of Last Resort*[88]:

---

[80]Engelhardt (2010), p. 61.

[81]Ibid.

[82]Article 7 lit. a of the UNESCO Convention on the means of prohibiting and preventing the illicit import, export and transfer of ownership of cultural property of 14 November 1970, UNTS 823, p. 231; Engelhardt (2010), p. 63.

[83]Engelhardt (2010), pp. 63–64.

[84]Engelhardt (2010), p. 64.

[85]Schoen (2007); Engelhardt (2010), p. 64; Anton (2010), p. 233.

[86]Engelhardt (2010), pp. 57–58; Engelhardt (2013), p. 255; Gersch (2015), pp. 17–18; Hollande (2016a).

[87]No. 9 Stiftung Preußischer Kulturbesitz (2003).

[88]No. 9 Stiftung Preußischer Kulturbesitz (2003); Engelhardt (2013), pp. 234–235; van Jaarsveldt (2015).

> Repositories of Last Resort: Nothing in this Code of Ethics should prevent a museum from acting as an authorised repository for unprovenanced, illicitly collected or recovered specimens or objects from the territory over which it has lawful responsibility.[89]

Both comprise far-reaching due-diligence provisions, in particular for *unprovenanced* cultural property.[90] Beyond these codes of ethics, the *Guidelines for the Implementation of the 1999 Second Protocol to the Hague Convention of 1954 for the Protection of Cultural Property in the Event of Armed Conflict*[91] do play a rather minor role.

To conclude with, safe havens can be regarded as an indicator of developing means of cultural property protection further.[92] From a more theory-driven approach of promising refuge to the more hands-on approach of safekeeping cultural property *de facto*, the 2008 *Guidelines for the Establishment and Conduct of Safe Havens* of the *International Law Association* do provide an appropriate complementary *soft-law* framework for practical embodiment.[93] They do provide crucial indications and specifications for implementing safe havens as part of a national initiative and therefore pass on to single states in order to act accordingly.[94]

4 Best Practices

In terms of cultural property protection in emergency and disaster cases, Switzerland is more than one step ahead of Germany since it comprises a fully-fledged state-owned contingency plan for cultural property.[95] Such existing provisions and precautionary measures turn Switzerland into the perfect role-model and best-practice country,[96] both of national and international cultural property protection.

Thus, it might be tempting to favor the Swiss cases as shining example and blueprint for universal implementation. However, this euphoria can be misleading because it neglects the comprehensive traditions and experiences made in terms of significance and protective status that cultural property enjoys in Switzerland. Of course, this is mainly due to the historical and geopolitical positioning that is hardly comparable to any equivalent, originally evolved foundation. To take an intuitive example: the term *Heimat*—which lacks literal translation into a couple of

[89] No. 2.11 International Council of Museums (2004), p. 4.

[90] Engelhardt (2013).

[91] N 48.

[92] Engelhardt (2013), pp. 264 et seq.; Engelhardt (2010), pp. 66–68.

[93] European Convention on the Protection of the Archaeological Heritage (n 55); International Law Association (2008a); Siehr and Bauer (2009).

[94] Engelhardt (2010), p. 68.

[95] Deutscher Bundestag (2013) Kulturgüterschutz stärken – Neuausrichtung des Kulturgüterschutzes in Deutschland jetzt beginnen: Drucksache 17/14115, p. 2.

[96] Zeller (2014).

languages—stands for the concept of national identity of proudly dealing with homeland security affairs (*Heimatschutz*) in a very specific, closely related way. What is occasionally stereotyped by strangers touches upon the essential insight that cultural property always has to do with people themselves, their origin, identity, evolution, and dignity as a matter of fact.[97]

4.1 Experiences and Challenges

So far there are no cases officially listed and documented for safe haven. Making use of such an option might become more realistic, though, once UNESCO is informed and being reported to. To that purpose, Switzerland has notified UNESCO Secretary-General of existing safe-haven provisions in accordance with respective guidelines. In this context, the specific role of the international organization needs to be elucidated further. Generally speaking, providing safe havens requires a bilateral agreement on contract basis between Switzerland as safe-haven state and any source state. However, UNESCO stays indirectly involved since such safe havens ought to be established under the auspices of the organization. However, this term is legally undefined, which leads to the assumption that real cases are going to point the way to the future of how the safe-haven triangle consisting of safe-haven state, source state, and UNESCO is going to be drafted accordingly. The Swiss context is particularly characterized by strong independently stipulated terms, whereas the embedding into the framework of international law and its respective organizational reference appears to be of subordinate importance. Such degree of freedom and independence is certainly an epitome for the confederate primacy or preference of contractual autonomy. It first and foremost includes a proactive, pragmatic, and progressive approach of sorting something out, giving something a try, testing procedures, and adapting them, if necessary. Advantages are evident: acting quickly and largely unbound, providing supply-side attitude, case-driven freedom of deciding, trendsetting opinion leadership, and material or nonmaterial reputational profits respectively (see Fig. 2).

A globally mandated solution of safekeeping under the auspices of an international organization (UNESCO) constitutes a demand-driven approach that includes all advantages and challenges that the system of the international community comprises. One of the assets claimed is the protected sovereignty of the source state, which is not necessarily guaranteed through individually agreed-upon contracts. In contrast, international approaches usually require considerable negotiation and ratification procedures, as the case may be with tolerating veto-mechanisms as far as responsibilities of the UN Security Council are concerned.

The decisive factor in favor of a bilateral solution vis-à-vis safe haven is closely related with contract design. One reason for preferring administrative agreements is

[97]Büchel (2015), p. 20.

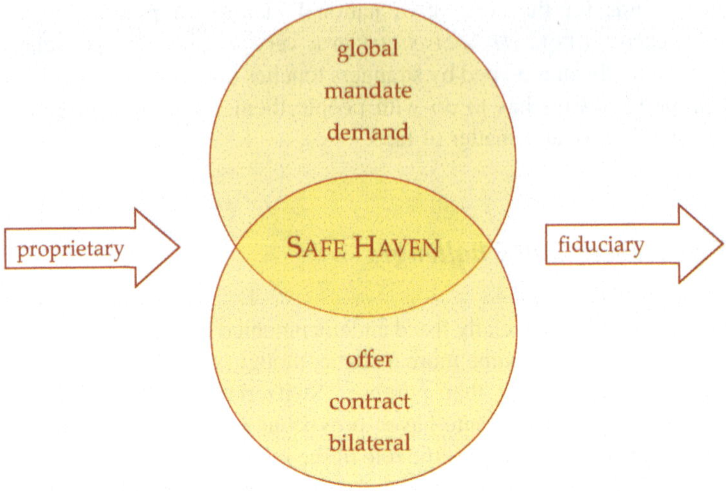

Fig. 2 Types of safe haven

that involving parliaments in international treaty making is highly complex and time-consuming. As to the contents to be regulated on a contractual basis, it is recommended not to incorporate a detailed and exhaustive catalog but to rather prefer a more proposing and exemplary wording instead. This enables and creates decision-making leeway, which is usually not legally prescribed. It needs to be agreed upon at least where and how cultural property is safeguarded,[98] who is to pay the costs for, and which conditions vis-à-vis restitution are required accordingly. Restituting foreign cultural property that is safe kept abroad is even guaranteed without covenant *expressis verbis* through respective German legislation.[99] This avoids legal uncertainty. Likewise, seeking for involving UNESCO *ex ante* for each particular case is widely regarded indispensable. Executive agreements without parliamentary involvement may be preferable for cases of urgent evacuation or emergency. These are the more typical circumstances for salvage; specific queries might be handled more efficiently, discretely, and smoothly. Generally speaking, in this context, the question remains vibrant whether to prefer a more confidential over a more public solution, including parliamentary involvement. The latter option is charming because it shows a high level of transparency, even though remarkable coordination between different responsibilities is requested, in budgetary realms in particular. Executive agreements, in contrast, can be financed through the ordinary budgetary allocations of the respective ministry. Thus, they allow for much more flexibility. Occasionally, already implemented, alternative approaches are so-called *secret safe havens*—clandestine or confidential refuges[100]: such hidden

[98]Engelhardt (2013), p. 210.
[99]Anton (2010), pp. 221–222.
[100]Spreckelsen (2015).

displacements elude publicity, they are covered by consciously spreading fake news (smoke grenades), and they are primarily supported by nonstate funds, foundations, or privately run businesses or individual donors (patronage) of civil society.[101] They by and large elude state controls, which represent advantage and disadvantage at the same time.[102] Therefore, either enormous confidence is to be taken for granted or an outstanding, self-regulating, informal network is essential, after all.[103]

So far, considerations always presumed displacing threatened cultural property abroad. However, this is highly risky; means of mitigating transportation risks represent only one aspect to be dealt with accordingly. In consequence, the question is evident whether respective cultural property should not remain within the source state and being kept safe in place. Hence, it needs to be investigated which means and instruments can appropriately and directly be applied within countries affected.[104] The rationale behind is that cultural property may best and most cost-effectively be safeguarded *in situ*. In that respect, protecting cultural property is primarily incumbent on the nation-state.[105] This *inland* salvage refers to the concept of *internally displaced heritage*. Such regional or culture-bound solutions are already been sought of[106]; they are either carried out or pursued as secret safe haven. Therefore, on the one hand, there are existing provisions based on well-established codes of ethics:

> Participating members agreed upon the basic principle that a certain museum for refuge can be determined for each region or nation state that might serve as legal deposit for those illicitly excavated antiquities which had exclusively been retrieved inside of the respective region or nation state.[107]

Probably the most common and prominent one is the *ICOM Code of Ethics for Museums* with prescribed *Repositories of Last Resort*.[108] Besides, there are more legally binding sectoral provisions driven by the intent to preferably foster inland solutions of cultural property, too.[109]

There is need to further conceptualize and prove in practice to what extent safe havens may both predominantly unfold preventive power and—comparable to evacuation and disaster scenarios—be applied in urgent cases of conflict or crises. For the latter case, one certainly needs to take into consideration overarching subject areas and competencies, in particular vis-à-vis military instruments. It analogously applies to the debatable question whether to realize an all-or-none protection principle for coherent collections, extensive pot excavations, or archival documents in

[101] Auswärtiges Amt (2015) and Hollande (2016a).

[102] Spreckelsen (2015) and Dutertre (2015).

[103] Schuler 2015), p. 25.

[104] Deutsches Archäologisches Institut (2014b), p. 12; Van Ess (2015).

[105] Siehr (2006), p. 42.

[106] De Caro (2015).

[107] No. 9 Stiftung Preußischer Kulturbesitz (2003).

[108] International Council of Museums (2004), p. 4.

[109] European Convention on the Protection of the Archaeological Heritage (n 55).

libraries. This ties to the—even among experts—highly delicate assessment of the *sui generis* quality of movable, intangible cultural property on how it is proposed through respective systems of listings at international level, for instance. Due to the inherent value, quite a few experts decide against listing individual items to be evacuated in the event of conflicts and crises; instead, they are in favor of ensemble objects to be protected. This approach appears to be reasonable considering the complexity of locations with an amount of artifacts and works of art.[110] It must consequently be taken into account that in the event of disaster, salvage is hardly manageable—against the established *modus operandi* in international cultural property law—with hierarchical listings, but needs to be executed under situational and pragmatic considerations. The so-called treasure trove consisting of a central system of deposit with capacity to *blanket coverage* provides a couple of advantages at first glance. However, in federally composed states, the trend is toward decentralized solutions; as a result, prioritized regionalism is particularly regarded innovative and reasonable since this approach actively contributes to spread and thus minimize risks in the event of conflicts and crises accordingly.

4.2 Current Trends

The increasing pressure to *de facto* protection of cultural property in conflicts and crises culminates in an evident momentum: only a couple of years after the first pioneering considerations made by internationally renowned experts,[111] there are remarkable developments taking place both at nation-state level and civil-society initiatives under private law:

- Switzerland: since 2015, safe-haven provision in national legislation, namely Article 12 of the *Bundesgesetz über den Schutz der Kulturgüter bei bewaffneten Konflikten, bei Katastrophen und in Notlagen* (KGSG)[112];
- France: since August 2016, corresponding provisions on *dépôts des biens culturels* prescribed in the *Code du patrimoine* preceded by *Cinquante propositions françaises pour protéger le patrimoine de l'humanité* in November 2015[113];
- USA: since September 2015, providing preliminary deposit jointly with the Association of Art Museum Directors, prescribed in AAMD Protocols for Safe Havens for Works of Cultural Significance from Countries in Crisis[114];
- Italy: since February 2016, Memorandum of Understanding on the Italian National Task Force between the Italian government and UNESCO to agree

[110]Lindner (2015); Beauftragte der Bundesregierung für Kultur und Medien and Bundesministerium des Inneren (2015), p. 51; Gersch (2015), p. 15.

[111]International Law Association (2008a, b) and Siehr and Bauer (2009).

[112]Schweizerische Bundeskanzlei (2014).

[113]Martinez (2015) and Hollande (2016b).

[114]Association of Art Museum Directors (2015), p. 2; Weber (2016).

upon providing "(assistance) in transferring movable cultural heritage property at risk to safe havens."[115]

So far, no request has become officially known to make use of such a safe-haven proposal. Cases for safe havens would have been desirable in the past. To take an example, the devastating earthquake in Haiti in 2011 dramatically raised the question of how to deal with all the historical records threatened through statically shaky library buildings.[116] The most obvious option would have been to make use of a safe haven in the nearby Santo Domingo. This attempt failed, however, due to lack of trust caused by bureaucracy, crime, and corruption faced with for transporting these materials. Instead, a mobile safe haven consisting of containers had been envisaged and finally established nearby the airport of the Haitian Port-au-Prince.[117] Artifacts from museums had been kept safe at place and restored in a secured institute for salvage and restoration. The second reported case took place in Mosul in 2014: the Iraqi territory was then controlled by IS/ISIL/Da'ish. Safe havens had been examined, considered favorably, but eventually refused due to high transportation risks and the general risk assessment for attendant specialists. Baghdad had been considered equally instable; therefore, a more discrete solution like in the Timbuktu case of the manuscripts had been envisaged, by carrying cultural property to Lebanon.[118] The most effective and unexpectedly effective means had been civil resistance toward IS/ISIL/Da'ish; this matter of fact finally affected protecting regional cultural treasures in a favorable way.

5 Conclusions

Summing up, different recommendations of managing cultural sustainability with respect to safe havens and cultural property can be proposed.

Safe Haven Should Be Established Individually at a Bilateral Basis and Promoted Globally In the first place, an option of temporarily safekeeping cultural property is to be legally envisaged through provisions enabling bilateral, single-case solutions. These should be in accordance with international law and be preferred to mandated ones. To recall the Swiss model, contract-based, single cases are tailored according to respective needs and give leeway to flexible contractual autonomy. The objective is to decide independently upon fiduciary safekeeping of cultural property (safe haven) in order to provide source states concerned an individual option. Therefore, a pragmatic, iterative and supply-oriented procedural approach needs to be favored that enables flexibly tailored options. As to external

[115]Government of the Italian Republic and UNESCO (2016); Renzi (2015), p. 6.

[116]International Council on Archives (2011); Kurin (2011), p. 44.

[117]Kurin (2011) and Association L'Arche du Bouclier Bleu (2015).

[118]Spreckelsen (2015).

representation, a framework agreement between safe haven and source states is desirable, which facilitates rapid and nonbureaucratic support both in long-term preventive perspective and in urgent cases of emergency. It is recommended to refer to the 2008 *Guidelines for the Establishment and Conduct of Safe Havens for Cultural Material* of the *International Law Association*[119] accordingly. This particularly involves specific conditions of restitution or return. As to internal representation, national responsibilities of safe havens must be sorted out and coordinated among federal entities. An alternative can be a leading coordination body mandated for this specific purpose, properly financed, and at best comprising of related expertise and resources, such as adequate real estate for safe havens.[120] Emergencies can be handled on the lines of national disaster management by adding complementary means of end-of-pipe evacuation scenarios that encompass rescue and salvage of cultural property from abroad.[121]

In second place, international recommendations for action need to be taken up and applied accordingly; embedding provisions for establishing safe havens in international law need to be developed further. Concurrently, with approaches on an individual-contractual basis, commitment is appreciated to help a universal safe-haven concept into existence in terms of being implemented both legally and in practice. To this end, respective legal requirements (Hague Convention and respective 1954 and 1999 Protocols) need to be consequently enhanced and strengthened through implementation. This includes national programs that are close to the notion of international efforts for protection[122] and that are directed toward tapping the full legal potential of provisional safekeeping.[123] Obviously, such protective thinking increasingly gains in importance. Following Switzerland, France recently provided the legal framework for fiduciary safekeeping of threatened cultural property, possibly in respective deposits or satellite premises of the Louvre museum.[124] Concerning a potential safe-haven strategy or safe-haven convention, UNESCO's role is of pivotal importance, which is based upon the organization's paramount global expertise in cultural property protection; related guidelines and calls for action ought to be intensely discussed, in particular in view of most sensitive issues of restitution and affected sovereignty.[125] Those issues might cause certain reluctance or even refusal among source states relating to safe-haven options. A feasible way to preclude such trends might represent a United Nations mandated mission on call order being financed through funds:

[119]International Law Association (2008a).

[120]Bundesamt für Bevölkerungsschutz und Katastrophenhilfe (2012).

[121]Dohrmann (2007), pp. 40–41; Workshop Kulturgutschutz (2007); Schuler (2015).

[122]Auswärtiges Amt (2015).

[123]Müller-Karpe (2010), p. 13; Müller-Karpe (2012), p. 202.

[124]Hollande (2016a, b); Articles L111-7, L111-11, R142-28 und R451-29 Legifrance (2016) Code du patrimoine; Bietry-Rivierre (2015).

[125]Nos. 22, 23 UNESCO (2015), p. 5.

> The commanders (...) assigned specifically to support UN humanitarian activities, and other deployed forces performing humanitarian support missions at the request of the UN, will avoid compromising the neutrality and impartiality of these agencies, their implementing and operational partners and other humanitarian actors responding to a (...) disaster. Likewise, all supporting activities will be conducted in a manner that respects the dignity, culture, religions, and laws of the affected population.[126]

In the event of conflict or crises, the full infrastructure of such a safekeeping mission would be available *ad hoc* to all signatory states[127]; respective approaches can be observed.[128] Thus, considering the analogous developments both in international cultural property protection law and international humanitarian law, the basis for multiple modes of mandated action appears to be defined already[129]:

> Last Resort: No other option is available to facilitate access and the timely delivery of humanitarian supplies, protection, and personnel required to meet critical humanitarian needs. All other options to reduce risks and ensure timely aid delivery are exhaustively explored and determined not viable.[130]

Culture-Bound Secret Safe Haven Should Be Envisaged in Order to Foster Cultural Sustainability Supporting efforts and concerted action for salvage and provisional safekeeping is preferably organized within the country of origin, i.e. the source state. Before taking into consideration safe-haven states for respective services, all strategic options of safeguarding threatened cultural property within the territory of the source state or its culture-bound region should be exhausted first and foremost. Such culture-bound solutions, roughly one safe haven per subcontinent, on the one hand may create synergies in terms of respective financing efforts and on the other hand may contribute to a lowered intercultural threshold of acceptance, which fully redounds to the advantage of cultural property and finally prevents from objections of cultural postcolonialism. In addition, discreet solutions are reasonable; too much publicity on the significance of threatened property inflicted by either state entities or international organizations (UNESCO) may be opposed to the purpose and can even harm smoothly functioning salvage operations. Hence, more quietly realized procedures driven by networks of credible secret carriers might eventually lead to successful mission accomplishment. Particularly promising are those cooperations with institutions and individuals who are already accredited by a reliable code of ethics.[131] In practice, such type of secret safe haven does not require military support in regions of armed conflict but primarily relies on comprehensively taking informal action of trustful teamwork among well-informed stakeholders of civil

[126]No. 95 Office for the Coordination of Humanitarian Affairs (2007).

[127]United Nations Security Council (2014) Resolution (2014) 2164: S/RES/2164 (2014); Lenzerini (2015); Dutertre (2015).

[128]UNESCO (2016a, b, c, d).

[129]United Nations Security Council (2014) Resolution (2014) 2164: S/RES/2164 (2014).

[130]Inter-Agency Standing Committee (2013), p. 3; Lenzerini (2015).

[131]International Council of Museums (2004); Henker and Westphal (2015); Schuler (2015); Gersch (2015), pp. 27–28; Dutertre (2015).

society and respective institutions; this makes its functioning strikingly unconventional, however tremendously powerful.[132] The essential prerequisites for culture-bound secret safe havens are trust, intergovernmental preparedness for cooperation,[133] and appropriate depositories.[134] Until now, Switzerland in this regard claims this unique option exclusively, officially under the auspices of UNESCO.[135] Irrespective of political commitment, many countries simply lack preparedness in terms of complying with essential prerequisites such as appropriate long-term documentation facilities,[136] the purposeful selection of existing safe havens, or virtual/digital safeguarding.[137] Given protective reasons, the minimal requirement is to safeguard contents with highest priority followed by covering structures. Safe-haven infrastructures must be tested before being officially announced. Besides providing the physical place of safe haven, a fail-safe infrastructure is required in the event of crisis-related breakdowns; it keeps operating when preventive mechanisms fail. To this purpose, contingency plans[138] and training facilities for civil servants and military affiliates must be compiled.[139]

Civil Heritage Protection Should Be Enhanced Embedding cultural property protection into its own national agenda or cultural framework respectively is regarded to be of utmost importance. Both thinking from well-acquainted contexts and sharing the notion of entailed obligations on property might serve as two leading principles before addressing to the full international dimension.[140] Protecting cultural property—including safe havens—fulfills the functioning of modern democracy by means of sociopolitical justification and coherent communicative mediation. Both are opened up through raised awareness and convinced activity orientation, for instance Unite4Heritage—Global Coalition for the Protection of Cultural Heritage.[141] That is why capacity building needs to be enforced. For decades, Switzerland has been leading in the realm of civil cultural property protection. By providing excellent educational and vocational services to professionals and ordinary people, momentum is achieved for decisions to be taken with both external and internal

[132]Spreckelsen (2015).

[133]No. 22 UNESCO (2015), p. 5.

[134]Article 4 European Convention on the Protection of the Archaeological Heritage (n 55).

[135]Schweizerische Depeschenagentur (2013); Schweizerische Bundeskanzlei (2013), p. 8987 (2013-1953, https://www.admin.ch/ch/d/ff/2013/8987.pdf, accessed 11 November 2017); Articles 2 and 12 Schweizerische Bundeskanzlei (2014); Zeller (2014).

[136]Dohrmann (2007).

[137]Deutsches Archäologisches Institut (2014a), pp. 21 ff.

[138]ICOM Deutschland e. V. (2014), pp. 20–24; Beauftragte der Bundesregierung für Kultur und Medien and Bundesministerium des Inneren (2015), pp. 10 et seq.

[139]Lenzerini (2015); No. 149 Bundesministerium der Verteidigung (2016); Bundesministerium der Verteidigung (2015), pp. 9–10; Bundesamt für Bevölkerungsschutz und Katastrophenhilfe (2016).

[140]Bundesministerium des Inneren (2016).

[141]United Nations Organization for Education, Science and Culture (2015); Beauftragte der Bundesregierung für Kultur und Medien and Bundesministerium des Inneren (2015), pp. 19–20.

impacts.[142] A feeling of solidarity and a common identity are decisive in defining the significance of cultural heritage.

Military Collaboration in the Field of Protecting Cultural Property Should Be Considered and Extended if Applicable The military mandate for cultural property protection should be fostered in two respects.[143] In first place, it is about sensitizing military affiliates to the outstanding value of cultural property in times of both peace and war:

> The United Nations force is prohibited from attacking monuments of art, architecture or history, archaeological sites, works of art, places of worship and museums and libraries which constitute the cultural or spiritual heritage of peoples. In its area of operation, the United Nations force shall not use such cultural property or their immediate surroundings for purposes which might expose them to destruction or damage. Theft, pillage, misappropriation and any act of vandalism directed against cultural property is strictly prohibited.[144]

This awareness includes the acquaintance with respective international norms and provisions, as well as a practical notion of locally important cultural property. Relevant training and instruction materials by far exceed the corresponding handouts that represent the ordinary basis for armed forces formation.[145] Austria and Switzerland are particularly leading in the military protection of cultural property; these efforts ought to be considered best practices. In the Austrian case, for instance, there are so-called cultural property protection officers on duty serving both the commander and for liaison purposes between civilian institutions and individuals; each military command disposes of two specifically trained officers for cultural property protection.[146] In the Swiss case, awareness raising vis-à-vis cultural property protection is an integral part of military formation; respective standing orders are conveyed to every affiliate to the Swiss army.[147] In addition, hands-on trainings on domestic and international cultural property protection are compulsory at least at leadership level. In second place it seems crucial to reason on providing synergies for cultural property protection by making use of strategic and logistic value added by the military:

> When there is a common goal and agreed strategy, and all parties accept to work together, cooperation may become possible, and coordination should focus on improving the effectiveness and efficiency of the combined efforts to serve humanitarian objectives. Experience has shown that when major natural, technological or environmental disasters occur in

---

[142]Bundesamt für Bevölkerungsschutz (2004a, 2013).

[143]Büchel and Hostettler (2002), p. 11.

[144]Annan (2008), p. 113; O'Keefe et al. (2016), pp. 32–33.

[145]Bundesministerium der Verteidigung (2016), pp. 490, 558, 901 et seq.; Bundesministerium der Verteidigung (2015), pp. 18–19.

[146]Schipper et al. (2010), pp. 151–156; Österreichische Gesellschaft für Kulturgüterschutz (2006); Bundesministerium für Landesverteidigung und Sport (2009), p. 7; Horn (2010).

[147]Schweizer Armee (2013); Kila (2008), pp. 221 et seq.

non-conflict environments, the use of foreign military and civil defence assets is generally readily accepted as less controversial and can even be essential.[148]

For instance, would it be feasible—compared to the Swiss case—to take advantage of specifically secured or abandoned real estate for potential safe havens? Even though intervention teams mandated by the United Nations, so-called *Blue Helmets*,[149] are barely considered realistic at the moment, however, it remains to be investigated whether support might be provided in terms of salvage and transportation of cultural property,[150] relying on humanitarian corridors, for instance:

> In a situation of active hostilities or an insecure operating environment, the use of armed escorts for humanitarian convoys will only be considered under exceptional circumstances. There are various other approaches to reaching affected persons, including (...) humanitarian corridors (...).[151]

In fact, neither the *Second Protocol to the Hague Convention of 1954 for the Protection of Cultural Property in the Event of Armed Conflict* nor the follow-up implementation guidelines[152] contain usable statements of practical relevance,[153] notwithstanding that the military component should be given consideration in addition to the civilian option:

> In any international humanitarian operation, priority should always be given to the use of civilian assets in responding to needs, but it is also necessary to plan for the possibility that foreign military and civil defence assets may be required.[154]

References

Adler G, Cerutti E (2015) Are foreign banks a 'Safe Haven'? Evidence from past banking crises. WP/15/43. http://www.imf.org/external/pubs/ft/wp/2015/wp1543.pdf. Accessed 30 July 2015

Annan KA (2008) Observance by United Nations Forces of International Humanitarian Law: Secretary-General's Bulletin ST/SGB/1999/13 (6 August 1999). In: United Nations (ed) Guidelines for complex emergencies. United Nations, New York, pp 109–116

Anton M (2010) Internationales Kulturgüterprivat- und Zivilverfahrensrecht. Rechtshandbuch Kulturgüterschutz und Kunstrestitutionsrecht, vol 3. De Gruyter, Berlin

Association L'Arche du Bouclier Bleu (2015) L'Arche du Bouclier Bleu – Haïti. http://www.arche-bouclierbleu.org/. Accessed 25 Aug 2015

[148] Office for the Coordination of Humanitarian Affairs (2012), p. 4.

[149] Schuler (2015), p. 26; Van Ess (2015).

[150] United Nations (2008).

[151] United Nations (2013).

[152] Guidelines for the Implementation of the 1999 Second Protocol to the Hague Convention of 1954 for the Protection of Cultural Property in the Event of Armed Conflict (n 48); No. 22 World Heritage Committee (2015), p. 3.

[153] Micewski and Sladek (2002), pp. 2, 3; Goes (2015), p. 57.

[154] Office for the Coordination of Humanitarian Affairs (2012).

Association of Art Museum Directors (2015) AAMD protocols for safe havens for works of cultural significance from countries in crisis. https://www.aamd.org/sites/default/files/document/Save%20Haven%20Protocols%2010%201%2015%20%282%29.pdf. Accessed 10 Sept 2016

Auswärtiges Amt (2015) Kulturerhalt in Krisenregionen – Auswärtiges Amt unterstützt Rettung historischer Handschriften aus Mali mit 350.000 Euro. http://www.auswaertiges-amt.de/DE/Infoservice/Presse/Meldungen/2015/150629-Kulturerhalt_Mali.html?nn=352220. Accessed 7 Nov 2017

Beauftragte der Bundesregierung für Kultur und Medien, Bundesministerium des Inneren (2015) Bestandsaufnahme zu Maßnahmen des Bundes zum Schutz von Kulturgut bei Katastrophen: (zum Beschluss des Bundestages "Kulturgüterschutz stärken – Neuausrichtung des Kulturgüterschutzes in Deutschland jetzt beginnen"). http://www.bundesregierung.de/Content/DE/_Anlagen/BKM/bestandaufnahme-kulturgutschutz-in-katastrophenf%C3%A4llen.pdf?__blob=publicationFile&v=1. Accessed 3 July 2015

Bernsdorff N, Kleine-Tebbe A (1996) Kulturgutschutz in Deutschland: Ein Kommentar. Carl Heymann Verlags KG, Köln

Bietry-Rivierre E (2015) Un "droit d'asile" pour les œuvres d'art menacées par Daech. Le Figaro

Brockschmidt R (2015) Wissen ist stärker als Waffen: Digitales Archiv gegen Kunstraub: Wie Archäologen aus Berlin und Syrien Schätze vor dem "Islamischen Staat" retten wollen. Der Tagesspiegel(22417), p 19

Büchel R (2015) Neuerungen als Chance für den Schweizer KGS. In: Bundesamt für Bevölkerungsschutz (ed) Das neue KGS-Gesetz ist in Kraft. 24/2015, Bern, pp 20–27

Büchel R, Hostettler P (2002) Protection of cultural property: reflections from a civilian and a military point of view. In: Micewski ER, Sladek G (eds) Protection of cultural property in the event of armed conflict: a challenge in peace support operations. Austrian Military Printing Press, Austria, pp 9–14

Buhse K-H (1959) Der Schutz von Kulturgut im Krieg: Unter besonderer Berücksichtigung der Konvention zum Schutze des Kulturguts im Falle eines bewaffneten Konfliktes vom 14. Mai 1954. Veröffentlichungen des Instituts für Internationales Recht an der Universität Kiel, vol 40. Hansischer Gildenverlag, Hamburg

Bundesamt für Bevölkerungsschutz (2004a) Bewahren, sichern, respektieren: Kulturgüterschutz in der Schweiz. BBL Verkauf Bundespublikation, Bern

Bundesamt für Bevölkerungsschutz (2004b) Erdbeben und Kulturgüter zur Erdbebenertüchtigung von immobilen und mobilen Kulturgütern von nationaler und internationaler Bedeutung auf dem Gebiet der Schweizerischen Eidgenossenschaft. https://www.bafu.admin.ch/dam/bafu/de/dokumente/naturgefahren/fachinfo-daten/erdbeben_und_kulturgueter-expertenberichtbabskgs.pdf.download.pdf/erdbeben_und_kulturgueter-expertenberichtbabskgs.pdf. Accessed 7 Nov 2017

Bundesamt für Bevölkerungsschutz (2013) Technisches Handbuch für das KGS-Personal. Instructions, vol 1. Bern

Bundesamt für Bevölkerungsschutz und Katastrophenhilfe (2012) Schutz von Kulturgut bei bewaffneten Konflikten. http://www.bbk.bund.de/SharedDocs/Downloads/BBK/DE/Publikationen/Broschueren_Flyer/Kulturgutschutz_7-Auflage.pdf?__blob=publicationFile. Accessed 7 Nov 2017

Bundesamt für Bevölkerungsschutz und Katastrophenhilfe (2016) Akademie für Krisenmanagement, Notfallplanung und Zivilschutz (AKNZ): Kulturgutschutz: Schutz von Kulturgut bei bewaffneten Konflikten. http://www.bbk.bund.de/DE/AufgabenundAusstattung/AKNZ/aknz_node.html. Accessed 6 Sept 2016

Bundesministerium der Verteidigung (2015) Die Rechtsausbildung der Soldatinnen und Soldaten. A-221/2

Bundesministerium der Verteidigung (2016) Humanitäres Völkerrecht in bewaffneten Konflikten. A-2141/1

Bundesministerium des Inneren (2016) Konzeption Zivile Verteidigung (KZV). http://www.bmi.bund.de/SharedDocs/Downloads/DE/Broschueren/2016/konzeption-zivile-verteidigung.pdf?__blob=publicationFile. Accessed 6 Sept 2016

Bundesministerium für Landesverteidigung und Sport (2009) Richtlinie für den militärischen Kulturgüterschutz und zur militärischen Bewahrung von Kulturellem Erbe. https://kulturgueterschutz.files.wordpress.com/2010/06/richtliniemilkgs1.pdf. Accessed 6 Jan 2016

Costa S (2015) Destruction and trafficking of cultural heritage Welcome address. http://www.europarl.europa.eu/ep-live/en/committees/video?event=20150713-1500-COMMITTEE-CULT. Accessed 15 July 2015

Cunliffe E, Muhesen N, Lostal M (2016) The destruction of cultural property in the Syrian conflict: legal implications and obligations. Int J Cult Prop 23(1):1–31

De Caro S (2015) Short- and long-term solutions for the protection of cultural heritage in armed conflicts Part I: destruction of cultural heritage. http://www.europarl.europa.eu/ep-live/en/committees/video?event=20150713-1500-COMMITTEE-CULT. Accessed 15 July 2015

Deutsche UNESCO-Kommission, Luxemburgische UNESCO-Kommission, Österreichische UNESCO-Kommission, Schweizerische UNESCO-Kommission (2009) Welterbe-Manual: Handbuch zur Umsetzung der Welterbekonvention in Deutschland, Luxemburg, Österreich und der Schweiz, 2nd edn. DUK, Bonn

Deutsches Archäologisches Institut (2014a) Archäologie Weltweit 2-2014. Archäologie Weltweit Zweiter Jahrgang(2)

Deutsches Archäologisches Institut (2014b) Review-Prozess: Sonderbeilage AW 4. Archäologie Weltweit 2. Jahrgang(9)

Dohrmann A (2007) Sicherheit und Katastrophenschutz für Museen, Archive und Bibliotheken. Typostudio SchumacherGebler Dresden, Dresden

Dutertre G (2015) War crimes and crimes against humanity and the possible actions of the ICC in relation to cases of destruction of cultural heritage Part I: destruction of cultural heritage. http://www.europarl.europa.eu/ep-live/en/committees/video?event=20150713-1500-COMMITTEE-CULT. Accessed 15 July 2015

Dutli MT (2002) Protection of cultural property in the event of armed conflict: report on the meeting of experts. https://www.icrc.org/en/download/file/1041/cutural-property-report-icrc_002_0805.pdf. Accessed 10 Nov 2017

El-Bitar J (2007) Der deutsche und der französische Kulturgüterschutz nach der Umsetzung der Kulturgüterrückgaberichtlinie: Eine materiellrechtliche und kollisionsrechtliche Untersuchung. Studien zum Vergleichenden und Internationalen Recht/Comparative and International Law Studies, vol 144. Peter Lang, Frankfurt am Main, New York

Engelhardt S (2010) Safe Haven für gefährdete Kulturgüter – Überblick über eine erste Vorlage zur Umsetzung sogenannter "sicherer Häfen" unter besonderer Berücksichtigung von Kulturgütern unbekannter Herkunft. In: Odendahl K (ed) Kulturgüterschutz – Kunstrecht – Kulturrecht: Festschrift für Kurt Siehr zum 75. Geburtstag aus dem Kreise des Doktoranden- und Habilitandenseminars "Kunst und Recht".Nomos; Dike; Facultas.wuv, Baden-Baden, pp 55–82

Engelhardt S (2013) Nachrichtenlose Kulturgüter. Schriften zum Kulturgüterschutz/Cultural property studies. De Gruyter, Berlin

Fechner F (1991) Rechtlicher Schutz archäologischen Kulturguts: Regelungen im innerstaatlichen Recht, im Europa- und Völkerrecht sowie Möglichkeiten zu ihrer Verbesserung. Tübinger Schriften zum internationalen und europäischen Recht, vol 25. Duncker & Humblot, Berlin

Fechner F (1996) Prinzipien des Kulturgüterschutzes: Eine Einführung. In: Fechner F, Oppermann T, Prott LV (eds) Prinzipien des Kulturgüterschutzes: Ansätze im deutschen, europäischen und internationalen Recht. Duncker & Humblot, Berlin, pp 11–46

Fiedler W (1996) Vom territorialen zum humanitären Kulturgüterschutz.: Zur Entwicklung des Kulturgüterschutzes nach kriegerischen Konflikten. In: Fechner F, Oppermann T, Prott LV (eds) Prinzipien des Kulturgüterschutzes: Ansätze im deutschen, europäischen und internationalen Recht. Duncker & Humblot, Berlin, pp 159–174

Francioni F, Lenzerini F (2003) The destruction of the Buddhas of Bamiyan and international law. EJIL 14(4):619–651
Friedrich D (2007) Ausgewählte Aspekte zum Thema Notfallplanung im Kulturgutschutz. In: Dohrmann A (ed) Sicherheit und Katastrophenschutz für Museen, Archive und Bibliotheken. Typostudio SchumacherGebler Dresden, Dresden, pp 40–41
Gerner M (2013) Lead Agency: UNESCO's global leadership and co-ordination role for the United Nations Decade of Education for Sustainable Development. Peter Lang Publishing Group, Frankfurt am Main
Gerner M (2017) Safe Haven in Deutschland?: Handlungsoptionen für Bergungsorte bedrohter Kulturgüter. ifa-Edition Kultur und Außenpolitik, Stuttgart
Gersch C (2015) Kulturgut in Gefahr: Raubgrabungen und illegaler Handel. Tagungsbericht, Stiftung preußischer Kulturbesitz, Berlin
Goes B (2015) La nouvelle Loi fédérale sur la PBC en Suisse. Vision comparée au regard de la situation en Belgique et de l'action du Comité intergouvernemental pour la protection des biens culturels en cas de conflit armé. In: Bundesamt für Bevölkerungsschutz (ed) Das neue KGS-Gesetz ist in Kraft. 24/2015, Bern, pp 47–64
Gornig G-H (2007) Der internationale Kulturgüterschutz. In: Gornig G-H, Horn H-D, Murswiek D (eds) Kulturgüterschutz – internationale und nationale Aspekte. Duncker & Humblot, Berlin, pp 17–63
Government of the Italian Republic, UNESCO (2016) Memorandum of Understanding on the Italian National "Task Force in the framework of UNESCO's Global Coalition Unite4Heritage" (hereafter referred to as the "Italian Task Force") for initiatives in favor of Countries facing emergencies that may affect the protection and safeguarding of culture and the promotion of cultural pluralism. http://www.beniculturali.it/mibac/multimedia/MiBAC/documents/1455616287505_2._Memorandum_of_Understanding___11_II_2016_DRAFT_Finale_UNESCO_versione_Italia.pdf. Accessed 20 Oct 2016
Henker M, Westphal J (eds) (2015) Mitteilungen 2015. ICOM Deutschland 22(37)
Hensel HM (2005) The protection of cultural objects during armed conflicts. In: Hensel HM (ed) The law of armed conflict: constraints on the contemporary use of military force. Ashgate Pub. Co., Aldershot, pp 39–104
Hilgert M (2015) Welterbe in Syrien – IS zerstört bedeutenden Baalschamin-Tempel in Palmyra. http://www.deutschlandfunk.de/kultur-heute-die-sendung-vom-24-august-2015.691.de.html?dram:article_id=329140. Accessed 26 Aug 2015
Hilgert M, Drost M (2016) Kulturzerstörung: Solche Verbrechen zu verfolgen, ist keine Selbstverständlichkeit. http://www.deutschlandfunk.de/kulturzerstoerung-solche-verbrechen-zu-verfolgen-ist-keine.691.de.html?dram:article_id=363784. Accessed 30 Aug 2016
Hipp A (2000) Schutz von Kulturgütern in Deutschland. Schriften zum Kulturgüterschutz Cultural property studies. De Gruyter, Berlin
Hofmann L (2015) The Prosecutor v Ahmad Al Faqi Al Mahdi: the first case to be brought before the ICC concerning alleged war crimes regarding the destruction of historical and religious monuments. http://www.ifhv.de/documents/bofaxe/bofaxe2015/477e.pdf. Accessed 9 May 2016
Hollande F (2016a) Discours à l'occasion de l'événement consacré au patrimoine culturel mondial menacé au Metropolitan Museum, New York
Hollande F (2016b) Discours lors de l'inauguration de l'exposition "L'Histoire commence en Mésopotamie". Lens, Pas-de-Calais
Horn D (2010) Der militärische Kulturgüterschutz und die militärische Bewahrung von Kulturellem Erbe. Truppendienst 316(4)
Howard R, Prohov J, Elliott M (2015) Digging in and trafficking out: how the destruction of cultural heritage funds terrorism: Combating Terrorism Center at West Point. Combating Terrorism Center Sentinel 8(2):14–18
ICOM Deutschland e. V. (2014) Präventive Konservierung: Ein Leitfaden. Beiträge zur Museologie, vol 5. ICOM Deutschland, Berlin

Inter-Agency Standing Committee (2013) IASC non-binding guidelines on the use of armed escorts for humanitarian convoys. https://docs.unocha.org/sites/dms/Documents/Armed%20Escort%20Guidelines%20-%20Final.pdf#page=1&zoom=auto,-158,781. Accessed 28 July 2015

International Committee of the Red Cross (2004) Practical advice for the protection of cultural property in the event of armed conflict. https://www.icrc.org/en/download/file/1040/advice-protection-cultural-property-armed-conflict.pdf. Accessed 20 Jan 2016

International Committee of the Red Cross (2008) War crimes under the Rome Statute of the International Criminal Court and their source in International Humanitarian Law: comparative table. https://www.icrc.org/en/download/file/1420/war-crimes-comparative-table.pdf. Accessed 20 Jan 2016

International Council of Museums (2004) ICOM Code of Ethics for Museums. ICOM Code of Professional Ethics. http://icom.museum/fileadmin/user_upload/pdf/Codes/code_ethics2013_eng.pdf. Accessed 27 June 2015

International Council on Archives (2011) Universal Declaration on Archives: 36th session of the general conference of UNESCO. http://www.ica.org/download.php?id=2406. Accessed 30 July 2015

International Criminal Court (2016) Summary of the Judgment and Sentence in the case of The Prosecutor v. Ahmad Al Faqi Al Mahdi. https://www.icc-cpi.int/itemsDocuments/160926Al-MahdiSummary.pdf. Accessed 3 Nov 2016

International Law Association (2008a) Guidelines for the establishment and conduct of safe havens: Resolution No 2/2008: Cultural Heritage Law. https://ila.vettoreweb.com/Storage/Download.aspx?DbStorageId=1087&StorageFileGuid=7a028bc4-aea5-42ec-8abe-8cea548d9445. Accessed 7 Nov 2017

International Law Association (2008b) Rio de Janeiro Conference (2008): Cultural Heritage Law: Draft Report. https://ila.vettoreweb.com/Storage/Download.aspx?DbStorageId=1086&StorageFileGuid=e3d37be1-36e0-4fc0-8a08-3828a3107a3d. Accessed 10 Nov 2017

Irmscher TH (2007) Kulturgüterschutz im humanitären Völkerrecht. In: Gornig G-H, Horn H-D, Murswiek D (eds) Kulturgüterschutz – internationale und nationale Aspekte. Duncker & Humblot, Berlin, pp 65–92

Jakubowski A (2015) State succession in cultural property. Cultural heritage law and policy series. Oxford University Press

Kila JD (2008) Utilizing military cultural experts in times of war and peace: an introduction: cultural property protection within the military, experiences in theatre, different perceptions of culture and practical problems. In: Meerts P (ed) Culture and international law. Hague Academic Press/T.M.C. Asser Press; Cambridge University Press, Hague, West Nyack, NY, pp 183–230

Konferenz nationaler Kultureinrichtungen (2012) kultur!gut!schützen!: sicherheit und katastrophenschutz für museen, archive und bibliotheken. konferenz nationaler kultureinrichtungen. Mitteldeutscher Verlag, Halle (Saale)

Kurin R (2011) Saving Haiti's heritage: cultural recovery after the earthquake. Smithsonian Institution, Washington

Lenzerini F (2015) The responsibility to protect: can third States and international organisations intervene in case of destruction of cultural heritage? Part I: destruction of cultural heritage. http://www.europarl.europa.eu/ep-live/en/committees/video?event=20150713-1500-COMMITTEE-CULT. Accessed 15 July 2015

Lindner E (2015) Raubkunst: Wettlauf mit der Zeit. Gespräch mit dem Archäologen Michael Müller-Karpe. Die ZEIT online 2015(9)

Liston D (1993) Museum security and protection: a handbook for cultural heritage institutions. ICOM, Routledge

Martinez J-L (2015) Cinquante propositions françaises pour protéger le patrimoine de l'humanité: Rapport au Président de la République sur la protection du patrimoine en situation de conflit armé. http://www.elysee.fr/assets/Uploads/Cinquante-propositions-francaises-pour-proteger-le-patrimoine-de-lhumanite.pdf. Accessed 9 Dec 2015

Micewski ER, Sladek G (2002) Protection of cultural property in the event of armed conflict: a challenge in peace support operations. Austrian Military Printing Press, Austria

Müller-Karpe M (2010) Deutschland als Paradies für zwielichtige Antikenhändler?: Machen sich die deutschen Behörden zu Handlangern von Kriminellen? Zum Umgang mit archäologischem Kulturgut "lückenhafter" Provenienz an einem Beispiel. In: Weschenfelder K, Westphal J (eds) Mitteilungen 2010. Oktoberdruck AG, Berlin, pp 10–13

Müller-Karpe M (2012) Antikenmarkt als Geldwäsche: Der Silberbecher des Königs Ebarat. KUR – Kunst und Recht|Journal für Kunstrecht, Urheberrecht und Kulturpolitik 14(6):195–202

Neumann B (2013) Bericht der Bundesregierung zum Kulturgutschutz in Deutschland: Bericht über die Auswirkungen des Gesetzes zur Ausführung des UNESCO-Übereinkommens vom 14. November 1970 über Maßnahmen zum Verbot und zur Verhütung der rechtswidrigen Einfuhr, Ausfuhr und Übereignung von Kulturgut (Ausführungsgesetz zum Kulturgutübereinkommen) und den Schutz von Kulturgut vor Abwanderung ins Ausland. http://www.bundesregierung.de/Content/DE/_Anlagen/BKM/2013-04-24-bericht-kulturgutschutz.pdf?__blob=publicationFile&v=2. Accessed 30 June 2015

O'Keefe R, Péron C, Musayev T, Ferrari G (2016) Protection of cultural property: military manual. UNESCO, Paris

Odendahl K (2005) Kulturgüterschutz: Entwicklung, Struktur und Dogmatik eines ebenenübergreifenden Normensystems. Jus publicum, vol 140. Mohr Siebeck, Tübingen

Odendahl K (2009) Der Schutz der wertvollsten Kulturgüter der Menschheit: aktuelle völkerrechtliche Entwicklungen. In: Weller M (ed) Kulturgüterschutz – Künstlerschutz: Tagungsband des Zweiten Heidelberger Kunstrechtstags am 5. und 6. September 2008 in Heidelberg, Nomos; Dike; Facultas.wuv, Baden-Baden, Zürich, Wien, pp 23–48

Oehlen M (2015) UNESCO-Konferenz in Bonn: "Die Zerstörungen von Welterbestätten sind Kriegsverbrechen": Interview mit der Vorsitzenden des Welterbekomitees Böhmer über zwingende Maßnahmen zum Schutz der wertvollen Kulturgüter. Kölner Stadtanzeiger 27.06.2015. http://www.auswaertiges-amt.de/nn_582138/sid_2188238AB3C5811605F54D46E72163C5/DE/Infoservice/Presse/Interviews/2015/150627-StM_B_KSA.html?nnm=582154. Accessed 10 Nov 2017

Office for the Coordination of Humanitarian Affairs (2007) Oslo guidelines: guidelines on the use of foreign military and civil defence assets in disaster relief. https://docs.unocha.org/sites/dms/Documents/Oslo%20Guidelines%20ENGLISH%20%28November%202007%29.pdf. Accessed 28 July 2015

Office for the Coordination of Humanitarian Affairs (2012) Last Resort Pamphlet. https://docs.unocha.org/sites/dms/Documents/Last%20Resort%20Pamphlet%20-%20FINAL%20April%202012.pdf. Accessed 28 July 2015

Open Society Justice Initiative (2016a) Ahmad Al Faqi Al Mahdi at the ICC: confirmation of charges. Briefing Paper. https://www.opensocietyfoundations.org/sites/default/files/briefing-almahdi-icc-confirmation-charges%2020160225.pdf. Accessed 30 Aug 2016

Open Society Justice Initiative (2016b) The Trial of Ahmad Al Faqi Al Mahdi at the International Criminal Court. Briefing Paper. https://www.opensocietyfoundations.org/sites/default/files/briefing-almahdi-icc-trial%2020160819_1.pdf. Accessed 30 Aug 2016

Österreichische Gesellschaft für Kulturgüterschutz (2006) Geschichte des Kulturgüterschutzes in Österreich. https://kulturgueterschutz.wordpress.com/kulturguterschutz/geschichte-des-kulturguterschutzes-in-osterreich/. Accessed 20 July 2015

Renzi M (2015) Statement to the 70th United Nations General Assembly by the Prime Minister of Italy the Honorable Matteo Renzi. United Nations General Assembly, New York

Rietschel S (2009) Internationale Vorgaben zum Kulturgüterschutz und ihre Umsetzung in Deutschland: Das KGÜAG-Meilenstein, oder, fauler Kompromiss in der Geschichte des deutschen Kulturgüterschutzes? Schriften zum Kulturgüterschutz Cultural property studies. De Gruyter Recht, Berlin

Scammell R (2015) Create UN force to protect ancient heritage from Isis, says Italy. The Guardian 2015
Schädler-Saub U (2008) Weltkulturerbe Deutschland: Präventive Konservierung und Erhaltungsperspektiven. Internationale Fachtagung des Deutschen Nationalkomitees von ICOMOS, Hildesheim, 23.–25. November 2006. Hefte des Deutschen Nationalkomitees/ ICOMOS, Internationaler Rat für Denkmäler und Schutzgebiete, vol 45. Schnell & Steiner, Regensburg
Schipper F, Schuller F, von Habsburg-Lothringen K, Eichberger H, Frank E, Fürstenhofer N (2010) Cultural property protection in the event of armed conflict – Austrian experiences. In: Rush LW (ed) Archaeology, cultural property, and the military. The Boydell Press, Woodbridge, pp 145–158
Schmidt-Radefeldt R (2007) Internationaler Schutz von Kulturgütern in bewaffneten Konflikten – Eine Einführung. UBWV (11), pp 401–408
Schoen S (2007) Die rechtsverbindliche Rückgabezusage – Das "Freie Geleit" für Kulturgut. In: Koordinierungsstelle für Kulturgutverluste Magdeburg, Beauftragter der Bundesregierung für Kultur und Medien (BKM) (eds) Im Labyrinth des Rechts? – Wege zum Kulturgüterschutz: Konferenz des Beauftragten der Bundesregierung für Kultur und Medien vom 9. bis 10. Oktober 2006 in Bonn. Koordinierungsstelle für Kulturgutverluste, Magdeburg, pp 79–102
Schorlemer Sv (1992) Internationaler Kulturgüterschutz: Ansätze zur Prävention im Frieden sowie im bewaffneten Konflikt. Schriften zum Völkerrecht, vol 102. Duncker & Humblot, Berlin
Schorlemer S (2015) Weltkulturerbe. In: Woyke W, Varwick J (eds) Handwörterbuch Internationale Politik, 13th edn. Budrich, Opladen, pp 518–526
Schorlemer Sv (2017) Kulturgutzerstörung: Die Auslöschung von Kulturerbe in Krisenländern als Herausforderung für die Vereinten Nationen, 1. Auflage. United Nations and Global Change, vol 11. Nomos, Baden-Baden
Schorlemer Sv, Maus S (2014) Climate change as a threat to peace: impacts on cultural heritage and cultural diversity, vol 19. Peter Lang, Frankfurt am Main
Schuler T (2015) Kulturgutschutz in Irak und Syrien. In: Henker M, Westphal J (eds) Mitteilungen 2015. Oktoberdruck AG, Berlin, pp 24–27
Schweizer Armee (2013) Die zehn Grundregeln des Kulturgüterschutzes: Reglement 51.007.05 d
Schweizerische Bundeskanzlei (2013) Botschaft zur Totalrevision des Bundesgesetzes über den Schutz der Kulturgüter bei bewaffneten Konflikten (BBl 2013)
Schweizerische Bundeskanzlei (2014) Bundesgesetz über den Schutz der Kulturgüter bei bewaffneten Konflikten, bei Katastrophen und in Notlagen: KGSG, SR 520.3
Schweizerische Depeschenagentur (2013) Schweiz schafft Voraussetzungen: Ein sicherer Hafen für Kulturgüter. Neue Zürcher Zeitung. https://www.nzz.ch/schweiz/kulturgueterschutz-kulturgueter-save-haven-schweiz-1.18047556. Accessed 10 Nov 2017
Siehr K (2006) Nationaler und übernationaler Rechtsschutz von Kulturgütern. In: AKMBnews 12 (2), pp 35–42. http://archiv.ub.uniheidelberg.de/artdok/657/1/siehr.pdf. Accessed 17 June 2015
Siehr K, Bauer A (2009) Guidelines for the establishment and conduct of safe havens: adopted by the International Law Association at its 73rd conference held in Rio De Janeiro, Brazil, 17–21 August 2008. Int J Cult Prop 16(04):371–378. https://doi.org/10.1017/S0940739109990300
Spreckelsen T (2015) Welterbe in Timbuktu: Afrikas Schatz in Stahlkisten verpackt. FAZ. 01.07.2015, p 11
Stachowiak R (2009) Der Schutz von Kulturgut: Gestern – Heute – Morgen. http://www.kulturgutschutz.eu/downloads/Publikation_Der_Schutz_von_Kulturgut.pdf. Accessed 14 July 2015
Stiftung Preußischer Kulturbesitz (2003) Berliner Resolution 2003: Illegale Archäologie? – Internationale Konferenz über zukünftige Probleme bei unerlaubtem Antikentransfer. https://www.preussischer-kulturbesitz.de/fileadmin/user_upload/documents/mediathek/schwerpunkte/provenienz_eigentum/rp/berliner_resolution_2003_dt.pdf. Accessed 27 June 2015

Turner S, Fiedler W (2003) Bibliographie zum Recht des internationalen Kulturgüterschutzes. Schriften zum Kulturgüterschutz. De Gruyter Recht, Berlin

UNESCO (2015) UNESCO Expert Meeting on the 'Responsibility to Protect' as applied to the protection of cultural heritage in armed conflict: Paris, 26–27 November 2015. Final Report. http://www.unesco.org/new/fileadmin/MULTIMEDIA/HQ/CLT/pdf/R2P-FinalReport-EN.pdf. Accessed 15 Aug 2016

UNESCO (2016a) Action Plan for the Implementation of the Strategy for the Reinforcement of UNESCO's Actions for the Protection of Culture and the Promotion of Cultural Pluralism in the event of armed conflict. CLT/HER/EPR/16/4926. http://en.unesco.org/sites/default/files/consultation_docs-heritage_at_risk_en.pdf. Accessed 9 Mar 2017

UNESCO (2016b) Follow-up to decisions and resolutions adopted by the Executive Board and the General Conference at their previous sessions: Action Plan for the Implementation of the Strategy for the Reinforcement of UNESCO's Actions for the Protection of Culture and the Promotion of Cultural Pluralism in the event of armed conflict. 200 EX/5 Part I Add. Annex I. http://unesdoc.unesco.org/images/0024/002457/245703e.pdf. Accessed 9 Mar 2017

UNESCO (2016c) Follow-up to decisions and resolutions adopted by the Executive Board and the General Conference at their previous sessions: Proposal for the Establishment and Maintenance of a Mechanism for the Rapid Intervention and Mobilization of National Experts (Roster "Unite4Heritage"). 200 EX/5 Part I Add. Annex II. http://unesdoc.unesco.org/images/0024/002457/245703e.pdf. Accessed 9 Mar 2017

UNESCO (2016d) Draft Action Plan for the Implementation of the Strategy for the reinforcement of UNESCO's action for the protection of culture and the promotion of cultural pluralism in the event of armed conflict: results of the Consultation with Member States. http://en.unesco.org/sites/default/files/results_web-heritage_at_risk.pdf. Accessed 9 Mar 2017

United Nations (2008) Guidelines for Complex Emergencies. https://docs.unocha.org/sites/dms/Documents/ENGLISH%20VERSION%20Guidelines%20for%20Complex%20Emergencies.pdf. Accessed 28 July 2015

United Nations (2013) Guidance on the Use of Foreign Military and Civil Defence Assets (MCDA) to Support Humanitarian Operations in the Context of the Current Military Intervention in Mali. https://docs.unocha.org/sites/dms/Documents/130201%20Guidance%20on%20the%20Use%20of%20MCDA%20in%20Mali%20FINAL.pdf. Accessed 28 July 2015

United Nations Organization for Education, Science and Culture (2015) Unite4Heritage: Global Coalition for the Protection of Cultural Heritage. http://www.unite4heritage.org/. Accessed 29 June 2015

van Beuren J (2008) Safe havens: art theft from fragile states. http://www.thebrokeronline.eu/Articles/Safe-havens. Accessed 7 Nov 2017

Van Ess M (2015) IS-Zerstörungen: In militärische Aktionen hinein Kulturgüterschutz verankern. Margarete van Ess im Gespräch mit Mascha Drost. http://www.deutschlandfunk.de/is-zerstoerungen-in-militaerische-aktionen-hinein.691.de.html?dram:article_id=314984. Accessed 20 Dec 2016

Van Jaarsveldt J (2015) Ukraine jumps into fray over Crimea artifacts in Amsterdam. NL Times. https://nltimes.nl/2015/01/21/ukraine-jumps-fray-crimea-artifacts-amsterdam. Accessed 10 Nov 2017

van Woudenberg N (2008) Second Protocol to the 1954 Hague Convention – Dutch Involvement. In: Meerts P (ed) Culture and international law. Hague Academic Press/T.M.C. Asser Press; Cambridge University Press, Hague, West Nyack, NY, pp 167–182

Weber E (2016) U.S. Museums may serve as safe havens to protect ISIS-looted antiquities from destruction. http://itsartlaw.com/2016/02/04/u-s-museums-may-serve-as-safe-havens-to-protect-isis-looted-antiquities-from-destruction/. Accessed 15 Mar 2016

Workshop Kulturgutschutz (2007) Ahrweiler Empfehlungen: Entwicklungsperspektiven für den Kulturgutschutz in Deutschland. http://www.museumspraxis.info/disaster/Ahrweiler.html. Accessed 25 Aug 2015

World Heritage Committee (2015) The Bonn Declaration on World Heritage: 39th session of the World Heritage Committee. http://www.auswaertiges-amt.de/cae/servlet/contentblob/709412/publicationFile/206411/150629-Bonner_Erklaerung-EN.pdf. Accessed 29 June 2015

Zeller R (2014) Musterland des Kulturgüterschutzes: Die Schweiz stellt im Zürcher Knonauer Amt ein Depot für gefährdete ausländische Schätze bereit. Neue Zürcher Zeitung 261, p 7

Zimmermann A (2010) Moderne Konfliktformen: Humanitäres Völkerrecht und privatrechtliche Folgen. Berichte der Deutschen Gesellschaft für Völkerrecht, vol 44. C.F. Müller, Heidelberg

Les défis culturels de la Cour pénale internationale

Jérémy Hall

Abstract Décriée par une minorité d'Etats de la communauté internationale, la Cour pénale internationale est sujette à de nombreuses controverses, à la fois politiques, économiques et juridiques. La notion de 'culture' se retrouve indirectement au cœur de ces controverses. La Cour doit donc faire face à plusieurs défis culturels dans l'exercice de son mandat juridictionnel. De tels défis avaient été anticipés par les rédacteurs du Statut de Rome dès le Préambule. La Cour doit opérer avec les outils prévus par son Statut pour résoudre ces défis particuliers. D'un côté, elle va tenter d'intégrer le métissage des cultures juridiques dans le cadre de son travail. D'un autre côté, la Cour va venir protéger la culture de manière indirecte en poursuivant des crimes internationaux.

1 Introduction

« On ne voit presque rien de juste ou d'injuste, qui ne change de qualité, en changeant de climat. Trois degrés d'élévation du Pôle renversent toute la Jurisprudence. Un méridien décide de la vérité, ou peu d'années de possession. Les lois fondamentales changent. Le Droit a ses époques. Plaisante Justice qu'une rivière ou une montagne borne. Vérité au-deçà des Pyrénées, Erreur au-delà »[1]. Cette pensée de Blaise Pascal montre l'importance du relativisme culturel en matière de justice entre différentes régions du monde. La justice ne possède pas la même valeur, ni n'emporte nécessairement les mêmes conséquences selon les États. Dès lors, la création d'une juridiction internationale sera imprégnée d'une certaine diversité culturelle. Par exemple, la Cour européenne des droits de l'homme a pu

[1]Pascal (1970), pp. 192-193.

J. Hall (✉)
Université de Grenoble, Saint-Martin d'Hères, France

© Springer International Publishing AG, part of Springer Nature 2018

E. Lagrange et al. (eds.), *Cultural Heritage and International Law*,
https://doi.org/10.1007/978-3-319-78789-3_10

accueillir la diversité culturelle européenne grâce au concept de marge nationale d'appréciation.

L'UNESCO, dans la Déclaration de Mexico sur les politiques culturelles, définit la notion de 'culture' « dans son sens le plus large, comme l'ensemble des traits distinctifs spirituels et matériels, intellectuels et affectifs, qui caractérisent une société ou un groupe social » et qui « englobe, outre les arts et les lettres, les modes de vie, les droits fondamentaux de l'être humain, les systèmes de valeurs, les traditions et les croyances »[2]. Ainsi, il existe dans la culture « une vie, un bouillonnement, une sensibilité tournée vers les traditions, le passé, mais aussi une soif d'avenir, un désir de mieux vivre ensemble demain »[3].

La culture peut être divisée en trois catégories principales:

- *« culture as capital »: « accumulation of material heritage of humankinds in its entirety »;*
- *« culture as creativity »: « culture is represented by scientific and artistic creations »;*
- *« 'anthropological' view of culture »: « total of all material and spiritual activities and product of a given social group that distinguishes it from other social groups »* [4].

Ces trois catégories illustrent la complexité inhérente à la définition de la notion de culture et permettent de spécifier le concept d'« héritage culturel », dont aucune définition n'est présente dans les traités internationaux. Le terme « heritage » « *refers to an inheritance received from the past, to be held 'in trust' by the current generation (that may enjoy its value in the present) to be handed down in at least as good as fate as it was received to the next generation* »[5]. A la différence du concept de bien culturel, la notion d'héritage culturel possède l'avantage de prendre en compte le patrimoine culturel à la fois matériel et immatériel[6], permettant d'appréhender l'incommensurable richesse de la diversité culturelle.

La mondialisation actuelle replace le droit au cœur de la diversité des cultures humaines[7]. Elle engendre des interactions complexes entre les cultures que le droit tente d'appréhender afin de les canaliser vers une coexistence en évitant un choc des

[2]UNESCO (26 Juillet-6 août 1982) Déclaration de Mexico sur les politiques culturelles. Conférence mondiale sur les politiques culturelles, Mexico City.

[3]Mestre (2010), p. 13.

[4]Blake (2015), p. 7.

[5]*Idem.*

[6]L'UNESCO définit le patrimoine immatériel comme « les traditions et croyances héritées des ancêtres et transmis à leurs descendants, comme les traditions orales, les arts du spectacle, les pratiques sociales, rituels et évènements festifs, les connaissances et pratiques concernant la nature et l'univers ou les connaissances et le savoir-faire nécessaires à l'artisanat traditionnel »: http://www.unesco.org/culture/ich/fr/qu-est-ce-que-le-patrimoine-culturel-immateriel-00003, Accès le 23 février 2017.

[7]Mestre (2010), p. 14.

cultures. Le souci de coexistence et le risque de choc des cultures animent justement la réflexion autour des interactions entre la culture et la CPI.

A l'aube de ses 15 ans, il est particulièrement reproché à cette juridiction pénale internationale de faire montre de néo-colonialisme par plusieurs États et commentateurs[8]. En effet, c'est actuellement la seule juridiction internationale qui doive faire face à d'importantes réticences politiques et divergences juridiques, comme l'illustrent les tentatives de retrait de l'Afrique du Sud, de la Gambie ou celui du Burundi, effectif depuis le 27 octobre 2017. Cette défiance révèle l'importance de la place qu'occupe la Cour dans les relations internationales. En effet, elle entretient des liens étroits avec les Nations Unies, ainsi qu'avec plus de 125 États, parties ou non au Statut de Rome. Les controverses à l'encontre de la Cour trouvent leur point de départ dans une vision divergente de certaines dispositions légales du Statut de Rome. Toutefois, ces divergences, qui se situent au point de rencontre de plusieurs cultures, ne prennent pas en compte la réalité juridique de la Cour, plongée dans la complexité de la politique internationale.

Le paragraphe 1er du Préambule du Statut de Rome rappelle que « tous les peuples sont unis par des liens étroits et que leurs cultures forment un patrimoine commun »; il précise que « cette mosaïque délicate [peut] être brisée à tout moment ». Il est ainsi clairement établi que l'ensemble des êtres humains forme une seule espèce d'êtres vivants, possédant les mêmes droits et libertés[9]. Les rédacteurs du Statut ont ainsi affirmé le rôle primordial de la Cour dans la lutte contre l'éclatement de cette mosaïque du fait de la commission de crimes internationaux. Ce faisant, une mission large de protection de la culture est dévolue à la Cour.

Il est donc essentiel que la Cour prenne en considération la culture, *lato sensu*, dans ses politiques judiciaires. Au demeurant, le Bureau du Procureur de la Cour pénale internationale (CPI) a affirmé qu'« il accordera une attention particulière aux crimes qui ont été traditionnellement sous-représentés dans les poursuites judiciaires » parmi lesquels sont listées « les attaques contre des biens culturels, religieux, historiques et autres biens protégés »[10]. Cette politique démontre la volonté du Procureur de protéger la culture en poursuivant les auteurs d'attaques criminelles contre des biens culturels. Elle s'est concrétisée par le jugement Al-Mahdi fin septembre 2016[11].

Cette appréhension de la culture permettra à la Cour de rechercher une plus grande légitimité aux yeux des États. En effet, la prise en compte des systèmes de valeur des populations locales dans les actions de la Cour permet de respecter la diversité culturelle tout en l'intégrant pour stimuler sa propre culture juridique. Il s'avère donc nécessaire que la Cour accepte de prendre en compte certains

---

[8]Vilmer (2014); Mégret (2013); Smith (2009).

[9]Triffterer, Bergsmo, Ambos (2016), p. 6.

[10]ICC OTP, Document de politique générale relatif à la sélection et à la hiérarchisation des affaires, 15 septembre 2016, par. 46.

[11]TCVIII, Situation en République du Mali, *Affaire le Procureur c. Ahmad Al Faqi Al Mahdi*, « Jugement portant condamnation », 27 septembre 2016, ICC-01/12-01/15-171-tFRA.

éléments au nom du relativisme culturel. « *However, the relationship between cultural diversity and international criminal law seems based on a paradox: everyone must respect cultural diversity, but no one may invoke it to violate international criminal law* »[12]. La rencontre, par le biais de la Cour, de différentes cultures fait-elle apparaître une franche opposition entre elles ou, à l'inverse, permet-elle une meilleure compréhension de leur pluralité, de leur créativité et de leur équilibre[13] ?

La Cour pénale internationale doit faire face à quatre défis. Luttant contre l'impunité, la Cour a pour fonction de poursuivre les personnes suspectées d'avoir commis des crimes internationaux. Lors de la mise en œuvre de sa compétence matérielle, la CPI contribue à protéger *a posteriori* la culture en poursuivant certains crimes commis contre la culture (2). Afin de remplir ses objectifs, les rédacteurs du Statut de Rome ont institué, au sein de la Cour, différents mécanismes processuels. Sa mise en œuvre permet une interaction importante entre différents systèmes de valeurs et de droits. Cette rencontre se traduit soit par une association, soit par un antagonisme entre diverses cultures juridiques nationales et la Cour. Ces corrélations apparaissent à la fois dans le cadre du fonctionnement interne de la juridiction (3) et à l'occasion de ses relations avec des entités externes (4). Finalement, lors du procès, les différentes parties peuvent appartenir à des cultures fondamentalement différentes. La Cour doit alors prendre en compte ces particularismes culturels (5), que ce soit en les intégrant à son système processuel, ou en les rejetant catégoriquement.

2 La poursuite limitée des crimes contre la culture

La Cour est compétente pour poursuivre des crimes ayant un certain lien avec la culture, dans l'objectif de tenter de préserver, *a posteriori*, cette culture. Cette compétence permet au Procureur d'attirer l'attention sur les atteintes culturelles commises en cas de conflit armé ou en temps de paix. Toutefois, les poursuites de crimes contre la culture restent limitées à deux cas très précis: les attaques contre des biens culturels, constitutives de crimes de guerre (2.1), et la persécution pour motifs culturels, caractéristique de crimes contre l'humanité (2.2). Cette limitation s'explique essentiellement par la préférence accordée à la protection de l'intégrité physique des personnes plutôt qu'à la protection de la culture, ce qui explique l'absence du « génocide culturel » dans le Statut de Rome (2.3).

---

[12]Raimondo (2011), p. 300.

[13]Mestre (2010), pp. 15-17.

2.1 Les attaques contre des biens culturels comme crime de guerre

Au-delà de la distinction classique entre les biens civils et militaires, et les dispositions *lex generalis*[14], l'article 8 incrimine spécifiquement les attaques intentionnelles dirigées contre « des bâtiments consacrés à la religion, à l'enseignement, à l'art, à la science ou à l'action caritative, ou des monuments historiques, [...], à condition qu'ils ne soient pas des objectifs militaires »[15]. Cette interdiction concerne les conflits armés présentant un caractère international ou non. Toutefois, cette incrimination ne prend pas en compte, de manière spécifique, les objets culturels meubles. En effet, l'infraction de pillage et celle de destruction et de saisie des biens de l'ennemi concernent les biens meubles de manière générale[16]. Cet oubli est regrettable alors que la destruction et le trafic d'objets culturels constituent des conséquences importantes d'un conflit armé[17], comme actuellement en Syrie.

A l'inverse des traités antérieurs, l'article 8 étend le champ d'application de ce crime puisqu'il vise de manière large l'attaque du bâtiment protégé, sans considération ni du résultat de l'attaque ou de la destruction du bâtiment[18], ni de la temporalité[19]. Toutefois, le Statut ne prévoit pas l'incrimination de l'utilisation des bâtiments culturels à des fins militaires, alors même que les Protocoles de 1977[20] et la jurisprudence du Tribunal pénal international pour l'ex-Yougoslavie (TPIY)[21] ont reconnu l'existence de ce crime. Selon l'article 8, l'attaque doit être dirigée intentionnellement contre un bâtiment protégé. L'auteur direct ou indirect de l'attaque devait donc être au courant du caractère protégé du bien et avoir la volonté précise de le viser, comme ce fut le cas dans l'affaire *Al Mahdi*[22].

Différents bâtiments envisagés à l'article 8 peuvent être considérés comme des « biens culturels »[23]. Le Bureau du Procureur a estimé que « le patrimoine culturel ou spirituel recouvre les biens dont la valeur dépasse les frontières et qui présentent un caractère unique en étant liés à l'histoire et à la culture d'un peuple »[24]. Cette définition renvoie sans équivoque aux sites inscrits sur la liste du patrimoine mondial de l'humanité de l'UNESCO. Dans l'affaire *Al-Mahdi*, la Chambre de première

---

[14]Interdiction d'attaquer des biens civils, interdiction du pillage, interdiction de saisir illégalement ou détruire les biens de l'ennemi.

[15]Article 8-2-b-ix et article 8-2-e-iv du Statut de Rome.

[16]Frulli (2011), pp. 204-212.

[17]Rubinstein (1999), pp. 83-85.

[18]Ehlert (2014), p. 80.

[19]TCVIII, affaire *Al Mahdi*, par. 15.

[20]Article 53 du Protocole I et article 16 du Protocole II.

[21]TPIY, TC, *Prosecutor v. Strugar, Judgement*, 31 janvier 2005, IT-01-42-T, par. 183 et 193-195.

[22]TCVIII, affaire *Al Mahdi*, par. 47-48.

[23]Concept défini au sens large par l'article 1er de la Convention de 1954 pour la protection des biens culturels en cas de conflit armé

[24]ICC OTP, Situation au Mali, Rapport établi au titre de l'article 53-1, 16 janvier 2013, par. 155.

instance VIII a affirmé que les bâtiments détruits, des mausolées et mosquées, constituent à la fois des bâtiments religieux et historiques de par leur rôle culturel local, et des éléments du patrimoine mondial de l'humanité[25]. Toutefois, un bien qui n'aurait de valeur culturelle que pour un certain nombre de personnes sur un territoire restreint pourrait ne pas être considéré comme faisant partie du patrimoine commun de l'humanité. Seuls les bâtiments ayant une importance pour l'ensemble de l'humanité seraient considérés par le Bureau du Procureur comme des bâtiments culturels spécialement protégés par les lois et coutumes de la guerre. Cette approche réduirait considérablement le spectre des bâtiments culturels au sens de l'article 8. Toutefois, elle s'explique par la détermination de la compétence de la Cour, qui doit principalement poursuivre les crimes les plus graves. De plus, le Statut de Rome ne prend pas en compte les différentes protections prévues par le droit international[26]. Il est vrai que ces protections sont actuellement limitées à un faible nombre de sites dans le monde[27]. Mais leur absence dans le Statut accentue l'approche *civil-use* adoptée lors de la rédaction du Statut. Cette approche privilégie le caractère civil d'un bâtiment, plutôt que son caractère spécial tel que son affectation culturelle ou sanitaire.

Les États ont préféré lister les bâtiments spécialement protégés par le droit international humanitaire. L'approche *civil-use* retenue par les États se fait au détriment de l'approche *cultural-value*, ce qui affaiblit la protection des biens culturels[28]. En incluant dans la même liste des bâtiments culturels et des bâtiments sanitaires, les États leur attribuent une protection similaire alors qu'ils n'ont pas le même caractère. D'autre part, le Statut de Rome prévoit une dérogation majeure à la protection spécifique des biens en cas de nécessité militaire[29]. Cette dérogation est essentielle pour certains bâtiments qui peuvent perdre leur caractère de bâtiment protégé, tels une école ou un hôpital. Or, il est difficile de considérer qu'un bâtiment puisse perdre son caractère culturel ou historique[30]. Pourtant, si un bâtiment historique était utilisé à des fins militaires, son caractère culturel ne serait plus protégé par le Statut. En effet, celui-ci serait écarté du fait que le bâtiment constituait un objectif militaire au moment de l'attaque. L'attaque contre ce bâtiment ne constituerait alors plus un crime de guerre. La protection statutaire se trouve donc affaiblie puisque la Cour est seulement compétente pour poursuivre des atteintes

[25]TCVIII, affaire *Al Mahdi*, par. 46.

[26]Convention de la Haye de 1907, Conventions des Genève de 1949, Convention pour la protection des biens culturels en cas de conflit armé de 1954.

[27]Voir pour la protection spéciale:
http://www.unesco.org/new/fileadmin/MULTIMEDIA/HQ/CLT/pdf/Register2015FR.pdf;
Et pour la protection renforcée:
http://www.unesco.org/new/fileadmin/MULTIMEDIA/HQ/CLT/pdf/19542P-enhanced-protection-list-fr_20140320.pdf

[28]Frulli (2011), pp. 212-213.

[29]Venturini (2010), pp. 45-78.

[30]Gottlieb (2004-2005), p. 865.

contre des bâtiments culturels en vertu de la distinction entre les objectifs civils et militaires.

2.2 *La persécution pour motif culturel comme crime contre l'humanité*

L'article 7 du Statut de Rome est la première tentative de définir substantiellement le crime de persécution dans une convention internationale. Il est nécessaire que celui-ci soit directement lié à la commission d'un autre crime prévu par le Statut de Rome. Cette approche est particulièrement extensive puisque ne sont pas seulement pris en compte les actes constitutifs d'un crime contre l'humanité mais également ceux qui sont constitutifs d'un crime de guerre ou d'un génocide[31]. Toutefois, un certain nombre d'actes, qualifiables de crimes de persécution dans le cadre d'un conflit armé, ne constitueraient plus un tel crime en temps de paix. Par exemple, les attaques contre des bâtiments culturels sont uniquement prévues en tant que crime de guerre. Une attaque contre des bâtiments culturels en temps de paix ne constituerait pas un crime de persécution puisqu'elle tomberait hors du champ des crimes prévus par le Statut de Rome[32].

Pour constituer un crime de persécution, les actes doivent être commis de manière intentionnelle dans le but d'établir une discrimination à l'égard d'un groupe de personnes. Il faut toutefois qu'ils soient commis « *as part of a widespread or systematic attack directed against any civilian population* »[33]. La persécution ne nécessite pas nécessairement un élément physique, puisque « *the issuance of discriminatory orders, policies, decisions or other regulations may constitute the* actus reus *of persecution* »[34]. Les actes constitutifs du crime de persécution peuvent causer une souffrance physique ou morale (meurtre, esclavage, terreur) ou une restriction de liberté (détention illégale, restrictions professionnelles, de mouvement ou de vie de famille)[35].

La persécution doit être intentionnellement dirigée au minimum contre un faible nombre de personnes, même si l'acte commis n'a d'effet direct que sur un seul individu[36]. Il est nécessaire que les individus visés constituent un groupe ou une collectivité identifiable. L'identification de ce groupe semble pouvoir être effectuée de manière objective ou subjective selon l'interprétation de l'auteur du crime. De plus, il n'est pas nécessaire que le groupe soit identifiable selon des critères raciaux,

---

[31]Hall, Van den Herik (2016), p. 282.

[32]Gottlieb (2004-2005), pp. 875-876.

[33]Abtahi (2004), pp.16-33.

[34]TPIY, *Prosecutor v. Tadic, Judgement*, 7 mai 1997, IT-94-1-T, par. 707.

[35]Hall, Van Den Herik (2016), pp. 277-280.

[36]CPI, Eléments des crimes, pp. 7-8.

politiques, ethniques, ou religieux comme le crime de génocide[37]. Par exemple, les universitaires, les femmes ou les homosexuels pourraient potentiellement constituer des groupes identifiables en raison, respectivement, de leur profession, leur sexe ou leur orientation sexuelle.

L'intention discriminatoire contre ce groupe identifiable doit être effectuée pour des motifs précisés par l'article 7, au rang desquels figurent des motifs culturels. La notion de culture ne possédant pas de définition universelle, il semble nécessaire de lui donner « *an ordinary broad meaning* » comprenant les traditions et coutumes, les valeurs et les arts[38]. Par exemple, le meurtre ou le déplacement forcé des artistes ou des représentants culturels d'une population locale pourrait permettre de déterminer la commission d'un crime de persécution. Il est donc possible que soit constitutif d'un crime de persécution l'attaque et la destruction de biens culturels en tant que crimes de guerre dans l'objectif intentionnel d'opprimer un groupe du fait de son appartenance culturelle. Dans l'affaire *Kordiz & Cerkez*, le TPIY a reconnu que les actes délibérés de destruction d'anciennes mosquées en Bosnie-Herzégovine, dans une intention discriminatoire, constituent une manifestation de la destruction d'une culture religieuse unique[39].

Dans son rapport de 2003 sur la situation au Mali, le Bureau du Procureur a considéré que les renseignements disponibles cette année-là ne permettaient pas d'envisager la poursuite de crimes contre l'humanité. On peut toutefois se demander si la destruction des mausolées, pour laquelle Al-Mahdi a été condamné en septembre 2016, ne constitue pas un crime de persécution. En effet, il semble que le groupe *Ansar Dine*, auquel appartenait Al-Mahdi, commettait des attaques contre la population de manière généralisée en connaissance de cause[40]. Il paraît évident que les tombes, mausolées et mosquées de Tombouctou, détruits par *Ansar Dine*, constituaient des bâtiments d'une valeur culturelle et religieuse importante pour ses habitants[41]. De plus, ce groupe terroriste a avancé des raisons culturelles et religieuses pour détruire ces bâtiments, en considérant que la population locale, constituée de musulmans modérés, ne respectait pas sa propre interprétation du Coran, en tant que groupe musulman radical[42]. Ces destructions engendrent une perte pour l'ensemble de l'Humanité, mais plus particulièrement un déni de l'identité culturelle, des croyances, de l'histoire et de la dignité de la population locale[43]. Par conséquent, il aurait été envisageable que la destruction des bâtiments culturels et religieux par *Ansar Dine* soit poursuivie en tant que crime de persécution. Il est fort probable que le Bureau du Procureur ne disposait pas de suffisamment d'éléments

[37]Hall, Powderly, Hayes (2016), p. 221.

[38]*Ibid.*, p. 224.

[39]TPIY, *Le Procureur c. Kordiz et Cerkez, Judgement*, 26 février 2001, IT-95-14/2-T, par. 207.

[40]Green Martinez (2015), pp. 1089-1092.

[41]*Ibid.*, p. 1094.

[42]*Ibid.*, p. 1096.

[43]Office of the High Commissioner for Human Rights, '*A Very Dark Future for the Local Populations in Northern Mali, Warn UN experts*', Communiqué de Presse, 10 July 2012.

probatoires pour permettre à une Chambre d'apprécier la commission du crime de persécution, qui s'avère plus difficile à prouver qu'une attaque contre des biens culturels constitutive d'un crime de guerre.

2.3 L'exclusion du crime de génocide culturel

L'article 6 du Statut de Rome définit le crime de génocide comme la commission de certains actes dans l'intention de détruire tout ou partie d'un groupe national, ethnique, racial ou religieux[44]. Le concept de 'génocide culturel' est donc absent du Statut. Exclu de la Convention sur le génocide de 1948[45], ce concept fut également rejeté par le TPIY dans l'affaire *Krstic* en 2001[46] et par la Cour internationale de Justice (CIJ) en 2007[47]. Mais « *cultural genocide is alive and spreading in our world* »[48]. D'ailleurs, en 2007, l'Assemblée générale des Nations-Unies a adopté une Déclaration sur les droits des peuples autochtones qui prévoit en son article 8 que « les autochtones, peuples et individus, ont le droit de ne pas subir d'assimilation forcée ou de destruction de leur culture »[49], ce qui fait resurgir le débat autour du concept d'ethnocide[50], proche de celui de génocide culturel. Le Secrétaire d'État américain John Kerry semble avoir considéré que Daech a créé un contexte général de génocide sur les territoires qu'il contrôle par le massacre de communautés entières, l'esclavage forcé de femmes dans un but sexuel, ainsi que la destruction de milliers d'années d'héritage culturel[51].

Un génocide culturel serait commis « when artistic, literary, and cultural activities are restricted or outlawed and when national treasures, libraries, archives, museums, artefacts, and arts galleries are destroyed or confiscated »[52]. Bien que la destruction d'un héritage culturel ne constitue pas en soi un génocide, elle peut constituer un acte de génocide ainsi qu'une preuve de l'intention génocidaire[53]. Cette dernière peut d'ailleurs être apportée par le témoignage des victimes quant au contexte culturel dans lequel s'est déroulé le génocide[54].

---

[44]Article 6 du Statut de Rome.

[45]Gerstenblith (2016), p. 343.

[46]TPIY, *Prosecutor v. Krstic*, Judgement, 2001, par. 580.

[47]CIJ, affaire relative à l'*Application de la Convention pour la prévention et la répression du crime de Génocide*, Bosnie c. Serbie, 26 février 2007, par. 194.

[48]Davidson (2012), p. 131.

[49]AGNU, Déclaration des Nations Unies sur les droits des peuples autochtones, 13 septembre 2007, A/RES/61/295, Article 8.

[50]Pruim (2014), pp. 269-308.

[51]John Kerry, US Secretary of State, « *Remarks on Daesh and Genocide* », 17 mars 2016, disponible sur: http://www.state.gov/secretary/remarks/2016/03/254782.htm.

[52]Nersessian (2005).

[53]Gerstenblith (2016), p. 389.

[54]Hon (2013), pp. 389-392.

En tout état de cause, il est possible de considérer que la définition même du génocide inclut le génocide culturel. En effet, la destruction d'un groupe ethnique ou religieux a pour finalité la destruction sociale du groupe visé, c'est-à-dire l'anéantissement d'une culture donnée. De plus, la destruction d'un groupe ethnique entraîne à la fois la destruction physique de ses membres, et l'annihilation de leur culture, comme leurs croyances et leurs connaissances traditionnelles sur la biodiversité. En précisant à l'article 6 qu'un acte constitutif de crime de génocide peut constituer une atteinte grave à l'intégrité mentale des groupes, les rédacteurs ne semblent pas avoir limité le crime de génocide à la destruction physique ou biologique des membres d'un groupe[55], contrairement à ce qu'a affirmé la CIJ[56]. Bien souvent, les commentateurs ont tendance à estimer la destruction physique d'un groupe plus grave que la disparition d'une culture. Toutefois, cette assertion est facilement inversable. En effet, sans culture, il ne peut y avoir de groupe ethnique, religieux voire politique. Par conséquent, il est nécessaire de considérer que les crimes contre la culture et les crimes contre l'intégrité physique peuvent coexister sans relation hiérarchique, et ce d'autant plus que l'essence de l'incrimination du génocide est « *to prevent draining the spiritual resources of humankind* »[57].

Les crimes spécifiquement commis contre la culture sont donc étroitement définis au sein du Statut de Rome, en particulier la destruction de l'héritage culturel en temps de paix. Toutefois, les actes incriminés par le Statut de Rome ne concernent pas seulement l'intégrité physique des personnes, mais affectent l'ensemble de la civilisation humaine puisque « *Cultural heritage destruction constitutes a crime against People* »[58]. Une telle opinion est particulièrement nécessaire aujourd'hui avec les destructions culturelles qui ont lieu dans de nombreux conflits, en particulier en Syrie et en Irak[59]. Le Procureur, en intégrant des aspects culturels dans ses politiques d'enquête et de poursuite, aspire à protéger la diversité culturelle de l'humanité. Cette finalité se retrouve également dans la rencontre entre diverses cultures juridiques dans le cadre du fonctionnement de la Cour.

3 Le métissage interne des cultures juridiques occidentales

La culture juridique s'entend comme le corpus formé par « les valeurs et les attitudes qui lient le système dans un ensemble, et qui déterminent la place du système juridique dans la culture de la société considérée comme un tout »[60]. Elle est formée

[55]Berster (2015), pp. 680-681.

[56]CIJ, affaire relative à l'*Application de la Convention pour la prévention et la répression du crime de Génocide*, Croatie c. Serbie, 3 février 2015, par. 136.

[57]Lemkin (1947), p. 147.

[58]Gerstenblith (2016), p. 392.

[59]*Ibid.*, pp. 354-362 et 372-381.

[60]Arnaud (1993), p. 141.

d'« un ensemble de principes, de valeurs et de concepts communs, un discours et une pratique partagés, entretenus par les modes d'enseignements et de pensée de chaque pays ou région du monde de telle sorte qu'ils s'inscrivent bien dans une certaine tradition de pensée »[61]. L'étude du Statut de Rome permet de considérer que la Cour crée un métissage entre les cultures juridiques occidentales, rendant difficile la détermination de sa propre culture juridique (3.1). Dès lors, il paraît nécessaire de qualifier le système juridique de la Cour comme 'système réseau', afin de prendre en compte la globalité de ces interactions (3.2).

3.1 La difficile détermination de la culture juridique de la Cour

Les cultures juridiques occidentales peuvent être regroupées autour de deux grands modèles, dits de *Common Law* et de *Civil Law*. Il convient de remarquer que le système accusatoire se réfère essentiellement à la tradition juridique de *Common Law* alors que le système inquisitoire est intégré au modèle de *Civil Law*. Le Statut de Rome est clairement le reflet de négociations basées sur ces cultures juridiques occidentales. De plus, la diversité entre les juges crée un « *melting pot* » culturel qui vient s'ajouter à l'engrenage du système de la Cour. Ce *melting pot*, associé à la marge de manœuvre laissée aux juges, permet d'expliquer les diverses approches processuelles adoptées par les diverses chambres de la Cour.

Par exemple, l'article 64 du Statut de Rome, relatif aux fonctions et pouvoirs de la Chambre de première instance, accorde une large discrétion aux juges pour réguler et guider la conduite de l'instance. En effet, les pouvoirs de la Chambre de première instance ne sont pas aussi restreints que ceux des juges de *Common Law*, ni aussi importants et substantiels que ceux des juges de *Civil Law*. En réalité, la discrétion laissée aux juges de la CPI est telle que les juges sont en mesure de décider de leur implication dans l'instance, c'est-à-dire de leur place au sein du procès face aux parties. Ce fut le cas dans l'affaire *Gbagbo & Blé Goudé* où le juge Président a été le premier juge à refuser aux parties le droit de poser des questions directrices (« *leading questions* ») lors des interrogatoires et contre-interrogatoires[62].

Dans la même optique, la procédure en cas d'aveu de culpabilité[63] montre l'absence d'accord entre les négociateurs sur le choix à opérer entre le modèle de *Common Law* et celui de *Civil Law*. Dans l'affaire *Al-Mahdi*, les juges ont pour la première fois interprété cet article, et ont affirmé son caractère hybride[64]. Les principales conditions pour enclencher la procédure d'aveu de culpabilité sont

[61]Jouannet (2008), p. 49.

[62]ICC-02/11-01/15-T-13-Red-ENG, 03 février 2016, p. 2, l. 3-4; et ICC-02/11-01/15-T-14-ENG, 04 février 2016, p. 1, l. 21 à p. 3, l. 25.

[63]Article 65 du Statut de Rome

[64]TCVIII, affaire *Al-Mahdi*, par. 23.

similaires à celles prévues par le droit de *Common Law*. Toutefois, une réserve, présente dans le système de *Civil Law*, a été incluse à l'alinéa 5[65]. L'article, dans sa version anglaise, précise que « *the Chamber may convict the accused based on his/her admission of guilt and end the trial; however, the Chamber is not required to do so* ». La Chambre peut donc ordonner que le procès se déroule selon les procédures normales, ce qui correspond plus à la culture juridique romano-germanique[66]. Une telle prérogative confirme l'importance des pouvoirs laissés aux juges et l'hybridité du système de la Cour.

Ce métissage des cultures juridiques occidentales constitue un obstacle pour déterminer la culture juridique propre de la Cour. Il convient de noter que « *each procedural tradition is far more complex than its discreet rules, or even the totality of its rules, and thus should be understood as an amalgation of rules and the understandings, institutions, and social types that come with them* »[67]. Par conséquent, déterminer la culture juridique de la Cour est un exercice d'autant plus difficile, d'une part, qu'elle est inconsciente et, d'autre part, que vouloir parler de culture juridique signifie que « l'on est soi-même déterminé par une culture juridique »[68]. Dès lors, il est nécessaire de se détacher au maximum de sa propre culture juridique afin de pouvoir étudier la globalité du système de la Cour, ce que tentent de faire plusieurs auteurs selon deux approches principales: l'analyse basée sur les cultures nationales ou l'analyse d'une culture *sui generis*.

Certains auteurs se sont concentrés sur l'idée d'un « clash culturel » entre les systèmes accusatoire et inquisitoire, inhérents aux cultures de *Common* et de *Civil Law*. Ce clash entre les cultures juridiques occidentales créerait un système incohérent, tel un « monstre de Frankenstein »[69], dans lequel prédominerait le système accusatoire. Mais, les concepts de systèmes accusatoire et inquisitoire restent « otages » du conflit entre le changement et la tradition procédurale au sein d'un État[70]. Ainsi, « *the inquisitorial-accusatorial divide [seems to have] only, if at all, a meaning in historic, pre-revolutionary terms* »[71]. Cette volonté de démontrer l'existence d'une rupture au sein du système de la CPI s'avère donc stérile[72], et s'avère souvent subordonnée à des considérations personnelles de la part des auteurs. « *Ultimately, this approach cannot theorize [International criminal law] as a truly international legal culture, since it will always be an impure and improper mixture of legal traditions* »[73].

[65] *Ibid.*, par. 25.
[66] *Ibid.*, par. 27-28.
[67] Mégret (2009), p. 46.
[68] *Ibid.* p. 50.
[69] Skilbeck (2010), p. 451.
[70] Damaška (2001), p. 481.
[71] Ambos (2003), pp. 3-4.
[72] Langer (2006), p. 835.
[73] Campbell (2013), p. 159.

D'autres auteurs ont préféré avancer l'argument selon lequel le système de la CPI constituerait un système *sui generis*. Cette nouvelle culture juridique serait la réponse aux exigences et défis des procès internationaux[74]. Toutefois, les auteurs se réfèrent toujours aux traditions légales nationales sans parvenir à expliquer les caractéristiques de cette culture juridique internationale[75]. Ainsi, considérer le système de la Cour comme un système *sui generis* n'est que le premier pas vers la détermination de sa culture juridique. En conséquence, il semble nécessaire d'adopter une troisième approche pour identifier la culture juridique de la Cour.

3.2 Le système juridique en réseau de la Cour

Kirsten Campbell propose une méthodologie particulière pour comprendre et identifier les traits d'une forme spécifique de culture, qui s'avérerait hégémonique au moment de l'étude. « *This cultural form works through very specific forms of representing and ordering social relations, such as the values and practices of law, legal institutions, and legal mechanisms for proceedings and judgment* »[76]. L'auteur décrit le concept de culture juridique comme un ensemble dynamique de valeurs et de pratiques. Ainsi, la culture juridique du droit international pénal « *develops its particular organizing categories on an ongoing basis* »[77]. L'auteur identifie trois principales caractéristiques de cette culture juridique internationale: les crimes internationaux, l'individu comme sujet du droit international et le caractère pénal de la recherche judiciaire de la vérité. Ces caractéristiques justifient les exigences particulières des procès devant les juridictions pénales internationales. De plus, la culture juridique développée par la CPI cherche à dépasser les cultures juridiques nationales vers une justice post-westphalienne sur la base de valeurs universelles communes à l'humanité[78]. Pour autant, cette nouvelle culture juridique ne peut pas être considérée comme universelle, mais demeure spécifique aux juridictions pénales internationales, en particulier la CPI. En réalité, elle constitue un nouveau mode d'interaction à l'échelle mondiale[79].

La théorie de ce mode d'interaction mondiale est particulièrement intéressante en ce qu'elle rend compte de l'interdépendance de l'ensemble des acteurs gravitant autour de la Cour. Mirjan Damaska a développé deux modèles d'adjudication dénommés *hierarchical* et*coordinated* (ou *participatory*) [80]. Le premier modèle se base sur une organisation verticale du pouvoir gravitant de manière centripète autour

[74]Ambos (2007).

[75]Campbell, (2013), p. 160.

[76]*Idem.*

[77]*Ibid.*, p. 161.

[78]Fraser (2009), p. 281.

[79]Campbell (2013), p. 168.

[80]Damaška (1975), p. 481, et Damaška (1986), p. 16.

d'un pouvoir centralisé[81], et appliquant un légalisme plutôt rigide[82]. Le second modèle voit l'effacement de l'État au profit d'une organisation horizontale gravitant de manière centrifuge par la mise en place d'un débat « véridictoire » entre les parties et des mécanismes de rationalité éthique[83]. Alors que ces deux systèmes paraissent antinomiques, la culture juridique de la Cour les réunit en créant une organisation à la fois verticale et horizontale et en accordant une place importante à la rationalité éthique, tout en instaurant des règles statutaires. La Cour a créé un système d'adjudication particulier qui s'explique par sa culture juridique spécifique, que l'on pourrait qualifier de système en réseau.

Le concept de « réseau » permet d'appréhender la complexité des interactions et des communications de la Cour dont le maillage permet de percevoir la dynamique, l'identité et la logique interne de sa culture juridique[84]. Dépassant la vision pyramidale de Kelsen, cette approche en réseau, que l'on peut qualifier d'holistique, fait apparaître les interconnexions multiples entre l'ensemble des éléments du système juridique qui réagissent et rétroagissent mutuellement[85]. « La production du droit via le procès [devant la Cour] ne se fait pas juste par le juge [ou les parties] de façon solipsiste, mais à travers la collaboration des procureurs, des avocats, des experts, et grâce au mécanisme de l'*amicus curiae*, de la Société civile [et des États] »[86]. Le droit au sein de la Cour est comme un élément dont la forme n'est jamais fixe, le résultat toujours instable et constitué d'une pluralité de connexions entre les différents acteurs du réseau étudié[87]. « Se découvre alors une mécanique relationnelle, complexe mais dynamique, dont les ressorts sont à la fois juridiques et culturels, qui stimule la circulation des modèles de droit [...] et favorise finalement la construction des principes et valeurs d'une justice universelle »[88].

Ce système en réseau s'accompagne d'une fragmentation du droit, d'un pluralisme juridique et d'une interdépendance entre les acteurs, qui sont des caractéristiques actuelles du droit international. Face à la mouvance perpétuelle du réseau, il est nécessaire que certains acteurs viennent contrôler la cohésion de la légalité hybride du système, en appliquant les concepts fondamentaux du raisonnable, d'équivalence et de cohérence[89]. Ce rôle serait alors dévolu aux juges, qui se situent dans une « tension dialectique entre contrainte et liberté, subordination et autonomie »[90]. Régulateurs du réseau, les juges sont en perpétuel conflit entre leur rôle juridique et les enjeux-socio-politiques entourant la Cour. Les nombreuses controverses entre les Chambres de la

[81]Damaška (1975), p. 484.
[82]*Ibid.*, pp. 506-507.
[83]*Ibid.*, pp. 511-521.
[84]Bernard (2014), p. 67.
[85]*Ibid.*, p. 66.
[86]Vogliotti (2004), p. 363.
[87]Vogliotti (2005), p. 15.
[88]Canivet (2005), p. 799.
[89]Bernard (2014), p. 133.
[90]Ost, Van de kerchove (2002), p. 98.

Cour et l'Union Africaine démontrent que les juges ont une influence directe sur la politique des États (retraits du Statut de Rome), et donc sur le système politico-juridique international. Dès lors, le rôle des juges est primordial puisqu'il vient réguler les interactions internes au réseau entre les parties au procès, mais également les interactions externes avec des cultures juridiques plurielles.

4 L'interaction externe avec des cultures juridiques plurielles

L'absence d'une réelle culture juridique cosmopolite laisse place à une multiplicité de visions nationales et régionales, individuelles et institutionnelles du droit international[91]. L'ordre juridique international est l'objet de revendications multiculturelles contre l'inévitable mondialisation de la société[92]. Pour faire face aux réticences de la communauté internationale, la Cour a su développer de manière flexible son réseau interactif (4.1). Ainsi, la Cour intervient dans ce contexte globalisé où les acteurs stimulent continuellement le relativisme culturel en appuyant les spécificités de leur culture juridique nationale (4.2).

4.1 Des interactions variées avec la communauté internationale

Deux exemples d'interactions avec la communauté internationale démontrent l'importance actuelle de la Cour, et la complexité de son système *sui generis*. D'un côté, la Cour doit composer avec la persistance d'intérêts divergents au sein du Conseil de Sécurité des Nations Unies. De l'autre, une vision différente des immunités présidentielles a engendré un processus de retrait auquel la Cour a dû faire face.

Alors que les Etats-Unis, la Russie et la Chine s'opposaient fermement à la création de la Cour, les politiques judiciaires de celle-ci ont su influencer ces États qui ont alors accepté que le Conseil de sécurité saisisse la Cour de la situation au Darfour[93] et en Libye[94]. Mais rapidement, certains États membres, en particulier la

[91]Jouannet (2008), p. 43.

[92]*Ibid.*, p. 44

[93]CSNU, 31 mars 2005, Résolution 1593 (2005), Rapports du Secrétaire Général sur le Soudan, saisine de la CPI à propos du Darfour, S/RES/1593 (2005). La France, le Royaume-Uni et la Russie ont voté en faveur de la résolution, alors que les Etats-Unis d'Amérique et la Chine se sont abstenus, tout comme l'Algérie et le Brésil.

[94]CSNU, 26 février 2011, Résolution 1970 (2011), Paix et Sécurité en Afrique, saisine de la CPI à propos de la situation en Libye, S/RES/1970 (é2011). Les quinze membres du Conseil de Sécurité ont voté en faveur de la résolution.

Russie, ont mis en avant des enjeux politiques et sécuritaires, conduisant à un blocage du Conseil sur la situation en Syrie. La Cour fait alors face à un antagonisme politico-culturel au Conseil de Sécurité, permettant à ses détracteurs de parler d'échec syrien. Toutefois, la Cour a créé d'autres lignes de conduite lui permettant de développer son réseau en direction d'autres États, via l'ouverture d'enquêtes sur la situation en Géorgie en 2008 et la situation en Palestine depuis 2014[95]. Dès lors, le Procureur, en tant qu'organe de poursuite, a su apprécier la situation politique au Conseil afin de la contourner pour ranimer le réseau juridique de la Cour et lui permettre de lutter contre l'impunité.

La Cour connaît également des difficultés notables avec les États africains quant à l'interprétation du droit international[96]. En effet, de nombreuses dissensions sont apparues au sein de la communauté internationale à propos de la poursuite d'un Chef d'État en exercice. La Cour a considéré que l'immunité d'inviolabilité personnelle d'un Chef d'État ne pouvait être invoquée pour s'exonérer temporellement de sa responsabilité pénale[97]. Toutefois, l'Union Africaine a défendu les intérêts des Chefs d'États visés, à savoir soudanais et kenyan, et s'est opposée de la manière la plus résolue à la Cour au point d'émettre des menaces de retrait collectif du Statut de Rome et de créer une cour pénale africaine au sein de la Cour africaine des droits de l'homme[98]. L'Union Africaine n'a pas mis ses menaces à exécution face au soutien du reste de la communauté internationale à la Cour. Le réseau de la Cour a alors tenté de renouer le dialogue avec les États africains afin de résoudre la situation, tout en continuant de pointer judiciairement du doigt les mauvais élèves. C'est ainsi que la Cour entra directement en conflit avec l'Afrique du Sud lorsque celle-ci refusa d'arrêter le président soudanais en voyage diplomatique sur son territoire[99]. Les juridictions sud-africaines furent saisies par la société civile et condamnèrent le gouvernement pour avoir failli à ses obligations internationales en vertu du Statut de Rome[100]. En représailles, le gouvernement décida de se retirer du Statut de Rome, bien que ce retrait soit essentiellement une réponse politique à la décision de la Cour suprême de Pretoria. D'ailleurs, cette dernière a récemment déclaré inconstitutionnelle la décision de retrait du

[95]Le Procureur a également demandé, le 3 novembre 2017, à la Chambre préliminaire III l'autorisation d'ouvrir une enquête sur la situation en Afghanistan.

[96]Mégret (2013).

[97]Hall (2012).

[98]Nmehielle (2014), pp. 7-42.

[99]ICC PTC II, Situation au Darfour, Soudan, affaire *The Prosecutor v. Omar Hassan Ahmad Al-Bashir*, « Decision following the Prosecutor's request for an order further clarifying that the Republic of South Africa is under the obligation to immediately arrest and surrender Omar Al-Bashir», 13 juin 2015, ICC-02/05-01/09-242.

[100]High Court of South Africa, Gauteng Division (24 juin 2015), *Southern African Litigation Centre v. Minister of Justice and Constitutional Development and Others*. 27740/2015. Voir Tladi (2015), pp. 1027-1047. The Supreme Court of Appeal of South Africa (15 mars 2016), *The Minister of Justice and Constitutional Development v. The Southern African Litigation Centre*. 867/15 [2016].

gouvernement[101], entraînant le retrait de la décision de retrait du Statut de l'Afrique du Sud[102]. Il est donc probable que la Cour ait tenté, via son réseau politico-juridique, d'influencer les organes de l'État, politiques ou juridictionnels, pour empêcher le retrait de l'Afrique du Sud du Statut de Rome.

En dépit de l'absence de culture juridique cosmopolite au niveau international, les interactions dynamiques entre la Cour et la communauté internationale appuient le développement d'une culture en réseau. Le maillage complexe de la Cour ne s'arrête pas à la société internationale: il s'étend aux systèmes juridiques nationaux auxquels la Cour est directement confrontée.

4.2 Des interactions externes avec des cultures juridiques nationales

La création de la Cour a engendré diverses interactions avec les États, que ce soit au moment de la ratification du Statut de Rome, ou lors de la mise en œuvre des compétences de la Cour. Ces différentes interactions externes mettent en avant, non pas une véritable différence culturelle, mais au contraire des ressemblances et des réticences politiques.

Lors de la ratification du Statut de Rome, certains États ont fait face à des conflits normatifs entre le Statut et leur Constitution nationale. Ainsi, la France a dû modifier sa Constitution pour ratifier le Statut[103]. Quant à lui, le Japon a été confronté à l'absence dans son droit pénal interne de certaines infractions prévues par le Statut de Rome[104]. Ainsi, avant même l'institution formelle de la Cour, du fait de la culture juridique spécifique qu'elle devait incarner, une légère harmonisation des législations nationales sur la base du Statut fut amorcée.

Un conflit normatif est apparu du fait de l'interaction entre la Cour et les systèmes juridiques islamiques. En effet, alors que la Cour utilise comme norme de référence un texte rédigé par l'homme, la culture juridique islamique prend pour norme de référence la loi divine du Coran, en application du code de la Sharia[105]. Malgré cette différence, les deux cultures juridiques semblent avoir de nombreux principes fondateurs en commun, ce qui pourrait les rapprocher[106]. Pour autant, certains

[101]High Court of South Africa, Gauteng Division (22 février 2017) *Democratic Alliance v. Minister of International Relations and Cooperation and Others*, 83145/2016 [2017].

[102]South Africa, Withdrawal of Notification of Withdrawal, 7 mars 2017, C.N.121.2017. TREATIES-XVIII.10 (Depositary Notification), disponible sur: https://treaties.un.org/doc/Publication/CN/2017/CN.121.2017-Eng.pdf.

[103]Lambert-Abdelgawad (2003), pp. 539-573.

[104]Noguchi (2006), pp. 585-604.

[105]Alarefi (2009), pp. 707-731.

[106]Malekian (2009), pp. 595-621.

États musulmans, comme l'Iran[107], ont une opinion ambivalente sur la conciliation du Statut de Rome avec certains principes religieux. Réticents également, les États asiatiques, comme l'Inde[108], voient de nombreuses contradictions entre le Statut et leurs cultures juridiques, telles que l'indépendance du Procureur ou l'application oblique du principe de complémentarité[109].

Le Préambule du Statut rappelle « qu'il est du devoir de chaque État de soumettre à sa juridiction criminelle les responsables de crimes internationaux ». La Cour se veut donc complémentaire des juridictions nationales, et n'interviendra qu'en cas de défaillance des systèmes nationaux. Le Bureau du Procureur a dès lors un rôle important de coopération avec les autorités nationales[110]. Pour cela, il est nécessaire que le Bureau « *use its different networks and engage with the various stakeholders involved in the process* »[111]. Lors de l'enquête préliminaire, le Bureau du Procureur doit opérer le test de complémentarité afin de déterminer si les autorités de l'État ont la capacité, la volonté et les ressources pour poursuivre les auteurs des crimes internationaux, et donc si une enquête ou des poursuites judiciaires sont en cours au niveau national[112]. En 2012, l'État libyen a contesté l'admissibilité des affaires *Al-Senussi* et *Saif Al-Islam Gaddafi* au motif que la justice nationale libyenne enquêtait de manière active sur les accusés pour des crimes commis dans le cadre d'une politique de l'État, équivalents à des crimes contre l'humanité[113]. La Chambre d'appel a rendu deux décisions divergentes relatives au principe de complémentarité, déclarant inadmissible l'affaire *Al-Senussi* devant la CPI et déclarant admissible l'affaire *Saif Al-Islam Gaddafi*[114]. La Cour a été directement confrontée à une culture juridique nationale, qu'elle a dû analyser et intégrer pour dynamiser son réseau. La proximité interactionnelle entre la Cour et les systèmes nationaux est alors particulièrement importante au moment du test de complémentarité, qu'il convient d'effectuer pour toutes les situations et affaires portées devant la Cour.

---

[107] Abtahi (2005), pp. 635-648.

[108] Ramanathan (2005), pp. 627-628.

[109] Schuldt (2015), pp. 75-104.

[110] ICC ASP, *Report of the Court on Complementarity*, 11 novembre 2011, ICC-ASP/10/23, p. 5.

[111] Tillier (2013), p. 510.

[112] Article 17-2-c du Statut de Rome.

[113] Situation in Libya in the Case of *The Prosecutor* v. *Saif Al-Islam and Abdullah Al-Senussi*, Application on behalf of the Government of Libya pursuant to Article 19 of the ICC Statute (ICC-01/11-01/11) 1 May 2012.

[114] Chambre d'Appel, Judgement on the appeal of Libya against the decision of Pre-Trial Chamber I of 31 may october 2013 entitled Decision on the admissibility of the case against Saif Al-Islam Gaddafi, 21 mai 2014, ICC-01/11-01/11-547-Red; Chambre d'Appel, Judgement on the appeal of Mr Abdullah Al-Senussi against the decision of Pre-Trial Chamber I of 11 october 2013 entitled "Decision on the admissibility of the case against Abdullah Al-Senussi", 24 juillet 2014, ICC-01/11-01/11-565.

La Cour rencontre également les cultures juridiques nationales dans la recherche et la collecte des éléments de preuves. Le Procureur a mis en place un cadre de coopération avec les États parties et non parties au Statut. Ce cadre de coopération vient donc alimenter de manière continue le réseau de la Cour, qui doit alors prendre en compte les procédures nationales de recherche et collecte de preuves. Lors de la phase des réparations, la Chambre de première instance II a rencontré un problème spécifique au moment de l'évaluation des preuves dans l'affaire *Katanga*[115]. En effet, les victimes ne pouvaient pas présenter de documents écrits attestant la possession de biens immeubles et/ou meubles lors de l'attaque du village. Ceci s'explique par le fait qu'en Ituri, il n'existe pas, à proprement parler, de culture juridique de système de droit écrit en matière de propriété. Dès lors, la Chambre a dû innover et prendre en compte la culture juridique locale. Elle a ainsi accepté que les victimes déposent des attestations de propriété datées postérieurement au conflit[116]. Contrairement à d'autres cultures juridiques, la Chambre n'aura pas d'autre choix que de leur attribuer une valeur probante raisonnable, actionnant alors les forces de la culture juridique en réseau de la Cour au profit des victimes. De telles problématiques seront rencontrées ultérieurement par la Cour lors de l'évaluation du préjudice subi par des enfants-soldats dans l'affaire *Lubanga* ou par des victimes de violences sexuelles dans l'affaire *Bemba*. La Cour devra donc élaborer la meilleure manière pour apprécier des éléments probatoires tronqués et difficiles à produire dans des situations de conflits armés, d'autant plus que la culture vient modeler la nature des crimes poursuivis par le Procureur.

5 Les particularismes culturels des parties au procès

Les crimes poursuivis par le Procureur de la Cour se sont déroulés sur des territoires délimités et dans des contextes diversifiés. Dès lors, le procureur et les juges sont confrontés à des situations insolites directement liées à la culture des accusés et des victimes. Chacun peut tenter de mettre en avant les particularités de sa culture, dans l'objectif que la Cour attribue un certain poids au relativisme culturel. Il peut parfois être nécessaire de le faire. Toutefois, le relativisme culturel ne doit pas être un argument pour disputer la compétence de la Cour ou justifier la commission des crimes. Les organes de la Cour ont par conséquent dû prendre en compte de manière sélective cette diversité culturelle, qui se manifeste de nombreuses manières, dans la langue (5.1) ou le contexte culturel des affaires (5.2).

---

[115]CPI, Chambre de première instance II, Situation en République démocratique du Congo, affaire *Le Procureur c. Germain Katanga*, Ordonnance de réparation en vertu de l'article 75 du Statut, 24 mars 2017, ICC-01/04-01/07-3728, pp. 26-33.

[116]*Ibid.*, par. 80-81.

5.1 Les difficultés d'interprétation d'ordre linguistique

Selon l'article 50 du Statut de Rome, les langues officielles de la Cour sont l'arabe, le chinois, l'anglais, le français, le russe et l'espagnol et les deux langues de travail sont l'anglais et le français. Le choix limité de ces langues s'explique par leur caractère de langues officielles au sein des Nations-Unies mais aussi pour des raisons financières et pratiques. Toutefois, plusieurs accusés et victimes ne parlent aucune de ces langues de manière courante. Or, cela semble contraire à l'article 14 du Pacte international relatif aux droits civils et politiques qui consacre le droit, pour l'accusé, de comprendre et de se défendre contre les charges dont il fait l'objet[117]. Par conséquent, il a fallu créer un système de traduction entre les dialectes africains (Swahili, Lingala) parlés par les témoins ou l'accusé et les organes de la Cour[118]. Le respect de la diversité linguistique entraîne des coûts supplémentaires auxquels doit faire face la Cour durant les différentes étapes procédurales.

Il convient de distinguer la traduction de l'interprétation en ce que la seconde « encompasses only oral communication and is defined as "situations in which one person speaks in the source language, an interpreter processes this input and produces output in the target language, and another person listens to the interpreted target language version of the original speaker's message" »[119]. L'interprétation est essentiellement exécutée de manière simultanée et nécessite donc, de la part de l'interprète, une connaissance approfondie des deux langues ainsi qu'une concentration extrême en vue d'interpréter rapidement le discours énoncé. C'est d'ailleurs l'une des raisons pour lesquelles des pauses régulières sont instaurées lors des audiences devant la Cour, ainsi qu'un transcrit numérique simultané puis ultérieurement corrigé. De plus, certains concepts juridiques et éléments factuels peuvent parfois être difficiles à interpréter d'une langue à l'autre. Par conséquent, la recherche de la vérité peut être distordue du fait d'une erreur d'interprétation. Ce fut le cas devant le TPIR dans l'affaire Akayesu où des incohérences au sein d'un témoignage entre l'enquête et l'audience furent le résultat de difficultés d'interprétation de la langue du kinyarwanda vers l'anglais et le français[120].

L'interprétation du discours est souvent insuffisante puisque l'interprète doit essayer de retranscrire le ton, l'hésitation et l'émotion du discours originel[121]. En effet, lors d'une audience, les juges et parties portent un casque afin d'écouter l'interprétation effectuée, et n'entendent donc pas nécessairement l'émotion dans le discours du témoin. Pourtant, « *in a trial, cross-cultural communication difficulties impact most significantly on the ability of triers of fact to assess the weight that should be given to different witnesses' testimony* »[122]. De plus, l'assistance

---

[117]Karton (2008), p. 12.

[118]Règle 42 du Règlement de Procédure et de Preuve de la CPI.

[119]Karton (2008), p. 17.

[120]Ngane (2015), p. 177.

[121]Karton (2008), p. 24.

[122]*Ibid.*, p. 29.

nécessaire d'un interprète empêche les avocats de contrôler les interrogatoires, en particulier le contre-interrogatoire qui a pour but de confronter le témoin aux incohérences de son témoignage. Or, le temps nécessaire pour interpréter les questions de l'avocat dans la langue du témoin permet à celui-ci une adaptation pour formuler sa réponse[123].

Une situation quelque peu insolite s'est déroulée à la CPI dans l'affaire *Ruto & Sang* lorsqu'un témoin de l'Accusation a parlé dans une autre langue que le swahili[124]. En effet, il n'y avait pas d'interprète compétent dans la salle d'audience pour traduire les phrases prononcées en kalenjin. Les juges ont donc accepté que ce soit l'un des membres de l'équipe de Défense de Ruto qui traduise les phrases prononcées par le témoin en kalenjin, alors que l'interprète du Greffe interprétait les phrases en swahili. La Cour a donc dû faire face à la diversité linguistique du continent africain. Des enquêtes ont été ouvertes pour des situations en Palestine et en Géorgie, ce qui signifie que la Cour rencontrera des défis linguistiques liés à d'autres langues encore peu pratiquées à la Cour, telles que l'hébreu, le géorgien ou le russe. Dès lors, les juges doivent être conscients des effets secondaires de l'interprétation linguistique afin d'évaluer correctement les témoignages pour respecter les droits de la défense.

5.2 *Les facteurs de complexité liés au contexte culturel des affaires*

Les situations portées devant la Cour se déroulent dans des régions dont les coutumes et traditions sont souvent méconnues des acteurs du procès. Par conséquent, il peut s'avérer nécessaire de faire appel à un 'témoin de contexte' afin d'expliquer certains éléments contextuels de l'affaire. Il doit être différencié des témoins directs qui ont vécu les événements sur place, et de l'expert scientifique qui, contrairement au témoin de contexte, a pour rôle d'aider les juges à apprécier des éléments de preuve. Une telle question fut soulevée devant la Cour par la défense dans l'affaire *Gbagbo & Blé Goudé*[125].

Le témoin de contexte, se voulant neutre et impartial, est réputé avoir un champ d'expertise particulier qui lui permet d'être considéré comme un expert des circonstances socio-politique lors de la survenance des crimes poursuivis. Par exemple, afin d'appréhender les circonstances ayant conduit au génocide rwandais, le Tribunal pénal international pour le Rwanda (TPIR) a entendu des témoins de

[123] *Ibid.*, p. 33.

[124] ICC Transcript, affaire *Ruto & Sang*, 24 février 2014, ICC-01/09-01/11-T-93-Red-FRA, p. 4 et suivantes.

[125] Transcript, affaire *Le Procureur c. Laurent Gbagbo et Charles Blé Goudé*, 12 mai 2016, ICC-02/11-01/15-T-38-Red-FRA, pp. 1-26.

contexte, tels qu'Alison Des Forges[126]. Il pourrait donc s'avérer parfois nécessaire pour les juges de la CPI de faire appel à un témoin de contexte afin de mieux appréhender les faits et preuves déposés. Dans son opinion dissidente, la juge Van den Wyngaert reproche à la majorité de ne pas avoir recherché plus d'informations contextuelles sur la question spécifique des féticheurs alors même que la Chambre les a estimés importants pour la communauté Walendu-Bindi, et donc pour déterminer la culpabilité de l'accusé[127].

Il semble nécessaire de prendre en compte le contexte culturel afin de juger équitablement l'accusé. Dès lors, le concept anglophone de « *cultural defenses* » pourrait être utilisé pour la défense d'un accusé[128]. Ce concept a pour objet d'exonérer tout ou partie de la responsabilité criminelle dès lors que les actes commis sont considérés comme légitimes dans la culture de l'accusé[129]. Ainsi, ce dernier pourrait faire valoir ses spécificités culturelles lors du procès au nom du relativisme culturel. Déterminée au cas par cas[130], l'admissibilité des preuves relatives à la culture de l'accusé pourrait permettre, au minimum, de mieux appréhender son comportement[131]. Ce moyen d'exonération criminelle n'est pas explicitement prévu par l'article 31 du Statut de Rome. Toutefois, ce dernier laisse une certaine marge de manœuvre aux juges pour prendre en considération d'autres motifs d'exonération pénale. Dans des situations de conflits, certains comportements peuvent être considérés comme traditionnels alors qu'ils constituent des crimes au sens du Statut de Rome. Par conséquent, le rôle de la Cour dans la poursuite des crimes internationaux entre en conflit avec son rôle de protection de la diversité culturelle. Le fait que les cultures évoluent « *does not automatically constitute a compelling reason for rejecting the use of cultural defence altogether* »[132].

Il est difficile d'appréhender la manière dont une différence culturelle permettrait d'exonérer de la responsabilité pour des crimes internationaux[133]. Cette défense pourrait être avancée pour le crime de conscription et d'enrôlement d'enfants[134]. En effet, dans certaines régions d'Afrique, des rites d'initiation guerriers existent pour le passage à l'âge adulte. Dès lors, la participation d'enfants à un conflit armé peut être perçue par leurs communautés comme une initiation vers l'âge adulte[135]. Un accusé

---

[126]TPIR, Chambre I, affaire *Le Procureur c. Jean-Paul Akayesu, Jugement*, 2 septembre 1998, ICTR-96-4-T, par. 118, 120 ou encore 126.

[127]ICC TCII, affaire *Le Procureur c. Germain Katanga*, Opinion dissidente de la juge Christine Van den Wyngaert, 1er août 2014, ICC-01/04-01/07-3436-AnxI-tFRA, p. 92.

[128]Erikkson (2004), pp. 269-290.

[129]Sheybani (1987), p. 752.

[130]Renteln (2011), p. 274.

[131]Renteln (2004), p. 6.

[132]Renteln (2011), p. 273.

[133]Phillips (2003), p. 515.

[134]http://debatewise.org/debates/2288-the-icc-should-allow-a-defence-of-cultural-relativism-to-the-crime-of-recruiting-and-using-child-soldiers/, accès le 22 février 2017.

[135]Kelsall (2009), pp. 151-155.

pourrait être tenté d'avancer cet argument culturel. Il convient toutefois de considérer que la *Cultural Defense* n'est pas un motif d'exonération accepté de manière universelle, et qu'il a au contraire été rejeté par certaines juridictions, comme le Tribunal spécial pour la Sierra Leone (TSSL)[136]. De la même manière, des arguments culturels peuvent être avancé pour les mariages forcés, dès lors que la famille de la victime a consenti au mariage[137]. Par exemple, il conviendrait de faire une distinction entre les arrangements maritaux courants dans certaines régions du globe et les mariages forcés où la victime et la famille, du fait de menaces, n'avaient pas d'autre choix que l'accepter[138]. De même, le TSSL a été confronté à la question de savoir si un accusé possédait le contrôle effectif sur ses subordonnés compte tenu du fait que ces derniers croyaient aux pouvoirs magiques prétendument possédés par l'accusé[139]. « *Judicial decisions on the cultural defence are likely to be tempered significantly by the need for pragmatism and practicality in Court* ». Par conséquent, bien qu'il semble nécessaire de rejeter ce concept à des fins d'exonération de la responsabilité pénale, il pourrait être utilisé lors de la fixation de la peine.

Dans la même optique, les règles 18-d et 19-e du Règlement de procédure et de preuve de la Cour prévoient que la division d'aide aux victimes et aux témoins doit prendre en compte les spécificités culturelles des témoins et victimes. De plus, il paraît nécessaire de considérer la culture des témoins lors de l'enquête, de l'interrogatoire, et de l'audience. Par exemple, le bureau du Procureur éprouve des difficultés à rencontrer des victimes d'abus sexuels acceptant de témoigner[140]. Le seul fait de se déclarer victime sexuelle peut conduire à l'exclusion de la communauté puisque la victime n'est plus vierge, ou est tombée enceinte[141]. Les relations sexuelles, bien que non consenties, peuvent être perçues par les victimes et leur famille comme le fait de participer à l'effort de guerre en soutenant moralement les soldats. Dès lors, des questions portées sur ces sujets tabous lors d'une audience peuvent entraîner une réticence des témoins à y répondre[142], d'autant plus que la défense a tendance à pointer les incohérences et faiblesses des témoignages de victimes d'abus sexuels. Ces dernières peuvent être alors perçues comme « *liars, cheats, mentally disturbed or fools and as themselves being accused* »[143]. La Cour devra donc déterminer la meilleure manière pour poursuivre les crimes sexuels, comme par exemple l'adoption du principe de l'autonomie sexuelle[144]. Dès lors,

[136]Pour le Tribunal Spécial pour la Sierra Leone, voir Kelsall (2009); pour les juridictions des Etats-Unis, voir Sams (1986), pp. 335-354.

[137]Renteln (2011), p. 282.

[138]Gong-Gershowitz (2009), p. 60.

[139]Raimondo (2011), p. 313.

[140]Bensouda (2007), pp. 401-417.

[141]Askin (2001), pp. 23-24.

[142]Almquist (2006), p. 757.

[143]FIDH (Nov. 2002), p. 8.

[144]Grewal (2012), pp. 373-396.

« *interrogators and international judges face a serious risks of making erroneous assessments of point of evidence* »[145].

6 Conclusion

La nature internationale des affaires portées devant la Cour rend inévitables les défis liés à la diversité culturelle de l'humanité. Il est donc nécessaire que la Cour prenne en compte les différentes cultures auxquelles elle est confrontée. Toutefois, la Cour ne doit pas nécessairement accueillir toutes les doléances fondées sur le relativisme culturel. Par ailleurs, alors que la Cour crée lentement sa propre culture juridique, elle intervient dans un contexte où l'impunité des responsables politiques et militaires est fréquente. D'ailleurs, la volonté de retrait de plusieurs pays d'Afrique montre que la culture de l'impunité au nom de la diplomatie prime encore sur la réparation des préjudices subis par les victimes. Pour autant, la CPI « *has confirmed the strength of the field of international criminal justice as the dynamic space within which the struggle for the definition of international crime occurs. This ability to create a meaningful space for social struggle, then, is what conditions the resilience of international criminal justice rather than its having achieved any of the things that international criminal lawyers are prone to present as necessary to its realization* »[146].

La Cour doit nécessairement intégrer à ses politiques judiciaires les différences culturelles de l'ensemble des acteurs des procès internationaux. Cette intégration lui permettrait de promouvoir et de protéger les cultures locales tout en les respectant. Ce faisant, les populations locales et la communauté internationale, au sein de laquelle le débat sur la diversité culturelle fait rage, auraient une meilleure compréhension du travail de la Cour. En réalité, en assurant la protection de l'humanité et de la diversité culturelle, la Cour se protégerait elle-même contre des critiques d'acculturation, comme si elle appliquait l'adage bien connu: « un pour tous, tous pour un ».

Références

Abtahi H (2004) From the Destruction of the Twin Buddhas to the Destruction of the Twin Towers: Crimes against Civilization under the ICC Statute. In: ICLA 4:1-63.
Abtahi H (2005) The Islamic Republic of Iran and the ICC. In: JICJ 3:635-648.
Alarefi AS (2009) Overview of Islamic Law. In: ICLA 9(4):707-731.
Almquist J (2006) The Impact of Cultural Diversity on International Criminal Proceedings. In: JICJ 4(4):745-764.

[145]Almquist (2006), p. 758.
[146]Mégret (2016).

Ambos K (2003) International Criminal Procedure: "Adversarial", "Inquisitorial", or Mixed?. In: ICLA 3:1-37.
Ambos K (2007) The Structure of International Criminal Procedure. In BOHLANDER M (ed) International Criminal Justice – A Critical Analysis of Institutions and Procedures. Brill Nihjoff, Leiden, pp. 429-503.
Arnaud AJ (dir.) (1993) Dictionnaire encyclopédique de théorie et de sociologie du droit, 2ème éd. LGDJ Paris
Askin KD (2001) Comfort Women – Shifting Shame and Stigma from Victims to Victimizers. In: ICLA 1:5-32
Bensouda F (2007) Gender and Sexual Violence under the Rome Statute. In Decaux E, Dieng A, Sow M (dir.), From Human Rights to International Criminal Law/Des droits de l'homme au droit international pénal. Brill Nijhoff, Leiden, pp. 401-418
Bernard D (2014) Trois propositions pour une théorie du droit international pénal. Presse de l'Université Saint-Louis, Bruxelles
Berster L (2015) The Alleged Non-Existence of Cultural Genocide – A Response to the Croatia v. Serbia Judgement. In: JICJ 13:677-692
Blake J (2015) International Cultural Heritage Law. OUP, Oxford
Campbell K (2013) The Making of Global Legal Culture and International Criminal Law. In: LJIL 26:155-172
Canivet G (2005) Les influences croisées entre juridictions nationales et internationales – Eloge de la « bénévolance » des juges. In: RSC 4:799-817
Damaška MR (1975) Structures of Authority and Comparative Criminal Procedure. In: The Yale Law Journal 1:480-544
Damaška MR (1986) The Faces of Justice and State authority: a comparative approach to the legal process. Yale University Press, Yale
Damaška MR (2001) Models of Criminal Procedure. In: ZBornik 51:477-484
Davidson L (2012) Cultural Genocide. Rutgers University Press, New Brunswick
Douglas Smith W (2009) The International Criminal Court: The Long Arm of Neocolonialism ?. In: International affaires Review. Disponible sur http://www.iar-gwu.org/node/87
Ehlert C (2014) Prosecuting the Destruction of Cultural property in International Criminal Law. Nijhoff, Leiden
Erikkson S (2004) International Humanitarian Law: Criminal Accountability, State Responsibility, and Cultural Considerations. In: Air Force Law Review 55:269-290
FIDH (Nov. 2002) Victims in the Balance: Challenges Ahead for the International Criminal Tribunal for Rwanda, Rapport n° 329/2
Fraser N (2009) Who Counts ? Dilemmas of Justice in a Post-Westphalian World. In: Antipode 41:281-297
Frulli M (2011) The Criminalization of Offences against Cultural Heritage in Times of Armed Conflict: The Quest for Consistency. In: EJIL 22(1):203-217
Gerstenblith P (2016) The Destruction of Cultural Heritage: A crime against Property or a Crime against People ? In: The John Marshall Review of Intellectual Property Law 15:336-393
Gong-Gershowitz J (2009) Forced Mariage: A New Crime Against Humanity ?. In: Northwestern Journal of International Human Rights 8:53-76
Gottlieb Y (2004-2005) Criminalizing Destruction of Cultural Property: A Proposal for Defining New Crimes under the Rome Statute. In: Penn State International Law Review 23(4):857-896
Green Martinez SA (2015) Destruction of Cultural heritage in Northern Mali – A Crime against Humanity ?. In: JICJ 13:1073-1097
Grewal K (2012) The Protection of sexual Autonomy under International Criminal Law – The International Criminal Court and the Challenge of Defining Rape. In: JICJ 10:373-396
Hall CK, Powderly J, Hayes N (2016) Article 7. In Triffterer O, Ambos K (dir.) The Rome Statute of International Criminal Court A Commentary, 3d éd. C.H. Beck, Hart et Nomos, Munich, p. 206-225

Hall CK, Van den Herik L (2016) Article 7. In Triffterer O, Ambos K (dir.) The Rome Statute of International Criminal Court A Commentary, 3e éd. C.H. Beck, Hart et Nomos, Munich, p. 282
Hall J (2012) La poursuite d'un Chef d'État en exercice devant la Cour pénale internationale – L'interaction entre l'exception aux immunités et la coopération étatique. Mémoire de Master 2, sous la direction de Mme Bannelier-Christakis, UPMF, 227 p.
Hon K (2013) Bringing Cultural Genocide in by the Backdoor: Victim Participation at the ICC. In: Seton Hal Law Review 43:359-407
Jeangene Vilmer JB (2014) Union Africaine versus Cour pénale internationale: répondre aux objections et sortir de la crise. In: Etudes internationales 45(1), pp. 5-26
Jouannet E (2008) Les visions françaises et américaine du droit international: cultures juridiques et droit international. In: SFDI Droit international et diversité des cultures juridiques. Pedone, Paris, pp. 43-90
Karton J (2008) Lost in Translation: International Criminal Tribunals and the Legal implication of Interpreted Testimony. In: Vand. J. Transnat'l L. 41(1):1-54
Kelsall T (2009) Culture Under Cross-examination: International Justice and the Special Court for Sierra Leone. CUP, New York
Langer M (2006) The Rise of Managerial Judging in International Criminal Law. In: AJIL 53:835-909
Lambert-Abdelgawad E (2003) Cour pénale internationale et adaptations constitutionnelles. In: RIDC 3:539-573
Lemkin R (1947) Genocide as a Crime in International Law. In: AJIL 41:145-151
Malekian F (2009) The Homogeneity of International Criminal Court with Islamic Jurisprudence. In: ICLA 9(4):595-621
Mégret F (2013) Cour pénale internationale et colonialisme, au-delà des évidences. Disponible sur SSRN, http://ssrn.com/abstract=2221424
Mégret F (2009) Beyond Fairness: Understanding the Determinants of International Criminal Procedure. In: JILFA 14:37-76
Mégret F (2016) International Criminal Justice as a Juridical Field. *Champ pénal/Penal Field*, Vol. XIII, disponible sur: https://champpenal.revues.org/9284, accès le 22 février 2017.
Mestre J (2010) Rapport de synthèse. In Association Henri Capitant (dir.) Droit et culture – Journées Louisianaises. Bruylant, Bruxelles
Nersessian D (2005) Rethinking Cultural Genocide Under International Law, disponible sur: https://www.carnegiecouncil.org/publications/archive/dialogue/2_12/section_1/5139
Ngane SN (2015) The Position of Witnesses before the International criminal Court. Brill Nijhoff, Leiden
Nmehielle VO (2014) Saddling the New African Regional Human Rights Court with International criminal Jurisdiction: Innovative, Obstructive, Expedient. In: AJLS 7(1):7-42
Noguchi M (2006) Criminal Justice in Asia and Japon and the International Criminal Court ». In: ICLA 6:585-604
Ost F, Van de kerchove M (2002) De la pyramide au réseau ? Pour une théorie dialectique du droit. Publications des Facultés universitaires Saint-Louis, Bruxelles
Pascal B (1970) Pensées – édition de Port Royal, Chap. XXV – Faiblesse de l'Homme. 1669 et janvier 1670. Gilbert, Paris
Phillips A (2003) When Culture Means Gender: Issues of Cultural Defence in the English Courts. In: Modern Law Review 66(4):510-531
Pruim S (2014) Ethnocide and Indigenous Peoples: Article 8 of the Declaration on the Rights of Indigenous People. In: Adelaïde Law Review 35:269-308
Raimondo FO (2011) For Further research on the Relationship between Cultural Diversity and International Criminal Law. In: ICLA 11:299-314
Ramanathan U (2005) India and the ICC. In: JICJ 3:627-634
Renteln AD (2004) The Cultural Defense. OUP, New York
Renteln AD (2011) Cultural Defenses in International Criminal Tribunals: a Preliminary Consideration of the Issues. In: Southwestern Journal of International Law 18:267-286

Rubinstein J (1999) Looting of Art and Cultural Property – a War Crime ?. In: International Legal Practitioner 24:83-86

Sams JP (1986) The Availability of the Cultural Defense as an Excuse for Criminal Behavior. In: GA. J. Int'l & Comp. L. 16:335-354

Skilbeck R (2010) Frankenstein Monster: Creating a New International Procedure. In: JICJ 8:451-462

Schuldt L (2015) Southeast Asian Hesitation: Asian Countries and the International Criminal Court. In: Ger. Law J 16:75-104

Sheybani MM (1987) Cultural Defence: One Person's Culture is Another's Crime. In: Loy. L.A. Int'l & Comp. L. Rev. 9:751-783

Tillier J (2013) The ICC Prosecutor and Positive Complementarity: Strengthening the Rule of Law ?. In: ICLA 13:507-592

Tladi D (2015) The Duty on South Africa to Arrest and Surrender President Al-Bashir under South African and International Law – A Perspective of International Law. In: JICJ, 13:1027-1047

Triffterer O, Bergsmo M, Ambos K (2016) Preamble. In Triffterer O, Ambos K (dir.) The Rome Statute of International Criminal Court A Commentary, 3d éd. C.H. Beck, Hart et Nomos, Munich, pp. 1-13

Venturini G (2010) Chapter 3 – Necessity in the Law of Armed Conflict and in International Criminal Law. In: Netherlands Yearbook of International Law 41:45-78

Vogliotti M (2004) Production du droit en réseau et juge « tisseur » - De quelques épiphanies de l'expérience juridique médiévale au sein de la justice pénale internationale. In: Delmas-Marty M, Fronza E, Lambert-Abdelgwad E (dir.) Les sources du droit international pénal – L'expérience des tribunaux pénaux internationaux et le statut de la Cour pénale internationale. SLC, Paris, pp. 361-369

Vogliotti M (2005) L'érosion de la pyramide pénale moderne et l'hypothèse du réseau. In: Revue interdisciplinaire d'études juridiques 55:1-16

Part IV
Cultural Identity

Leitkultur Meets German *Angst*: On the Role of Values and Needs in the German Debate on the Integration of Refugees and Migrants

Claudia Maria Hofmann

Abstract The term 'culture' is an open one. Various meanings can be attached to it. This chapter focuses on the connection of certain aspects of 'culture' to what is perceived as individual and collective identity. The example of a German 'guiding culture' serves as a point of departure to address the following questions: First, how can 'culture' in general be defined, and how is it linked to what is perceived as individual or collective identity? Second, do we need policies defending a particular culture, and (how) can a 'guiding culture' be justified? Third, what has—international and national—law got to do with it? Fourth, what lies beneath cultural defence politics, and which lessons can be drawn from a more thorough understanding of these underlying motives? It is suggested to add a needs-based view to the debate about the integration of migrants and refugees in a society.

1 Background: *Leitkultur* Re-re-revisited

Bassam Tibi coined the term *Leitkultur*[1]—which can be translated as 'guiding', 'leading' or 'dominant culture'—in 1996. As a response to a perceived arbitrariness or value relativism in the idea of multiculturalism, he called for a European *Leitkultur* to which all members of European society should subscribe.[2] According to Tibi, a European *Leitkultur* consists of a catalogue of norms and values based on the European cultural modernity.[3] This catalogue includes in particular the primacy of reason over religious views and absolute truths, individual (i.e., not collective)

[1]Tibi (1996), p. 28.

[2]Tibi elaborated the concept in 1998 in his book 'Europa ohne Identität?' ('Europe without Identity?'), which was reprinted with an additional introduction in 2016. See also Tibi (2001).

[3]Tibi (2016), p. 294.

C. M. Hofmann (✉)
Public Law and Politics (Professor A. Graser), Faculty of Law, University of Regensburg, Regensburg, Germany
e-mail: claudia.m.hofmann@ur.de

© Springer International Publishing AG, part of Springer Nature 2018

E. Lagrange et al. (eds.), *Cultural Heritage and International Law*,
https://doi.org/10.1007/978-3-319-78789-3_11

human rights, secular democracies based on the separation of church and state, generally acknowledged pluralism and mutual tolerance.[4]

In Germany, the idea of a *Leitkultur* has been taken up in political discourse not only once but also on several occasions.[5] Tibi's concept of a European *Leitkultur*, however, was gutted and filled with German content, a content that varied with the political background of the respective participants of the debate. Common denominator was the notion that a German 'guiding culture' was necessary with regard to the integration of migrants and refugees into German society.[6] Initially, harsh critique led to the dismissal of the concept of a German *Leitkultur* guiding integration policies.[7] However, the critique seems to have lost its effect over time.

Twenty years after Tibi's first use of the term, it has found its way into German state legislation. In 2016, Bavaria passed the 'Bavarian Integration Act' (Bayerisches Integrationsgesetz).[8] Since 2010, four German states have enacted legislation concerning the social integration of people with migrant or refugee backgrounds.[9] The general aim of these laws is to regulate integration policies, define certain integration goals, create integration programmes and coordinate the work of the institutions involved. Yet only the Bavarian Integration Act turns to the concept of a guiding culture in this regard. Its preamble defines *Leitkultur* as a 'fundamental cultural order of society' and lists certain core values and historic and structural circumstances that shape this consensus:

> Bavaria forms part of the German nation with a common language and culture. It is deeply embedded in the values and traditions of the Christian occident and is at the same time aware of the Jewish contribution to its identity. The human dignity, the personal liberty and the equality of all men, the right of everyone to a life in self-determination but also accountability, the separation of church and state are – as fruits of the Enlightenment – the foundation of our legal and social order. The National Socialist despotism, the crimes of the Third Reich and the horrors of the Second World War have taught that only a constitutionally governed rule of law prevents from terror, dictatorship and division and is a precondition for peace and freedom. Everyone has therefore a duty to uphold the law and a duty to be loyal to the people, the constitution, the state and its laws. Conversely, in a democratically constituted community all state power is bound to the voice of the people. Solidarity with the weak and those in need of help is a commandment for the community as well as every individual, but at the same time assumes that first and foremost everyone is obliged to take responsibility for oneself and one's family and to do the utmost to make a contribution in this respect. The community can only offer what is generated by all, and

[4]Ibid., p. 295.

[5]Cf. Meier-Walser (2017), pp. 5 et seq.; Ohlert (2015), pp. 18 et seq. The debate peaked in particular in 2000, in 2005 and in the course of the refugee crisis in 2016 and 2017.

[6]Although the more comprehensive term 'inclusion' has in many cases replaced the term 'integration' in public debate and policy instruments, in German legislation the latter term still prevails. The usage of the term 'integration' in this text is due to this fact.

[7]Cf. Meier-Walser (2017), pp. 6 et seq.

[8]Bayerisches Integrationsgesetz of 13 December 2016, Bayerisches Gesetz- und Verordnungsblatt 2016, p. 335.

[9]These states are Baden-Wuerttemberg, Bavaria, Berlin and North Rhine-Westphalia; cf. Wohlfarth (2017), p. 4.

> therefore may expect everyone's contribution. All of Bavaria is shaped by habits, customs and traditions. The liberal way of life in an open and plural society requires equally mutual tolerance and respect for the cultural character of our country. In the past decades, it has become the new home for many who have settled in here and have participated actively in society. The long historical struggle of our nation and our continent for unity, justice, peace and freedom entails an obligation to the achieved pan-European heritage and the goal of a common European path. This identity-forming basic consensus is lived and embraced on a daily basis in our country and forms the fundamental cultural order of society (guiding culture). To safeguard this, to secure social cohesion and to empower migrants to a life in our society is the purpose of this law.[10]

The lengthy and somewhat cumbersome wording of this preamble reflects the difficulty to define what a 'guiding culture' is. In sum, according to the preamble, a guiding culture is influenced by a common history; by certain common values, traits and traditions; and by the way they have manifested in societal, legal and governmental structures. This definition presupposes two things: First, it is generally assumed that the mentioned values and traditions are actually shared by (at least the majority of) the members of a particular community. This might be plausible but it does not necessarily have to be the case. Second, the dominance of a certain culture, i.e. the right to prescribe a specific culture to others, is justified by the previous assumption. In addition, the drawn linkage between culture and identity is noteworthy.

Several questions come to mind in this respect: First, how can 'culture' in general be defined, and how is it linked to what is perceived as individual or collective identity? Second, do we need policies defending a particular culture, and (how) can a 'guiding culture' be justified? Third, what has—international and national—law got to do with it? Fourth, what lies beneath cultural defence politics, and which lessons can be drawn from a more thorough understanding of these underlying motives? These questions shall be addressed in the subsequent sections.

2 Culture: Can It Be Defined?

In search of a definition of the term 'culture', it is almost impossible not to get lost. In 1952, Kroeber and Kluckhohn compiled a list of 164 definitions.[11] It is not hard to imagine that the number of definitions has increased since then. Given the plethora of conceptual approaches, one is tempted to think that 'culture is everything'[12] and to follow German sociologist Dirk Baecker's advice that 'culture' cannot be defined. To him, those who try to do so only show that they cannot cope with the term.[13] For the purpose of this article, at least some facets of the term shall be highlighted.

---

[10](Partially analogous) Translation by the author.

[11]Kroeber and Kluckhohn (1952), pp. 39 et seq.

[12]Cf. D'Andrade (1999), p. 87 who holds the opposite opinion though.

[13]Baecker (2003), p. 33.

In common parlance, the term 'culture' in relation to a specific group or community is used to describe a set of social practices, conventions, attitudes, values and common traits.[14] Depending on the respective disciplinary lens, there is much more to be seen, though. To name but a few aspects,[15] anthropologists may understand culture as a form of human expression or as a strategy to cope with the complex demands of everyday life. As Albert Camus famously put it,: '*Culture: cri des hommes devant leur destin*'.[16] From the perspective of social psychology, culture can be perceived as both creating and expressing a network. Philosophers may explore culture as a construct or ponder the dialectics between culture and nature, whereas political scientists might analyse culture as a social order or an educational programme. From a sociological point of view, culture can be seen rather as a (communicative) process than as a generic term for certain values, traditions and traits. Culture stands on the one hand for something stable that survives time; on the other hand, it is exposed to constant change. The stability of cultural practices depends on their daily re-creation. This too is reflected by the notion of 'culture as a process'.[17]

'Culture' as a legal term both has a descriptive and a normative nature. In view of a complexity that can only be hinted at here, lawmakers and practitioners are faced with a seemingly impossible mission when they want to define 'culture' in a legal instrument.[18] Naturally, they must generalise. The United Nations Committee on Economic, Social and Cultural Rights (CESCR), i.e. the treaty body responsible for supervising the implementation of the International Covenant on Economic, Social and Cultural Rights (ICESCR), addresses the difficulties of this task openly and turns to an all-encompassing approach. For the interpretation of Article 15 para. 1 (a) ICESCR (right of everyone to take part in cultural life) in the General Comment No. 21, the Committee comes to the following conclusion:

> 11. In the Committee's view, culture is a broad, inclusive concept encompassing all manifestations of human existence. The expression 'cultural life' is an explicit reference to culture as a living process, historical, dynamic and evolving, with a past, a present and a future.
>
> 12. The concept of culture must be seen not as a series of isolated manifestations or hermetic compartments, but as an interactive process whereby individuals and communities, while preserving their specificities and purposes, give expression to the culture of humanity. This concept takes account of the individuality and otherness of culture as the creation and product of society.
>
> 13. The Committee considers that culture, for the purpose of implementing article 15 (1) (a), encompasses, inter alia, ways of life, language, oral and written literature, music and song, non-verbal communication, religion or belief systems, rites and ceremonies, sport and

[14]Cf. the definition of 'culture' In: Merriam-Webster.com (9 February 2018).

[15]See for the following the various approaches compiled by Treichel and Mayer (2011).

[16]Camus (1962), p. 31.

[17]Cf. Treichel (2011), pp. 256 et seq.

[18]Unsurprisingly, some authors consider the term 'culture' unsuitable for legal provisions; see for a critique in the context of constitutional law Huster (2005), pp. 75 et seq. (with further references).

> games, methods of production or technology, natural and man-made environments, food, clothing and shelter and the arts, customs and traditions through which individuals, groups of individuals and communities express their humanity and the meaning they give to their existence, and build their world view representing their encounter with the external forces affecting their lives. Culture shapes and mirrors the values of well-being and the economic, social and political life of individuals, groups of individuals and communities.[19]

Although this definition indicates a certain connection, no explicit mention is made on values as a part of culture at this point. However, within the text of General Comment No. 21, several references can be found in this regard.[20] When looking at the connection between law and culture, two aspects stand out: (1) Culture can be perceived as an expression of certain values, and these values again may form a part of culture. (2) Law itself is an expression of culture and, hence, of the aforementioned values.

3 Some Reflections on the Linkage Between Culture and Identity

Having addressed the many aspects of 'culture', we now turn to a term of similar complexity. Personal 'identity' equally can be viewed from many different angles.[21] And the search for the answer to the question 'Who am I?' is perhaps as old as humanity itself. As the term 'human *being*' indicates, from the moment we are born, we are in a constant process of being. Much of this process is spent in search and in the creation of our individual identity. Identity too is a construct, not only a personal but in many cases also a social construct. Some people may choose to spend years in the exile of the Himalayan mountains to 'find themselves'. But probably for most of us, much of finding our personal identity lies in the interaction with others. Other persons may serve as a mirror for our self. We perceive their reactions to us, and we compare our attitudes and actions to theirs, and by doing so we are able to draw conclusions as to the question of who we are.

Just as this is part of constructing individual identity, it also forms collective identities—i.e., the understanding of who we are as a community, who we as individuals are in relation to this community and its members, as well as in relation to other communities and their members. With regard to collective identity, Tomlinson points out that 'identity is not in fact merely some fragile communal-psychic attachment, but a considerable dimension of *institutionalized* social life in modernity'.[22] It is this process of institutionalisation and the institutions created that can be understood as an expression of culture. With regard to the individual, cultural

[19]Committee on Economic, Social and Cultural Rights (2009), paras. 11–13.

[20]Ibid., at paras. 2, 16, 26, 27, 28, 36, 43, 69.

[21]Cf. for instance Olson (2017), at para 1.

[22]Tomlinson (2003), pp. 270 et seq. (emphasis in original).

practices can be a way of expressing identity, as well as they can shape the belief of who we are. This notion is also reflected in the above-mentioned General Comment No. 21 when the CESCR points out that 'intangible cultural goods, such as languages, customs, traditions, beliefs, knowledge and history, as well as values [. . .] make up identity and contribute to the cultural diversity of individuals and communities'.[23] Thus, the expression 'cultural identity' is somewhat imprecise since it merges the aforementioned aspects of culture being both an expression of and a source of imprinting individual and collective identity.

4 Does Culture Need to Be Defended?

When asking whether there is a need to defend culture, we first have to identify a threat. No threat, no need for defence. In this regard, various threat scenarios may be conceived: the most significant threat is, of course, the deliberate attack. Some might perceive such an attack in the actions of international terrorists. In addition, we can find threats that appear slightly softer, maybe not in respect of their effects but in respect of their modes of action. The most prominent example is globalisation. The sentiment that the societal, political or economic changes brought about in an increasingly interconnected world pose a risk to the cultural distinctiveness of individuals, as well as communities, is shared by many, be they academics, political stakeholders or the 'man on the street'. They raise the spectre of a consumption-oriented Western cultural imperialism, which eventually homogenises and levels all local particularities.[24]

However, this notion is not exempt from criticism. Tomlinson, for instance, argues 'that cultural identity, properly understood, is much more the *product* of globalization than its victim'.[25] The processes of communication and exchange certainly have altered rapidly, especially in the twentieth century. And it is an important aim to protect the cultural heritage of humanity. Yet as we are in constant interaction with each other, it is naïve to think that we can freeze and preserve certain forms of these interactions from being influenced by the outside world. Change is natural, just as it is frightening from time to time.

This brings us to another perceived threat to culture, a threat that is to some extend connected to globalisation and a threat that has the potential to trigger various fears. Global migration flows have impacted on societies throughout history. One could say that in a globalised world, the channels for these flows have even increased, as perhaps have the causes for migration. As people from diverse ethnic, religious or linguistic backgrounds start living together, they get exposed to many that were unknown to them before: new faces, new languages, new social practices. This can

[23]Committee on Economic, Social and Cultural Rights (2009), para. 16.
[24]Cf. Tomlinson (2003), p. 269.
[25]Ibid.

be disturbing at times.[26] But for some, it is even more than that. They detect the danger of a foreign infiltration and call for the protection of their 'cultural identity'. Tibi, for instance, who fathered the term *Leitkultur*, used the title 'Europe without Identity?' for a book in which he advocated a European guiding culture as a response to the perceived danger of an increasing Islamisation of Western Europe.[27]

Identity in respect of collective culture comes with a sense of belonging.[28] Hence, sharing traditions, beliefs, values or a common language may induce the feeling of 'I am one of them' or 'this person is one of us'. The complex relations and causes are still to be explored by social psychology and neuroscience. Perhaps there are parts of our brain that still perceive the felt connection to others to be an insurance to the threats of a sabre-toothed tiger. Perhaps our brains are simply 'wired to connect'.[29] Suffice it to say here that identity process theory tells us whenever 'identity is threatened [...] the individual will engage in strategies for coping with the threat'.[30] In this regard, the following coping strategies are being described: intrapsychic (e.g., denial, re-conceptualisation), interpersonal (e.g., isolation) or intergroup (e.g., social mobilisation). Prescribing a guiding culture that migrants or refugees have to adhere to can be viewed as an example for the latter strategy.

However, it is highly doubtful whether this prescription is necessary or whether it is rather a Don Quixotean fight against windmills. As regards minority cultures, we can find several arguments for the necessity to protect them[31]: due to the minority aspect, there is the danger of extinction.[32] Their protection can be justified on the basis of the equal human rights of the member of the minority group. And cultural plurality as a value can also serve as a reason for safeguarding minority cultures. Conversely, the need to protect the cultural practices of a majority is questionable. Since they are backed by a majority, one might say that they 'can take care of themselves'.[33] Orgad, however, identifies four different scenarios that have the potential to justify also the protection of majority cultures: (a) diminishing majorities, (b) regional-minority majorities, (c) victimised majorities and (d) minoritised majorities.[34] With a view to the cultural defence policies of certain European countries, one is left wondering whether these justification scenarios apply to the respective cases.

---

[26]Cf. for instance Carleton (2016).

[27]This perception is also reflected in the additional subtitle to the 2016 edition of the book which reads 'Europäisierung oder Islamisierung' ('Europeanisation or Islamisation').

[28]Cf. Vignoles et al. (2006).

[29]Lieberman (2013).

[30]Jaspal (2014), p. 5.

[31]See also Monteiro de Matos, in this volume.

[32]With regard to regional and minority languages see Oeter, in this volume, Sect. 2.

[33]Orgad (2015), p. 8.

[34]Ibid., p. 9.

5 What's Law Got to Do with It?

Cultural defence policies can be found not only in Germany. In the Netherlands, for example, there is the process of *inburgering*.[35] In France, immigrants must sign an integration contract (*contrat d'intégration républicaine*) in which they declare to respect the fundamental values of the French Republic, and civic education courses need to be attended in order to learn about these values.[36] But since we have opened with a German example, we shall have a closer look at it.

The Bavarian Integration Act aims, on the one hand, at fostering integration—based on the general premise that the successful integration is the prerequisite for a 'good life' in society; on the other hand, the Act creates a duty to integrate—demanding integration efforts of those who are subject to the Act (Article 1). Under the Act, migrants are also bound by the guiding culture. Actions that can be perceived as a disregard of the values of a liberal democracy can be sanctioned with civic education courses (Article 13).

Education generally is the main instrument of the Bavarian Integration Act: for every stage of education (pre-school, primary, secondary and tertiary education), the Act makes provision for the respective services and specific educational content. Thus, from an early age onwards, migrants are to be taught the German language (Articles 4 and 5), the 'central elements of the Christian-occidental culture' (Article 6) and the 'fundamental legal and value system of the constitution' (Article 7). The Act also obliges media and business in terms of the integration goals and also in terms of conveying the contents of the guiding culture (Articles 10 and 11). In sum, migrants are to be constantly exposed to the *Leitkultur*.

As has been said before, law can be viewed as an expression of culture. Here, however, law serves as an instrument to impose a specific culture. In contrast to the national laws implementing cultural defence policies, we find a range of provisions in international law protecting cultural diversity and minority cultures. In general, international human rights—as they are elaborated, for instance, in the United Nations core human rights treaties—just as national basic rights protect certain elements of culture, e.g. the freedom of opinion and expression, the freedom of religion and belief, the right to equality and non-discrimination, the freedom of association or the people's right to self-determination. This is of particular relevance since minority rights cannot necessarily be invoked by migrants or refugees.[37]

In addition, there are international human rights dealing specifically with culture such as the right to participate freely in the cultural life of the community (Article 27 para. 1 of the Universal Declaration of Human Rights), the right to take part in cultural life (Article 15 para 1 lit. a ICESCR) or the obligation of non-discrimination

---

[35] See for an overview of the procedure Orgad (2015), pp. 100 et seq.

[36] See information on the website of the French Office of Immigration and Integration, URL: http://www.ofii.fr/le-contrat-d-integration-republicaine (9 February 2018). Cf. for the previous *contrat d'accieul et d'intégration* Orgad (2015), pp. 89 ff.

[37] Cf. Langenfeld (2001), pp. 360 et seq.

with respect to cultural rights (Article 2 para. 2 ICESCR and Article 5 lit. e (vi) of the International Convention on the Elimination of All Forms of Racial Discrimination). Furthermore, Article 27 of the International Covenant on Civil and Political Rights provides for a right for members of minorities to 'enjoy their own culture, to profess and practice their own religion, or to use their own language'. These individual rights are complemented by the United Nations Declaration on the Rights of Persons Belonging to National or Ethnic, Religious and Linguistic Minorities and, of course, by the various conventions and declarations of the United Nations Educational, Scientific and Cultural Organization (UNESCO).

With regard to the aforementioned range of individual human rights, it is safe to say that 'cultural plurality' is one of the values expressed and promoted by the international human rights framework. National cultural defence policies stand in contrast with these individual rights in particular and the value expressed in general. In this respect, the legal system with its various levels serves as a playing field for social negotiations about conflicting goals and values. It is therefore not surprising that Bavarian Integration Act is being challenged in court—for now solely on the ground of a potential violation of national laws.[38] This is, however, due to the fact that the Bavarian Constitutional Court, which was invoked in this matter, can only check legislation for a possible infringement of the Bavarian constitution.

6 Needs-Based View on Cultural Defence Politics

In view of the actions undertaken, for instance, in Bavaria, the images of a shadow play come to mind where shadow puppets are moved behind a translucent screen. On the surface, the audience only sees the puppets acting out a specific story. The puppeteer, however, as author of story and actions remains hidden from the viewers. Of course, human actions are caused by a complex set of causes, with many yet to be detected. What is offered here only refers to one potential cause in this respect: human needs. Applied to the situation discussed in this article, it is suggested that human needs are the 'hidden puppeteer' that drives cultural defence politics. The aim to protect a certain culture only lies on the surface, whereas underneath more fundamental objectives are at work. Adopting a needs-based view, i.e. analysing the respective underlying needs and addressing them in a transparent manner, opens a forum for a dialogue that is less prone to inclusion and exclusion ('us vs. them', 'our culture vs. their culture') but open to a discussion about features that all humans share.

When speaking of human needs, Maslow's hierarchy of needs is probably one of the first associations. His famous distinction between physiological needs, safety needs, the need for belonging and love, for esteem, for self-actualisation and for self-transcendence often serves as a point of reference in discussions about human

[38] Schnell and Wittl (2017).

Table 1 Matrix of needs and satisfiers according to Max-Neef et al. (shortened version)

Need	Being	Having	Doing	Interacting
Subsistence	Physical and mental health, equilibrium	Food, shelter, work	Feed, clothe, rest, work	Living environment social setting
Protection	Care, adaptability, autonomy	Insurance systems, social security, health systems, rights, work, family	Cooperate, plan, prevent, take care of, help, cure	Living space, social environment, dwelling
Affection	Respect, sense of humour, generosity, sensuality	Friendships, family, relationships with nature	Make love, express emotions, share, take care of, cultivate	Privacy, intimate spaces of togetherness
Understanding	Critical conscience, curiosity, intuition	Literature, teachers, policies, education	Analyse, study, meditate, investigate	Schools, families, universities, communities
Participation	Receptiveness, dedication, sense of humour	Responsibilities, duties, privileges, work	Cooperate, dissent, interact, express opinions	Associations, parties, churches, neighbourhoods
Leisure	Imagination, tranquillity, spontaneity	Games, parties, peace of mind	Daydream, remember, relax, have fun	Landscapes, intimate spaces, places to be alone
Creation	Imagination, boldness, inventiveness, curiosity	Abilities, skills, work, techniques	Work, invent, build, design, compose, interpret	Workshops, spaces for expression, cultural groups, audiences
Identity	Sense of belonging, self-esteem, consistency	Language, religions, work, customs, values, norms	Get to know oneself, grow, commit oneself	Everyday settings, settings that one belongs to, maturation stages
Freedom	Autonomy, passion, self-esteem, open-mindedness	Equal rights	Dissent, choose, run risks, develop awareness	Temporal, spacial

needs.[39] Self-determination theory proposes a triad of needs: the need for competence, for relatedness and for autonomy.[40] Another, more differentiated categorisation of human needs is offered by the Chilean economist Max-Neef and his colleagues (Table 1).[41]

What does a needs-based view imply in the context of the *Leitkultur* debate? Most importantly, we can observe that all of the aspects invoked in this debate serve various kinds of needs: some elements of culture may serve need for social

[39]Maslow (1943), pp. 372 et seq.

[40]Deci and Ryan (2000), pp. 233 et seq.

[41]Max-Neef et al. (1989), p. 33.

interaction, affection or even basic physical needs (i.e., the way we prepare our food or we build our houses[42]). Cultural practices such as artistic activities may meet the need for esteem, for self-actualisation, for leisure or for creation. Shared values and traditions or the participation in cultural groups may satisfy a need to belong.[43] There is an inextricable link between culture and us making sense of life; creating cultural goods may even give us a sense of immortality.

Probably all of the aspects just mentioned are also connected to our individual and collective identity. The search for this identity is also need driven. It may serve the need for self-esteem or consistency, and it may give us a sense of belonging. In this regard, the triangular relation between culture, identity and needs is subject to permanent tension. Obviously, just as we as humans are in constant interaction, various cultural practices are in a process of constant exchange and—sometimes more, sometimes less—in a competition for dominance. Hence, cultural defence policies serve specific needs as well: codified values in form of a *Leitkultur* may address the aforementioned need for dominance, as well as the need for security. In the German context, the latter need is mirrored in the proverbial German *Angst.*[44] Thus, in the face of the German refugee crisis in 2015, the creation of laws that impose values and worldviews can be seen as a direct response to this *Angst.* Legislation gives the impression of control, even if it is just an illusionary one. Furthermore, whenever cultural practices are institutionalised, as is the case particularly with religious communities or states, the institutionalisation can be understood as an expression of the search for security and the quest for supremacy.

7 Conclusion

As has been suggested before, a needs-based view may add an element of empathy to the discussion about the integration of migrants and refugees in a society, and that is empathy for both sides. The needs underlying the idea of a *Leitkultur* must be assessed on a neutral basis. In general, they too deserve to be respected. However, cultural defence policies must be examined in the light of the rights guaranteed by the international human rights framework, by regional human rights instruments, as well as by national laws. A 'liberal state' cannot protect itself by illiberal means. This again contradicts other fundamental values such as equality, pluralism or the right to live a life in freedom and self-determination. Perhaps the approaches suggested by multiculturalism still leave many problems of multi-ethnic societies unresolved. Meeting others with empathy, an open mind, genuine interest and curiosity can neither be demanded by the members of the respective societies, nor can it be induced by legislation. Thus, a needs-based dialogue can serve as a tool to

[42]Many of these aspects can be found in the UNESCO list of Intangible Cultural Heritage.

[43]Specifically on the need to belong see Baumeister and Leary (1995).

[44]See for an exploration of the historic context of the 'German Angst' Bode (2006).

deconstruct certain bases of fear and to construct a sense of identity: the collective identity of us as human beings.

References

Baecker D (2003) Wozu Kultur? 3rd edn. Kadmos, Berlin
Baumeister RF, Leary MR (1995) The need to belong: desire for interpersonal attachments as a fundamental human motivation. Psychol Bull 117:497–592
Bode S (2006) Die deutsche Krankheit – German Angst. Klett-Cotta, Stuttgart
Camus A (1962) Carnets. Mai 1935 - Mars 1951. Éditions Gallimard, Paris
Carleton RN (2016) Fear of the unknown: one fear to rule them all? J Anxiety Disord 41:5–21
Committee on Economic, Social and Cultural Rights (2009), General Comment No. 21. Right of Everyone to Take Part in Cultural Life (art. 15, para. 1 (a) of the International Covenant on Economic, Social and Cultural Rights, 21 December 2009, UN Doc. E/C.12/GC/21
D'Andrade R (1999) Culture is not everything. In: Cerroni-Long EL (ed) Anthropological theory in North America. Bergin & Gavey, Westport, pp 85–103
Deci EL, Ryan RM (2000) The 'What' and 'Why' of goal pursuits: human needs and the self-determination of behaviour. Psychol Inq 11:227–268
Huster S (2005) Kultur im Verfassungsstaat, Veröffentlichungen der Vereinigung der Deutschen Staatsrechtslehrer 65:53–82
Jaspal R (2014) Social psychological debates about identity. In: Jaspal R (ed) Identity process theory. Identity, social action and social change. Cambridge University Press, Cambridge, pp 3–19
Kroeber AL, Kluckhohn C (1952) Culture. A critical review of concepts and definitions. Harvard University Printing Office, Cambridge
Langenfeld C (2001) Integration und kulturelle Identität zugewanderter Minderheiten. Eine Untersuchung am Beispiel des allgemeinbildenden Schulwesens in der Bundesrepublik Deutschland. Mohr Siebeck, Tübingen
Lieberman MD (2013) Social. Why our brains are wired to connect. Broadway Books, New York
Maslow AH (1943) A theory of human motivation. Psychol Rev 50:370–396
Max-Neef M, Elizalde A, Hopenhayn M (1989) Human scale development: an option for the future. Dev Dialogue 1:5–80
Meier-Walser R (2017) Die Diskussion um eine Leitkultur. Hintergrund, Positionen und aktueller Stand, Hanns-Seidel-Stiftung e.V., Munich
Ohlert M (2015) Zwischen 'Multikulturalismus' und 'Leitkultur'. Integrationsleitbild und -politik der im 17. Deutschen Bundestag vertretenen Parteien, Springer, Wiesbaden
Olson ET (2017) Personal identity. In: Zalta EN (ed) The Stanford encyclopedia of philosophy (Summer 2017 edn). https://plato.stanford.edu/archives/sum2017/entries/identity-personal/. Accessed 9 Feb 2018
Orgad L (2015) The cultural defense of nations. A liberal theory of majority rights. Oxford University Press, Oxford
Schnell L, Wittl W (2017) Ein Gesetz der usgrenzung. Süddeutsche Zeitung online, 2 May 2017. http://www.sueddeutsche.de/bayern/leitkultur-ein-gesetz-der-ausgrenzung-1.3486476. Accessed 9 Feb 2018
Tibi B (1996) Multikultureller Werte-Relativismus und Werteverlust. Aus Politik und Zeitgeschichte (B 52–53):27–36
Tibi B (2001) Leitkultur als Wertekonsens. Bilanz einer missglückten Debatte. Aus Politik und Zeitgeschichte (1–2):23–26
Tibi B (2016) Europa ohne Identität? Europäisierung oder Islamisierung, ibidem, Stuttgart

Tomlinson J (2003) Globalization and cultural identity. In: McGrew AG, Held D (eds) The globalization transformations reader: an introduction to the globalization debate. Blackwell Pub, Cambridge

Treichel D (2011) Methoden der Kulturanalyse. In: Treichel D, Mayer C-H (eds) Lehrbuch Kultur. Lehr- und Lernmaterialien zur Vermittlung kultureller Kompetenzen. Waxmann, Münster, pp 228–268

Treichel D, Mayer C-H (eds) (2011) Lehrbuch Kultur. Lehr- und Lernmaterialien zur Vermittlung kultureller Kompetenzen. Waxmann, Münster

Vignoles VL, Regalia C, Manzi C, Golledge J, Scabini E (2006) Beyond self-esteem: influence of multiple motives on identity construction. J Pers Soc Psychol 90(2):308–333

Wohlfarth C (2017) Papiertiger oder Meilenstein? Die Integrationsgesetze der Bundesländer im Vergleich, Policy Brief des SVR-Forschungsbereichs 2017-1, Berlin

Le droit international public et le respect de l'identité culturelle en matière de statut familial

Lukas Rass-Masson

Abstract Le droit international public comporte de nombreuses sources consacrant et renforçant le respect de l'identité culturelle. Il semble naturel que ces sources s'étendent au droit de la famille et au statut familial de l'étranger. Pourtant, à l'analyse, ces sources internationales restent trop incomplètes pour fonder de véritables droits individuels, qui seraient la traduction d'un droit au respect de l'identité culturelle en matière de statut familial. L'influence directe du droit international public sur le droit international privé de la famille est donc fortement limitée. Cela ne signifie cependant pas que le droit international public n'ait aucune influence sur le droit international privé de la famille. Les fondements du droit international public sont en effet des vecteurs puissants d'une obligation pour les États de reconnaître l'identité culturelle en matière de statut familial. En ce que la théorie du droit international public souligne que ce droit doit être construit autour d'un universel cosmopolitique respectueux des particularités nationales, elle permet aussi de comprendre que ces fondements se prolongent nécessairement par l'obligation de concevoir le droit international privé de la famille d'une façon ouverte à la pluralité culturelle.

1 Introduction

Parmi les défis culturels auxquels la communauté internationale fait face figure certainement la question de la place à accorder aux différences de structures familiales, que celles-ci soient appréhendées sur le plan social, ou sur un plan plus strictement juridique. Le phénomène familial a en effet une influence primordiale sur

L. Rass-Masson (✉)
Université Toulouse 1 Capitole, Toulouse, France
e-mail: lukas.rass-masson@ut-capitole.fr

© Springer International Publishing AG, part of Springer Nature 2018

E. Lagrange et al. (eds.), *Cultural Heritage and International Law*,
https://doi.org/10.1007/978-3-319-78789-3_12

la cohésion d'une société, et par conséquent sur l'évolution et l'histoire de nos États[1]. Or, « la dimension culturelle du statut personnel »[2] est une donnée largement acceptée aujourd'hui, et « il est évident qu'appliquer une loi étrangère, c'est aussi appliquer un système de valeurs étranger et à cet égard, le droit international privé est sans aucun doute un poste d'observation pertinent pour s'interroger sur l'éternel débat entre l'universalisme des valeurs et la relativité des cultures; pour contempler par-là, ce qui fait les identités des sociétés humaines »[3].

Partant de cette idée, il est nécessaire d'analyser l'influence du droit international public sur le droit international privé des relations familiales internationales, notamment à travers l'étude d'une éventuelle obligation tirée du droit international public d'appliquer le droit de la famille étranger, afin de respecter l'identité culturelle des personnes concernées. Il faut d'ailleurs préciser ici que la notion d'« identité culturelle », consacrée en droit international privé[4], est appréhendée sans aucun *a priori* sur la façon de concevoir cette identité, qui peut aussi bien être une identité ouverte qu'une identité refermée sur elle-même[5]. Cette question est au cœur des enjeux contemporains, puisque, pour reprendre la formule d'Erik Jayme, « l'époque postmoderne est caractérisée par le rôle primordial que les individus accordent à leur identité culturelle, dont les expressions extérieures sont la langue, la religion, les mœurs et les autres membres de la communauté à laquelle un fort sentiment de loyauté les lie. L'on défend cette identité par tous les moyens, parfois en sacrifiant son existence et même sa vie »[6].

Si le sujet connaît depuis quelques années un regain d'intérêt, en raison de la crise des réfugiés que connaît actuellement l'Europe, il n'en demeure pas moins que cette question soulève des débats de principe qui doivent pouvoir s'émanciper de l'actualité pour mieux guider les choix juridiques et politiques retenus dans le but de répondre aux défis de l'actualité. Et le droit international privé est particulièrement bien placé pour servir de modèle d'analyse, puisque « la discipline du conflit de lois a précisément pour objet de gérer la tension entre le besoin de cohésion sociale et la nécessité de faire place à l'altérité »[7]. Ainsi, s'il est vrai qu'il « serait vain de rechercher l'existence *de lege lata* d'un droit général et autonome à l'identité culturelle [et qu'] en l'état du droit positif, aucun texte à valeur juridiquement contraignante pour les Etats n'autorise un individu à exciper d'une violation d'un tel droit devant les juges [européens], pour autant, l'exigence de protection de l'identité culturelle des

---

[1]Pour une analyse du phénomène pour le continent européen, voy. Todd (1996).

[2]Bollée, Pataut (2016), p. 1.

[3]*Ibid.*

[4]Jayme (1995).

[5]Qui est celle que François Jullien condamne lorsqu'il critique la notion d'identité culturelle; voy. Jullien (2016).

[6]Jayme (1995), p. 167.

[7]Muir Watt (2016), p. 15.

individus, non plus considérée comme un droit invocable en justice mais comme un but à atteindre, trouve progressivement un régime juridique propre »[8].

La question permet également de proposer une réflexion sur la nature particulière du droit international public lorsque le destinataire des règles n'est pas un État étranger, mais un citoyen. L'identité culturelle dans le contexte du droit privé est une excellente illustration de la difficulté pour le droit international public de définir sa place dans ces situations hybrides dans lesquelles le droit international public propose des règles ayant vocation à s'appliquer uniquement dans des relations privées[9]. Si le respect de l'identité culturelle est indéniablement un objectif du droit international public, s'il y a de nombreuses conventions internationales prévoyant des règles de droit international privé de la famille et s'il est incontesté que le statut personnel et familial relève également de l'identité culturelle de la personne, il n'en reste pas moins que le droit international public semble bien ne pas étendre l'obligation du respect de l'identité culturelle à une obligation pour les États de prévoir des règles de droit international privé par lesquelles l'identité culturelle est protégée dans le cadre des relations familiales transfrontières.

Il convient donc d'analyser les raisons pour lesquelles le droit international public n'a pas cette influence directe, ce qui est une situation d'autant plus surprenante, au premier regard, que le droit international privé fut longtemps conçu, suite à l'École hollandaise[10] et encore par Mancini[11], dans la dépendance directe du droit international public[12]. L'absence de consécration directe d'une exigence de reconnaissance de l'identité culturelle dans le cadre du statut familial laisse cependant en suspens la question de l'influence que peut avoir le droit international public général, à travers ses concepts fondateurs et des principes que les États s'engagent nécessairement à respecter dans le cadre des relations internationales.

Nous proposons de répondre à ces questions en analysant, dans un premier temps, l'absence de consécration par le droit international public d'un authentique droit à la reconnaissance de l'identité culturelle dans le cadre du statut familial, en raison de l'absence d'obligation véritable en ce sens imposée par le droit international public. Puis, dans un second temps, nous nous intéresserons à la question de savoir si certains des fondements du droit international public ne seraient pas le vecteur d'une obligation pour les États de construire leur droit international privé de la famille d'une façon ouverte à la pluralité culturelle, ce qui pourrait alors comporter une forme de « réintroduction » de l'exigence du respect de l'identité culturelle.

---

[8]Colavitti (2013), p. 195.

[9]Lagrange (2012).

[10]Ancel (2017), pp. 321-422.

[11]Mancini (1874).

[12]De Boer (2010).

2 L'absence de consécration d'un droit à la reconnaissance de l'identité culturelle en matière de statut familial

Le droit international public comporte des éléments qui peuvent avoir potentiellement une influence décisive sur le droit international privé en vue de l'application d'un droit étranger en matière familiale, et donc en vue de la consécration d'un droit à la reconnaissance de l'identité culturelle en matière familiale. Mais à l'analyse, ces éléments restent trop incomplets pour en déduire de véritables droits qui pourraient être invoqués par les particuliers, voire par les États dans leurs relations réciproques, ce qui réduit alors fortement l'influence réelle du droit international public sur le droit international privé de la famille.

2.1 La diversité des sources internationales potentiellement porteuses d'une exigence de reconnaissance de l'identité culturelle dans le cadre du statut familial

Force est de constater que le droit international public appréhende la question du statut familial et qu'il le fait en insistant sur la nécessité de respecter l'identité culturelle dans le cadre du statut familial. Un bref inventaire, non exhaustif, des sources qui existent suffira pour prouver que le droit international public s'intéresse à la question du statut familial, en le voyant comme un prolongement de l'identité culturelle.

La Convention de 1951 relative au statut des réfugiés prévoit ainsi à l'alinéa 2 de son article 12 relatif au statut personnel le maintien des droits découlant du statut personnel du réfugié[13]. Cette « pétrification » du statut personnel et familial, que le cas du mariage illustre bien[14], correspond parfaitement à la traduction concrète d'une exigence de respect de l'identité culturelle dans le cadre du statut personnel et familial.

Cette idée est prolongée par la Déclaration universelle de l'Unesco sur la diversité culturelle de 2001 qui, dans son préambule, insiste sur l'importance de plusieurs éléments qui ont également des conséquences tangibles sur le statut familial, tels que « les modes de vie, les façons de vivre ensemble » ou les « débats contemporains sur

---

[13]Voy. l'art. article 12 de la Convention de 1951 relative au statut des réfugiés, qui prévoit que « 1. Le statut personnel de tout réfugié sera régi par la loi du pays de son domicile ou, à défaut de domicile, par la loi du pays de sa résidence.

2. Les droits précédemment acquis par le réfugié et découlant du statut personnel, et notamment ceux qui résultent du mariage, seront respectés par tout Etat contractant, sous réserve, le cas échéant, de l'accomplissement des formalités prévues par la législation dudit Etat, étant entendu, toutefois, que le droit en cause doit être de ceux qui auraient été reconnus par la législation dudit Etat si l'intéressé n'était devenu un réfugié. »

[14]Sur cette « théorie de la pétrification », voy. p. ex. Bureau, Muir Watt (2014), pp. 590-591.

l'identité »[15]. Et la Convention sur la protection et la promotion de la diversité des expressions culturelles de 2005 lui emboîte le pas, particulièrement lorsqu'elle souligne « que la culture prend diverses formes dans le temps et dans l'espace et que cette diversité s'incarne dans l'originalité et la pluralité des identités »[16].

Toujours en précisant et en illustrant ce constat du droit international public porteur d'une exigence de reconnaissance de l'identité culturelle dans le cadre du statut familial, de nombreuses conventions de droit international privé visent à permettre une certaine stabilité de la relation familiale en garantissant les droits qui existent en application d'un droit étranger. Il en va ainsi de conventions à vocation universelle, et notamment des Conventions de La Haye, telles que la Convention du 25 octobre 1980 sur les aspects civils de l'enlèvement international d'enfants, la Convention du 29 mai 1993 sur la protection des enfants et la coopération en matière d'adoption internationale ou la Convention du 19 octobre 1996 concernant la compétence, la loi applicable, la reconnaissance, l'exécution et la coopération en matière de responsabilité parentale et de mesures de protection des enfants, pour se limiter aux conventions les plus largement ratifiées en matière familiale. Ce tissu normatif est complété par des conventions à vocation continentale, comme l'illustrent les efforts du Conseil de l'Europe, ou l'adoption de conventions bilatérales visant également au maintien de la diversité culturelle en matière de statut familial[17].

Ces différents éléments normatifs de source internationale sont les germes d'une exigence de reconnaissance de l'identité culturelle dans le cadre du statut familial auxquels les juges sont réceptifs. Une illustration particulièrement évocatrice est l'hypothèse de l'adoption. La Cour européenne des droits de l'homme considère en effet dans ce domaine que les juges doivent reconnaître le « statut juridique créé valablement à l'étranger et correspondant à une vie familiale au sens de l'article 8 de la Convention »[18] et ne peuvent donc, sans motif légitime, « refuser la reconnaissance des liens familiaux qui préexistaient *de facto* [à l'étranger] ». Cette supposée obligation de reconnaissance[19] montre bien l'importance qui est accordée à l'exigence du respect de la diversité culturelle en matière de statut familial. Mais la Cour de Strasbourg va plus loin encore dans l'attachement à la diversité, puisqu'elle accepte, notamment dans l'arrêt *Harroudj c. France*, que l'on puisse refuser la consécration de la situation familiale voulue par les parties, ici la

---

[15]Préambule de la Déclaration universelle de l'Unesco sur la diversité culturelle de 2001, paras. 5 et 6.

[16]Préambule de la Convention sur la protection et la promotion de la diversité des expressions culturelles de 2005, para. 7.

[17]En ce qui concerne la France et la question des enlèvements d'enfants, par exemple, voy. les 19 conventions bilatérales sur le site justice.gouv.fr (http://www.justice.gouv.fr/justice-civile-11861/enlevement-parental-12063/source-les-conventions-applicables-conventions-bilaterales-21128.html, consulté le 10 novembre 2017).

[18]CEDH 28 juin 2007, *Wagner et J.M.W.L. c. Luxembourg*, n° 76240/01, para. 133.

[19]Sur les mutations méthodologiques contemporaines entraînées notamment par cette exigence de reconnaissance, voy. not. Bureau, Muir Watt (2014), pp. 603-718.

transposition d'une *kafala*[20] en adoption, en raison du fait qu'« en effaçant ainsi progressivement la prohibition de l'adoption, l'Etat défendeur, qui entend favoriser l'intégration d'enfants d'origine étrangère sans les couper immédiatement des règles de leur pays d'origine, respecte le pluralisme culturel et ménage un juste équilibre entre l'intérêt public et celui de la requérante » [21].

Il y a donc des éléments de droit international public qui, malgré leur caractère assez embryonnaire, renferment la nécessité de respecter l'identité culturelle des individus dans le cadre de leur statut familial. Mais à côté de ces éléments en faveur du respect de la diversité culturelle et familiale, il y a également un assez grand nombre d'éléments révélateurs des limites du droit international public en ce domaine, et qui montrent que le droit international public est loin d'imposer de véritables obligations aux États en matière familiale.

2.2 *Les limites des sources internationales porteuses d'une exigence de reconnaissance de l'identité culturelle dans le cadre du statut familial*

Plusieurs facteurs contribuent à enlever aux sources internationales leur influence, au point d'interdire d'y voir une obligation internationale pour les États de reconnaître l'identité culturelle en matière familiale. Un premier élément tient au fait que les conventions qui portent directement sur l'unification des règles de droit international privé sont généralement des conventions qui ne sont ratifiées que par une partie limitée de la communauté internationale[22], voire des conventions qui dès le départ n'ont qu'une vocation régionale ou bilatérale[23]. En outre, les conventions qui obtiennent le plus grand succès en termes de ratifications sont des conventions qui ne consacrent pas de règles de conflit de lois à proprement parler, mais qui se concentrent sur les mécanismes de coopération[24]. Leur influence sur la consécration

[20]La *kafala*, également désignée comme « recueil légal », est une institution de droit coranique qui a pour objet d'offrir à un enfant une protection en assurant son accueil dans une famille, sans créer de lien de filiation entre lui et la personne qui le recueille. Comme il n'y a pas de création d'un lien de filiation, la *kafala* ne peut pas être assimilée à une adoption, institution interdite par le Coran.

[21]CEDH 4 oct. 2012, *Harroudj c. France*, n° 43631/09, para. 51.

[22]Pour s'en convaincre, il suffit de regarder le nombre de ratifications des Conventions de La Haye en matière de droit de la famille. Celles qui ont connu le plus grand succès, les conventions du 25 octobre 1980 sur les aspects civils de l'enlèvement international d'enfants et du 29 mai 1993 sur la protection des enfants et la coopération en matière d'adoption internationale, ont toutes les deux 98 Etats contractants, ce qui est certes déjà notable, mais ne leur confère certainement pas une dimension universelle (source: www.hcch.net).

[23]Ce qui est le cas donc de tous les instruments adoptés au sein d'une organisation à vocation régionale, telle que le Conseil de l'Europe, ou de façon bilatérale par deux Etats.

[24]C'est en effet le cas des Conventions de La Haye de 1980 sur les enlèvements international d'enfants et de 1993 sur l'adoption.

d'une véritable obligation de reconnaissance de l'identité culturelle en matière de statut familial est donc limitée.

Un second élément tient à l'absence d'obligation prévue par les traités de reconnaître juridiquement l'identité culturelle. C'est ici en effet la nature hybride des obligations prévues par les instruments qui est un frein important. En ce que ces instruments s'adressent surtout aux particuliers, premiers concernés par ces règles de droit international privé, les Etats n'ont qu'un intérêt indirect à leur application par d'autres Etats contractants. Comme l'État n'est pas le sujet de ces obligations en matière de statut familial, l'on voit bien que la mise en œuvre effective de ces obligations dépend *in fine* du bon vouloir des Etats qui les acceptent. Or cette effectivité est souvent variable, faute pour le droit international public de prévoir des recours ou des mécanismes permettant d'assurer la bonne exécution de ces obligations. Et ce constat de la très relative effectivité du droit international public en matière familiale ne peut qu'être renforcé si l'on tient compte de la marge nationale d'appréciation ou des nécessités de transposition, qui sont particulièrement fortes en matière de statut familial. Ainsi, « il faut bien voir que l'avancée du droit international public sur les terres du droit international privé reste parfaitement relative, et dans une large mesure encore très résiduelle »[25].

Pour s'en convaincre, la position des juges internationaux est ici encore révélatrice, particulièrement celle de la Cour internationale de Justice[26]. Dans l'arrêt *Boll* de 1958, opposant les Pays-Bas et la Suède au sujet de la convention de 1902 pour régler la tutelle des mineures, que la Suède avait laissée inappliquée au bénéfice de ses règles internes, ce qui est aujourd'hui connu sous la technique des lois de police, les juges ont en effet souligné qu'« il est à peine besoin d'ajouter qu'aboutir à une solution qui mettrait obstacle à l'application de la loi suédoise sur la protection de l'enfance et de la jeunesse à un mineur étranger vivant en Suède serait méconnaître le but social de cette loi, but social dont l'importance a été ressentie dans de nombreux pays, surtout après la signature de la Convention de 1902. Le problème social de la jeunesse délinquante ou même simplement dévoyée et des enfants dont la santé, l'état mental ou le développement moral est compromis, bref mal adaptés à la vie sociale, a été souvent posé; des lois telles que la loi suédoise actuellement en cause ont été édictées dans plusieurs pays pour y pourvoir. La Cour ne pourrait aisément souscrire à une interprétation qui ferait de la Convention de 1902 un obstacle sur ce point au progrès social »[27]. Ce n'est donc pas le droit

---

[25]Forteau (2015), p. 62.

[26]Sur laquelle, voy. not. van Loon, de Dycker (2013).

[27]Recueil des arrêts, avis consultatifs et ordonnances, jugement du 28 novembre 1958, p. 71; ce raisonnement a par ailleurs autorisé la Cour à ne pas se prononcer sur la question de savoir si « cette convention doit s'entendre comme comportant une réserve implicite autorisant à faire échec, pour motif d'ordre public, à l'application de la loi étrangère reconnue normalement compétente pour régir le rapport de droit considéré », réserve implicite qui est aujourd'hui largement considérée comme contenue dans les conventions internationales, y compris bilatérales, signées par les Etats en matière de droit international privé (voy. sur ce point not. Gannagé (2001) et Ancel, Lequette (2006), pp. 605-607).

international public qui va venir encadrer la souveraineté nationale au moment où l'Etat construit son droit international privé de la famille.

Les Etats disposent alors d'une telle liberté qu'une reconnaissance de l'identité culturelle étrangère ne saurait leur être imposée par les mécanismes classiques du droit international public. Le droit international public peut donc bien être un droit commun des États, mais aucune obligation normative n'en découle pour l'élaboration du droit international privé en matière familiale. Et compte tenu de l'organisation actuelle de la communauté internationale, un consensus entre les Etats sur des questions aussi intimement liées à des enjeux de société reste hypothétique. Au contraire, tant qu'il y aura une diversité culturelle, cette diversité s'opposera sans doute à l'émergence d'une société internationale sur le modèle des sociétés nationales ou étatiques, qui reposent, à des degrés variables, sur une certaine homogénéité, et donc identité, culturelle. La liberté des ordres juridiques nationaux reste quasiment absolue. Un Etat peut ainsi refuser la reconnaissance de l'identité culturelle de la famille étrangère par une attitude exclusiviste, c'est-à-dire une attitude qui n'accepte que la juridicité des situations internes ou intégrées à cet Etat, et qui ignore donc la situation familiale étrangère. Il peut aussi à l'inverse adopter une attitude universaliste et appliquer ses conceptions culturelles à toute situation familiale internationale, en se dotant ainsi d'un champ d'application universel incompatible avec toute reconnaissance de la diversité culturelle. Aucune de ces deux attitudes ne permet le développement d'un système de droit international privé dans lequel l'identité de l'étranger soit respectée dans sa diversité. Mais les deux attitudes sont possibles au regard du droit international public. Du point de vue strictement normatif, le seul apport du droit international public est donc de dire qu'il appartient aux ordres juridiques nationaux de construire pour leur propre compte un système de droit international privé, sans leur imposer la reconnaissance de l'identité culturelle de l'étranger en matière de statut familial. Tous ces éléments confirment en effet que « l'existence même du droit international privé révèle tout à la fois les limites existentielles du droit international public (tant qu'il y aura un droit international privé, ce sera le signe qu'il existe toujours un droit international public entendu comme le droit d'une société moins intégrée que ne le serait un Etat mondial), mais aussi ses limites politiques (dans le monde contemporain, il existe un vaste champ de réglementation que les sociétés internes n'acceptent pas encore de voir relever de son orbite) »[28].

En tant que tel, le droit international public est donc stérile en matière de statut familial et n'impose pas aux Etats d'appliquer un droit de la famille étranger afin de protéger l'identité culturelle des personnes concernées. L'autonomie constitutionnelle de l'Etat entraîne en effet tout à la fois l'absence d'obligation d'incorporation, d'obligation relative à l'applicabilité directe des normes internationales et d'obligation de reconnaître la primauté du droit international dans l'ordre interne[29]. Faire du droit international public une source de respect de la diversité culturelle en matière de droit

[28]Forteau (2015), p. 65.

[29]Lagrange (2012), pp. 325-334.

de la famille implique donc de dépasser son influence purement normative. Si l'influence ne vient pas des règles, il se pourrait bien en effet qu'elle vienne des concepts, notamment des concepts qui fondent et structurent le droit international public et qui pourraient avoir des prolongements nécessaires en droit international privé de la famille. C'est donc, au-delà de l'influence normative, la question de l'influence conceptuelle qui est posée.

3 Les fondements du droit international public, vecteurs d'une obligation pour les États de reconnaître l'identité culturelle en matière de statut familial

Il est ici question de savoir si l'influence du droit international public sur le droit international privé de la famille peut venir des fondements mêmes du droit international public. Ces fondements peuvent en effet, en cas d'adhésion des Etats à ceux-ci, avoir comme prolongement nécessaire l'obligation de construire le droit international privé de la famille d'une façon ouverte à la pluralité culturelle. En ce que la théorie du droit international public souligne que le droit international public doit être construit autour d'un universel cosmopolitique respectueux des particularités nationales[30], ce que confirme au demeurant fort bien l'exigence du respect de l'identité culturelle, et met l'accent sur le fait que « particularisme et cosmopolitisme sont les deux faces du droit international, qui reconnaît notre commune humanité en nous protégeant dans nos différences »[31], le droit international public recèle à l'évidence des éléments de comparaison *a priori* très fructueux pour le droit international privé de la famille.

Avant de pouvoir procéder à l'analyse de l'influence des concepts de cosmopolitisme et de particularisme, il faut d'abord s'attarder sur l'importance accordée, aussi bien en droit international public que privé au postulat de la singularité des ordres juridiques. En droit international public, il n'est guère douteux que la souveraineté des Etats, et donc leur singularité, reste le fondement essentiel du droit. Et pour le droit privé, l'Etat est aussi l'ordre et l'autorité de référence. C'est à travers l'Etat qu'une société affirme, par un acte constituant, qu'elle constitue un ordre légitime et autonome disposant de la plénitude des pouvoirs. C'est donc cet ordre étatique qui est la source primaire et centrale du droit, ce qui a été conceptualisé en droit international privé par le recours à la notion d'« antériorité de l'ordre juridique interne par rapport à l'ordre international »[32]. Il faut donc d'abord comprendre dans quelle mesure cette antériorité, autre forme d'expression de la souveraineté des Etats, permet encore l'ouverture à la diversité qui est nécessaire au respect de l'identité

[30]Cosmopolitisme qui se prolonge aussi par l'universel; voy. not. Beck (2006), p. 16 et s.

[31]« *Parochialism and cosmopolitanism are two faces of international law, which recognizes our common humanity by protecting us in our differences* » (Sellers (2012), p. 275).

[32]Francescakis (1955 et 1985), p. 133.

culturelle. Ce n'est qu'ensuite qu'il est possible de découvrir l'influence que les principes de cosmopolitisme et de particularisme, que nous rapprocherons des concepts d'universalité et de singularité, ont sur la conception du droit international privé, outre leur valeur axiomatique en droit international public. Le droit international privé, pour pleinement respecter ces principes, doit en effet nécessairement être conçu de façon ouverte à la pluralité, ce qu'il convient de confirmer par une analyse de la conception contemporaine du statut familial international des personnes qui se déplacent à travers les frontières.

3.1 Souveraineté et antériorité des ordres juridiques nationaux, sources de coordination de la diversité culturelle

L'antériorité de l'ordre juridique national se pose d'abord comme antériorité du droit par rapport aux faits, puisque, pour connaître la signification juridique d'une situation, il faut confronter le fait à l'ensemble préconstitué du droit objectif. Le droit objectif, qu'il soit interne ou international, est donc primordial en tant que norme sociale. C'est une norme de traduction, ou « métanorme », qui fait communiquer les autres domaines de la vie sociale, les évalue et conditionne leur acceptabilité pour la société[33]. Pour les relations entre droit international public et privé, cette antériorité signifie que, compte tenu de l'idée que « l'ordre interne s'est établi historiquement avant l'ordre international, lequel n'a encore ni autorité législative proprement dite, ni par suite sanctions directement organisées, il est [...] légitime que l'ordre interne développe spontanément et efficacement des règles sur des question auxquelles l'ordre international n'est pas en mesure de formuler des solutions et dont il pourrait d'ailleurs ensuite difficilement assurer l'observation »[34]. Le Doyen Batiffol, sans doute le plus grand spécialiste français de droit international privé du XXème siècle, conceptualise ainsi l'antériorité de l'ordre juridique interne pour ce qu'elle est, c'est-à-dire une nécessité théorique. Il dépasse la conception politique et excessivement restrictive retenue en théorie du droit international privé à la suite de Niboyet, sur fond d'attachement à la souveraineté[35]. Batiffol distingue ainsi deux conceptions du droit, pour dire que « rationnellement, quant à son essence, l'ordre interne est subordonné à l'ordre international, mais par l'élément impératif, il a devancé, sur le plan de l'existence, l'ordre international »[36]. Or l'élément qui est

[33]Cette question soulève des débats théoriques très importants, qui sont discutés notamment par Habermas (1992 et 1998), pp. 69-78, critiquant la vision autopoïétique du droit; sur celle-ci, voy. not. Teubner (1989).

[34]Batiffol (1956), p. 205.

[35]L'idée d'une certaine antériorité était en effet déjà présente chez Niboyet, autour du postulat de politique législative de la primauté de la collectivité nationale sur la collectivité internationale, voy. Niboyet (1944).

[36]Batiffol, Lagarde (1993), p. 38.

déterminant pour la juridicité d'une règle, d'après la conception aujourd'hui prédominante en théorie du droit, est celui de l'impérativité, au sens de « sanctionnabilité », de la règle. L'antériorité de l'ordre juridique national pour déterminer la juridicité d'une situation, y compris internationale, est donc un axiome de la théorie générale du droit, et du droit international privé en particulier. Pour obtenir la sanction d'une règle, il faut *in fine* toujours se tourner vers les organes et techniques institués par l'État. L'État national se pose à ce titre comme irréductiblement premier, antérieur, par rapport aux organes internationaux et aux relations privées internationales. Il pourrait parfaitement considérer que son droit de la famille est le seul qui mérite d'être juridiquement reconnu, et que le statut familial des étrangers doit s'y conformer, ce qui reviendrait donc à nier l'identité culturelle en ce domaine.

Le fondement du particularisme ou de la singularité qui s'exprime par l'antériorité de l'ordre juridique national doit donc être bien compris pour saisir ses conséquences sur le respect de l'identité culturelle en matière de statut familial. Or, « les relations internationales s'insérant normalement dans le contexte du droit interne – et devant s'y insérer sans perturbation – l'ordre interne doit être admis en priorité à faire prévaloir sur les lois étrangères ceux de ses éléments qui mettent en cause sa cohésion »[37]. Autrement dit, « la règle de conflit remplit une fonction médiatrice: elle relie à la vie sociale interne, que contrôle et constitue l'ordre du for, les rapports de droit privé qui, par quelque côté, y échappent pour se développer aussi dans d'autres ordres juridiques. Cette fonction lui est assignée par l'ordre du for dont la tâche première et la raison d'être ne sont pas d'assurer le gouvernement de la société internationale en lieu et place d'institutions défaillantes, mais d'organiser la vie sociale interne. [La règle de conflit] établit entre l'ordre du for et les ordres juridiques étrangers une interconnexion réalisant la conciliation des exigences de cohésion de l'ordre qui accueille la relation et des aspirations à la différence de traitement que fonde le caractère international de celle-ci »[38]. Il faut à ce titre veiller à bien comprendre que le respect de la cohésion de l'ordre juridique interne n'est en rien un synonyme de dérive nationaliste et unilatéraliste d'un particularisme trop marqué. Ce respect n'empêche pas, en effet, de tenir compte d'objectifs internationalistes que l'ordre juridique du for peut très bien poursuivre en même temps qu'il défend le respect de sa cohérence interne. L'ordre juridique national peut tout à fait, au nom même de son antériorité, procéder à une mise en balance des objectifs de son propre droit de la famille avec la volonté du respect de l'identité culturelle et familiales des étrangers, pour trouver un équilibre entre la défense de sa singularité et l'ouverture aux autres Etats. Cette recherche d'équilibre conduit à ce que « la règle de conflit de lois dépend, dans une mesure plus ou moins large, à la fois

[37]Batiffol, Francescakis (1959), pp. 270-271; Batiffol et Francescakis (1959), pp. 259 et s., spéc. pp. 270 à 271; idée que Francescakis a également développée dans sa thèse (Francescakis (1958), et not. p. 259: « Les rapports internationaux de droit privé doivent normalement pouvoir s'intégrer dans le commerce interne »).

[38]Ancel, Lequette (2006), p. 250.

de la teneur du droit interne de l'État qui la consacre et de la conception que cet État se fait de la teneur concrète des rapports internationaux »[39].

L'antériorité de l'ordre juridique national n'empêche donc nullement la prise en considération des objectifs spécifiques liés au respect de l'identité culturelle en matière de statut familial. Comme nous avons déjà eu l'occasion de le dire, « l'antériorité ne signifie pas du tout fermeture et repli sur soi, parce que l'objectif d'ouverture à la diversité des relations privées internationales peut parfaitement s'y intégrer »[40]. Mais à s'en tenir à cette seule considération, le respect de l'identité culturelle en matière de statut familial ne serait qu'un simple objectif politique, dont la mise en œuvre serait laissée aux Etats qui seraient parfaitement libres de ne pas y adhérer. L'antériorité n'empêche donc pas une conception ouverte du droit de la famille, mais ne l'impose pas non plus. L'exigence de reconnaissance de l'identité culturelle doit venir d'ailleurs, ou du moins de l'articulation de l'antériorité avec un autre concept fondamental. Et c'est la confrontation avec le concept d'universel, qui doit être respecté au nom justement de l'antériorité de l'ordre juridique national, qui est particulièrement fertile à cet égard.

3.2 Universalité et singularité en droit international public, des concepts porteurs d'une nécessaire ouverture à l'altérité, révélée par le droit international privé de la famille

Les principes généraux tirés des fondements du droit international public doivent nécessairement être transposés et mis en œuvre au niveau national. C'est donc en s'adressant au droit national et en en appelant au législateur national qu'il convient d'élaborer des lignes directrices, nécessairement variables d'un ordre juridique à un autre, mais construit sur le respect des principes fondateurs communs qui imposent, notamment à travers le respect de la souveraineté des autres Etats, de reconnaître la pluralité des ordres juridiques. Dans le contexte du statut familial international, cette ouverture à la pluralité se prolonge par le respect de l'identité culturelle des personnes concernées. Le point de départ du raisonnement réside dans le fait que la juridicité d'une situation de fait dépend nécessairement d'un ordre juridique dont les règles de droit objectif conditionnent l'acceptation de la situation. Le droit international privé nous enseigne cependant qu'une situation contenant un élément d'extranéité peut être privée de juridicité en raison de cette extranéité, ce qui explique pourquoi historiquement la reconnaissance de la qualité de sujet de droit a été un attribut de la citoyenneté et donc un avantage refusé pendant longtemps aux étrangers[41]. Il faut découvrir les raisons pour lesquelles l'ordre juridique doit

[39]Francescakis (1958), p. 259.

[40]Notre thèse, 2015, para. 183.

[41]Voy. sur ce point notre thèse, 2015, paras. 42-177.

appréhender juridiquement toute situation, y compris internationale, et analyser en quoi les concepts fondateurs du droit international public peuvent lui imposer une forme de prétention à l'universalité, avant de comprendre le sens de cette prétention notamment au regard de l'identité culturelle en matière de statut familial.

En droit privé, la prétention à l'universalité de l'ordre juridique peut être fondée sur l'universel du respect de la dignité de tout homme. Il est en effet désormais acquis que « le développement de l'organisation juridique n'est pas concevable sans l'admission que la notion d'homme correspond à une réalité »[42] et que « le comportement du système juridique des rapports privés internationaux ne décèle aujourd'hui aucune trace d'une hésitation sur ce que tout homme est sujet de droit »[43]. Le respect de l'autre et de l'étranger découle alors directement de la notion de droits de l'homme, et le sens véritable des droits de l'homme peut même radicalement être ce respect de l'autre[44]. Pour le droit international privé, il en a été déduit que la valeur que le droit international privé est appelé à servir est le « respect dû à l'étranger »[45]. En droit international public, on retrouve cette même exigence de respect dû à la diversité. On la retrouve de façon générale en raison du fait que les Etats doivent respecter la souveraineté des autres Etats. Mais on la retrouve également de façon plus précise face au respect de l'identité culturelle par les nombreux outils, expliqués ci-dessus, qui en sont une expression au niveau international. Le droit international public conforte cependant le constat que l'acceptation de la pluralité ne peut se faire que dans la mesure où l'Etat, en tant qu'ordre juridique singulier, l'autorise, c'est-à-dire uniquement dans la mesure où la différence est compatible avec les valeurs fondamentales de l'ordre juridique national requis.

Pour l'ordre juridique qui se réfère à l'universel, que ce soit celui du droit international public ou celui des droits de l'homme, il devient alors indispensable de concevoir des « notions universelles, que l'on rencontrerait comme telles à la base de toutes les cultures, et ce même si d'autres cultures n'en ont pas pensé – abstrait – le mode d'universalité »[46], « notions et représentations de base considérées comme ne pouvant pas ne pas être présentes dans toutes les cultures, [...] proprement (strictement) 'universelles', puisque impliquant un devoir-être; [...] il faut, de façon non conditionnelle, et sans même que l'on ait à le vérifier, poser cette nécessit-é-universalité de principe; celle-ci a statut axiomatique. Au risque, sinon, de mettre

---

[42]Batiffol (1979), p. 167. Comme le dit également Hannah Arendt dans *Le système totalitaire*, « le premier pas essentiel sur la route qui mène à la domination totale consiste à tuer en l'homme la personnalité juridique »; Arendt (1972), p. 185.

[43]Batiffol (1979), p. 170.

[44]Comme a pu le dire Emmanuel Levinas, « que les droits de l'homme soient originellement les droits de l'autre homme et qu'ils expriment par-delà l'épanouissement des identités dans leur identité même et leur instinct de conservation, le pour–l'autre du social, du pour–l'étranger – tel me semble être le sens de leur nouveauté » (Levinas (2006), p. 153).

[45]« Die Achtung vor dem Fremden » (Werner Goldschmidt, cité d'après Evrigenis (1966), p. 105). Voy. égal. Batiffol (1957), p. 229–272 et Francescakis (1957), p. 205-219.

[46]Jullien (2008), p. 127.

en péril toute communication et compréhension entre les hommes: de mettre en péril, par conséquent, toute humanité »[47]. Les droits de l'homme imposent alors un strict respect de tout homme, jusque dans une radicale altérité. Et le droit international public montre que l'on peut même aller plus loin dans l'analyse. Dans la mesure où la participation de l'Etat à la vie internationale implique l'acceptation de concepts universels, notamment ceux de la souveraineté des Etats et du principe *pacta sunt servanda*, sans le respect desquels les relations entre les Etats ne peuvent être autre chose que la seule traduction d'un rapport de forces, ce qui serait dès lors incompatible avec le concept de droit[48], l'universel devient une exigence qui s'émancipe de la notion de droits de l'homme. Parler de « droit international » plutôt que de « relations internationales » évoque très justement la nécessité d'appréhender les rapports entre les Etats sur un autre modèle que celui du seul fait politique. Or, un tel modèle juridique repose sur une logique qui, en cherchant une source de légitimité de la règle, suppose l'acceptation de la possibilité d'un universel fondateur, même si le contenu précis de cet universel est indéterminé, voire reste nécessairement indéterminable. Or, « une fois apparue, l'exigence d'universalité n'est plus relégable »[49]. Appliquée au droit international privé, cette exigence d'universalité implique de tenir compte de la situation particulière de l'étranger, afin de tendre vers la justice, justice qui « est compromise quand la relation avec autrui est visiblement profanée »[50].

Le droit international public contribue donc à renforcer l'universel, qui en droit international privé se conçoit autour de « la reconnaissance de l'homme comme tel par le droit en tant que tel »[51]. Cette référence à l'homme soulève une difficulté qui relève à l'évidence de la diversité culturelle, et elle permet de trouver un terrain d'entente permettant la coexistence de cultures différentes, puisque « c'est dans le sens commun de l'humain que s'entendraient originairement les cultures et qu'elles peuvent traverser leur idiotisme pour s'ouvrir à ce que Kant a nommé si justement une 'communicabilité' ou 'partagibilité' universelle, *allgemeine Mitteilbarkeit* »[52]. L'acception du sens précis du commun ne peut donc jamais être donnée par un ordre juridique seul. Il faut au contraire trouver ce commun autour d'un « sens commun de l'humanité dans lequel les cultures peuvent s'ouvrir à une 'partagiblité' universelle »[53]. En ce qui concerne le dialogue entre les cultures et, par extension, entre les ordres juridiques, il n'y a donc pas une culture commune ou un droit commun qui puisse être imposé aux autres en invoquant un prétendu fondement universel. Le

---

[47] *Ibid.*, p. 128.

[48] Autour de la conception rousseauiste du droit notamment, qui démontre bien que le droit qui n'est que le droit du plus fort n'est plus du droit, puisqu'un renversement du rapport de forces entraînerait immédiatement une modification du sens de la règle en faveur du « nouveau » fort.

[49] *Ibid.*, p. 143.

[50] Levinas (2006), p. 177.

[51] Batiffol (1979), p. 166.

[52] Jullien (2008), p. 159.

[53] *Ibid.*

droit international public n'impose donc pas une identité culturelle commune. Au contraire, la question de l'universel confronté au statut familial ne peut se poser que par rapport à chaque ordre juridique singulier, seul susceptible de reconnaître ce statut familial. Il n'y a alors ni contradiction entre universel et singulier, ni même contradiction dans l'affirmation du caractère relatif de l'universel. Chaque Etat doit poser pour lui-même les critères de ce qu'il entend par « sens commun de l'humain », c'est-à-dire les critères qui lui permettent de communiquer avec d'autres cultures et donc de tenir compte de l'identité culturelle de l'étranger en matière de statut familial. Mais le droit international public renforce l'importance qu'il y a de prendre conscience de l'aspiration à l'universel de l'ordre juridique. Affirmer que l'ordre juridique doive prétendre à l'universel implique alors que chaque ordre juridique se donne des critères d'un sens commun de l'humain dépassant les seules valeurs de l'ordre juridique du for, et au regard de l'identité culturelle en matière de statut familial implique que l'ordre juridique soit ouvert à l'idée de l'application potentielle d'un droit de la famille étranger. Cela confirme alors également toute la pertinence qu'il y a d'avoir recours au concept d'« Etat ouvert », comme un Etat ouvert à la diversité des ordres juridiques, y compris interne et international. En effet, « l'efficacité des normes internationales concernant la situation des personnes privées dépend toujours en premier lieu, et parfois *de facto* exclusivement, des normes constitutionnelles, mais de normes qui, dans un 'Etat ouvert', tendent, à des degrés divers et avec ici ou là de fortes résistances voire des reculs, à être conçues par le pouvoir constituant et/ou interprétées par les pouvoirs constitués non plus comme un écran entre l'ordre interne et l'ordre international, mais comme une interface entre deux droits complémentaires, le droit interne et le droit international »[54].

La question de l'identité culturelle en matière de statut familial permet alors de comprendre avec plus de précision les conséquences de la prétention à l'universalité de l'ordre juridique. Celle-ci doit en effet aller de pair avec la prise de conscience de la relativité des conceptions familiales propres de l'ordre juridique. L'universalité doit être construite sur une certaine « partagibilité »[55], qui implique la recherche des outils qui permettent la traduction des conceptions familiales de l'ordre juridique étranger vers les conceptions de l'ordre juridique du for[56]. Le droit international privé de la famille assure alors une universalité fondamentale, car le droit international privé doit se transformer en « métalangage juridique » par lequel l'ordre juridique du for « communique » avec les ordres juridiques étrangers[57]. Il devient ainsi l'outil par lequel l'ordre juridique du for est « véritablement universel » au sens de « capable d'être universellement partageable ». Pour pouvoir communiquer avec

[54]Lagrange (2011), pp. 306-307.

[55]Jullien (2008), p. 159.

[56]En adhérant aux exigences d'une méthode universelle et plurielle, le droit international privé tient ainsi compte, juridiquement, du besoin d'évitement de l'uniformisation, sur un modèle qui peut être rapproché de celui sur lequel repose fondamentalement la logique de la traduction (sur laquelle, voy. not. Ost (2009), p. 55; à rapprocher de Glenn (2012)).

[57]Ce que Savigny pressentait déjà, notamment en matière d'institutions inconnues du for (Savigny (1849), p. 37 et s.).

les autres ordres juridiques et les cultures qui les fondent, il faut en effet être en mesure de comprendre les conceptions des autres ordres juridiques. Le droit international public enseigne que cette capacité de compréhension requiert l'existence d'un langage adapté. Pour les relations entre Etats, le droit international public remplit ce rôle de langage commun qui permet aux Etats de communiquer autour d'un respect réciproque minimal. Et pour le statut familial, ce langage est le droit international privé de la famille, en ce qu'il permet de traduire une situation familiale étrangère en une situation de droit reconnue par l'ordre juridique national. Le droit international privé a dans ce cadre « un rôle fondamental de médiation avec l'universel, car en s'affirmant comme le langage traduisant l'universel, il fixe aussi les limites à l'intérieur desquelles l'ordre juridique du for peut comprendre et communiquer avec les ordres juridiques étrangers »[58].

Le droit international public permet cependant de prendre conscience d'un important élément de précision de l'universel. Puisque l'universel ne peut pas être imposé de force à un Etat, ce que la question du statut familial illustre très bien, il ne doit pas se transformer en « universalisme »[59], au sens d'une vérité absolue objectivement constatable et imposée à tous les Etats. Il faut au contraire maintenir un équilibre entre, d'un côté, la prétention à l'universalité, qui implique la reconnaissance de l'identité de chaque culture, y compris dans la mesure où elle à vocation à s'étendre, et, de l'autre côté, le sens du commun, qui s'exprime en droit international public par l'appartenance partagée de tous les Etats à la communauté internationale. Dès lors, le droit international public confirme bien que « l'intérêt fonctionnel de l'universel est qu'il maintient une transcendance, mais qui demeure interne; qu'il pose un absolu – comme inconditionné ou, mieux, inconditionnable –, mais qui n'est pas religieux. Ainsi, c'est lui notamment qui tire après lui le commun et le promeut: grâce à lui le commun (du politique) ne s'enlise dans aucune appartenance établie, ne se confine dans aucun partage acquis, mais est porté à s'étendre [...] dans le sens d'un élargissement qui ne se connaît pas de fin. [...] C'est lui, l'universel, qui par sa rigueur, de la logique à l'Histoire, pousse vers cette 'communauté universelle', *civitas universa* – des genres, des peuples, des Elus; donc qui détourne le commun du communautarisme »[60].

Les concepts d'universalité et de singularité sont donc des concepts dont la coexistence est source de tension, ce que montre bien le droit international public autour des obligations universelles qui se heurtent à la souveraineté de chaque Etat. Mais ils n'en jouent pas moins un rôle fondamental pour la conception de l'ordre juridique dans son ensemble, tout comme le font l'universel et l'antériorité des ordres juridiques nationaux en droit international privé. Ainsi, en ce que l'« opérativité de

---

[58]Notre thèse (2015), para. 189. Le droit international privé se présente ainsi comme un véritable « droit du traduire » (voy. plus généralement Ost (2009)), dont l'objectif est de gérer un pluralisme de droits, mais également de valeurs (voy. plus généralement sur ce point Vanderlinden (2013)).

[59]Le suffixe « -isme » suggérant, voire impliquant, déjà une radicalité et une prétention à l'absoluité de la notion qui versent presque inéluctablement dans une pensée totale, sinon totalitaire.

[60]Jullien (2008), p. 149.

l'universel [est] de vider toute formation-institution de son assurance, née de la totalisation dont elle se suffit, et de rouvrir une brèche dans ce confort de la clôture, [...] la fonction de l'universel est d'inquiéter toute saturation-satisfaction »[61]. L'universel, inhérent au droit international public, devient ainsi « moteur: dans la pensée mais aussi dans l'Histoire » [62], et ce n'est qu'à condition de pleinement le reconnaître que l'universel se pose alors comme un rempart contre la pensée totalitaire ou totalisante qui se caractérise par le dogme d'une vérité absolue qui puisse être imposée aux autres pays et cultures du monde et qui correspond au risque de l'« universalisme »[63]. Pour conjuguer ce risque, « c'est l'universel – et non le particularisme – qui fournit le seul démenti véritable aux universalismes établis »[64]. Nous avons déjà cherché à démontrer que « l'universel invite sans cesse à la réflexion et à la vigilance, nécessaires pour garantir que le droit puisse toujours tendre vers l'idéal de la justice, tout en garantissant le respect des diversités et singularités que l'universalisme prétend justement anéantir »[65]. Ainsi, « c'est parce que l'universel maintient l'humanité en quête, et non parce qu'il prétendrait venir à bout de l'individuel ou du singulier qu'il fait figure d'idéal »[66]. L'universel, notamment en matière d'identité culturelle, impose d'avoir conscience de la relativité avec laquelle chaque ordre juridique l'affirme. Cette conscience de la relativité de la culture et du droit impose ensuite le respect de la diversité, tout comme elle impose de posséder l'aptitude à la remise en cause et au dépassement de soi. En matière d'identité culturelle, elle implique donc, d'une part, d'avoir une conception ouverte de sa propre culture ou identité culturelle, et, d'autre part, d'accepter la diversité culturelle et le fait que d'autres Etats puissent avoir une conception différente de leur identité culturelle.

L'universel permet ainsi de ne pas tomber dans la contradiction de l'universalisme et introduit une part de nécessaire dynamisme afin de garantir l'adaptation de l'ordre juridique aux besoins sociaux. L'identité culturelle devient donc dynamique lorsqu'elle assume ce concept d'universel, puisque le fait de « concevoir l'universel comme un strict agent et vecteur – comme tel inépuisable – de promotion »[67] confère l'aptitude au dépassement, afin de rapprocher l'ordre juridique de l'idéal de justice. Et la promotion est ici tout autant une promotion de chaque ordre juridique qu'une promotion de la diversité culturelle. Or, le droit international public confirme parfaitement que l'idéal de justice, déjà insaisissable dans les relations sociales internes, devient encore plus fuyant dans les relations sociales se nouant entre plusieurs Etats. L'universel permet alors, y compris et surtout en ce qui concerne le dialogue entre les différentes cultures du monde, de

---

[61] *Ibid.*, p. 144.
[62] *Ibid.*, p. 148.
[63] *Ibid.*, p. 146.
[64] *Ibid.*
[65] Notre thèse (2015), para. 191.
[66] Jullien (2008), p. 149.
[67] *Ibid.*, p. 145.

« sortir de l'impasse des premiers écueils de l'interculturel[,] d'un côté l'universalisme facile et, de l'autre, le relativisme paresseux »[68]. La prise de conscience de la dimension singulière et universelle du droit, confortée par la valeur fondamentale des concepts d'universalité et de singularité en droit international public, précise le droit international privé, y compris en matière familiale, pour y voir « un ensemble de règles capable de concevoir l'universel – la prétention à l'universalité – au sein même de chaque ordre juridique national afin de permettre à l'ordre juridique d'organiser son ouverture au monde et de concevoir juridiquement les relations avec l'Autre dans le respect de l'altérité »[69]. La prétention à l'universalité de l'ordre juridique singulier a donc comme conséquence de concevoir l'universel de l'ordre juridique de façon ouverte à la pluralité, et donc en matière de statut familial de façon ouverte à la diversité des identités culturelles en ce domaine.

Cela permet de comprendre que les concepts fondateurs du droit international public sont porteurs d'une nécessaire ouverture à l'altérité, donc d'une nécessaire prise en compte de l'identité culturelle des individus dans le cadre du statut familial. Pour le droit international privé de la famille, le fondement de l'universel, affirmé de façon singulière et unilatérale par l'ordre juridique national, y compris en le déduisant des fondements du droit international public, ne signifie donc pas l'application universelle par l'ordre juridique du for de ses propres jugements de valeurs, mais impose le respect du pluriel et l'ouverture aux jugements de valeurs des cultures étrangères. Cet universel pluriel impose ainsi l'obligation positive de la reconnaissance de l'identité culturelle en matière de statut familial. Cette exigence de reconnaissance doit s'inscrire dans un système de droit international privé qui est universel par deux aspects au moins. Il l'est, d'un côté, en ce que toute situation familiale qui se présente à l'ordre juridique sera dotée d'une certaine juridicité. Et il l'est, d'un autre côté, en ce que le statut juridique d'une famille présentant des contacts avec un ordre juridique étranger peut potentiellement être appréciée au regard des valeurs matérielles de l'ordre juridique étranger. La prétention à l'universalité des ordres juridiques leur impose en effet l'ouverture à la pluralité et le respect de la diversité, y compris en matière d'identité culturelle dans le domaine du statut familial. Autrement dit, « ce que fait en réalité le droit international privé [. . .] c'est gérer un pluralisme juridique »[70]. L'universel de l'ordre juridique singulier rejoint alors le droit international public en ce qu'il en ressort un système de droit international privé qui est intermédiaire entre l'exclusivisme et l'universalisme total. L'ordre juridique qui apprécie le statut familial d'une personne doit avoir conscience de la nécessité qu'il peut y avoir, face à une situation internationale, de ne pas appliquer ses conceptions culturelles propres, mais qu'en raison de l'intégration de cette situation familiale internationale à un autre ordre juridique et une autre culture, il convient de faire prévaloir les conceptions culturelles de cet ordre juridique étranger. En comprenant et en assumant l'influence de ses concepts fondateurs sur

[68] *Ibid.*, p. 155.

[69] Notre thèse (2015), para. 193.

[70] Francescakis (2002), p. XVI.

le droit international privé de la famille, le droit international public devient alors un outil précieux afin de respecter l'identité culturelle en matière de statut familial.

Références

Ancel B (2017) Eléments d'histoire du droit international privé. Editions Panthéon-Assas, Paris

Arendt H (1972), *Le système totalitaire, Paris,* Le Seuil, 1972

Batiffol H (1956) Aspects philosophiques du droit international privé. Paris, Dalloz, 1956

Batiffol H (1957) compte-rendu des « Observations sur les Aspects philosophiques de droit international privé » de Jacques Maury. In: Rev. crit. DIP 229–272

Batiffol H (1979) Problèmes de base de philosophie du droit. Paris, LGDJ, Paris

Batiffol H et Lagarde P (1993), Traité de droit international privé, 8ème éd., LGDJ, Paris

Batiffol H et Francescakis Ph (1959) L'arrêt Boll. In: Rev crit.DIP 259-276

Beck U (2006) Qu'est-ce que le cosmopolitisme ? Traduit par Aurélie Duthoo. Paris, Aubier, 2006

Bollée S et Pataut E (2016) Avant-propos. In: Bollée S et Pataut E (2016) L'identité à l'épreuve de la mondialisation. IRJS éditions, Paris

Bureau D et Muir Watt H (2014) Droit international privé. 3ème éd. mise à jour. Thémis. Droit privé, Paris

Colavitti R (2013) La protection des identités culturelles dans le contexte européen. In: Foblets, M-C, Yassari N, et Ben Lamine M Approches juridiques de la diversité culturelle. Les livres de droit de l'Académie, Leiden, Nijhoff, 2013, pp. 183-247

De Boer Th M (2010) Living Apart Together: the Relationship Between Public and Private International Law. In: Netherlands International Law Review 183-207

Evrigenis D J (1966) Tendances doctrinales actuelles en droit international privé. In: RCADI, t. 118, pp. 313-433

Forteau M (2015) Le droit international privé, reflet des limites (mais aussi de la nature) du droit international public. In: Les limites du droit international: essais en l'honneur de Joe Verhoeven, Bruylant, Bruxelles, pp. 55-68

Franceskakis Ph (1955) Perspectives du droit international privé français actuel. In: Revue internationale de droit comparé 349-360

Francescakis Ph (1957) Philosophie du droit et droit international privé. In: Archives de philosophie du droit 205-219

Francescakis Ph (2002), « Introduction à l'édition française ». In: Santi ROMANO, L'ordre juridique, Traduction française de la 2e édition de l'Ordinamento giuridico par Lucien François et Pierre Gothot, Réédition présentée par Pierre Mayer, Paris, Dalloz, 2e édition, 2002, pp. i-xxii

Francescakis Ph (1958), La théorie du renvoi et les conflits de systèmes en droit international privé. Paris, Sirey

Gannagé L (2001) La hiérarchie des normes et les méthodes du droit international privé: étude de droit international privé de la famille. LGDJ, Paris

Glenn H P (2012), La conciliation des lois. In: RCADI, t. 364, pp. 187-470

Habermas J (1992 et 1998) Faktizität und Geltung: Beiträge zur Diskurstheorie des Rechts und des demokratischen Rechtsstaats, 1° éd. (identique à la 4° éd. rev. et compl. 1994, 1° éd. 1992), coll. Taschenbuch Wissenschaft, Suhrkamp Verlag, Frankfurt-am-Main, 1998

Jayme E (1995) Identité culturelle et intégration : le droit international privé postmoderne. In: RCADI, t. 251, pp. 9-267

Jullien F (2008) De l'universel, de l'uniforme, du commun et du dialogue entre les cultures, Fayard, Paris

Jullien F (2016) Il n'y a pas d'identité culturelle. Herne, Paris

Lagrange E (2012) L'efficacité des normes internationales concernant la situation des personnes privées dans les ordres juridiques internes. RCADI, t. 356, pp. 239-552

Levinas E (2006), Altérité et transcendance, coll. Biblio Essais, Le Livre de Poche, Paris
Mancini P S (1874) De l'utilité de rendre obligatoire pour tous les États, sous la forme d'un ou de plusieurs traités internationaux, un certain nombre de règles générales de Droit international privé pour assurer la décision uniforme des conflits entre les différentes législations civiles et criminelles. In: JDI 221-239 et 285-304
Muir Watt H (2016) Identité et droit international privé dans la globalisation: introduction. In: Bollée S et Pataut E (2016) L'identité à l'épreuve de la mondialisation. IRJS Editions, Paris, pp. 5-24
Niboyet J-P (1944), Traité de droit international privé français, t. III, Recueil Sirey, Paris
Ost Fr (2009) Traduire – Défense et illustration du multilinguisme, Fayard, Paris
Savigny F C von (1849) System des heutigen Römischen Rechts. Bd. 8. Berlin
Sellers M (2012) Parochialism, Cosmopolitanism, and Justice ». In: Mortimer N S Sellers Parochialism, Cosmopolitanism, and the Foundations of International Law. New York, Cambridge University Press, 2012, pp. 250-275
Teubner G (1989), Recht als autopoietisches System, Suhrkamp, Frankfurt-am-Main
Todd E (1996) L'invention de l'Europe. Seuil, Paris
Van Loon H, et De Dycker St (2013) The Role of the International Court of Justice *in* the Development of Private International Law », 2013. In: Lesaffer, RCH. One century Peace Palace, from Past to Present. Asser Press, Den Haag
Vanderlinden J (2013) Les pluralismes juridiques, Bruylant, Bruxelles

Cultural Identity and Self-Determination as Key Concepts in Concurring Legal Frameworks for the International Protection of the Rights of Indigenous Peoples

Mariana Monteiro de Matos

Abstract This chapter analyzes the protection of the rights of indigenous peoples in light of both the United Nations Declaration on the Rights of Indigenous Peoples and the International Covenant on Civil and Political Rights. This analysis demonstrates that there are two key concepts in international human rights law that build the protection of indigenous peoples: cultural identity and self-determination. These concepts evoke respectively the cultural-identity-based framework and the self-determination-based framework. This chapter concludes that the relationship between both frameworks is inexplicit and very fragile. Additionally, the cultural-identity-based framework holds a more comprehensive protection for indigenous peoples and their lands than the self-determination-based framework.

1 Introduction

In 2007, the United Nations General Assembly adopted with an overwhelming majority of 144 states in favor the United Nations Declaration on the Rights of Indigenous Peoples (UNDRIPS or the Declaration).[1] This document was the first international instrument with universal character to recognize specific rights for indigenous peoples.[2] Prior to UNDRIPS' adoption, international legal instruments recognizing specific rights to indigenous peoples referred to the ILO Conventions

[1]For the official record of adoption see United Nations Division for Social Policy and Development (2017).

[2]This paper uses the concepts of "indigenous peoples" and "indigenous communities" as interchangeable terms. An analysis about the differences between these concepts lays beyond the scope of this research.

M. M. de Matos (✉)
Institute of International and European Law, Georg-August University of Goettingen, Goettingen, Germany

© Springer International Publishing AG, part of Springer Nature 2018

E. Lagrange et al. (eds.), *Cultural Heritage and International Law*,
https://doi.org/10.1007/978-3-319-78789-3_13

107 and 169, which unfortunately received only a few ratifications.[3] By analyzing its provisions, it becomes clear that the UNDRIPS inaugurated a new path for the protection of the rights of indigenous peoples.

The UNDRIPS establishes a self-determination-based framework to protect indigenous peoples. The Declaration is the first international legal instrument to recognize a connection between the right to self-determination and indigenous communities. Article 3 UNDRIPS sets forth that indigenous peoples have the right to self-determination. This right has a special meaning in the context of indigenous issues whose different aspects appear throughout several provisions of the UNDRIPS.

The UNDRIPS' self-determination-based framework contrasts with the consolidated framework in international human rights law for the protection of indigenous peoples. Human rights instruments such as the International Covenant on Civil and Political Rights (ICCPR) and the American Convention on Human Rights lack any provision concerning indigenous peoples and their right to self-determination. Yet these instruments provide complaint procedure mechanisms that enable individuals to file a complaint against the violation of their rights before judicial and quasi-judicial human rights bodies. Due to the lack of specific legal remedies available for dealing with indigenous issues, members of indigenous communities have been using those complaint procedures to express grievances about violations of their rights.[4] Consequently, international human rights bodies developed a substantial jurisprudence on indigenous issues that is essential to fully grasp the rights of indigenous peoples.

This research addresses the question of how international human rights law protects the rights of indigenous peoples. It explains and contrasts the UNDRIPS' framework with the framework resulting from the jurisprudence of international human rights bodies. By canvassing a narrow approach, this chapter focuses on the jurisprudence of the ICCPR's individual complaint procedure.

The cases the Human Rights Committee (HRC) received, alleging violations of the rights set down in the ICCPR, have a significant value. First, they frame the struggle of indigenous peoples and their members all around the world. Second, the HRC's decisions entail a similar rationale to the one of other human rights bodies, e.g. the Inter-American Commission on Human Rights and the Inter-American

---

[3]As of May 2017, the ILO Convention 169 had 22 ratifications and the ILO Convention 107 had 27 ratifications. For more information see: http://www.ilo.org/dyn/normlex/en/f?p=NORMLEXPUB:11300:0::NO::P11300_INSTRUMENT_ID:312314. Accessed 31 May 2017.

[4]Neither the UNDRIPS nor the ILO Conventions have monitoring bodies to receive complaints concerning the violation of their provisions in individual cases. A monitoring body is responsible for supervising the implementation of the ILO Conventions. Yet this body does not have the mandate to receive complaints by indigenous peoples and their organizations. For more information about the ILO supervisory system see: http://www.oit.org/global/about-the-ilo/how-the-ilo-works/ilo-supervisory-system-mechanism/lang--en/index.htm. Accessed 31 May 2017.

Court of Human Rights.[5] Therefore, the HRC's jurisprudence is a good example of how the jurisprudence of international human rights bodies work. Text limitations make an in-depth exploration of the jurisprudence of all these bodies infeasible for this paper.

This chapter is divided in two analytical parts. After the introduction, the first part fleshes out the key concepts in international human rights law for the protection of indigenous peoples in accordance with the UNDRIPS and the ICCPR. Each instrument evokes a framework of protection based on a different concept. For the sake of this analysis, these frameworks are called self-determination-based framework and cultural-identity-based framework. Next, the second part explores the relationship between these frameworks. It divides itself in two subparts that compare the similarities and differences between both frameworks regarding their normative contents of protection toward indigenous lands and natural resources therein. Lastly, final remarks summarize the main findings of this research.

2 Key Concepts for the Protection of the Rights of Indigenous Peoples in International Law

This part elucidates the main concepts in international law for the protection of indigenous peoples. Section one explains the concept of self-determination in accordance with the UNDRIPS. Section two enlightens the concept of cultural identity in the context of the ICCPR and the HRC's jurisprudence.

2.1 The Self-Determination-Based Framework: UNDRIPS

The official denomination of the UNDRIPS is Resolution 61/295 of 13 September 2007 adopted by the United Nations General Assembly (UNGA).[6] It represents a milestone for the rights of indigenous peoples. Notably, the UNDRIPS enjoys a high political significance that is a result of its long-standing negotiation process in which states and representatives of indigenous organizations actively engaged.[7] Besides its

[5]Among others see Inter-Am. Ct.H.R., Case of the Kichwa Indigenous People of Sarayaku against Ecuador, Merits and Reparations, Judgment of 27 Jun 2012, Series C No. 245; Inter-Am. Ct.H.R., Comunidad Moiwana against Suriname, Preliminary Exceptions, Merits, Reparations and Costs, Judgment of 15 Jun 2005, Series C No. 124; Inter-Am. C.H.R., Demanda de la Comisión Interamericana de Derechos Humanos presentada ante la Corte Interamericana de Derechos Humanos, Comunidad Indígena Mayagna (Sumo) Awas Tingni contra la República de Nicaragua, 4 Jun 1998.

[6]United Nations Division for Social Policy and Development (2017).

[7]For details on the drafting process of the UNDRIPS see Ahrén (2009), pp. 206–209; Anaya (2009), p. 56; Charters (2009), pp. 285–287; Errico (2007), p. 743; Kingsbury (2017), paras 11–13; Xanthaki (2007), pp. 120–121.

political value, some authors claim that the UNDRIPS, or at least its provisions regarding land rights, represents customary international law or contains general principles of law.[8]

The UNDRIPS is not a legally binding instrument. Pursuant to Article 10, read in conjunction with Article 13 Charter of the United Nations, the UNGA has competence for making recommendations to the members of the United Nations (UN) on different matters, i.a. on promoting international cooperation. In other words, the UNGA lacks competence for creating binding international rules.[9] Since the UNGA adopted the UNDRIPS as a resolution, this document is not legally binding. The UNDRIPS is a so-called soft law document. Pursuant to Article 38(1) ICJ Statute, soft law documents are not a formal source of international law.

Despite its soft law nature, the UNDRIPS has a significant normative value. Such a value may be seen in its very denomination. The UNDRIPS is not an UNGA "recommendation" but a "declaration." While the UNGA adopts hundreds of recommendations every year, it reserves the term "declaration" to name a very few of them. According to the UN Office of Legal Affairs, declarations are a special category of recommendations that the UNGA adopted. Declarations have a unique importance because they reflect significant values that the international community recognizes as worthy of safeguarding. This was the case for the adoption of the Universal Declaration of Human Rights.[10] Additionally, the stakeholders within the UN fora, through a near-unanimous decision, crafted the text of the UNDRIPS, which displays legally binding language.[11] Those aspects demonstrate the normative value of the UNDRIPS.[12]

The UNDRIPS has been having a strong impact on international human rights law. Pursuant to Article 42 UNDRIPS, the UN shall promote respect for and full application of the Declaration. Accordingly, the Declaration has been an inspirational source to develop initiatives in the field of indigenous rights among UN bodies and specialized agencies.[13] This is the case of the Special Rapporteur on the Rights of Indigenous Peoples, the Food and Agriculture Organization, and the Committee on Economic, Social and Cultural Rights. Moreover, the UNDRIPS has influenced the development of legal instruments on the rights of indigenous peoples such as the American Declaration on the Rights of Indigenous Peoples.[14]

---

[8]Shortly after the adoption of the UNDRIPS there was a wide discussion in the literature about the normative value of the UNDRIPS. For details see Baldwin and Morel (2011), pp. 123–126; Charters (2010), p. 23; Lenzerini (2010a), p. 43; Wiessner (2008), p. 1162; Campbell and Anaya (2008), p. 398; Kingsbury (2017), para. 15.

[9]Legality of the Threat or Use of Nuclear Weapons, Advisory Opinion, I.C.J. Reports 1996, 226, para. 70.

[10]For a similar argument see Barelli (2009), p. 972; Lenzerini (2010b), pp. 21–22.

[11]Barelli (2009), pp. 968–983.

[12]Cf. Legality of the Threat or Use of Nuclear Weapons, Advisory Opinion, I.C.J. Reports 1996, 226, para. 70.

[13]Barelli (2016), pp. 43–68.

[14]Clavero (2016).

Regarding its content, the UNDRIPS is a landmark for the recognition of indigenous peoples as subjects entitled to the right to self-determination. Article 3 UNDRIPS sets down that indigenous peoples have the right to self-determination and that by virtue of that right they freely determine their political status and freely pursue their economic, social, and cultural development. This provision is the key aspect that distinguishes the UNDRIPS from other instruments dealing with indigenous peoples.[15] The provision places the Declaration in a human rights context by connecting UNDRIPS' provisions with other human rights instruments.[16]

The right to self-determination is the heart and soul of the Declaration whose different aspects are spread through UNDRIPS' provisions.[17] For instance, Article 4 UNDRIPS establishes that indigenous peoples, in exercising their right to self-determination, have the right to autonomy or self-government. In addition, Article 5 UNDRIPS recognizes their right to participate fully in the political, economic, social, and cultural life of the state. Pursuant to Article 46.1 UNDRIPS, indigenous peoples should exercise the right to self-determination enshrined in the UNDRIPS within state's borders.[18] This restricted exercise gives this right a *sui generis* meaning different from the historical one.[19]

The right to self-determination pursuant to the UNDRIPS has two main aspects. First, the internal aspect refers to autonomy of indigenous communities for dealing with local affairs. In this context, states should respect and not interfere with indigenous self-government, including their distinct political, legal, economic, social, and cultural institutions. Second, the external aspect refers to the relationship between state and indigenous peoples. This relationship should be voluntary for indigenous peoples. Such external aspect entails their right to participate in all issues related to the state's life.

---

[15]Cf. Article 1.3 ILO Convention 169.

[16]Cf. Article 1.1 ICCPR and Article 1.1 International Covenant on Economic, Social and Cultural Rights.

[17]Anaya (2009), pp. 73–74; Crawford (2012), p. 650; Oeter (2012), p. 494; Thornberry (2002), pp. 382–385.

[18]The exercise of the right to self-determination by indigenous peoples within state's borders is a highly controversial issue in international human rights law. For a substantive comprehension on this topic see Castellino (2005).

[19]The right to self-determination dates back to the decolonization time and the related declarations of independence of former colonies. By that time, the UNGA adopted the recommendation 2625 of 24 Oct 1970 (U.N. Doc. A/Res/25/2625) which recognized the principle of self-determination of peoples. The adoption of the UNDRIPS by the UNGA gives a new meaning to the right to self-determination.

2.2 The Cultural-Identity-Based Framework: ICCPR

The ICCPR and its optional protocol are milestones for international human rights law. Among the distinguished features of these instruments, there is Article 28 ICCPR. The first part of this provision established a Human Rights Committee in order to monitor states' compliance with the ICCPR. With the aim of fulfilling its mandate, the HRC had to deal with issues related to indigenous peoples.

The HRC consists of 18 members who are human rights experts. It has three main competences. First, the HRC may receive reports from States Parties about measures they have adopted to give effect to the rights recognized in the ICCPR (Article 40.1 ICCPR). Second, the HRC may publish general comments that help with the clarification of the content of specific provisions of the ICCPR (Article 40.4 ICCPR). Third, the HRC may receive and consider individual complaints alleging violation of rights laid down in the ICCPR (Article 1 Optional Protocol to the ICCPR).

There are a few special features regarding the individual complaint procedure that the HRC supervises. Notably, only States Parties to the Optional Protocol to the ICCPR (and not all States Parties to the ICCPR) recognize the competence of the HRC to receive complaints. After the HRC analyzes the complaints, it publicizes its conclusions as official UN documents with the title "views of the committee." The structure of these documents has similar characteristics to judicial decisions, and therefore scholars refer to them as "decisions." In contrast to proper judicial decisions, the HRC decisions are only persuasive recommendations, i.e. they are not legally binding. Yet states have the obligation to consider them in good faith.[20]

For the sake of dealing with indigenous issues, the HRC has developed a framework based on the concept of cultural identity in accordance with Article 27 ICCPR. Since the 1980s, the HRC has been receiving communications from indigenous communities alleging violation of their rights. The ICCPR lacks any provision addressing indigenous peoples or their rights. To fill this gap, the HRC began to answer their issues based on the individualistic framed right of members of minority groups to enjoy their own culture pursuant to Article 27 ICCPR.[21] Accordingly, the HRC stated that the scope of this right is to ensure the very survival and continued development of cultural, religious, and social identity of minorities.[22] Cultural identity is a comprehensive concept because culture has a broad meaning. According to the HRC, culture may relate to the development of a particular way of life and traditional economic activities as in the case of indigenous peoples.[23] Thus,

---

[20]HRC, General Comment Nr. 33: The obligations of State Parties under the Optional Protocol to the International Covenant on Civil and Political Rights, 05 Nov 2008, 94th Session, UN Doc. CCPR/C/GC/33, para. 15.

[21]The inclusion of indigenous communities in the category of minority groups is a highly controversial issue in international human rights law. For a good analysis on this topic see Kymlicka (2010).

[22]HRC, General Comment Nr. 23: The rights of minorities (Art. 27), 08 Apr 1994, 50th Session, UN Doc. CCPR/C/21/Rev.1/Add.5, para. 9.

[23]HRC, General Comment Nr. 23: The rights of minorities (Art. 27), 08 Apr 1994, 50th Session, UN Doc. CCPR/C/21/Rev.1/Add.5, para. 7.

the HRC uses the concept of cultural identity to tackle claims that indigenous peoples make under the complaint procedure.

3 Self-Determination-Based Framework and Cultural-Identity-Based Framework: A Hidden and Fragile Relationship

This part dives into the relationship between the self-determination-based framework and the cultural-identity-based framework. It focuses on the similarities and differences of a common topic in both frameworks, the protection of indigenous lands and natural resources therein. Conflicts related to indigenous territories are the most controversial issue touching upon the rights of indigenous peoples. The first section of this part looks at procedural issues, and the second section explores substantial issues concerning both frameworks.

3.1 Procedural Issues Regarding the Protection of Indigenous Lands and Natural Resources According to the Frameworks

The self-determination-based framework relates to Article 3 UNDRIPS, which entails a very similar wording to Article 1 ICCPR (right of self-determination). Such a similarity could be a way to make the UNDRIPS and the ICCPR work in a complementary manner by submitting complaints about the violation of indigenous land rights pursuant to Articles 27 and 1 ICCPR and articulating this alleged violation with reference to Article 3 UNDRIPS. Accordingly, the HRC could apply these provisions to analyze communications about the violation of indigenous land rights. Yet the jurisprudence of the HRC demonstrates that such an attempt would most probably fail. In practice, the HRC does not admit complaints pursuant to Article 1 ICCPR.[24] This inadmissibility constitutes the procedural block against a dialog between the self-determination-based model and the cultural-identity-based model. The rationale behind it deserves special attention.

[24]There is a long-standing jurisprudence confirming the inadmissibility of complaints pursuant to Article 1 ICCPR. Among them see HRC, Ivan Kitok against Sweden, 27 Jul 1988, UN Doc. CCPR/C/33/D/197/1985, para. 6.3; HRC, Lubicon Lake Band against Canada, 26 Mar 1990, UN Doc. CCPR/C/38/D/167/1984, para. 32.2; HRC, Apirana Mahuika et al. against New Zealand, 27 Oct 2000, UN Doc. CCPR/C/70/D/547/1993, para. 9.2; HRC, Marie-Helene Gillot against France, 15 Jul 2002, UN Doc. CCPR/C/75/D/932/2000, para. 13.4; HRC, Angela Poma Poma against Peru, 27 Mar 2009, UN Doc. CCPR/C/95/D/1457/2006, para. 6.3.

According to the HRC, the Optional Protocol to the ICCPR allows individuals to bring claims of alleged violations of individual rights pursuant to the ICCPR. These rights do not include Article 1 ICCPR. Rather, they refer to Articles 6 to 27 ICCPR. In the decision of Lubicon Lake Band against Canada, the HRC elucidated its understanding in this regard (emphasis added):

> The question has arisen of whether any claim under article 1 of the Covenant remains, the Committee's decision on admissibility notwithstanding. While all peoples have the right of self-determination and the right freely to determine their political status, pursue their economic, social and cultural development and dispose of their natural wealth and resources, as stipulated in article 1 of the Covenant, *the question whether the Lubicon Lake Band constitutes a "people" is not an issue for the Committee to address under the Optional Protocol to the Covenant. The Optional Protocol provides a procedure under which individuals can claim that their individual rights have been violated.* These rights are set out in part III of the Covenant, articles 6 to 27, inclusive. There is, however, no objection to a group of individuals, who claim to be similarly affected, collectively to submit a communication about alleged breaches of their rights.[25]

This HRC's understanding evokes several criticisms in the scholarship that argues for more flexible admissibility requirements. Accordingly, the complaint procedure should enable a comprehensive protection of human rights. The first criticism regarding this HRC's understanding relates to the requirement of alleging violations of individual rights laid down in the ICCPR. This HRC's interpretation restricts the *ratione materiae* of the complaints to individual rights of the ICCPR. In contrast, Article 1 Optional Protocol to the ICCPR lacks any distinction between the rights set forth in the ICCPR that petitioners may invoke under the complaint procedure. It uses the wording "any rights set forth in the Covenant." Thus, a literal interpretation of the Optional Protocol to the ICCPR would enable the admission of complaints alleging violations of both individual and group rights.[26]

The second criticism refers to the HRC's interpretation that the issue whether a group constitutes a people is not under the HRC's competence to decide. In response, one may argue that the HRC may admit a complaint without ruling on this topic by referring to international legal instruments that recognize a specific group as people. This argument is applicable to the case of indigenous peoples because both Article 3 UNDRIPS and Article 3 American Declaration on the Rights of Indigenous Peoples recognize them as peoples. Hence, the HRC may easily admit complaints by indigenous peoples with reference to these legal instruments adopted by states.

The third criticism relates to the HRC's understanding that individuals lack legal standing to claim group rights. As a consequence, since the right to self-determination is a group right, individuals cannot claim to be victims of a violation

[25] HRC, Lubicon Lake Band against Canada, 26 Mar 1990, UN Doc. CCPR/C/38/D/167/1984, para. 32.1.

[26] For a similar understanding see Tyagi (2011), pp. 598–599; Nowak (2005), p. 19.

in this regard.[27] While the collective nature of the right to self-determination is undeniable, it is arguable that an individual or a group of individuals on behalf of a people may claim a violation of the right of self-determination. The representation of a people by individuals is in accordance with the text of the ICCPR and its systematic interpretation.[28] However, the HRC has been reluctant to admit such a complaint in its jurisprudence.

In spite of all the above-explained criticisms regarding the HRC's admissibility criteria, it is very unlikely that the HRC will adopt significant changes in this regard. As demonstrated, the HRC's admissibility requirements raise controversial issues that could be easily solved for the sake of a comprehensive protection of human rights, including the right of indigenous peoples to self-determination. To that end, the HRC needs to expand its jurisdiction *ratione materiae* and recognize the legal standing of individuals on behalf of a group (or people) under the complaint procedure. Yet considering that the HRC has been adopting more rigid admissibility criteria since the 1990s, a change of requirements seems very improbable.

To sum up, it is important to remark that the self-determination-based framework and the cultural-identity-based framework do not engage in a direct dialog. The reason behind it is the HRC's admissibility criteria in the complaint procedure that do not admit complaints alleging the violation of the right to self-determination.

3.2 *Substantial Issues Regarding the Protection of Indigenous Lands and Natural Resources According to the Frameworks*

This part analyzes whether the protection regarding indigenous lands and natural resources therein contained in the self-determination-based framework and in the cultural-identity-based framework has similarities or differences that affect a dialog between both frameworks. To that end, this section takes a closer look first at (1) the scope of protection of indigenous lands and then at (2) the criteria to solve conflicts over the exploitation of natural resources in indigenous lands.

---

[27]Group rights have no universal definition in international law. As a working definition, with group rights this paper refers to the rights, which the right holder is the group itself. For a discussion in this regard see Buchanan (1993), pp. 93–95; Pogge (1997), pp. 191–193; Wenzel (2008), pp. 19–27.

[28]For a more detailed explanation of this argument see Nowak (2005), pp. 829–831; Cassese (1995), pp. 144–145.

3.2.1 Scope of Protection of Indigenous Lands and Natural Resources: Development of Cultural Activities and the Issue of Mineral Resources

Self-Determination-Based Framework: Indigenous Territory and Surface Resources Article 26.2 UNDRIPS is the main provision for the protection of indigenous lands in the self-determination-based framework. The scope of protection refers to the ownership, use, development, and control of lands and resources that indigenous peoples have already acquired or currently possess. Such indigenous current possession must fulfill additional requirements. Indigenous current possession must be a consequence of (1) traditional ownership or (2) traditional occupation or use. Hence, the UNDRIPS protects not only the geographical space where indigenous communal life flourishes but also the entire territory that is necessary for developing indigenous religion, cultural, and economic activities.

Regarding natural resources in indigenous lands, the scope of protection in the self-determination-based framework is less clear. Different from other legal instruments concerning the rights of indigenous peoples, the UNDRIPS does not specify to which type of resources indigenous peoples have rights.[29] The text of the UNDRIPS differentiates between "resources" (Article 26 UNDRIPS) and "other resources" (Article 32 UNDRIPS) without explaining where the difference lays. This is a problem because domestic laws in many countries restrict the ownership of mineral resources to states.

In accordance with the general rules of treaty interpretation (Article 31 Vienna Convention on the Law of Treaties), the interpretation of obscure provisions in the UNDRIPS should observe UNDRIPS' objective and purpose. This refers to the guarantee of the right to self-determination in accordance with UNDRIPS' provisions.[30] In that sense, the right to self-determination should guide the interpretation of the provisions on natural resources within indigenous lands.

In light of the right to self-determination, the scope of protection entails all natural resources found in indigenous lands. Articles 26–27 UNDRIPS establish that states shall give legal recognition and protection for natural resources in indigenous lands in accordance with indigenous peoples' laws, traditions, customs, and land tenure systems. As a result, these provisions request states to interpret indigenous land rights according to indigenous customary law. Indigenous customary law lacks a differentiation between types of natural resources because indigenous peoples understand their territory in a holistic way.[31] Hence, indigenous property is an all-encompassing concept referring to lands and natural resources therein.

Nevertheless, an interpretation of the scope of protection of natural resources in indigenous lands as an all-encompassing concept raises controversial issues. First,

---

[29] Cf. Art. 15.2 ILO Convention 169 and Art. 28-29 American Declaration on the Rights of Indigenous Peoples.

[30] See above Sect. 2.1.

[31] Among others see Descola (2000), pp. 15–103; Viveiros de Castro (2013), pp. 317–400.

this interpretation goes against domestic laws of many countries that recognize states as legitimate owners of subsurface resources. Second, it undermines a systematic interpretation of the UNDRIPS because the Declaration clearly points out to a differentiation between natural resources found in indigenous lands.[32] Third, it contradicts the historical background of the UNDRIPS. Notably, the UNDRIPS' draft text made explicit reference to the resources included within the scope of indigenous natural resources, i.e. air, water, sea coasts, flora, and fauna. Yet states did not accept such exhaustive provision and successfully achieved its removal from the text.[33] In other words, states did not agree to recognize the ownership of indigenous peoples over all natural resources in their lands. For all these reasons, such an interpretation based only on the right to self-determination is unreasonable.

A solid interpretation of the scope of protection of natural resources in accordance with the UNDRIPS refers only to surface resources. In order to clarify the meaning of an unreasonable interpretation, pursuant to Article 32 Vienna Convention on the Law of Treaties, one should consider the preparatory work of the treaty and the circumstances of its conclusion. As stated above, the *travaux préparatoires* of the UNDRIPS demonstrate that states strongly opposed the recognition of indigenous peoples' ownership over all natural resources found in indigenous lands. Moreover, during the adoption of the UNDRIPS, some states such as Japan, Mexico, and Namibia remarked that the interpretation of provisions concerning indigenous land rights have limits in domestic laws.[34] Since these laws often restrict the ownership of indigenous peoples to surface resources, the UNDRIPS has to be interpreted accordingly. Hence, the scope of protection of natural resources in indigenous lands restricts itself to surface resources.

To sum up, the self-determination-based framework pursuant to the UNDRIPS establishes limits to the scope of protection of lands and natural resources therein. Regarding lands, the scope of protection refers to lands that indigenous peoples have already acquired or currently possess and that are necessary for developing indigenous religion, cultural, and economic activities. Regarding natural resources, the scope of protection relates to surface resources.

Cultural-Identity-Based Framework: Economic Activities, Indigenous Lands and Culture The ICCPR lacks any provision addressing indigenous peoples. Despite that, in its jurisprudence, the HRC has been consistent in recognizing criteria to evaluate the scope of protection of indigenous lands and natural resources therein.[35] The HRC applies those criteria on a case-by-case basis in order to analyze alleged violations of Article 27 ICCPR touching upon the use and exploitation of indigenous lands and natural resources. Those criteria refer to the existence of a "distinctive culture" that is a result of the "development of economic activities."

---

[32]Cf. Article 26 and 32 UNDRIPS.

[33]For more details on this issue see Errico (2011), pp. 340–341; Xanthaki (2007), pp. 117–118.

[34]United Nations Division for Social Policy and Development (2017).

[35]Scheinin (2005), pp. 3–8.

In that sense, the HRC recognizes that the scope of protection of Article 27 ICCPR comprises indigenous lands and natural resources therein that are necessary for the development of a distinctive culture. The most important aspect in this regard refers to the relationship between economic activities, lands, and culture. While the burden of proof is not clear, sufficient pieces of evidence are usually found in decisions dealing with damages to the natural environment that impact on the cultural life of the group.[36] In the decision of the case Angela Poma Poma against Peru, the HRC explained (emphasis added):

> In previous cases, the Committee has recognized that the rights protected by article 27 include the right of persons, in community with others, *to engage in economic and social activities which are part of the culture of the community to which they belong*. In the present case, it is undisputed that the author is a member of an ethnic minority and that raising llamas is an essential element of the culture of the Aymara community, since it is a form of subsistence and an ancestral tradition handed down from parent to child. The author herself is engaged in this activity.[37]

Self-Determination-Based Framework and Cultural-Identity-Based Framework: Similarities, Differences and an Unspoken Connection Regarding the Scope of Protection of Indigenous Lands and Natural Resources Based on the foregoing analysis, it is necessary to conclude that the scope of protection of indigenous lands in both frameworks is very similar. Accordingly, indigenous lands that are necessary for communities to develop their economic and cultural activities are protected. Despite the common scope of protection between both frameworks, the HRC has never referred to the UNDRIPS in its decisions. Hence, there is an unspoken dialog between both frameworks related to the protection of cultural aspects of indigenous groups.

The difference between both frameworks lays on the scope of protection of natural resources in indigenous lands. While the protection contained in the UNDRIPS refers only to surface resources, the HRC may extend the scope of protection to subsurface resources in some cases. To that end, an indigenous community would have to prove that its distinctive culture depends on the development of economic activities related to the exploitation of mineral resources. Such a complaint has never appeared before the HRC, but there is no doubt that its criteria are applicable to such cases.

By looking at the similarities and differences, there are compelling reasons to recognize that the cultural-identity-based approach entails a more far-reaching scope of protection of indigenous lands and natural resources therein than the self-determination-based approach. Since the HRC adopts the decisions on an individual basis, it may adequate the scope of protection in view of the actual needs of the community. The cultural-identity-based framework offers therefore flexibility and

---

[36] HRC, J.G.A. Diergaard et al. against Namibia, 25 Jul 2000, UN Doc. CCPR/C/69/D/760/1997, Individual Opinion of Elizabeth Evatt and Cecilia Medina Quiroga. Similarly see Thornberry (2002), pp. 160.

[37] HRC, Angela Poma Poma against Peru, 27 Mar 2009, UN Doc. CCPR/C/95/D/1457/2006, para. 7.3.

involve the protection of the use of mineral resources by indigenous communities. The self-determination-based framework does not entail such a comprehensive protection. It has a scope of protection that does not consider concrete situations.

3.2.2 Conflict of Interests Between States and Indigenous Peoples Regarding Indigenous Lands and Natural Resources: Participation of Indigenous Peoples in State Decisions and Beyond

The jurisprudence on international human rights law indicates the existence of a standard conflict of interests between states and indigenous peoples. The survival and development of indigenous peoples is attached to their possessed lands and natural resources therein. Yet they do not have the title of ownership of these lands or they lack effective control over it. Conversely, states have the interest of exploiting directly or indirectly the natural resources within indigenous lands. This section evaluates the solutions contained in the self-determination-based framework and in the cultural-identity-based framework to deal with such conflict.

Self-Determination-Based Framework: Consultation with Specific Procedural Requirements The UNDRIPS establishes a criterion to deal with the situation of conflicts of interests between the state and indigenous peoples. The Declaration contains provisions that recognize so-called participatory rights in favor of indigenous peoples and evoke several state's obligations.

Article 32 UNDRIPS sets forth the state's obligation to consult and to cooperate in good faith with indigenous peoples in case of the development of a state's project affecting their lands or resources therein. The fulfillment of this obligation is the key to strike a balance between the interests of indigenous peoples and the state. To that end, the state has to engage in a process of consultation with indigenous peoples that requires a specific type of conduct toward the achievement of a certain result.

Article 32 UNDRIPS lays down additional requirements for the state's conduct, whose meaning is not as straightforward. In this regard, ILO Convention 169 may be helpful to interpret those requirements. ILO Convention 169 is applicable to situations that the UNDRIPS addresses, and many of the Convention's provisions have a wording similar to the UNDRIPS. The concepts contained in Article 32 UNDRIPS such as "good faith" and "indigenous peoples concerned" are akin to those of the ILO Convention 169, e.g. Articles 2, 6 and 15. There is no focused literature exploring the requirements of Article 32 UNDRIPS, yet there is a substantial scholarship regarding ILO Convention 169. States may look at this scholarship to understand the meaning of the requirements set down in the UNDRIPS and to find the adequate conduct for due compliance.

Regarding the achievement of a result following the process of consultation with indigenous peoples, Article 32 UNDRIPS evokes two different lines of interpretation. First, that the state has the obligation to obtain the consent of indigenous peoples before developing any project in their lands. As a result, this provision would entail a veto power of indigenous peoples.[38] Accordingly, the state's obligation would be to obtain the consent of indigenous peoples for the development of activities in their territory. Second, one can interpret this provision as seeking consent for the purpose of consultation.[39] The state would consult with the aim of obtaining consent to fulfill its obligation under Article 32 UNDRIPS. In this case, even if the state does not obtain the consent of indigenous peoples, it may proceed with the development of its project in indigenous lands.

Pursuant to Article 31 Vienna Convention on the Law of the Treaties, the right to self-determination, as described in the UNDRIPS, should guide the interpretation of Article 32 UNDRIPS. Accordingly, indigenous peoples may freely pursue their economic, social, and cultural development. Such development relates to the use and control of indigenous peoples' territory and natural resources therein. Therefore, one could raise the argument that the obtention of consent of indigenous peoples would be a necessary requirement to guarantee the right to self-determination. Some scholars claim that the link between the right to self-determination and the veto power of indigenous peoples finds support in international law.[40]

Nevertheless, such an understanding of Article 32 UNDRIPS as encompassing a veto power of indigenous peoples is a very controversial issue. The bottom of this controversy touches upon the permanent sovereignty over natural resources. States have been historically exercising the free use and exploitation of their natural resources. As a result, they are very reluctant to any attempt to modify this role, i.a. the inclusion of new obligations such as to obtain indigenous peoples' consent.[41] Furthermore, the recognition of indigenous peoples' right to consent raises questions about the existence of related obligations in this regard. For instance, it is controversial whether indigenous peoples' consent has to observe the sustainable use of natural resources. May indigenous peoples withhold their consent in case the suggested modifications to a state's project affecting their territory go against environmental laws? Scholarship has barely explored the issue of the existence of binding obligations to indigenous peoples.[42]

The preparatory work of the UNDRIPS offers a clearer explanation to the interpretation of Article 32 UNDRIPS. The draft version of Article 32 UNDRIPS entailed an explicit recognition of the state's obligation to obtain the consent of indigenous peoples in case of any project affecting their lands, including a veto power of indigenous communities.[43] Yet states involved in the drafting process did

[38]For this interpretation see, among others, Barelli (2016), pp. 37–40; Errico (2007), p. 753; Gilbert (2007), p. 223.

[39]For this argument see, among others, Barelli (2012), p. 11; Engle (2011), p. 157; Pentassuglia (2011), pp. 179–180.

[40]For a detailed explanation see Gilbert and Doyle (2011), pp. 304–320.

[41]A comprehensive analysis on the issue of permanent sovereignty over natural resources refers to Schrijver (1997).

[42]An unparalleled substantial analysis regarding the existence of binding obligations for indigenous peoples refers to Wenzel (2008), pp. 404–460.

[43]For this particular aspect of Article 32 UNDRIPS see Barelli (2012), p. 10.

not accept such a text and demanded its modification. States suggested replacing the wording "obtain consent" for "seek the consent." Indigenous peoples did not agree with this states' proposal because they considered the veto power essential. At the end, all involved parties agreed with the chairperson's proposal, which contained the wording "to obtain the ... consent."[44] This wording reflects the final version of Article 32 UNDRIPS.

In light of the drafting history of the UNDRIPS, it is compelling to recognize that states have the obligation to carry out a consultation and cooperation with indigenous peoples in order to obtain their consent. While Article 32 UNDRIPS does not recognize a veto power, its threshold goes beyond a mere consultation. States must truly aim to obtain the consent of indigenous peoples. This aim should reflect in the states' conduct that must follow established requirements in Article 32 UNDRIPS. For instance, the state must engage in the process with the representative institutions of indigenous peoples and not with any member of the group. In addition, there is the state's obligation to fulfill the requirements set down in Article 32 UNDRIPS before authorizing third parties to develop projects impacting on indigenous lands.

Besides that, states must redress and mitigate adverse impacts on indigenous territories resulting from the development of projects affecting their lands. This obligation appears in Article 32 UNDRIPS in a broad way and without specific criteria for its fulfillment. The state has the obligation to issue a "just and fair redress" and to take "appropriate measures" for mitigation of impact. Since the concepts of "fair" and "appropriate" are relational concepts, the state must assert them on an individual basis.

Cultural-Identity-Based Framework: Effective Participation with Guarantee of Sustainability of Indigenous Peoples' Economic Activities Exploitation of indigenous lands by states lays in the heart of indigenous peoples' complaints. In view of the lack of provisions in the ICCPR to deal with such issue, the HRC has elaborated criteria in its jurisprudence. It asserts on a case-by-case basis whether the development of states' projects that affect indigenous lands may amount to a violation of Article 27 ICCPR. These criteria refer to two obligations that states' must comply with in order to develop activities within indigenous lands.

The first state obligation refers to the sustainability of indigenous peoples' economic activities. The HRC recognizes that only state measures with a limited impact on the way of life and livelihood of persons belonging to indigenous communities are compatible with Article 27 ICCPR. In this regard, the HRC's threshold of analysis refers to the guarantee of survival of the indigenous community and its members. The HRC requires that state measures do not affect the community in a way that exhausts the possibility for the community to benefit from their traditional economy. The HRC requires thus that states guarantee the permanent sustainable development of indigenous communities' economic activities.

[44]In order to take an insider look on the drafting process of the UNDRIPS see Chávez (2009).

The first obligation refers in an implicit way to the subsistence of indigenous communities. The HRC does not use the word "subsistence." Instead, it mentions "survival." While both words are very similar, there is an important difference between them. According to Black Law's dictionary, the word "survival" relates to "remaining alive," whereas "subsistence" concerns "means of support."[45] The word "subsistence" holds hence the idea of the material support for own existence. This idea appears to be behind the HRC's assessment in cases related to alleged violations of Article 27 ICCPR.

A deep analysis of the HRC's jurisprudence points out to the relationship between the state's first obligation and the subsistence of indigenous communities. Notably, the Spanish version of the HRC's decision in the case of Poma Poma against Peru uses the word "subsistencia," which corresponds to the English "subsistence."[46] However, the English version of this decision applies the word "survival." "Survival" corresponds to the Spanish "supervivencia." There is no explanation for this translation's inconsistency regarding the use of "survival" rather than "subsistence," yet there can be no doubt that they are interrelated. Futhermore, the HRC's examination of violations of Article 27 ICCPR undoubtedly contains a material component.[47] The HRC stated in a decision *expressis verbis* (emphasis added):

> Moreover, the State did not require studies to be undertaken by a competent independent body in order to determine the impact that the construction of the wells would have on traditional economic activity, nor did it take measures to minimize the negative consequences and repair the harm done. The Committee also observes that the author has been unable to continue benefiting from her *traditional economic activity owing to the drying out of the land and loss of her livestock.*[48]

The second state obligation concerns the effective participation of indigenous peoples in any state decision about measures affecting their territories and natural resources therein. In its early jurisprudence, the HRC analyzed states' compliance with this obligation by looking at evidence (or its absence) regarding consultation with affected indigenous communities. In the decision of the case Poma Poma against Peru, the HRC changed the threshold of analysis and clarified that to avoid a violation of Article 27 ICCPR, states must obtain the free, prior, and informed consent of indigenous communities before adopting measures that may affect their territories.[49]

The HRC's interpretation of effective participation of indigenous peoples evokes a veto power of these peoples that boosts their protection. This veto power enables indigenous peoples to be in effective control of their lands, and it is an adequate way

---

[45]Garner (2014), pp. 1656; 1675.

[46]HRC, Angela Poma Poma against Peru, 27 Mar 2009, UN Doc. CCPR/C/95/D/1457/2006, para. 7.6.

[47]HRC, Ilmari Lansman et al. against Finland, 26 Oct 1994, UN Doc. CCPR/C/52/D/511/1992, paras 9.4–9.5.

[48]HRC, Angela Poma Poma against Peru, 27 Mar 2009, UN Doc. CCPR/C/95/D/1457/2006, para. 7.7.

[49]HRC, Angela Poma Poma against Peru, 27 Mar 2009, UN Doc. CCPR/C/95/D/1457/2006, para. 7.6.

to promote their self-determination.[50] Yet the HRC does not mention the concept of "self-determination" in its analysis. HRC's high threshold of analysis requires efforts by states to comply with Article 27 ICCPR. While the requirement of consent appeared for the first time in a decision of 2009, the HRC expressed it prior to this decision in the comments on the reports that States Parties submitted.[51]

Finally, states' obligations to guarantee the sustainability of indigenous peoples' economic activities and the effective participation in states' decisions are cumulative requirements. In case states fail to comply with one of them, the HRC may assert a violation of Article 27 ICCPR. These obligations are necessary measures to safeguard the right of members of minorities to cultural identity as in the case of members of indigenous communities.

Self-Determination-Based Framework and Cultural-Identity-Based Framework: Together and Apart Regarding Conflict of Interests Between States and Indigenous Peoples From the foregoing analysis, it follows that both frameworks establish states' obligation to negotiate with indigenous peoples before developing or authorizing third parties to develop any project affecting indigenous peoples' lands. The difference between both frameworks lays on the degree of the required negotiation. As explained above, on the one hand, the UNDRIPS sets forth some procedural requirements by requiring states to consult in order to obtain the consent of indigenous peoples. On the other hand, Article 27 ICCPR evokes a more demanding negotiation with indigenous communities. The cultural-identity-based framework requires that states effectively obtain the free, prior, and informed consent of indigenous peoples.

The cultural-identity-based framework displays a higher degree of protection for indigenous peoples. The requirement of consent enables indigenous peoples to be in effective control of their lands and resources and to determine their priorities. In this regard, scholars claim that this requirement of consent promotes the self-determination of indigenous peoples. This is the reason why the framework of cultural identity offers a far-reaching protection for indigenous lands and natural resources therein. The self-determination-based framework lacks such a requirement of consent.

States' obligation concerning the sustainability of indigenous peoples' economic activities contained in the cultural-identity-based framework connects to the self-

[50]For a detailed explanation on the relationship between the effective control of lands by indigenous peoples and self-determination see Ludescher (2004), pp. 363–398.

[51]See the HRC on this issue: Examen de los informes presentados por los Estados partes en virtud del articulo 40 del Pacto, Observaciones finales del Comite de Derechos Humanos, UN Doc. CCPR/C/COL/CO/6, 2010, para. 25; Consideration of reports submitted by States parties under Article 40 of the Covenant, Concluding observations of the HRC, UN Doc. CCPR/C/SLV/CO/6, 2010, para. 18; Consideration of reports submitted by States parties under Article 40 of the Covenant, Concluding observations of the HRC, UN Doc. CCPR/C/TGO/CO/4, 2011, para. 21; Consideration of reports submitted by States parties under Article 40 of the Covenant, Concluding observations of the HRC, UN Doc. CCPR/C/KEN/CO/3, 2012, para. 24; Concluding observations on Belize in the absence of a report, UN Doc. CCPR/C/BLZ/CO/1, 2013, para. 25; Concluding observations on the fourth periodic report of the United States of America, UN Doc. CCPR/C/USA/CO/4, 2014, para. 25.

determination-based framework. The UNDRIPS does not contain this state obligation. However, as explained above, while the HRC does not state it explicitly, this obligation relates to the guarantee of subsistence of indigenous communities. The important point regarding "subsistence" is its direct link with the right to self-determination according to Article 1 ICCPR and Article 3 UNDRIPS.

Finally, it is possible to conclude that both frameworks use similar concepts without referring to each other. The frameworks request the participation of indigenous peoples in state decisions affecting their lands and natural resources therein. Moreover, they relate to the right of self-determination pursuant to Article 1 ICCPR. Yet the HRC does not explicitly mention "self-determination" that is hidden behind the protection of indigenous lands in accordance with the right of members of minorities to cultural identity.

4 Final Remarks

The analysis of UNDRIPS' provisions and the HRC's jurisprudence of the ICCPR demonstrated that these legal instruments evoke different frameworks for the protection of indigenous peoples in international human rights law. As demonstrated in the second part, the UNDRIPS raised a framework based on the right to self-determination. The HRC created a framework based on the right of members of minorities to cultural identity in accordance with the ICCPR. It is thus compelling to recognize that there are two different frameworks: the self-determination-based framework and the cultural-identity-based framework.

Both frameworks do not engage in a direct dialog due to procedural issues. Yet they have similar substantial issues that flag a hidden relationship between them. Since the HRC does not admit complaints pursuant to the right of self-determination, both frameworks do not explicitly work in a related way. However, as demonstrated in the third part, the self-determination-based framework and the cultural-identity-based framework come close to each other. The reason behind this is that they entail a similar content regarding the protection of indigenous lands and natural resources therein. Both frameworks protect indigenous lands that are necessary for the development of indigenous cultural and economic activities. In addition, they raise an obligation to guarantee the participation of indigenous peoples in state decisions affecting indigenous lands. Despite similarities, the HRC has never referred to the UNDRIPS in any of its decisions. Both frameworks develop in a concurring way in relation to one another.

The cultural-identity-based framework entails a more comprehensive protection for indigenous peoples and their lands than the self-determination-based framework. As demonstrated in the third part of this analysis, the criteria that the HRC developed enable indigenous peoples to control directly their lands and natural resources in a way that may include the control over mineral resources. Indeed, indigenous peoples and their members may complain about their land issues in accordance with the cultural-identity-based framework. The UNDRIPS' obscure provisions evoke a less degree of protection as part of the self-determination-based framework.

Accordingly, this framework relates only to surface resources found in indigenous lands and indigenous peoples' indirect control in this regard.

References

Ahrén M (2009) The provisions on lands, territories and natural resources in the UN Declaration on the Rights of Indigenous Peoples: an introduction. In: Charters C, Stavenhagen R (eds) Making the declaration work: the United Nations Declaration on the Rights of Indigenous Peoples. International Work Group for Indigenous Affairs, Copenhagen, pp 200–215

Anaya SJ (2009) International human rights and indigenous peoples. Elective series. Wolters Kluwer Law & Business, Austin

Baldwin C, Morel C (2011) Using the United Nations Declaration on the Rights of Indigenous Peoples in litigation. In: Allen S, Xanthaki A (eds) Reflections on the UN Declaration on the Rights of Indigenous Peoples. Hart Publishing, Oxford, pp 121–143

Barelli M (2009) The role of soft law in the international legal system: the case of the United Nations Declaration on the Rights of Indigenous Peoples. Int Comp Law Q 58:957–983

Barelli M (2012) Free, prior and informed consent in the aftermath of the UN Declaration on the Rights of Indigenous Peoples: developments and challenges ahead. Int J Hum Rights 16(1): 1–24

Barelli M (2016) Seeking justice in international law: the significance and implications of the UN Declaration on the Rights of Indigenous Peoples. Routledge Research in International Law. Routledge, Abingdon

Buchanan A (1993) The role of collective rights in the theory of indigenous peoples' rights. Transnat Law Contemp Probl 3:89–108

Campbell MS, Anaya SJ (2008) The case of the Maya villages of Belize: reversing the trend of government neglect to secure indigenous land rights. Hum Rights Law Rev 8:377–399

Cassese A (1995) Self-determination of peoples: a legal reappraisal. Cambridge University Press, Cambridge

Castellino J (2005) The "Right" to land, international law & indigenous peoples. In: Castellino J, Walsh N (eds) International law and indigenous peoples. Martinus Nijhoff, Leiden, pp 89–116

Charters C (2009) The legitimacy of the UN Declaration on the Rights of Indigenous Peoples. In: Charters C, Stavenhagen R (eds) Making the declaration work: the United Nations Declaration on the Rights of Indigenous Peoples. International Work Group for Indigenous Affairs, Copenhagen, pp 280–303

Charters CWN (2010) Land rights. In: International Law Association (ed) Rights of indigenous peoples. Wellington, pp 20–25

Chávez LE (2009) The declaration on the rights of indigenous peoples breaking the impasse: the middle ground. In: Charters C, Stavenhagen R (eds) Making the declaration work: the United Nations Declaration on the Rights of Indigenous Peoples. International Work Group for Indigenous Affairs, Copenhagen, pp 96–107

Clavero B (2016) La Declaración Americana sobre Derechos de Los Pueblos Indígenas: El Reto de la Interpretación de Una Norma Contradictoria, Peru

Crawford J (2012) Brownlie's principles of public international law, 8th edn. Oxford University Press, Oxford

Descola P (2000) In the society of nature: a native ecology in Amazonia. Cambridge studies in social and cultural anthropology, vol 93. Cambridge University Press, Cambridge

Engle K (2011) On fragile architecture: the UN Declaration on the Rights of Indigenous Peoples in the context of human rights. Eur J Int Law 22(1):141–163

Errico S (2007) The draft UN Declaration on the Rights of Indigenous Peoples: an overview. Hum Rights Law Rev 7:741–755

Errico S (2011) The controversial issue of natural resources: balancing states' sovereignty with indigenous peoples' rights. In: Allen S, Xanthaki A (eds) Reflections on the UN Declaration on the Rights of Indigenous Peoples. Hart Publishing, Oxford, pp 329–366

Garner BA (ed) (2014) Black's law dictionary, 10th edn. Thomson Reuters, St. Paul

Gilbert J (2007) Indigenous rights in the making: the United Nations Declaration on the Rights of Indigenous Peoples. Int J Minor Group Rights 14:207–230

Gilbert J, Doyle C (2011) A new dawn over the land: shedding light on collective ownership and consent. In: Allen S, Xanthaki A (eds) Reflections on the UN Declaration on the Rights of Indigenous Peoples. Hart Publishing, Oxford, pp 289–328

Kingsbury B (2017) Indigenous peoples. In: Wolfrum R (ed) Max Planck encyclopedia of public international law. Oxford University Press, Oxford, pp 1–16

Kymlicka W (2010) Minority rights in political and philosophy and international law. In: Besson S, Tasioulas J (eds) The philosophy of international law. Oxford University Press, Oxford, pp 377–396

Lenzerini F (2010a) Rights of indigenous peoples under customary international law. In: International Law Association (ed) Rights of indigenous peoples, pp 43–52

Lenzerini F (2010b) The United Nations Declaration on the Rights of Indigenous Peoples: amending five centuries of wrongs. In: Te Rito JS, Healy SM (eds) Kei Muri i te Awe Kāpara he Tangata Kē: Recognising, engaging, understanding difference: 4th International Traditional Knowledge Conference 2010. Knowledge Exchange Programme of Ngā Pae o te Māramatanga New Zealand's Māori Centre of Research Excellence, Auckland, pp 19–28

Ludescher M (2004) Menschenrechte und indigene Völker. Peter Lang, Frankfurt a.M.

Nowak M (ed) (2005) U.N. Covenant on Civil and Political Rights: CCPR commentary, 2nd revised edition. N.P. Engel, Kehl

Oeter S (2012) The protection of indigenous peoples in international law revisited: from non-discrimination to self-determination. In: Hestermeyer HP, König D, Matz-Lück N, Röben V, Seibert-Fohr A, Stoll P-T, Vöneky S (eds) Coexistence, cooperation and solidarity: Liber Amicorum Ruediger Wolfrum. Martinus Nijhoff Publishers, Leiden, pp 477–502

Pentassuglia G (2011) Towards a jurisprudential articulation of indigenous land rights. Eur J Int Law 22(1):165–202

Pogge T (1997) Group rights and ethnicity. Am Soc Polit Leg Philos 39:187–221

Scheinin M (2005) Indigenous Peoples' Rights under the International Covenant on Civil and Political Rights. In: Castellino J, Walsh N (eds) International law and indigenous peoples. Martinus Nijhoff, Leiden, pp 3–15

Schrijver N (1997) Sovereignty over natural resources: balancing rights and duties. Cambridge University Press, Cambridge

Thornberry P (2002) Indigenous peoples and human rights. Manchester University Press, Juris Publishing, Manchester

Tyagi Y (2011) The UN Human Rights Committee: practice and procedure. Cambridge University Press, Cambridge

United Nations Division for Social Policy and Development (2017) United Nations Declaration on the Rights of Indigenous Peoples. https://www.un.org/development/desa/indigenouspeoples/declaration-on-the-rights-of-indigenous-peoples.html. Accessed 31 May 2017

Viveiros de Castro E (2013) A inconstancia da alma selvagem: e outros ensaios de antropologia, 5th edn. Cosacnaify, Sao Paulo

Wenzel N (2008) Das Spannungsverhältnis zwischen Gruppenschutz und Individualschutz im Völkerrecht: The protection of groups in international law in tension with the protection of the individual. Beiträge zum ausländischen öffentlichen Recht und Völkerrecht, vol 191. Springer, Berlin

Wiessner S (2008) Indigenous sovereignty: a reassessment in the light of the UN Declaration on the Rights of Indigenous Peoples. Vanderbilt J Transnat Law 41:1141–1176

Xanthaki A (2007) Indigenous rights and United Nations standards: self-determination, culture and land. Cambridge University Press, Cambridge

The manufacturer's authorised representative in the EU is Springer
Nature Customer Service Centre GmbH, Europaplatz 3, 69115 Heidelberg,
Germany. If you have any concerns regarding our products, please
contact ProductSafety@springernature.com

Printed and bound by CPI Group (UK) Ltd, Croydon, CR0 4YY
25/09/2026
02222850-0003